SEASONS IN THE LITERATURES
OF THE MEDIEVAL NORTH

Seasons in the Literatures of the Medieval North

P. S. Langeslag

D. S. BREWER

© P. S. Langeslag 2015

All Rights Reserved. Except as permitted under current legislation no part of this work may be photocopied, stored in a retrieval system, published, performed in public, adapted, broadcast, transmitted, recorded or reproduced in any form or by any means, without the prior permission of the copyright owner

The right of P. S. Langeslag to be identified as the author of this work has been asserted in accordance with sections 77 and 78 of the Copyright, Designs and Patents Act 1988

First published 2015
D. S. Brewer, Cambridge
Paperback edition 2019

ISBN 978 1 84384 425 9 hardback
ISBN 978 1 84384 525 6 paperback

D. S. Brewer is an imprint of Boydell & Brewer Ltd
PO Box 9, Woodbridge, Suffolk IP12 3DF, UK
and of Boydell & Brewer Inc.
668 Mt Hope Avenue, Rochester, NY 14620–2731, USA
website: www.boydellandbrewer.com

The publisher has no responsibility for the continued existence or accuracy of URLs for external or third-party internet websites referred to in this book, and does not guarantee that any content on such websites is, or will remain, accurate or appropriate

A CIP catalogue record for this book is available from the British Library

Typeset by Word and Page, Chester, UK

Contents

Acknowledgements	vii
Abbreviations and Citation Practice	viii
Introduction	1
A Monster of Our Making	1
Measuring Time	4
The Associative Year	9
Climate History	13
The Economic Year	17
Domesticating Time	26
1. Myth and Ritual	29
Accounting for the Seasons	29
Performing the Seasons	47
Conclusions	61
2. Winter Mindscapes	63
Introduction	63
Mind, Space, and Season	67
Anglo-Saxon Elegy	69
Cold Water	80
Sites of Fear and Mourning in *Beowulf*	89
Hostile Categories in Old Norse Literature	100
Conclusions	110
3. Winter Institutions	113
Hauntings	114
The Grendel Season	128
Seasonal Progression in *Beowulf*	137
The Bonds of Winter	142
Winter Conflict	148
Prognostication and Prophecy	154
Conclusions	157
4. Summer Adventure	161
Introduction	161
Visions and Debates	164
The Forest of Romance	173
Conclusions	204
Conclusions	207
Bibliography	213
Index	245

Acknowledgements

This book was written in conditions of great privilege. Throughout the processes of research, drafting, and revision, I received guidance from some of the most accomplished scholars in the field. I am deeply grateful to Andy Orchard, Richard North, Ian McDougall, William Robins, and David Klausner for their invaluable recommendations, to Terry Gunnell and Torfi Tulinius for guiding my early thought on literary representations of the seasons, and to Daniel Jamison and Jeroen Nieboer for offering their expertise in areas in which I felt out of my depth. My research environment, too, has been stellar. I have made extensive use of the library resources of the universities of Toronto, Iceland, and Göttingen, whose richness is reflected in my footnotes and bibliography. In particular, I would like to mention the Dictionary of Old English Project and the Jackman Humanities Institute, the two towers I was permitted to make my home by the generosity of Hal Jackman and the kindness of Antonette diPaolo Healey. By way of the Dictionary, I had access not only to a unique set of library resources, but also to the friendship and immense learning of Ian and David McDougall. Their places at the Dictionary have since been taken by Robert Getz and Stephen Pelle, the only scholars of my acquaintance able to fill Dave and Ian's shoes. Though Rob and Stephen have not contributed to this book in any direct way, I think of our Old Germanic reading sessions across the landscapes and seasons of Toronto's Saint George campus as the heart of the intellectual culture that fostered my work during the drafting stage. More generally, I owe much of my academic profile to Karin Olsen, who first introduced me to the languages and literatures of medieval north-western Europe, and Alaric Hall, who mentored me with great patience. Alasdair MacDonald, too, has been a great mentor and friend. Winfried Rudolf, head of Medieval Studies at the University of Göttingen's Department of English Philology, deserves a solemn acknowledgement for his untiring work to safeguard my private research time in the final stages of the book's preparation.

Countless volunteers have contributed to the software environments that have made much of my workflow so pleasant. I would like to single out the maintainers of XMonad, VIM, and biblatex for providing the invisible framework behind this book.

My final word of thanks must go to my students, who are the point.

Abbreviations and Citation Practice

CV	*An Icelandic-English Dictionary*, ed. Cleasby and Vigfusson
DOE	*Dictionary of Old English: A to G*, ed. Cameron, Amos, Healey, *et al.*
EETS	Early English Text Society
ES, OS, SS	Extra Series, Original Series, Supplementary Series
Fritzner	*Ordbog over det gamle norske Sprog*, ed. Fritzner
KLNM	*Kulturhistorisk leksikon for nordisk middelalder*

Biblical references use abbreviations as found in Weber's edition of the Vulgate.[1] I use *DOE* short titles for otherwise untitled manuscript scribbles (*Notes*). In reprinting from text editions, I have silently altered punctuation and capitalization to meet the requirements of syntax and style, and removed such editorial cues as italics and brackets. Occasionally, I have altered word spacing to reflect my reading of the text. Translations are my own.

---

[1] Robert Weber, ed., *Biblia sacra iuxta vulgatam versionem*, 5th ed., rev. Roger Gryson (Stuttgart: Deutsche Bibelgesellschaft, 2007).

Introduction

A Monster of Our Making

Our understanding of the seasonal cycle at higher latitudes, with its annual oscillation in temperature and sun hours, owes a great deal to the development of controlled fire. It was a knowledge of this technology, along with advances in body insulation, that permitted early hominids to push into new territories where temperatures varied greatly between the seasons, and where the cold of winter would have precluded human survival had it not been for artificial heating and heat preservation. By moving away from the equator, our ancestors effectively created a new enemy for themselves in the shape of the winter season. At this time of year more than any other, their survival in moderate and subarctic zones depended on technology, a shared and therefore social acquisition that has left a more profound mark on the genus of homo than anything else has. With it, humankind learned to shut out the world outside and create a space of its own.[1]

Energy infrastructure has undergone dramatic developments since the taming of fire. Consequently, developed societies today enjoy the most seasonally uniform lifestyle in the history of human life outside the tropics. Architectural developments, the exploitation of new sources of heat, and ever-improving insulation technologies are only a few facets of this feat. In some of our cities with their year-round climate control, heated parking garages, and seamless underground transportation infrastructure – winter cities, as Adam Gopnik calls them[2] – it is now possible to avoid direct contact with the elements altogether if one so chooses. Meanwhile, the airlifting of produce has done away with seasonal limitations on the availability of virtually any food while vastly expanding the dietary range available to us. On an existential level, therefore, the cycle of the seasons has lost much of its immediacy for those with access to advanced infrastructure. What remains of our susceptibility to the seasons largely belongs to such domains as mood and leisure: cultural and psychological responses to a material reality.

---

[1] C. O. Sauer, 'Fire and Early Man', *Paideuma* 7, no. 8 (November 1961): 404–5; Juli G. Pausas and Jon E. Keeley, 'A Burning Story: The Role of Fire in the History of Life', *BioScience* 59, no. 7 (July–August 2009): 597; Bent Sørensen, *A History of Energy: Northern Europe from the Stone Age to the Present Day* (Abingdon and New York: Earthscan, 2012), 20–77; cf. Leland M. Roth, *Understanding Architecture: Its Elements, History, and Meaning*, 2nd ed. (Boulder, CO: Westview, 2007), 161–2.

[2] Adam Gopnik, *Winter: Five Windows on the Season*, CBC Massey Lectures (Toronto: Anansi, 2011), 185.

This book concerns such responses to the seasons, but it looks for them in the medieval literatures of England and Scandinavia, whose authors could not so easily dismiss seasonal variation as a matter of November gloom and February skiing. Even after coal heating and the chimney became more widely used in the thirteenth century,[3] the seasonal experience remained one of considerably greater exposure than is typical of post-industrial societies. Moreover, these technological improvements coincided with the start of a gradual climatic cooling that was to become substantial, and particularly erratic, by the fourteenth century.[4] Accordingly, life throughout the period involved regular exposure to seasonal extremes through their tactile representatives, heat and, above all, cold. Morbidity was likewise affected by the seasons, as winter is conducive to respiratory infections while summer favours insect-borne diseases.[5] More than anything, however, the seasons mattered because they dictated food supplies and the labour calendar for most economic sectors. Yields of crops and animal products alike were strongly seasonal.[6] Though long-term nutritional deficiencies seem to have had no statistically discernible effect on mortality in pre-industrial Europe,[7] the local nature of the food economy did leave the population vulnerable to crop failures and the year-by-year seasonal fluctuations that gave rise to them.[8] Even at the best of times, the seasonal nature of agricultural production imposed restrictions on the diets of the poorer classes in particular while structuring the day-to-day lives of many.[9]

Although hard evidence for the effects of this cycle on the daily lives of medieval individuals is hard to come by, the combined efforts of social historians, archaeologists, palaeopathologists, and others are beginning to add up to some profound insights. Alongside material finds, these scholars make use of documentary evidence by which to quantify variables in

---

[3] LeRoy Dresbeck, 'Winter Climate and Society in the Northern Middle Ages: The Technological Impact', in *On Pre-Modern Technology and Science: A Volume of Studies in Honour of Lynn White, Jr.*, ed. Bert S. Hall and Delno C. West (Malibu: Undena, 1976), 182–6; LeRoy Dresbeck, 'Techne, labor et natura: Ideas and Active Life in the Medieval Winter', *Studies in Medieval and Renaissance History*, s.s. 2 (1979): 103–11.

[4] Jean M. Grove, 'The Initiation of the "Little Ice Age" in Regions round the North Atlantic', *Climatic Change* 48 (1999): 53–82; Jean M. Grove, *Little Ice Ages: Ancient and Modern*, 2nd ed., 2 vols (London and New York: Routledge, 2008).

[5] John Landers, *The Field and the Forge: Population, Production, and Power in the Pre-Industrial West* (Oxford: Oxford University Press, 2003), 29–30.

[6] Debby Banham and Rosamond Faith, *Anglo-Saxon Farms and Farming*, Medieval History and Archaeology (Oxford: Oxford University Press, 2014), 50–8, 113, 118.

[7] Stephen J. Kunitz, 'Speculations on the European Mortality Decline', *The Economic History Review*, n.s., 36, no. 3 (July 1983): 349–64.

[8] Edward Miller and John Hatcher, *Medieval England: Rural Society and Economic Change 1086–1348* (London: Longman, 1978), vii–viii.

[9] Kathy L. Pearson, 'Nutrition and the Early-Medieval Diet', *Speculum* 72, no. 1 (January 1997): 1–32; C. C. Dyer, 'Seasonal Patterns in Food Consumption in the Later Middle Ages', in *Food in Medieval England: Diet and Nutrition*, ed. C. M. Woolgar, D. Serjeantson, and T. Waldron (Oxford: Oxford University Press, 2006), 201–14.

matters of diet, death, disease, and weather extremes. Especially in the study of climate history, narrative texts are either discarded or subjected to a critical vetting before their testimony is admitted as evidence,[10] and with good reason. Not only are documents of this kind especially likely to be invested with authorial purpose beyond the strict registration of facts, they are also occasional compositions, regularly of obscure origin, contrasting with the better-defined and more methodical annalistic sources that offer some limited statistical validity.

Narrative and lyric texts can nevertheless contribute to our understanding of medieval seasonal experience on a more subjective level. In the absence of medieval treatises on environmental psychology, these works provide the best available access to medieval cognitive and emotive responses to the seasonal cycle. By cataloguing the literary functions of seasonal motifs across genres and corpora, moreover, it is possible to identify seasonal associations of some cultural validity.

This book identifies and interprets seasonal devices in medieval English and Scandinavian literature as evidenced primarily in Old English poetry from the eighth century to the eleventh, Old Icelandic writings from the thirteenth and fourteenth centuries, and Middle English poetry principally from the second half of the fourteenth century. Through these sources, it offers an insight into attitudes to season and environment in medieval north-western Europe. As will be seen, the conceptual integration of time and space is of critical importance to the investigation, since the seasons commonly manifest themselves in literature as associative overlays onto geographic space.

Medieval north-western Europe is an appropriate test case for the study of seasonal associations in literature because a number of relevant conditions converge here. To begin with, it is a higher-latitude region, ensuring considerable contrasts between the seasons. Such contrasts are a necessary condition for a study of this sort, but they also translate into cultural concepts worth exploring in this context. For instance, there is a tendency in the narrative and lyric literature of this region to divide the year into two seasons, while four were used in astronomical and some administrative taxonomies. Since sets of two differ greatly in their figurative associations from sets of four, there is an opportunity here to compare figurative uses of both divisions.

A second advantage to the study of these particular traditions is that they were productive at a time when climate and season penetrated deeply into the lives of people, ensuring the material relevance of these phenomena

---

[10] For example A. E. J. Ogilvie, 'Climate and Society in Iceland From the Medieval Period to the Late Eighteenth Century' (unpublished doctoral thesis, University of East Anglia, 1981); A. E. J. Ogilvie, 'Climatic Changes in Iceland AD c. 865 to 1598', *Acta Archaeologica* 61 (1990): 233–51; A. E. J. Ogilvie and Graham Farmer, 'Documenting the Medieval Climate', in *Climates of the British Isles: Present, Past and Future*, ed. Mike Hulme (London: Routledge, 1997), 112–33.

for authors and the general population alike. This seasonal susceptibility ultimately follows from the energy infrastructure of the time, as medieval economies were supported in the first instance by organic matter as opposed to fossil fuels. This dependence severely limited societies' defence against seasonal extremes not only in terms of fuel for heating, but also because the manpower required to feed the population severely curtailed investment opportunities for diverse technological improvements that might have served that defence.[11] Conclusions here reached concerning the literary functions of the seasons will therefore be a useful point of comparison to set against later traditions. In addition, the timespan between *Beowulf* and *Sir Gawain and the Green Knight* witnessed the onset of a notable climate deterioration, so that Old English poetry was composed in a period of milder and more stable mean conditions than the Middle English material. Some cautious comparative work may therefore be carried out within the investigated period as well.

Finally, medieval north-western Europe is an appropriate field of focus because it constitutes a loose cultural sphere with sufficient shared material to permit the detailed comparison of its constituent parts, yet enough that sets these apart to be able to discuss them as individual cultures. The Old English, Middle English, and Old Norse corpora each engage extensively with their seasonal environments, and they do so in distinct yet overlapping ways. The resulting field is one that allows for the discussion of a range of seasonal themes while retaining a unified focus. Following a thematic tendency found in all three corpora, that focus concerns the seasons as environments associated with the unfamiliar and uncanny aspects of extra-societal space.

Measuring Time

There is an inevitable discrepancy between the science that informs our conceptual understanding of the world around us and the phenomenological intuition that guides our everyday experience. When we speak of the seasons of the year, for instance, the discussion may be coloured at some level by their astronomical definition, reflecting an uneven and variable distribution of sunlight caused by the angle between the earth's spin and solar orbit. In casual conversation, however, we slip almost imperceptibly back and forth between that definition and the related but more relatable concepts of heat and cold, light and dark, sun and rain. A quantified set of observations of this sort in turn feeds into a second formal definition known as the meteorological year, whose function is not to measure time but to track local weather patterns along an annual mean. These statistics

---

[11] Landers, *The Field and the Forge*, 1–122.

as reported by mass media have a considerable presence in our reflection on the weather, if primarily to confirm our subjective experience: *that was a really hot day*.

However, the acknowledgement of extreme weather events has a distinctly linear character: *this has been the hottest spring since records began*. When it comes to the cyclical experience of weather patterns, statistics fade into the background and we are guided rather by our own experience and memories, which are necessarily less refined. In medium and high latitudes, we associate summer with heat and long days, winter with cold and dark. 18 and 22 December do not feel like different seasons to us, and we base our expectations of Christmas weather rather on our own experiences than on the longitudinal data kept by meteorologists.

These observations demonstrate that the seasons of the year are subject to a plurality of definitions. Some of these are rooted in astronomical constants, but others are more subjective. One cannot assert that this or that system is culturally dominant without specifying the cultural domain one has in mind. The knowledge that spring begins around 20 March by astronomical reckoning is of no value to the gardener, who knows that nocturnal frosts typically do not occur beyond a certain point in the season, whose connection with the vernal equinox is of limited practical relevance to the survival of her crops. On the other hand, keeping astronomical time is the safest way to ensure she visits her client on the appointed day.

Just as a book on gardening will reference the meteorological rather than the astronomical year, a book on medieval culture may reference a different seasonal reality depending on its thematic domain. A book on seasonal themes above all must begin by defining its terms. This is the more pressing in a book on the seasons in medieval north-western Europe, because the definitions used by the relevant cultures differed from today's.

To begin with, it is worth recalling the calendrical tradition that has dominated Western Europe in the Common Era. Its premodern form is known as the Julian calendar, itself a modified version of an older Roman calendar. Instituted by Julius Caesar in 45 BCE, it spread across Europe as an administrative tool of the Roman Empire. As a solar calendar containing twelve months and 365.25 days, it differed little from today's construct. Officially, even the start of the year was the same that is observed today, although in practice there was a good deal of local variation. In ecclesiastical and most administrative circles, the Julian calendar was used throughout the Middle Ages, and the start of the year remained variable. In England, for instance, 25 December was widely observed during the Anglo-Saxon period. Following an Anglo-Norman interlude at 1 January, 25 March gained traction in the twelfth and thirteenth centuries, and remained in use until 1752.[12] By the thirteenth

---

[12] Bede, *De temporum ratione*, ch. 15: Charles W. Jones, ed., *Opera didascalica II: De temporum*

century, 25 March seems to have enjoyed some popularity in mainland Scandinavia as well.[13]

Today's Gregorian calendar differs from its Julian predecessor only in a slight reduction in the frequency of leap years. Instituted by Pope Gregory XIII in 1582 and not adopted in England until 1752, its main motivation was to call a halt to the backwards march of Easter that had been observed since the Nicaean Council definitively fixed its timing to the solar year in 325 CE. By the time of the reform, this difference amounted to ten days, which were accordingly excised from the year 1582; by the time England adopted it in 1752, eleven days had to be omitted.[14]

From a Roman perspective, then, no significant calendrical change has taken place since the days of the Republic. Of course, the perspective to which this book aspires is more peripheral, as it concerns cultures that adopted Roman ways late and not equally into all domains. It is in this adoption that notable change seems to have taken place.

Two descriptive types of source provide evidence on calendrical systems in use by early Germanic speakers: the peoples' own observations and those of foreign observers. The latter type has the longer history, as it begins with the Roman historiographer Tacitus, who in the closing years of the first century CE remarked of the Germanic peoples:

> Arva per annos mutant, et superest ager. Nec enim cum ubertate et amplitudine soli labore contendunt, ut pomaria conserant, ut prata separent, ut hortos rigent; sola terrae seges imperatur. Unde annum quoque ipsum non in totidem digerunt species: hiems et ver et aestas intellectum ac vocabula habent, autumni perinde nomen ac bona ignorantur. (*Germania*, ch. 26)[15]
>
> They vary their fields year by year, and there is land to spare. For with the fertility and abundance of soil they do not strive in labour to plant orchards, divide up their pastures, or irrigate gardens; only the land's grain harvest is claimed. Accordingly, they do not divide the year itself into as many constituent parts: winter, spring, and summer have both concept and name, but they know neither the name nor the products of autumn.

---

ratione liber, Corpus Christianorum, Series Latina, 123B: Bedae venerabilis opera, 6 (Turnhout: Brepols, 1977), 330; H. Grotefend, *Zeitrechnung des deutschen Mittelalters und der Neuzeit*, 2 vols (Hannover: Hahn, 1891–8), 1:s.vv. 'Annunciationsstil', 'Circumcisionsstil', 'Jahresanfang', 'Julianisches Jahr', 'Weihnachtsanfang'; Sacha Stern, *Calendars in Antiquity: Empires, States, and Societies* (Oxford: Oxford University Press, 2012), 204–27.

[13] Finn Hødnebø, 'Juleskrå', in *Kulturhistorisk leksikon for nordisk middelalder*, ed. John Danstrup et al. (Copenhagen: Rosenkilde / Bagger, 1963–78; hereafter cited as *KLNM*), 8 (1963): 19–20; Sam Owen Jansson, 'Nyår', *KLNM* 12 (1967): 410–11; Árni Björnsson, *Saga daganna*, 2nd ed. (Reykjavik: Mál og menning, 2000), 393–4.

[14] Grotefend, *Zeitrechnung*, 1:s.v. 'Neuer Stil'.

[15] Allan A. Lund, ed., *P. Cornelius Tacitus: 'Germania'* (Heidelberg: Winter, 1988), 90; for the dating, see 17, n. 3.

This passage provides a first indication that the premodern seasons were not always identical to our own. It is, however, doubtful whether Tacitus's account can be taken at face value. In his day, northern Europe was home to a smaller population than the Mediterranean, and it had supported that population for a shorter period of time. Accordingly, the soil had been used less intensively but more extensively (using crop rotation and fallow, as Tacitus makes clear), and it had not suffered the salinization through irrigation that had turned much of the southern Mediterranean into desert, nor quite as much deforestation leading to erosion.[16] As such, much of the land in the north was indeed more fertile, but its yield was surely less than it could have been in the hands of intensive Mediterranean farmers. Its exploitation would thus have looked primitive from the agro-economic viewpoint one expects from the economic elite of a powerful society supported by advanced agricultural technology.[17] Tacitus's decision to emphasize the quality of the soil rather than the primitive character of its exploitation must have been conscious as well as unconventional. As such, it is characteristic of his political designs, which involved a critical assessment of Roman society by comparison with its tribal neighbours.[18] Read in the context of the wider passage, the observation regarding the absence of autumn fits into this depiction of the noble savage so well provided for by nature that he is unfamiliar with the unnecessary toils of horticulture, much less its conceptual field. Seasonal taxonomy here seems to be used as supporting evidence for the ease of the Germanic agricultural life.

Tacitus's claim is best read in the light of observations made by members of Germanic societies themselves. Although such writings do not appear until the early Middle Ages, they suggest that Tacitus's account may be rooted in a real and notable difference between Roman and Germanic time-reckoning. Bede puts it succinctly:

> Quotiescumque communis esset annus ternos menses lunares singulis anni temporibus dabant [antiqui Anglorum populi]. [. . .] Item principaliter annum totum in duo tempora, hiemis uidelicet et aestatis, dispertiebant – sex illos menses quibus longiores sunt noctibus dies aestati tribuendo, sex reliquos hiemi. (*De temporum ratione*, ch. 15)[19]

---

[16] Jared Diamond, 'Ecological Collapses of Past Civilizations', *Proceedings of the American Philosophical Society* 138, no. 3 (1994): 369; J. Donald Hughes, *The Mediterranean: An Environmental History, Nature and Human Societies* (Santa Barbara, CA: ABC-Clio, 2005), passim, esp. 17–44, 194–5, and cf. 71; Roger Sands, *Forestry in a Global Context* (Cambridge, MA: CABI, 2005), 1–31; Uriel N. Safriel, 'Dryland Development, Desertification and Security in the Mediterranean', in *Desertification in the Mediterranean Region: A Security Issue*, ed. William G. Kepner *et al.*, NATO Security through Science Series, C: Environmental Security (Dordrecht: Springer, 2006), and other papers in the same volume.
[17] Lund, *Germania*, 67.
[18] Ibid., 56–69, esp. 67.
[19] Jones, *De temporum ratione*, 330–1.

Whenever it was a common year, they [the ancient English people] gave each season of the year three lunar months. [. . .] Furthermore, they originally divided the full year into two seasons, namely winter and summer, assigning the six months whose days are longer than the nights to summer, the other six to winter.

Whereas no external source confirms Tacitus's ternary claim, support for Bede's binary division of the year is extensive. The overwhelming majority of such evidence hails from the Old Norse cultural sphere, where legal and computistical works are among the earliest texts asserting the existence of a bipartite year.[20] The notion of a six-month unit *misseri* finds ample support in the sagas, and remained in use in Iceland well into the modern period.[21] Evidence of the existence of the cognate term *missere* and its usage in Anglo-Saxon England survives in three poetic sources conventionally dated 'early'.[22] These attestations lend credence to the inference that a calendrical division of the year into two parts was prevalent before Germanic culture branched off into North and West Germanic subgroups, and remained influential at least until the Julian year took over most of its official functions.

The exact relationship between the system practised in medieval Europe and that described by Tacitus is uncertain. Early scholars in particular have attempted to give Tacitus's three seasons a place in early Germanic history,[23] but a diachronic perspective suggests rather that the account is based on a misunderstanding, a misrepresentation, or the customs of an unrepresentative tribe.[24]

---

[20] *Grágás*, ch. 19: Vilhjálmur Finsen, ed., *Grágás: Islændernes lovbog i fristatens tid* (Copenhagen: Berling, 1852; reprinted in one volume Odense: Odense universitetsforlag, 1974), 1:37; *Bókarbót*: N. Beckman and Kr. Kålund, eds, *Alfræði íslenzk II: Rímtöl* (Copenhagen: Møller, 1914–18), 78.

[21] Árni Björnsson, *Saga dagganna*, 31–47, 261–9.

[22] *Genesis A* 1168, 1743: A. N. Doane, ed., *Genesis A: A New Edition*, rev. ed. (Madison, WI: University of Wisconsin Press, 2013); *Exodus* 49: J. R. R. Tolkien and Joan Turville-Petre, eds, *The Old English 'Exodus': Text, Translation, and Commentary* (Oxford: Clarendon, 1981); *Beowulf* 153, 1498, 1769, 2620: R. D. Fulk, Robert E. Bjork, and John D. Niles, eds, *Klaeber's '"Beowulf" and "The Fight at Finnsburg"'* (Toronto: University of Toronto Press, 2008). Although many scholars now approach the dating of these poems with great caution, the strongest linguistic and metrical studies place them firmly in the same, comparatively early period. The eighth century is still most commonly mentioned for all three. See Peter J. Lucas, ed., *Exodus* (London: Methuen, 1977), 69–71; Doane, *Genesis A*, 42–55; Leonard Neidorf, ed., *The Dating of 'Beowulf': A Reassessment* (Cambridge: Brewer, 2014).

[23] Alexander Tille, *Yule and Christmas: Their Place in the Germanic Year* (London: Nutt, 1899); Martin P. Nilsson, *Primitive Time-Reckoning: A Study in the Origins and First Development of the Art of Counting Time Among the Primitive and Early Culture Peoples* (Lund: Berling, 1920), 71–7; Nils Erik Enkvist, *The Seasons of the Year: Chapters on a Motif from 'Beowulf' to 'The Shepherd's Calendar'* (Helsinki: Societas Scientiarum Fennica, 1957), 4; Andreas Fischer, 'Sumer is icumen in: The Seasons of the Year in Middle English and Early Modern English', in *Studies in Early Modern English*, ed. Dieter Kastovsky, Topics in English Linguistics 13 (Berlin and New York: Mouton de Gruyter, 1994), 90; cf. Earl R. Anderson, 'The Seasons of the Year in Old English', *Anglo-Saxon England* 26 (1997): 242–4.

[24] Jacob Grimm, *Deutsche Mythologie*, 4th ed., ed. Elard Hugo Meyer, 3 vols (Berlin: Dümmler, 1875–8), 717–18; Enkvist, *The Seasons of the Year*, 4.

The lexical field of seasonal terms likewise supports the bipartite year, not the tripartite. Words for winter (*wintrus, winter, vetr*) and summer (*sumer, sumar*) are cognates across the Germanic languages, but spring (*lencten, vár*) has no such stable presence.[25] Although autumn is uniformly attested by *hærfest* and its cognates across the West and North Germanic languages, the persistent ambiguity of that term between the season and its chief agricultural labour of harvest, to which the word originally referred, makes it difficult to determine its age as a seasonal-taxonomical concept. The fact that no word for autumn or spring survives in Gothic may also be taken to suggest that an older calendar had only two parts, winter and summer,[26] but the modest size of the Gothic corpus beckons caution in that regard.

The Associative Year

Bede's account makes clear that the English administrative year in his day had four parts, and this has been the case ever since. Nevertheless, scholars have observed that the bipartite year was not so promptly abandoned by poets. Both the Old English poem *The Seafarer* and the Middle English lyric *Sumer is icumen in* have the cuckoo herald summer, for instance, an inaccuracy in a carefully referenced Julian system, since today's cuckoo migrates to England by April.[27] Earl Anderson is right to point out that this difficulty is easily resolved if it is understood that the authors had the bipartite year in mind, a folk-taxonomy that survived in common usage alongside the quadripartite year.[28] However, it would be misguided to reduce poetic references of this sort to remnants of a disappearing administrative system. Even if medieval authors thought of summer as starting in April, for instance, this does not explain why the birds in Chaucer's *Parliament of Fowls* welcome summer on Valentine's Day:

> Now welcome, somer, with thy sonne softe,
> That hast thes wintres wedres overshake,
> And driven away the longe nyghtes blake![29]   (lines 680–2)

---

[25] Although Old Norse *vár* has cognates with seasonal reference in other Indo-European languages (notably Latin *ver* and Old Frisian *wars*), the variance in seasonal terms between the Germanic languages suggests a lesser degree of conceptual prominence for this season in the early Germanic cultures.

[26] Earl R. Anderson, *Folk-Taxonomies in Early English* (Cranbury, NJ, London, and Mississauga, ON: Associated University Presses, 2003), 219–34.

[27] Janet Bately, 'Time and the Passing of Time in *The Wanderer* and Related OE Texts', *Essays & Studies*, n.s., no. 37 (1984): 5–6; Fischer, '*Sumer is icumen in*', 79; Marguerite-Marie Dubois, 'Le rondeau du coucou', in *La ronde des saisons: Les saisons dans la littérature et la société anglaises au Moyen Age*, ed. Leo Carruthers, Cultures et Civilisations Médiévales 16 (Paris: Presses de l'Université de Paris-Sorbonne, 1998), 18–19.

[28] Anderson, *Folk-Taxonomies*, 262–4.

[29] Larry Dean Benson, ed., *The Riverside Chaucer*, 3rd ed. (Boston: Houghton Mifflin, 1987), 385–94.

Indeed, examples can be found in modern literature where summer is understood to commence with the warmer weather of spring. The authors of these texts are unlikely to have known of a formal start to a six-month summer as observed in either medieval England or modern Iceland. When Shakespeare writes

> Shall I compare thee to a Summers day?
> Thou art more louely and more temperate:
> Rough windes do shake the darling buds of Maie,
> And Sommers lease hath all too short a date   (Sonnet 18, lines 1–4)[30]

his summer includes May and the process of budding, yet it has a short lease. Clearly, he is not perpetuating an ancient Germanic administrative calendar last attested in English literature 900 years before his own day. Instead, the cycle he is referencing is associative, not chronological: it is the warm and sunny days of the English year that have 'too short a date', more so than the three months labelled 'summer' by men and women of numbers.

Shakespeare's summer illustrates that the division of the solar year is not a monolithic convention but an elastic taxonomy, whose resolution and constitution adapt to the speaker's needs. In daily life, we alternate between Bede's astronomical understanding of the year (for example to make a dentist appointment) and Shakespeare's associative set of seasons (for example when we witness the annual return of birdsong), but we use no lexical markers to distinguish between the two; only context may reveal what we mean by 'summer'. To avoid perpetuating the scholarly confusion between the two systems, I will here attempt to shed some light on the cognitive processes underlying the variation in seasonal taxonomy.

Cognitive representations of reality are bounded by limited knowledge, time, and processing power;[31] they are thus necessarily reductive.[32] Indeed, recent models assume that compression is one of the central functions of the cognitive apparatus.[33] At both intuitive and deliberative levels of processing, the brain makes extensive use of heuristics, shortcuts employed with the objective of striking the optimal balance between accuracy and economy in judgement and decision-making. Heuristics bypass the majority of relevant computational processes, relying instead on simple cues that

---

[30] Paul Hammond, ed., *Shakespeare's Sonnets: An Original-Spelling Text* (Oxford: Oxford University Press, 2012), 145.

[31] Gerd Gigerenzer and Peter M. Todd, 'Fast and Frugal Heuristics: The Adaptive Toolbox', in *Simple Heuristics that Make us Smart*, ed. Gerd Gigerenzer and Peter M. Todd (Oxford: Oxford University Press, 1999), 5.

[32] Cf. Kenneth Burke, *A Grammar of Motives* (London: Prentice-Hall, 1945; Berkeley and Los Angeles: University of California Press, 1969), 59–61.

[33] Nick Chater and Paul Vitányi, 'Simplicity: A Unifying Principle in Cognitive Science?', *TRENDS in Cognitive Sciences* 7, no. 1 (January 2003): 19–20.

we associate with accurate prediction, though actual success rates vary greatly according to the heuristic used and the context of employment.[34]

Heuristic strategies have mostly been studied in preferential choice settings, but they have also been used to model categorization. To maximize successful categorization, one has to compare all relevant features of an object against the criteria of the available categories. However, someone who finds herself face to face with a potentially dangerous predator cannot afford to run through the complete checklist of hooves, teeth, and stripes, but will rather rely on a small number of potent cues.[35] She also cannot afford to come to a systematic ranking of features in descending order of predictive value (known as cue validity), as this takes time and processing power, both of which the heuristic process seeks to minimize. In intuitive processes, it is therefore more appropriate to speak of a feature's salience, or ability to attract the subject's attention. The salience of a feature may be learned or evolved to match its cue validity, but this relationship cannot be taken for granted.

Researchers stress the adaptive nature of the heuristic toolkit: test subjects apply different simplification strategies in different settings.[36] The salience of any one feature may thus depend on the task at hand. In deliberative tasks, of course, the mind does more processing in absolute measures, though its proportional reliance on heuristics seems to be no less than in low-level tasks.[37] The production of literature and learning belongs firmly in the deliberative realm, but many conceptual sets relayed in these traditions have been canonized through both deliberative and intuitive heuristic processes.

The earth's spin (the day) and solar orbit (the year) are high-resolution cycles with measurable effects on sun hours, meteorology, flora, and fauna at higher latitudes. In these parts of the world, communities rely on a detailed understanding of the solar year for a viable food economy. However, it would be an inefficient use of computational resources to bring an overly high resolution of the year to bear on operations that require less planning.

Our intuition, evolved before the days of agricultural planning, responds to immediate environmental stimuli. The most salient stimuli effected by

---

[34] Gerd Gigerenzer, 'Fast and Frugal Heuristics: The Tools of Bounded Rationality', in *Blackwell Handbook of Judgment and Decision Making*, ed. Derek J. Koehler and Nigel Harvey (Malden, MA: Blackwell, 2004), 63–4; Benjamin E. Hilbig, Sabine G. Scholl, and Rüdiger F. Pohl, 'Think or Blink: Is the Recognition Heuristic an "Intuitive" Strategy?', *Judgment and Decision Making* 5, no. 4 (July 2010): 300–9; Jean Czerlinski, Gerd Gigerenzer, and Daniel G. Goldstein, 'How Good are Simple Heuristics?' In Gigerenzer and Todd, *Simple Heuristics*, 97–118.

[35] Patricia M. Berretty, Peter M. Todd, and Laura Martignon, 'Categorization by Elimination: Using Few Cues to Choose', in Gigerenzer and Todd, *Simple Heuristics*, 235–54.

[36] John W. Payne, James R. Bettman, and Eric J. Johnson, *The Adaptive Decision Maker* (Cambridge: Cambridge University press, 1993).

[37] Hilbig, Scholl, and Pohl, 'Think or Blink'.

the cycles of year and day are warm and cold, light and dark. Although these are all points or ranges on their respective spectra, the fight-or-flight mechanism needs only a binary cue to know whether to undertake action.[38] Intuition accordingly responds to *too* cold to rest, *too* dark to travel, simplifying these spectra into binary switches.

From a cyclical-phenomenological viewpoint, what stands out in these ranges is their extreme manifestations. Autumn is not an outlier in terms of its temperature or sun hours, and its profile in this respect does not differ much from that of spring except in the direction of its trend. An experiential view of the year offers a simpler taxonomy: cold and dark connote winter; warm and bright connote summer. On an intuitive level and in processing tasks not concerned with accurate planning, therefore, these are the salient seasons.

Since chronological tasks are just one of many ways in which humans engage with their environment, it is a premise of this book that the phenomenological or associative year is central to seasonal thinking in many domains of human thought, including literature. This is not to say that these domains do not acknowledge a year of more detail than just two seasons. Instead, it means that when a seasonal or annual event is invoked, its non-chronological associations typically play a more prominent role than just where it falls on the abstracted calendar. Thus in much of Western culture, Christmas is associated rather with leisure, family, and woodfires than with the timing of the winter solstice. The question 'what are your summer plans?' prompts an account of leisure activities or a scheduled conference tour, not a sketch of the continuation of the year-round working rhythm that inevitably also continues into the astronomical summer. Similarly, the first annual co-occurrence of birdsong, flowers, and warmer temperatures connotes both summer and spring in many temperate zones, regardless of the precise date. An overzealous focus on the formal, chronological composition of the year risks losing sight of the more connotative and less quantifiable form the calendar assumes when it is not being consulted for the purpose of scheduling an appointment. The quantified solar calendar is an abstract and regularized overlay onto a rougher rhythm that would carry on just the same without accurate timekeeping. The tendency of associative thought to divide the year into two parts is a result of its disregard for scheduling combined with the greater phenomenological salience of the dichotomous set.

If associative and binary thinking plays an important role in the phenomenological year of today's thoroughly quantified societies, it should come as no surprise that this mode of thought was likewise prominent among cultures in transition from a two-season administrative (or broadly

---

[38] Daniel Nettle, 'Error Management', in *Evolution and the Mechanisms of Decision Making*, ed. Peter Hammerstein and Jeffrey R. Stevens (Cambridge, MA: MIT Press, 2012), 69–79.

practical) year. No author is limited to the dominant taxonomy of the day, of course: writers may choose a bipartite or quadripartite system and select figurative associations to match, as complexity is no objection in a creative endeavour. This is true of medieval as well as modern authors, though it stands to reason that two-season models will be especially productive in cultures that regularly make use of a binary practical calendar.

Since a two-season year was still remembered in Bede's lifetime, and the Icelanders used it in various domains throughout the Middle Ages, we should expect to see a fair number of references to bipartite seasonal taxonomies in addition to the Julian models found in the literatures of both these cultures. As the human mind tends to see contrast in binary sets while sets of four are more commonly analysed in terms of interdependence or progression, an author's choice of calendar division primes his choice of figurative application. These considerations predict a substantial number of summer/winter contrasts in medieval English and Icelandic literature.

Climate History

Literary seasonality may be informed by two types of source: literary convention and an author's own responses to the cycle of the year. Both ultimately derive from a personal experience of the physical climate, whether the author's or that of an ultimate source. It is thus worth reviewing what is known about medieval climatic conditions.

Climatology is an increasingly nuanced science. The coming of age of the field has yielded improved accuracy of results, but it has also led to greater difficulty communicating those results to interested parties not accustomed to the scientific culture typifying climatology today. The public is interested above all in the spatiotemporal generalization of data sets: which centuries were warmer, which were colder? Once such abstractions are attained, the desire is to be able to translate them back to the level of individual experience, so that they may inform our understanding of the challenges and opportunities faced by a king like Alfred or an explorer like Ohthere.

Climatologists' reluctance to satisfy these demands follows largely from the recognition that the desired data conversion breaks several of the rules of the field. Induction on the basis of multiple observations is not as widely valid here as it is in other disciplines, since five local warming trends may result from ten different causes, some cyclical and others aperiodic. This inherent complexity of the climate system means that the reverse process, deducing local conditions in a given year or decade exclusively from longitudinal regional data, is likewise problematic.[39]

---

[39] James W. Jordan, 'Arctic Climate and Landscape ca. AD 800–1400', in *The Northern World AD 900–1400*, ed. Herbert Maschner, Owen Mason, and Robert McGhee (Salt Lake City: University of Utah Press, 2009), 7–8.

Today's narrative framework surrounding medieval climate stems from a paradigm established by climatologist Hubert Lamb. From the 1960s onward, Lamb synthesized an array of proxy records alongside documentary evidence to show that the medieval-to-modern temperature record is characterized by a peak-and-trough progression in surface temperature that has since come to be known as the twin events of Medieval Warm Period and Little Ice Age.[40]

Although Lamb's narrative has had a tremendous impact on the field, his work is not cited by climatologists today except for reasons of historical interest. With the field's substantial increase in scientific rigour since the 1990s came higher standards of calibration and quantitative analysis, so that works more than two decades old are now rarely cited. A particularly problematic type of source employed by Lamb was documentary data, which are subjective, hard to date or verify, and too sporadic to be quantified in accordance with scientific standards. In addition, Lamb was given to generalizing on the basis of regional trends, a practice now avoided.[41] His emphasis on England overlaps with the geographic focus of this book, however, so that this last objection is less problematic for present purposes.

These considerations have made many climatologists reluctant to use the concepts of Medieval Warm Period and Little Ice Age. Nevertheless, recent proxy data continue to bear out patterns of early-medieval warming and late-medieval cooling in many parts of the northern hemisphere, and the 2013 report by the authoritative Intergovernmental Panel on Climate Change continues to use the concepts, although it adopts the more cautious term 'Medieval Climate Anomaly' for the former event.[42]

If documentary sources are disregarded, a medieval warm and/or arid period is still evidenced in the geological record, which indicates that the period between 900 and 1250 was one of net glacial retreat worldwide.[43] That this period was comparatively warm on either side of the North Atlantic is confirmed by numerous studies of marine sediments and other

---

[40] H. H. Lamb, 'Britain's Climate in the Past', in *The Changing Climate: Selected Papers* (London: Methuen, 1966), 170–95; H. H. Lamb, *Climate: Present, Past, and Future*, 2 vols (London: Methuen, 1972–7), 2:423–73; H. H. Lamb, *Climate, History and the Modern World*, 2nd ed. (London and New York: Routledge, 1995), 171–241; H. H. Lamb, 'Northern Europe: The Last Thousand Years', in *Weather, Climate and Human Affairs: A Book of Essays and Other Papers* (London: Routledge, 1998), 27–39.
[41] Raymond S. Bradley, Malcolm K. Hughes, and Henry F. Diaz, 'Climate in Medieval Time', *Science*, n.s., 302, no. 5644 (17 October 2003): 404–5; Eystein Jansen *et al.*, 'Palaeoclimate: The Physical Science Basis', *Contribution of Working Group I to the Fourth Assessment Report of the Intergovernmental Panel on Climate Change*, ed. S. Solomon *et al.* (Cambridge: Cambridge University Press, 2007), 468–9.
[42] V. Masson-Delmotte *et al.*, 'Information from Palaeoclimate Archives: The Physical Science Basis', *Working Group I Contribution to the Fifth Assessment Report of the Intergovernmental Panel on Climate Change*, ed. Thomas F. Stocker *et al.* (Cambridge: Cambridge University Press, 2013), 409–15.
[43] Jean M. Grove, 'Glacial Geological Evidence for the Medieval Warm Period', *Climatic Change* 26 (1994): 143–69.

proxy records, though high-resolution records tend to reveal a succession of shorter trends with greater regional variability. On average, temperatures for this period and region are comparable to early-twentieth-century levels but did not reach those of the late-twentieth century except at a small number of sites in the western North Atlantic.[44]

The subsequent cooling is not in doubt, though this period too is best defined regionally and not as a straightforward, continuously downward trend. Following a gradual onset, Europe and the North Atlantic experienced a first trough, and exceptional seasonal variability, in the fourteenth century. After a warming spell in the fifteenth, the climate resumed its downward trend to a low about the eighteenth century. For several regions, including Iceland, the period can be said to have extended into the mid-1800s, when it was replaced by the current warming trend.[45]

Although climatologists cannot rely on documentary data for the reconstruction of past climate, historians may compare historical writings to climatological reconstructions as long as they acknowledge the limited applicability of their evidence and avoid such traps as false deduction and confirmation bias. With these caveats and recent developments in the field of climatology in mind, it may be pointed out that scholars in the later-twentieth century gathered the relevant documentary data for England, Iceland, and Continental Europe and judged these records to be consistent with an early-medieval warming and late-medieval cooling.[46]

[44] Malcolm K. Hughes and Henry F. Diaz, 'Was there a "Medieval Warm Period", and if so, where and when?', *Climatic Change* 26 (1994): 114–25; T. M. Cronin *et al.*, 'Medieval Warm Period, Little Ice Age and 20th Century Temperature Variability from Chesapeake Bay', *Global and Planetary Change* 36 (2003): 17–29; K. V. Kremenetski *et al.*, 'Medieval Climate Warming and Aridity as Indicated by Multiproxy Evidence from the Kola Peninsula, Russia', *Palaeogeography, Palaeoclimatology, Palaeoecology* 209 (2004): 113–25; Hans W. Linderholm and Björn E. Gunnarson, 'Summer Temperature Variability in Central Scandinavia during the Last 3600 Years', *Geografiska Annaler* 87a1 (2005): 231–41; Gerald R. North *et al.*, *Surface Temperature Reconstructions for the last 2,000 Years* (Washington, DC: National Academic Press, 2006), accessed 15 March 2015, http://www.nap.edu/catalog/11676.html; Michael E. Mann *et al.*, 'Proxy-Based Reconstructions of Hemispheric and Global Surface Temperature Variations Over the Past Two Millennia', *PNAS* 105, no. 36 (September 2008): 13252–7; Jordan, 'Arctic Climate'; Karen Knudsen *et al.*, 'Palaeoceanography and Climate Changes off North Iceland during the Last Millennium: Comparison of Foraminifera, Diatoms and Ice-Rafted Debris with Instrumental and Documentary Data', *Journal of Quaternary Science* 24 (2009): 457–68; T. M. Cronin *et al.*, 'The Medieval Climate Anomaly and Little Ice Age in Chesapeake Bay and the North Atlantic Ocean', *Palaeogeography, Palaeoclimatology, Palaeoecology* 297 (2010): 299–310.

[45] A. E. J. Ogilvie and Trausti Jónsson, '"Little Ice Age" Research: A Perspective from Iceland', *Climatic Change* 48 (2001): 9–52; Cronin *et al.*, 'Temperature Variability', 26; Linderholm and Björn E. Gunnarson, 'Summer Temperature Variability'; Grove, *Little Ice Ages*; Yarrow Axford *et al.*, 'Climate of the Little Ice Age and the Past 2000 Years in Northeast Iceland Inferred from Chironomids and Other Lake Sediment Proxies', *Journal of Paleolimnology* 41 (2009): 7–24.

[46] Lamb, *Climate*, 2:423–549; Ogilvie, 'Climate and Society', 171–264; Ogilvie, 'Climatic Changes'; Lamb, *Climate, History and the Modern World*; Ogilvie and Farmer, 'Documenting the Medieval Climate'; C. Pfister, G. Schwarz-Zanetti, and M. Wegmann, 'Winter Severity in Europe: The Fourteenth Century', *Climatic Change* 34 (1996): 91–108; C. Pfister *et al.*, 'Winter Air Temperature Variations in Western Europe during the Early and High Middle Ages (AD 750–1300)', *The Holocene* 8, no. 5 (1998): 535–52.

What, then, can historical climatology tell us about the seasons as experienced by the cultures under investigation? The evidence suggests that the productive literary culture of the late Anglo-Saxon period, at least from around 950 onwards, unfolded amidst frequent series of relatively warm summers and mild winters. The resulting mean temperature for 950–1100 seems to have been higher than that of preceding centuries and comparable to the earlier, though not the later, twentieth century. The same may be said of the later waves of Norse expansion and the time in which the sagas of Icelanders are set. However, these narratives and most other Old Icelandic literature began to be written down as temperatures began to decline during the severe fluctuations of the fourteenth century. The bulk of Middle English poetry was likewise composed in this time of rapid and erratic climatic downturn.

It is important to recognize that these statistics translate into no significant difference in phenomenological climate perception between medieval and modern periods. Individuals in all eras will mark extreme weather events and notable deviations from a mean, but adjustments of that mean itself are perceptible only if their gradient is comparable to that of the current anthropogenic warming trend, which is unprecedented in historical times. The difference between medieval and modern temperatures and precipitation patterns would instead have been visible indirectly, in the viability and yields of various crops. Above all, people would have been struck by the increased variability of crop yields.[47] One can imagine this fact of fourteenth-century life leaving a strong impression of the arbitrariness of worldly fortunes, comparable with the Boethian sentiment so avidly promulgated by Chaucer. In addition, the greater number of colder winters in some decades must have had an impact on the seasonality of manuscript production, as neither scribes nor ink performed well in cold conditions.[48]

This last observation signals a more important point. Differences in direct climate perception between medieval and modern observers are due less to climate change than to technological differences and the nature of the energy infrastructure. There are longitudinal climatic differences between our own lifetime and those of medieval English and Icelandic authors,

---

[47] Cf. Miller and Hatcher, *Medieval England*, 60.

[48] Abbot Guthberht of Wearmouth–Jarrow remarks on the winter's effect on the hand of the scribe and on consequent limits to book production in a letter of 764, the year of a severe winter across western Europe: Michael Tangl, ed., *Epistolae selectae in usum scholarum I: S. Bonifatii et Lulli epistolae* (Berlin: Weidmann, 1916), 251. For documentary evidence of the winter's severity, see, for example, Seán Mac Airt and Gearóid Mac Niocaill, eds and trans., *The Annals of Ulster (to AD 1131)*, vol. 1, *Text and Translation* (Dublin: Dublin Institute for Advanced Studies, 1983), s.a. 764.1; *Anglo-Saxon Chronicle*, MS A, s.a. 761: Janet Bately, ed., *The Anglo-Saxon Chronicle: A Collaborative Edition*, vol. 3: *MS A* (Cambridge: Brewer, 1986); and further evidence collected in Michael McCormick, *Origins of the European Economy: Communications and Commerce*, A.D. 300–900 (Cambridge: Cambridge University Press, 2001), 878–81. The low temperatures of this particular winter have been plausibly linked with volcanic activity: ibid., 881. See further Dresbeck, 'Winter Climate and Society', 180; 191, n. 34; Dresbeck, 'Techne, labor et natura', 87–8.

but the immediately observable differences are due in the first instance to improvements in heating and insulation as well as a vast reduction in the proportion of economic activity conducted out of doors.

The Economic Year

As was observed above, the astronomical and meteorological definitions of the solar year are today considered the most authoritative. Since the description of seasonal progression is a human activity, however, it should come as no surprise that more anthropocentric definitions exist, tracing the impact of temperature and the growth cycle on society. Historically, the most important of these is the economic year, as this cycle holds the key to societal sustainability, not least in sedentary societies.[49] Culture, including the processes of law, politics, religion, and literature, is conditional upon and largely conditioned by the societal base of economic production.[50] The viability of these processes thus depends to various degrees on economic prosperity.

Given the low per-capita production value of organic economies, the bulk of medieval labour was carried out in the primary sector, and more specifically in farming.[51] Land cultivation and animal husbandry were normally carried out in conjunction, as crops required animals for ploughing and manure, while animals fed on arable products and by-products. The primary food intake in Anglo-Saxon England was from plants, however, especially grains, and especially in the later period.[52] The agricultural calendar dictated the economic year accordingly. Since agricultural production was especially closely tied to the solar year while the economic year in turn played a central role in shaping the social calendar, the agricultural cycle may be seen as an interface elastically subjecting the cultural year to the material demands of the seasons.

Although the agricultural sector has undergone great technological advances since the Middle Ages, the environmental variables of outdoor cultivation have remained comparatively stable. Broadly speaking, therefore, the English agricultural year answered to the still familiar cycle of ploughing, sowing, haymaking, and harvesting.[53] Innovations through the centuries

---

[49] Cristiano Grottanelli, 'Agriculture', in *Encyclopedia of Religion*, 2nd ed., ed. Lindsay Jones (Detroit, MI: MacMillan, 2005), 186–8.

[50] See Marx's preface to his *Zur Kritik der politischen Ökonomie*: Karl Marx and Friedrich Engels, *Werke*, 13 vols, ed. not given; commissioned by the Institut für Marxismus-Leninismus beim ZK der SED (Berlin: Dietz, 1956–90), 13:8–9; cf. C. C. Dyer, *Making a Living in the Middle Ages: The People of Britain 850–1520* (New Haven and London: Yale University Press, 2002), 1.

[51] Dyer, *Making a Living*, 13; Banham and Faith, *Farms and Farming*, 2.

[52] Banham and Faith, *Farms and Farming*, 19–20, 39–40, 76.

[53] Ibid., 50–66. Some detail may be found in the eleventh-century Old English text *Be gesceadwisan gerefan*, which lists a selection of the various tasks to be carried out under the

included technological developments and changes to the balance between crops and livestock, or different crops;[54] some may also have responded to the changing climate.[55] This was a likely factor in the rise of viticulture, first sparingly evidenced in southern England in the tenth century but reaching true economic viability only with the arrival of Norman aristocrats[56] and, shortly thereafter, peak climatic conditions (c. 1100–1300).[57]

The Icelandic economy differed from that of medieval England in its greater reliance on animal husbandry.[58] The island's climate supports fewer species of crop than England and is more susceptible to poor yields due to sustained winters.[59] For these reasons, pre-industrial Icelanders primarily cultivated hay as winter fodder for their livestock,[60] supplementing their diet of dairy and meat from husbandry with fish and game.[61] The seasonality of fishery and the hunt depended to a degree on the migratory patterns of cod and birds, but also relied on lulls in the agricultural cycle. Up until the nineteenth century, fishing seems to have been one of many labours practised at a balanced farming estate,[62] although professional fishing, including a domestic fish trade and some exportation of stockfish, existed

---

supervision of the estate manager, dividing them by the quarter-year: F. Liebermann, ed., *Die Gesetze der Angelsachsen*, 3 vols (Halle: Niemeyer, 1903–16), 1:454; for the dating, see Liebermann, *Gesetze*, 3:244–7; Dorothy Bethurum, 'Episcopal Magnificence in the Eleventh Century', in *Studies in Old English Literature in Honor of Arthur G. Brodeur*, ed. Stanley B. Greenfield (Eugene, OR: University of Oregon Books, 1963), 162–70; P. D. A. Harvey, '*Rectitudines singularum personarum* and *Gerefa*', *English Historical Review* 108, no. 426 (1993): 4–7.

[54] Banham and Faith, *Farms and Farming*, 28–9, 38–9, 44–51, 57–8, 68–74, 76–7, 107–8, 113.

[55] Ibid., 34.

[56] Tim Unwin, 'Saxon and Early Norman Viticulture in England', *Journal of Wine Research* 1, no. 1 (1990): 64–70.

[57] Lamb, *Climate*, 2:276–9; Lamb, *Climate, History and the Modern World*, 179–80.

[58] Jón Jóhannesson, *Íslendinga saga: A History of the Icelandic Commonwealth* (Winnipeg: University of Manitoba Press, 1974), 288–96; Daniel E. Vasey, 'Population, Agriculture, and Famine: Iceland, 1784–1785', *Human Ecology* 19, no. 3 (September 1991): 323–50; William R. Short, *Icelanders in the Viking Age: The People of the Sagas* (Jefferson, NC, and London: McFarland, 2010), 74–88. For a detailed study of the traditional Icelandic diet, see Hallgerður Gísladóttir, *Íslensk matarhefð* (Reykjavik: Mál og menning, 1999).

[59] S. Axel Anderson, 'Iceland's Industries', *Economic Geography* 7, no. 3 (July 1931): 284–90; Vasey, 'Population'.

[60] Gunnar Karlsson, *Iceland's 1100 Years: History of a Marginal Society* (Reykjavik: Mál og menning, 2000), 45–6. Hay remains the country's primary crop today: Rannveig Sigurdardóttir *et al.*, *The Economy of Iceland* (Reykjavik: Sedlabanki, 2007), 27; see also Anderson, 'Iceland's Industries', 285–6.

[61] Anderson, 'Iceland's Industries'; Vasey, 'Population', 324; Hallgerður Gísladóttir, *Matarhefð*; Thomas H. McGovern *et al.*, 'Landscapes of Settlement in Northern Iceland: Historical Ecology of Human Impact and Climate Fluctuation on the Millennial Scale', *American Anthropologist* 109, no. 1 (March 2007): 29; W. Paul Adderley, Ian A. Simpson, and Orri Vésteinsson, 'Local-Scale Adaptations: A Modeled Assessment of Soil, Landscape, Microclimatic, and Management Factors in Norse Home-Field Productivities', *Geoarchaeology* 34, no. 4 (2008): 500–27; Short, *Icelanders*, 74–88.

[62] Anderson, 'Iceland's Industries', 290; Lúðvík Kristjánsson, 'Fiskveiðar Íslendinga 1874–1940: Lauslegt yfirlit', *Almanak hins Íslenzka þjóðvinafélags* (Reykjavik) 70 (1944): 65–111; Gunnar Karlsson, *Iceland's 1100 Years*, 106–10; cf. *Egils saga*, ch. 29: Bjarni Einarsson, ed., *Egils saga* (London: Viking Society for Northern Research / University College London, 2003), 40.

by the thirteenth and fourteenth centuries and became a major part of the economy in the fifteenth century.[63]

A noteworthy difference between the medieval English and Icelandic economies consisted in better conditions for soil productivity and trade in the former, comparing to a closer approximation of subsistence farming in the latter.[64] England's longer growing season and milder winters naturally translated into larger yields. Indeed, a surplus was required of English peasants, as they typically owed land rents and taxes.[65] Any produce left over would have found a market in the towns, whose very existence required specialization and trade. By contrast, Icelandic freemen, minimally burdened by a system of public officials,[66] owed little tax prior to annexation by the Norwegian crown in 1262,[67] although religious tithing was practised after the adoption of Christianity and was in literary times at least believed to have been in use before the Conversion as well.[68] The social topography of the country was characterized by isolated farms and settled valleys. With urbanization wholly absent and international trade a seasonal industry, there was comparatively little impetus to set up a domestic market for vital resources other than the distribution of fish to inland areas,[69] although the local exchange of food and artefacts must have been ubiquitous.

Iceland's main export in the Commonwealth era was not a food product but wool, which was traded primarily for grain and wood.[70] This should not be taken to mean that the population at large depended on these imported grains for subsistence, however: even at the time of annexation, the legislated minimum of trading ships between Iceland and Norway was

---

[63] Jón Jóhannesson, *Íslendinga saga*, 303–5; Bridget Ann Henisch, *Fast and Feast: Food in Medieval Society* (University Park, PA: Pennsylvania State University Press, 1976), 33–5; Bruce E. Gelsinger, *Icelandic Enterprise: Commerce and Economy in the Middle Ages* (Columbia, SC: University of South Carolina Press, 1981), 181–94; Gunnar Karlsson, *Iceland's 1100 Years*, 106–7; but cf. the reservations concerning the scale of stockfish exports expressed in Jón Jóhannesson, *Íslendinga saga*, 313–15.

[64] Kevin P. Smith, 'Landnám: The Settlement of Iceland in Archaeological and Historical Perspective', *World Archaeology* 26, no. 3 (February 1995): 319–47; Ian A. Simpson et al., 'Soil Limitations to Agrarian Land Production in Premodern Iceland', *Human Ecology* 30, no. 4 (December 2002): 423–43; cf. Vasey, 'Population', 326.

[65] Dyer, *Making a Living*, 14, 26–42.

[66] Jón Jóhannesson, *Íslendinga saga*, 35–93, esp. 53–63; Gunnar Karlsson, *Iceland's 1100 Years*, 20–7.

[67] Björn Þorsteinsson, *Íslenzka þjóðveldið* (Reykjavik: Heimskringla, 1953), esp. 100; Jón Jóhannesson, *Íslendinga saga*, 61–2; Jesse Byock, ed., *Medieval Iceland: Society, Sagas, and Power* (Berkeley, CA: University of California Press, 1988), 78–9; Gunnar Karlsson, *Iceland's 1100 Years*, 83–6.

[68] *Egils saga*, ch. 86: Bjarni Einarsson, *Egils saga*, 178; *Vápnfirðinga saga*, ch. 5: Jón Jóhannesson, ed., *Austfirðinga sǫgur*, Íslenzk fornrit 11 (Reykjavik: Hið íslenzka fornritafélag, 1950), 33; *Grágás*, chs 255–60: Vilhjálmur Finsen, *Grágás*, 2:205–15; Björn Þorsteinsson, 'Tollr', *KLNM* 18 (1974): 452–4; Jón Jóhannesson, *Íslendinga saga*, 62.

[69] Cf. Gelsinger, *Icelandic Enterprise*, 181–94, which argues that fish took the place of wool as Iceland's primary export product from the fourteenth century onwards.

[70] Ibid.; Helgi Þorláksson, *Vaðmál og verðlag: Vaðmál í utanlandsviðskiptum og búskap Íslendinga á 13. og 14. öld* (Reykjavik: Helgi Þorláksson, 1991), 3–28.

as low as six per annum, translating into an estimated twelve kilograms of imported goods per capita.[71] At best, if it is assumed that only the social elite profited from international trade, the wealthier landowners chose to enrich their diet by these foreign sources.[72] This is almost certainly what happened, as a lack of competition among traders and the short sailing season must have translated into high prices.[73] This disconnect between trade and subsistence had a parallel among the Norse Greenlanders, who seem to have been extensively engaged in the export of furs, hides, ivory, and valuable birds,[74] yet they traded these valuables for non-vital commodities rather than the grain their own soil could not support.[75]

North Atlantic agriculture thus placed a strong emphasis on local subsistence, while individual farmers aimed for self-sufficiency in the first instance.[76] This impression is reinforced by the fact that high-latitude societies generally depend more heavily on food storage to last them through the winter. Even if the thirteenth-century interference of Norwegian kings and the subsequent annexation represented a first clear impetus towards a more strongly profit-driven economy,[77] Iceland's paucity of natural resources and its peripheral location relative to trading partners meant that food production remained very much the consuming farmer's own responsibility.[78] Perceived within the framework of the economic cycle, the accumulation of winter provisions, and therefore the feat of making it through the winter without unnecessary discomfort or losses in livestock, constituted a year-long personal challenge for the farmers described in the sagas.

In both England and Scandinavia, any failure to meet the challenge of winter provisions would have hit hardest in spring, when stocks of food and fodder ran low and the population could find themselves at the season's

---

[71] Gunnar Karlsson, *Iceland's 1100 Years*, 50.

[72] Contrast Gelsinger, *Icelandic Enterprise*, for example 14–15, 150–1.

[73] Cf. Vasey, 'Population', 326; Gunnar Karlsson, *Iceland's 1100 Years*, 50.

[74] P. C. Buckland *et al.*, 'Bioarchaeological and Climatological Evidence for the Fate of Norse Farmers in Medieval Greenland', *Antiquity* 70 (1996): 90; Kirsten Seaver, *The Frozen Echo: Greenland and the Exploration of North America ca. AD 1000–1500* (Stanford, CA: Stanford University Press, 1996), 47–8, 80–9.

[75] Thomas H. McGovern, 'Management for Extinction in Norse Greenland', in *Historical Ecology: Cultural Knowledge and Changing Landscapes*, ed. C. Crumley (Santa Fe: School of American Research Monographs, 1994), 138; cf. Seaver, *Frozen Echo*, 47.

[76] Cf. Vasey, 'Population', 326. One may compare with this situation Tacitus's Roman perspective on Germanic agricultural practice, based on self-sufficiency rather than profit (*Germania*, ch. 26: Lund, *Germania*, 90; see also Lund's cultural interpretation on p. 67 of his edition).

[77] Sophia Perdikaris and Thomas H. McGovern, 'Cod Fish, Walrus, and Chieftains: Economic Intensification in the Norse North Atlantic', in *Seeking a Richer Harvest: The Archaeology of Subsistence Intensification, Innovation, and Change*, ed. Tina L. Thurston and Christopher T. Fisher (New York: Springer, 2006), 193–216.

[78] An impression of the socio-economic dynamics of scarcity is presented in *Hœnsa-Þóris saga*, which suggests that resources were redistributed through local trade as required (chs 4–5): Sigurður Nordal and Guðni Jónsson, eds, *Borgfirðinga sǫgur*, Íslenzk fornrit 3 (Reykjavik: Hið íslenzka fornritafélag, 1916–18), 11–16.

mercy. Accordingly, morbidity and mortality rates were greatest not in the three months of the Julian winter when the temperatures reached their annual minima, but in spring when provisions ran low and the succession of cold months became a test of endurance.[79] Tellingly, the Old English collection of metrical aphorisms known as *Maxims II* observes that

> Winter byð cealdost,
> lencten hrimigost (he byð lengest ceald). (lines 5–6)[80]

Winter is coldest, spring most hoarfrosted (it is cold the longest).

It has been proposed that this notion of a prolonged ground frost in spring has an explanation in Ælfric's *De temporibus anni*,[81] which notes that the earth takes time to warm up after being pervaded by the cold of winter.[82] Even so, the observations of Ælfric and the *Maxims* poet alike may well have been inspired by the social and economic realities of spring that made the season seem so slow to pass. The Lent fast, though it stimulated fishery in north-western Europe and eventually, by the fifteenth century, helped spawn a large-scale international fish trade,[83] cannot have been beneficial to either health or economy in all respects and localities. After all, the dairy produce that had to be forgone came from livestock that still had to be fed, and any dietary impoverishment at the time of year when least fresh food is available to begin with poses a threat to health. Although the Advent fast likewise represented dietary impoverishment, the early-winter ritual followed the time of greatest plenty (harvest and slaughtering season) and was followed by a season of less activity and large food stores; it may thus be expected to have had less impact on morbidity rates. Economically and medically, therefore, the season of greatest hardship was spring, while the darkest days of the year were eased by large provisions.

---

[79] Barbara Harvey and Jim Oeppen, 'Patterns of Morbidity in Late Medieval England: A Sample from Westminster Abbey', *Economic History Review* 54, no. 2 (2001): 230–1 (seasonal morbidity among monks of fourteenth-century Westminster Abbey compared to seasonal patterns in early-modern mortality); cf. Vasey, 'Population', esp. 327–36, 344–8 (mortality in Iceland as a consequence of the famine following the nine-month eruption of the Lakagígar fissure in southern Iceland beginning in June 1783). A different pattern may have existed among the wealthy, who were less affected by food shortages. Cf. William Wayne Farris, *Japan's Medieval Population: Famine, Fertility, and Warfare in a Transformative Age* ([Honolulu]: University of Hawai'i Press, 2006), 189. A different pattern existed also in years of pestilence, as the bubonic plague caused most deaths in late summer and autumn but was tempered by the northern winter weather: Ole J. Benedictow, *The Black Death 1346–1353: The Complete History* (Woodbridge: Boydell, 2004), for example 24, 30, 103–4.

[80] Elliott van Kirk Dobbie, ed., *The Anglo-Saxon Minor Poems*, Anglo-Saxon Poetic Records 6 (New York: Columbia University Press, 1942), 55–7.

[81] Martin Blake, ed., *Ælfric's 'De temporibus anni'*, Anglo-Saxon Texts 6 (Cambridge: Brewer, 2009).

[82] Anderson, *Folk-Taxonomies*, 248. 'Se langigenda dæg is ceald forðan þe seo eorðe bið mid ðam winterlicum cyle þurhgan, ꝛ bið langsum ær ðan ðe heo eft gebeðod sy' ('the lengthening day is cold because the earth is pervaded by the winter cold, and it is long before it is heated up again', Ælfric, *De temporibus anni*, lines 204–5).

[83] Henisch, *Fast and Feast*, 33–5.

LITERARY ECONOMICS

The key role played by spring processes in the sustainability of the Icelandic food economy finds confirmation in the narrative literature. The emphasis here is on gathering sufficient winter fodder to last the livestock until the grazing season, the time of whose arrival is variable and therefore highly anticipated. *Landnámabók* tells how Flóki Vilgerðarson, one of Iceland's traditional explorers, neglects to gather sufficient hay on account of the country's abundance in fish, resulting in the death of all his livestock during his first winter in Iceland.[84] The anecdote bears witness to the need for adaptation to the new habitat by underlining the need to stock up for a long winter. In his failure to do so, Flóki is confronted with the long infertile season characteristic of his new habitat. By contrast, the author of *Egils saga* explains Skalla-Grímr's success as an early settler of Iceland by the multifaceted nature of his farming and his clever use of space, but notable among his successes is certainly the discovery that his sheep are able to survive in their valley pastures by themselves all winter (ch. 29).[85] Icelandic farmers indeed relied on winter grazing when possible, but snow and lack of growth commonly interfered, so that spring severity remained a threat throughout pre-industrial history.[86] Accordingly, winters that were hard on livestock (*fellivetr, hrosfellisvetr, nautadauðavetr, nautfellisvetr*) are commonly recorded in both narrative and annalistic sources.[87] In *Eyrbyggja saga*, Úlfar kappi is considered exceptionally lucky with his livestock (*fésæll*) because it never dies of starvation or blizzards (ch. 30).[88] These references taken

---

[84] Jakob Benediktsson, ed., *Íslendingabók, Landnámabók*, Íslenzk fornrit 1 (Reykjavik: Hið íslenzka fornritafélag, 1986), 36–8.

[85] Bjarni Einarsson, *Egils saga*, 40.

[86] A. E. J. Ogilvie, 'Climate and Farming in Northern Iceland, ca. 1700–1850', in *Aspects of Arctic and Sub-Arctic History: Proceedings of the International Congress on the History of the Arctic and Sub-Arctic Region, Reykjavík, 18–21 June 1998*, ed. Ingi Sigurðsson and Jón Skaptason (Reykjavik: University of Iceland Press, 2000), 289–99; Páll Bergþórsson, 'The Effect of Climatic Variations on Farming in Iceland', in Ingi Sigurðsson and Jón Skaptason, *Aspects*, 264–9; A. E. J. Ogilvie and Gísli Pálsson, 'Mood, Magic, and Metaphor: Allusions to Weather and Climate in the Sagas of Icelanders', in *Weather, Climate, Culture*, ed. Sarah Strauss and Benjamin Orlove (Oxford and New York: Berg, 2003), 258–9.

[87] A detailed account of a hay shortage is given in *Hœnsa-Þóris saga*, esp. chs 4–5: Sigurður Nordal and Guðni Jónsson, *Borgfirðinga sǫgur*, 11–16; see also *Fóstbrœðra saga*, ch. 6: Björn K. Þórólfsson and Guðni Jónsson, eds, *Vestfirðinga sǫgur*, Íslenzk fornrit 6 (Reykjavik: Hið íslenzka fornritafélag, 1943), 147; *Prestssaga Guðmundar Arasonar*, ch. 11: Jón Jóhannesson, Magnús Finnbogason, and Kristján Eldjárn, eds, *Sturlunga saga*, 2 vols (Reykjavik: Sturlunguútgáfan, 1946), 1:136; Annals I, IV, V, VIII s.a. 1187: Gustav Stork, ed., *Islandske annaler indtil 1578* (Christiania [Oslo]: Grøndahl, 1888), 22, 119, 180, 324; IV s.a. 1313: ibid., 150; X s.a. 1313–14: ibid., 488; VII s.a. 1314: ibid., 265; VIII s.a. 1362: ibid., 359. Cf. legal documents suggesting hay disputes, for example *Grágás*, ch. 198: Vilhjálmur Finsen, *Grágás*, 2:106–8. See further Paul Schach, 'The Use of Scenery in the *Íslendinga sǫgur*' (unpublished doctoral dissertation, University of Pennsylvania, 1949), 18; Ogilvie, 'Climate and Society', 256–60; Ogilvie and Gísli Pálsson, 'Mood, Magic, and Metaphor', 259–61; Short, *Icelanders*, 77–9.

[88] Einar Ólafur Sveinsson and Matthías Þórðarson, eds, *Eyrbyggja saga*, Íslenzk fornrit 4 (Reykjavik: Hið íslenzka fornritafélag, 1935), 81.

together underline the critical economic significance of livestock survival during the medieval Icelandic winter.

The importance of spring grazing is further brought out by the concept's presence in weather miracles that are in other respects representative of the widespread motif of saintly mediation between season and economy. The concern is addressed in both the early-thirteenth-century[89] *Jóns saga ins helga*, on Jón Ǫgmundarson (1052–1121), and the early-fourteenth-century[90] saga of Guðmundr Arason (1161–1237). Chapter 13 of the first work tells how, on account of the cold weather, the land in northern Iceland has not yet commenced its springtime growth by the time of the spring assembly in May. Jón travels to the assembly grounds and vows to erect a church there, even marking the spot where the church is to be built. Following his promise, the ice breaks up and the grass grows up so quickly that there is sufficient grazing before the week is over.[91] Just two chapters on follows another anecdote, perhaps a variant account of the same incident, which tells how one spring the weather is so dry that the land supports little growth by the time of the Moving Days (i.e. late May on the Julian calendar), and even by the time of the *alþingi* in late June. Jón rides to the assembly and promises an improvement in weather conditions. On the same day the weather turns from cloudless to a downpouring, and for the remainder of the summer the land is irrigated by nocturnal dews while the days are sunny, resulting in an average harvest yield (ch. 15).[92] *Guðmundar saga Arasonar* conveys the same motif one year when the Virgin Mary predicts that the snow will disappear so rapidly that there will be sufficient grazing by Easter Sunday (ch. 79).[93] Similar episodes occur elsewhere without reference to grazing, as in the later-fourteenth-century[94] saga of Lárentíus Kálfsson (1267–1331), which tells of the snow and ice melting just in time for the Easter Day procession (ch. 33)[95] and how the weather turns mild and

---

[89] Sigurgeir Steingrímsson, Ólafur Halldórsson, and Peter Foote, eds, *Biskupa sögur I*, 2 vols, Íslenzk fornrit 15 (Reykjavik: Hið íslenzka fornritafélag, 2003), 1:ccxiv–ccxv.
[90] The various redactions make extensive use of early-thirteenth-century sources, but these do not contain the miracle here described. See Stefán Karlsson, 'Bóklausir menn: A Note on Two Versions of *Guðmundar saga*', in *Sagnaskemmtun: Studies in Honour of Hermann Pálsson*, ed. Rudolf Simek, Jónas Kristjánsson, and Hans Bekker-Nielsen (Vienna: Böhlau, 1986), 277–86; Margaret Cormac, 'Christian Biography', in *A Companion to Old Norse–Icelandic Literature and Culture*, ed. Rory McTurk (Oxford: Blackwell, 2005), 37–8.
[91] Sigurgeir Steingrímsson, Ólafur Halldórsson, and Foote, *Biskupa sögur I*, 2:227–8. Cf. the miraculous absence of snow from the south-western face of Þorgrímr's grave mound in *Gísla saga*, presented as a token of Freyr's loyalty to Þorgrímr (ch. 18: Björn K. Þórólfsson and Guðni Jónsson, *Vestfirðinga sǫgur*, 57 and n. 2).
[92] Sigurgeir Steingrímsson, Ólafur Halldórsson, and Foote, *Biskupa sögur I*, 2:229–30.
[93] Jón Sigurðsson and Guðbrand[u]r Vígfusson, eds, *Biskupa sögur*, 2 vols (Copenhagen: Hið íslenzka bókmenntafélag, 1858–78), 167.
[94] Guðrun Ása Grímsdóttir, ed., *Biskupa sögur III*, Íslenzk fornrit 17 (Reykjavik: Hið íslenzka fornritafélag, 1998), lxvii.
[95] Ibid., 340.

the snow melts for the occasion of Jón Ǫgmundarson's translation (ch. 35).⁹⁶

None of these miracles is exceptional among the European corpus of saintly interventions in general outline;⁹⁷ indeed, Jón's feat in conjuring rain from a cloudless sky closely follows its model in the *Dialogues* of Gregory the Great.⁹⁸ What is peculiar to their form in the bishops' sagas is the authors' concern for spring grazing, reflecting the key role played by this component of the Icelandic economic cycle.

THE MILITARY SEASON

Another aspect of the economic cycle commonly invoked with regard to ancient and medieval Europe is warfare. Though numerous exceptions have been documented, the legions of the Roman Empire normally ceased combat operations when fodder availability became problematic. This closed season is generally defined as December through February for the Mediterranean region;⁹⁹ for northern Europe it has been suggested that the arrival of the rainy season about the beginning of October may have been more commonly normative.¹⁰⁰ The Mediterranean Sea was largely closed to travel, generally including military expeditions, from 10 November to 10 March on account of severe weather.¹⁰¹ North Sea conditions necessitated a shorter season still.¹⁰² In addition, raiding and sustained warfare alike often depended on the exploitation of the enemy's food stocks for the sustenance of the invading army.¹⁰³ This suggests that late summer should be the central season for large-scale warfare in agricultural societies, when crops are ripening but still in the fields where they will naturally fall to the invaders and can easily be denied to the besieged population. Winter, by contrast, should be the season of least military activity on account of the severe weather conditions and limited access to food and fodder, although occasional land-based raids on food stocks might be expected.

---

⁹⁶ Sigurgeir Steingrímsson, Ólafur Halldórsson, and Foote, *Biskupa sögur I*, 2:229–30.

⁹⁷ Cf. E. Cobham Brewer, *A Dictionary of Miracles: Imitative, Realistic, and Dogmatic* (Philadelphia, PA: Lippincott, 1884), 129–31.

⁹⁸ Gregory the Great, *Dialogues* 2.33: Adalbert De Vogüé and Paul Antin, eds, *Grégoire le grande: 'Dialogues'*, 3 vols, Sources chrétiennes, 251, 260, 265 (Paris: Cerf, 1978–80), 2:230–5; Sigurgeir Steingrímsson, Ólafur Halldórsson, and Foote, *Biskupa sögur I*, 2:230, n. 1.

⁹⁹ Jonathan P. Roth, *The Logistics of the Roman Army at War*, Columbia Studies in the Classical Tradition 23 (Leiden: Brill, 1998), 177–82.

¹⁰⁰ Tille, *Yule and Christmas*, 24.

¹⁰¹ McCormick, *Origins*, 450–1, 459. The same chapter notes, however, that military campaigns, and raids in particular, are among the most common exceptions to this convention (466–7).

¹⁰² For a Roman perspective on the dangers of the North Sea, see Tacitus, *Annales* 2.23–4: Henry Furneaux, ed., *Cornelii Taciti 'Annalium libri I–IV'*, 2nd ed. (Oxford: Clarendon, 1904), 96–7. An insight into Atlantic practice is offered in *Konungs skuggsjá*, chs 22–3: Oscar Brenner, ed., *Speculum regale: Ein altnorwegischer Dialog nach Cod. Arnamagn. 243 Fol. B und den ältesten Fragmenten* (Munich: Kaiser, 1881), 59–63.

¹⁰³ Andrew Baume, 'Lancastrian Normandy and the Calendar of Medieval Warfare', in Carruthers, *La ronde des saisons*, 61–8.

A survey of military seasonality from Roman Britain to Norman England falls outside the scope of this book. However, it may be observed that while the convention of late-summer warfare is borne out for a number of large-scale campaigns in Britain, there is also evidence that the sailing or travelling season was a more prominent consideration than the state of the crops.[104] Within Scandinavia, as will be seen below (pp. 148–53), a large number of narratives tell of winter conflicts, many of which must be supposed to have a basis in fact. This high incidence of winter combat in Scandinavian literature calls attention to the potential for surprise campaigns in the northern winter, when frozen lakes and marshes opened up new roads while the dark and the snow hindered retreat.

This cursory overview of the effects of the earth's trajectory on the economic year serves to sketch the seasonal realities to which the cultures under study were subjected, but without establishing too deterministic a framework. Since the vast majority of biological processes on earth depend on a narrow band of environmental values, human survival does indeed depend on the continued uniformity of the seasonal cycle. Beyond that, however, there is no firm causation. The geographic distribution of agriculturalism and pastoralism around the North Atlantic may have largely developed in harmony with regional climatic variables, but a local choice of one over the other was rarely a strict requirement for survival. Indeed, the Norse endured for some time as a pastoral-maricultural economy in Greenland, where it would have been more efficient to give up their livestock and expand the hunt for sea mammals.[105] Today's infrastructure even makes it possible for select but sizeable cultures to subsist primarily on trade and services, outsourcing seasonal concerns to agricultural regions, whether domestic or foreign. For organic economies like medieval England and Iceland, however, the climate and the seasonal cycle exercised a soft determinism, favouring certain economic emphases and the lifestyles entailed by the associated activities.

---

[104] Although Caesar twice invaded Britain in late summer, his more ambitious second attempt, in 54 BCE, relied on an external supply of grain and was originally intended to commence earlier in the year: Sheppard Frere, *Britannia: A History of Roman Britain* (London: Routledge / Kegan Paul, 1967), 33. Rome's definitive conquest of Britain in 43 CE was likewise planned as a spring expedition but it was delayed by unrest among the troops, probably until July. Dio Cassius, *Roman History*, ch. 60.19: Herbert Baldwin Foster, ed., *Dio's 'Roman History'*, trans. Earnest Cary (London: Heinemann, 1924), 414–16; Donald R. Dudley and Graham Webster, *The Roman Conquest of Britain AD 43–57* (Chester Springs, PA: Dufour, 1965), 18–19. In the ninth century, Alfred's measures to ensure there was both a military and an agricultural force available at all times are indicative of military activity at times of year demanding of agricultural labour (*Anglo-Saxon Chronicle*, MS A, s.a. 893; Paul Hill, *The Viking Wars of Alfred the Great* (Barnsley: Pen & Sword, 2008), 100). On the other hand, the battles fought against the Vikings by the houses of East Anglia and Wessex in the winter and spring of 870–1 make clear that seasonal considerations, though surely a factor in military planning, should rarely be thought of as necessary conditions for military campaigns, particularly where any sea crossings involved were comparatively short (*Anglo-Saxon Chronicle*, MS A s.aa. 870–1).

[105] Buckland *et al.*, 'The Fate of Norse Farmers'.

Domesticating Time

The passing of time is a recurring theme in human thought. Shakespeare's sonnets give expression to a widespread preoccupation with ageing, a process whose reversal through rejuvenation is now increasingly regarded as the holy grail of medical research. Time travel has been a mainstay in science fiction since the dawn of the genre (anticipated in some respects by medieval visions of heaven and hell), and it remains one of the most compelling implications of general relativity. Our fascination with these ideals stems from our inevitable mortality combined with a simple axiom of classical physics: that the passing of time is beyond our control.

While relativity and medical advances have begun to undermine the inexorability of forward time and biological ageing at least on a theoretical plane, climate science has made clear that the meteorological qualities of cyclical time likewise are not as autonomous as once thought. Anthropogenic climate change is not just visible in instrument and proxy records dating back to the start of Western industrialization: even as simple a decision as grounding all commercial flights in a large country, as was done in the United States in September 2001, appears to have an immediate effect on regional surface temperatures.[106] Anglo-Saxons and early Icelanders could hope to achieve similar effects through charms and saintly intervention, but the fact that such achievements were hailed as miracles demonstrates that it took a higher power to influence weather, season, and time. Under normal circumstances, these were all givens.

Since seasonal and chronological progression could not be avoided, it was embedded into the texture of medieval cultures in a variety of ways. I have already outlined the more practical interfaces of economics and timekeeping found in medieval England and Iceland, and I have observed with more universal implications that seasonality also has a more associative, less quantifiable psychological presence. The remainder of this book will analyse the ways in which aspects of seasonality surface in the literatures of medieval England and Scandinavia.

The book proposes that seasonal imagery in these cultures frequently serves the psychological contrast between familiar and foreign space. This argument is developed in Chapters 2 to 4. Chapter 1 provides a bridge between the literary realm of the central thesis and its theoretical underpinnings in the introduction by investigating mythological interpretations and ritual enactments of seasonality. Myth merits analysis as literature, but authoritative myth furthermore provides a framework within which a culture's philosophy and literature operate. This duality

---

[106] David J. Travis, Andrew M. Carleton, and Ryan G. Lauritsen, 'Contrails Reduce Daily Temperature Range', *Nature* 418, no. 6898 (August 2002): 601. The study's authority is limited by the fact that the conditions of the event cannot easily be replicated.

makes the mythological canon one of a culture's most widely acknowledged interpretations of the laws by which the world is governed, framing the reality within which other narratives should be understood to take place. The analysis of literary seasonality is therefore helped by a consideration of relevant seasonal mythologies.

Associations of the seasons in medieval literature come in various forms. Some are highly stylized and conventional, building on such traditions as the classical *locus amoenus*. Others take the form of myth or exegesis and seek to explain the origins and purpose of seasonality. Others yet relay widespread associations between landscapes, seasons, and dangerous outside forces, reflecting an associative logic that may be parsed in terms of economic activity. All such observations on seasonal elements combine to outline the roles played by seasonal variation in the thought world of medieval European cultures. Accordingly, this book may be seen as a window on medieval minds intuiting and processing the world around them.

— 1 —
Myth and Ritual

In an organic economy at higher latitudes, the seasonal cycle is an unavoidable interface between planetary physics and the indispensable fruits of agriculture. This dynamic is a powerful factor in the creation of origin myths of the seasons. By the same token, it explains ritual traditions that acknowledge the seasons' yields and petition for their cooperation.

Rather than perpetuate the misleading nomenclature of Christian and pagan, I will discuss the medieval literature of north-western Europe along an axis from orthodox (Bede, Ælfric) to heterodox (*Genesis B*), with suspected non-Christian religious elements (the eddic material) at the furthest extreme. As the chosen examples suggest, these categories often coincide with corpus and genre boundaries. Most notably, only the Scandinavian material contains extensive creation and origin myths squarely at odds with the official Church narrative. Accordingly, the discussion that follows divides quite naturally into Christian and Scandinavian ritual and myth.

Accounting for the Seasons

SEASONALITY AS PUNISHMENT

Prior to the popularization of purgatory, a concept that became especially authoritative in the twelfth century,[1] Western Christian theology knew two blessed realms: Eden and the heavenly Jerusalem, and two lesser spiritual environments: hell and the postlapsarian earth. Taking its cue from biblical accounts, literature from this sphere of influence commonly juxtaposes these desirable and undesirable environments through depictions of physical contrast. The Book of Genesis describes the terrestrial paradise as a 'garden of pleasure' (*paradisus voluptatis*), filled with 'every tree that is beautiful of appearance and sweet for eating' (Gn 2:8–9).[2] The beauty of this world is complete and self-contained: the production of crops requires no labour, and even the disturbance of rain does not enter into paradise (Gn 2:5–6). At mankind's expulsion from Eden, God pronounces a curse over

---

[1] Jacques le Goff, *La naissance du purgatoire*, Bibliothèque des histoires (Paris: Gallimard, 1981).
[2] 'Omne lignum pulchrum visu et ad vescendum suave.' All biblical references are to Weber, *Biblia sacra*.

the earth to the effect that its yield will now depend on human toil, while the natural world is no longer limited to pleasant and beneficial flora but comes to include thorns and thistles (Gn 3:18).

By implication, the expulsion introduces seasonality. Although some prelapsarian horticulture is implied in the stipulation that Adam 'should cultivate and govern' the garden of pleasure (Gn 2:15),[3] toil and sweat are understood to have no part in the process until after the fall (Gn 3:17–19). Since the practice of agriculture is to a high degree dictated by the seasons, the novelty of postlapsarian toil suggests that previously, ripe crops had always been there for the taking.[4] Thus a contrast is implied between the prelapsarian *operari paradisum voluptatis* ('cultivating the garden of pleasure') and the postlapsarian *operari terram* ('cultivating the land', Gn 3:23): after all, crops grew even before the creation of man, when 'there was no man to cultivate the land' (Gn 2:5).[5] Augustine points out that labour as penance was introduced only after the advent of sin, explaining *operari paradisum voluptatis* as a joyful participation in God's work at a time when there were no agricultural adversities and tilling the land was therefore considerably more pleasant than in today's world (Augustine, *De Genesi ad litteram* 8.8, 8.10).[6] Although the creation account introduces the heavenly luminaries two days prior to the creation of man (Gn 1:14–31), and the role of the sun in seasonal variation was well understood by influential theologians,[7] macroseasonal variation in general and cold and winter in particular were considered absent from paradise.[8] The absence of agricultural seasons was understood to return only in the heavenly Jerusalem, where the seventh age

---

[3] 'Operaretur et custodiret [paradisum voluptatis].'

[4] In Augustine's words, 'uiuebat itaque homo in paradiso [...] sine ulla egestate [...]. Cibus aderat ne esuriret, potus ne sitiret' ('and so man lived in paradise [...] without any hardship [...]. Food was available so he would not suffer hunger, drink was available so he would not suffer thirst'), Augustine, *De civitate Dei* 14.26: Bernardus [Bernard] Dombart and Alphonsus [Alphonse] Kalb, eds, *Sancti Aurelii Augustini 'De civitate Dei'*, 2 vols, Corpus Christianorum, Series Latina, 47–8: Aurelii Augustini opera, 14 (Turnhout: Brepols, 1955), 499. Cf. Gloria Cigman, 'The Seasons in Late Medieval Literature: Mutability and Metaphors of Good and Evil', *Études anglaises* 51, no. 2 (1998): 132. *Stjórn*, the early-fourteenth-century Old Norse compilation of biblical commentary, acknowledges prelapsarian labour, but without difficulty and for man's delightful nourishment ('ser til lystiligrar næringar'): Reidar Astås, ed., *Stjórn: Tekst etter håndskriftene*, 2 vols, Norrøne tekster 8 (Oslo: Riksarkivet, 2009), 1:50.

[5] 'Homo non erat qui operaretur terram.'

[6] Iosephus [Joseph] Zycha, ed., *De Genesi ad litteram libri duodecim*, Corpus Scriptorum Ecclesiasticorum Latinorum, 28 (3, no. 2) (Vienna: Tempsky, 1894), 242–3, 245–6.

[7] Isidore of Seville, *De natura rerum* 17.1–3: Jacques Fontaine, ed., *Isidore de Seville: Traité de la nature*, Bibliothèque de l'École des hautes études hispaniques 28 (Bordeaux: Féret, 1960), 233–5; Bede, *De temporum ratione*, chs 32, 35: Jones, *De temporum ratione*, 380–1, 391.

[8] 'In paradiso nullus aestus aut frigus' ('there was no heat or cold in paradise', Augustine, *De civitate Dei* 14.26: Dombart and Kalb, *De civitate Dei*, 449); cf. Remigius of Lyon, J.-P. Migne, ed., *Patrologiae cursus completus: Series Latina* (Paris: Migne, 1841–65), 121:1089c (hereafter cited as *Patrologia Latina*); John Scotus, *Patrologia Latina*, 122:806b; and, in the later Middle Ages, Martin of Leon, *Patrologia Latina*, 208:556c.

was to consist in a perpetual Sabbath (Augustine, *De civitate Dei* 22.30)[9] and the tree of life would be continuously fruit-bearing (Apc 22:2). However, heaven was thought to be devoid of seasonality in the astronomical as well as the agricultural sense, as there would be no more need for the heavenly bodies, and no more night (Apc 21:23–5, 22:5).

Humankind was thus subjected to seasonality on multiple levels. Individuals experienced the regular climate of the postlapsarian world as manifested in the cycles of night and day, winter and summer. However, salvation history itself could likewise be thought of as a seasonal cycle, proceeding from a *locus amoenus* via a flawed and harmful landscape back to a pleasant place; from bright to dark and back into the light; and from a condition without true seasons (though participating in the sequence of day and night) to a seasonal world and back into aseasonality. Thus understood, all life in the present age may be regarded as a penitential winter characterized by a dual perspective, backward and forward to seasons without sorrow.

A contrast between pleasant and unpleasant environments was commonly posited not only in a diachronic configuration, but also in the broadly synchronic opposition between heaven and hell. The Gospel of Matthew, for instance, contrasts the kingdom of heaven with 'outer darkness' (*tenebrae exteriores*), where spiritual outcasts engage in 'weeping and gnashing of teeth' (*fletus et stridor dentium*).[10] The opposition implies not only a spatial centrality on the part of heaven as the opposite of *exterior*, but also an afterworld that is divided between the perpetual day of heaven and the perpetual night of hell.[11] Light and dark, day and night, are seasonal images not only because together they constitute the microseason of the twenty-four-hour cycle, but also because light is associated with summer while dark connotes winter. These seasonal alliances are thus implicit in contrasts between heaven and hell. The postlapsarian world occupies a middle ground between these extremes, contrasting with both environments while partaking of each in a limited way.

These contrasts were eagerly exploited in medieval theology as well as narrative literature. One of its most influential applications in theology may be found in Augustine's *De civitate Dei*, which employs a spiritual chiaroscuro like that found in the Gospel of Matthew, tracing the parallel history of two spiritual communities, one associated with light and the other with darkness. Augustine makes the connection quite literal, declaring that God's angels constitute the light spoken into being on the first day of creation,[12] and accordingly that those who turned away from the good

---

[9] Dombart and Kalb, *De civitate Dei*, 866.
[10] Mt 8:11–12, 22:13, 25:30; cf. 13:40–50, 24:51; Lc 13:28.
[11] Cf. Apc 22:5.
[12] 'Nimirum ergo si ad istorum dierum opera Dei pertinent angeli, ipsi sunt illa lux, quae diei nomen accepit' ('without a doubt, therefore, if the angels belong to the works of God of those

became darkness,[13] separated from the light as one of God's first deeds of creation (Gn 1:4).[14] Gregory the Great likewise made use of the spiritual contrast between light and dark, following in the footsteps of Plato, Aristotle, and Cicero in associating them with knowledge and ignorance.[15] Hot and cold were similarly distributed: Gregory the Great and Augustine both seized on these seasonal attributes to distinguish between religious charity (hot) and sinfulness (cold),[16] concepts typically discussed within the framework of the present world but whose seasonal associations carried over into descriptions of the afterlife.

HEAVENLY STASIS

Narrative depictions of heaven and hell are described at length in vision literature. As narrative accommodates more descriptive content than the exegetical mode, visions predictably make extensive use of the spiritual dimension of the narrative environment. Already the *Visio Pauli* in its early-medieval Latin forms[17] exploits the opposition between pleasant and hostile surroundings, following but also elaborating on biblical models. Starting from the four rivers that irrigate Eden, for instance (Gn 2:10–14), it posits two corresponding sets in the otherworld. One of these is infernal, recruiting three or four of the rivers of the Greek underworld;[18] the other belongs to the kingdom of heaven, sporting the same four rivers found in the earthly paradise, now flowing with honey, milk, oil, and wine.[19]

---

days, they are the light which received the name of day'), Augustine, *De civitate Dei* 11.9: Dombart and Kalb, *De civitate Dei*, 329; similarly 11.19–20 on pp. 338–9.

[13] 'Sunt omnes, qui uocantur inmundi spiritus, nec iam lux in Domino, sed in se ipsis tenebrae, priuati participatione lucis aeternae' ('neither are all those who are called unclean spirits any longer light in the Lord, but they are darkness in themselves, deprived of the participation of the eternal light'), Augustine, *De civitate Dei* 11.9: ibid., 330.

[14] Cf. Augustine, *De Genesi ad litteram* 1.17: Zycha, *De Genesi ad litteram*, 23–6.

[15] The contrast and its heritage is most strikingly expressed in Gregory's adaptation of the cave analogy in *Dialogues* 4.1: De Vogüé and Antin, *Dialogues*, 3:20.

[16] See Thomas D. Hill, 'The Tropological Context of Heat and Cold Imagery in Anglo-Saxon Poetry', *Neuphilologische Mitteilungen* 69 (1968): 522–32 and the literature there cited.

[17] The Greek original of this vision was composed in the third century CE. A full Latin translation seems to have existed by the sixth century, though the earliest manuscripts to survive are from the ninth. Abbreviated versions, describing the scenes in hell only, were in existence by the fifth century: Lenka Jiroušková, *Die 'Visio Pauli': Wege und Wandlungen einer orientalischen Apokryphe im lateinischen Mittelalter*, Mittellateinische Studien und Texte 34 (Leiden and Boston: Brill, 2006), 7–17. In view of the complexity of the tradition, motifs from various textual witnesses will here be cited, thus representing the wider textual tradition and its genre rather than a single text.

[18] Theodore Silverstein, *Visio Sancti Pauli: The History of the Apocalypse in Latin together with Nine Texts* (London: Christophers, 1935), 153 (Vienna, Nationalbibliothek, MS 362); 205 (Paris, Bibliothèque Nationale, MS lat. 2851).

[19] Montague Rhodes James, ed., *Apocrypha anecdota: A Collection of Thirteen Apocryphal Books and Fragments* (London: Christophers, 1935), 25–6 (Paris, Bibliothèque Nationale, MS Nouv. acq. lat. 1631).

The *Visio Pauli* also incorporates the contrast between light and dark. At one extreme, hell lacks all light;[20] at the other end, even the second heaven, a bright 'land more beautiful than all gold' (*terra omni auro pulcrior*),[21] serves only as a strawman, paling before the brightness and beauty of the third heaven.[22] Similar contrasts are found in later visions, which share many particulars with the *Visio Pauli*. Thus in Bede's eighth-century account of the vision of Dryhthelm, the visionary describes the transition overseen by his angelic guide as follows: 'having brought me out of the darkness, he led me without delay into an atmosphere of serene light' (Bede, *Historia ecclesiastica* 5.12).[23] The twelfth-century Hiberno-Latin *Visio Tnugdali* involves a plurality of senses in the contrast, characterizing hell by darkness, smoke, stench, and wailing, in addition to the repulsive sights of physical punishment.[24] In heaven, on the other hand, the visionary's soul is met by pleasant music, beauty of dress, faces bright as the sun, and a sweet smell unmatched by earthly odours.[25] Heaven and hell are thus consistently depicted as environments surpassing the comforts and discomforts of the present life, a contrast that may be conveniently described through seasonal imagery.

The concept of seasonality concretely enters narrative depictions of hell in the nature of its punishments, while occurring in discussions of heaven in the negative only. Once again, this understanding builds on the biblical tradition: the implication that both the earthly and the heavenly paradise lack seasonal variation suggests that the seasons of postlapsarian life are a punishment, and therefore a preview of hell. In this respect, a difference between earth and hell is that in the latter, the visual aspect of seasonality is divorced from the tactile: the extremes of heat and cold are both punishments, but hell is always dark (and thus associated with both night and winter), even when filled with fire.[26] In this context, the Old English poem *Christ and Satan*[27] deploys the paradox *se wonna læg* ('the dark flame', 713).[28]

Several English texts acknowledge that the heavenly exclusion of seasonal extremes also entails a ban on summer. The Old Saxon poetic

---

[20] Silverstein, *Visio Sancti Pauli*, 153 (Vienna, Nationalbibliothek, MS 362 (redaction I, on fol. 7rv)).
[21] Ibid., 149 (Vienna, Nationalbibliothek, MS 362 (fragment, on fols 7v–8v)).
[22] Ibid., 149–51 (Vienna, Nationalbibliothek, MS 362 (fragment, on fols 7v–8v)).
[23] 'Nec mora, exemtum tenebris in auras me serenae lucis eduxit', Bertram Colgrave and R. A. B. Mynors, eds, *Bede's 'Ecclesiastical History of the English People'* (Oxford: Clarendon, 1969), 492.
[24] Albrecht Wagner, ed., *Visio Tnugdali: Lateinisch und altdeutsch* (Erlangen: Deichert, 1882), 12–40.
[25] Ibid., 45–54.
[26] For example 2 Enoch, ch. 10: R. H. Charles, ed., *The Book of the Secrets of Enoch: Translated from the Slavonic*, trans. W. R. Morfill (Oxford: Clarendon, 1896), 9–10.
[27] George Philip Krapp, ed., *The Junius Manuscript*, Anglo-Saxon Poetic Records 1 (New York: Columbia University Press, 1931), 133–58.
[28] Cf. *Beowulf* 3115.

Genesis, surviving in its fullest form in the Old English *Genesis B*,[29] conveys this understanding:

> Hu sculon wit nu libban oððe on þis lande wesan,
> gif her wind cymð, westan oððe eastan,
> suðan oððe norðan? Gesweorc up færeð,
> cymeð hægles scur hefone getenge,
> færeð forst on gemang,[30] se byð fyrnum ceald.
> Hwilum of heofnum hate scineð,
> blicð þeos beorhte sunne, and wit her baru standað,
> unwered wædo. Nys unc wuht beforan
> to scursceade, ne sceattes wiht
> to mete gemearcod, ac unc is mihtig God,
> waldend, wraðmod. (lines 805–15)

> How shall we now live or be in this land if wind comes here, from west or east, south or north? A cloud will rise up, a hailstorm will approach close by the heaven, frost will accompany it; it will be terribly cold. Heat will shine down from the heavens at times, this bright sun will blaze, and we will stand here naked, unprotected by clothing. We have nothing before us as a shield against the rain, nor any money set aside for food, but mighty God the ruler is angry with us.

The lament makes clear that all seasonal extremes are harmful: the heat of summer is portrayed alongside the frost and hail of winter as an evil against which mankind stands unprotected. Specifically, Adam and Eve are *unwered wædo* ('unprotected by clothing'), implying that the introduction of dress is a response to the advent of seasonal extremes as much as it serves to counter the shame of nudity.[31]

The same categorical rejection of seasonal extremes occurs in the Old English *Phoenix*.[32] This text, which portrays the mythical bird as an allegory of Christ (583–98), describes its paradisal habitat as devoid of all seasonal evils:

---

[29] A. N. Doane, ed., *The Saxon Genesis: An Edition of the West Saxon 'Genesis B' and the Old Saxon 'Vatican Genesis'* (Madison, WI: University of Wisconsin Press, 1991), 207–31.

[30] The Old Saxon *Genesis* reads 'ferid ford an gimang' ('[a hailstorm] goes forth along with [the wind]', 18), but Doane believes the *Genesis B* reading may be closer to the original (*The Saxon Genesis*, 300).

[31] Cf. lines 838–46, where no reason is given for the adoption of the covering of leaves. *Genesis A* follows the biblical account in having Adam confess he dare not show himself because he is naked, though the Old English text shows rather greater interest in the concept of clothing, of which it makes repeated mention (*Genesis A* 867–81; Gn 3:10–11). It may here also be noted that the Old English prose *Genesis* describes the dress of the first parents as *wædbrec* ('trousers'), a northern invention that compares to the *perizoma* ('girdle') of the Vulgate account as a more insulating garment. *Genesis* 3.7: Richard Marsden, ed., *The 'Old English Heptateuch' and Ælfric's 'Libellus de veteri testamento et novo'*, vol. 1, Introduction and Text, EETS, os 330 (Oxford: Oxford University Press, 2008), 12.

[32] George Philip Krapp and Elliott van Kirk Dobbie, eds, *The Exeter Book*, Anglo-Saxon Poetic Records 3 (New York: Columbia University Press, 1936), 94–113.

Ne mæg þær ren ne snaw,
ne forstes fnæst, ne fyres blæst,
ne hægles hryre, ne hrimes dryre,
ne sunnan hætu, ne sincaldu,
ne wearm weder, ne winterscur
wihte gewyrdan, ac se wong seomað
eadig ond onsund.   (lines 14–20)

Neither rain nor snow can do any harm there, nor the onset of frost, nor fire's blast, nor downpour of hail, nor fall of hoarfrost, nor heat of the sun, nor continuous cold, nor warm weather, nor winter precipitation, but the field lies blessed and perfect.

Although the description of a *locus amoenus* through the absence of evils is a classical topos inspired by the poem's Latin model,[33] Lactantius's *Carmen de ave phoenice*,[34] the absence of hot weather (and by implication of the summer season) is a deviation from Lactantius, who mentions only the absence of tempest, clouds, and winter weather:

Luctus acerbus abest et egestas obsita pannis
  et curae insomnes et violenta fames.
Non ibi tempestas nec vis furit horrida venti
  nec gelido terram rore pruina tegit,
nulla super campos tendit sua vellera nubes,
  nec cadit ex alto turbidus umor aquae.   (lines 19–24)

Bitter affliction is absent, as is rag-covered poverty and sleepless worries and severe hunger. There are no storms, nor does the terrible force of the wind rage there, nor does hoarfrost cover the earth with its icy dew. No cloud stretches its fleece across the fields, nor does the stormy liquid of water fall from above.

The understanding of seasonal variation, including heat, as punishment was certainly not unique to Anglo-Saxon England.[35] Nevertheless, it seems to have been a popular motif in Anglo-Saxon tradition, to the extent that the imported narrative of *The Phoenix* was adapted to conform to this pattern. It was known to fourteenth-century readers as well: the air in Chaucer's garden of love is so temperate 'that nevere was grevaunce of hot ne cold' ('that there never was the discomfort of hot or cold', *Parliament of Fowls* 205).

The aseasonality of paradise is one of the strongest elements to suggest a Christian influence on the eddic poem *Vǫluspá*, probably composed about

---

[33] Janie Steen, *Verse and Virtuosity: The Adaptation of Latin Rhetoric in Old English Poetry* (Toronto: University of Toronto Press, 2008), 43–7.

[34] Mary Cletus FitzPatrick, ed. and trans., 'Lactanti *De ave phoenice*: With an Introduction, Text, Translation, and Commentary' (unpublished doctoral dissertation, University of Pennsylvania, 1933).

[35] For example Augustine, *De civitate Dei* 14.26: Dombart and Kalb, *De civitate Dei*, 449; Avitus, *De mundo initio* 222: Rudolf Peiper, ed., *Alcimi Ecdicii Aviti Viennensis episcopi opera quae supersunt*, vol. 2, Monumenta Germaniae Historica, Auctores antiquissimi 6 (Berlin: Weidmann, 1883), 203–12.

1000 CE and thus about the time of the christianization of Iceland.³⁶ This poem prophesies an end-time conflict already reminiscent of the events of the Apocalypse. After the sun turns black and the earth is drowned in the ocean, however, the seeress reports seeing a new earth rise up from the waters which she describes as *iðjagrœnn* ('perpetually green', *Vǫluspá*, st. 59), suggesting it is not subject to winter. The scene is even more reminiscent of the earthly and the heavenly paradise of Christian tradition when she goes on to claim that 'fields will grow unsown there'³⁷ – as in Eden.

THE HEIGHTENED SEASONALITY OF HELL

A penitentiary understanding of the seasonal cycle is further found in descriptions of hell. These commonly feature a radical equivalent to the seasons as a punitive device, often applied to a single class of sinners. Thus in the *Visio Pauli*, those who have killed widows and orphans and sought their own gain without mercy are burned by a fire on one side, while their other side is subjected to freezing.³⁸ A similar punishment is inflicted in Bede's account of the vision of Dryhthelm:

> Deuenimus ad uallem multae latitudinis ac profunditatis, infinitae autem longitudinis, quae ad leuam nobis sita unum latus flammis feruentibus nimium terribile, alterum furenti grandine ac frigore niuium omnia perflante atque uerrente non minus intolerabile praeferebat. Vtrumque autem erat animabus hominum plenum, quae uicissim huc inde uidebantur quasi tempestatis impetu iactari. Cum enim uim feruoris immensi tolerare non possent, prosiliebant miserae in medium rigoris infesti: et cum neque ibi quippiam requiei inuenire ualerent, resiliebant rursus urendae in medium flammarum inextinguibilium.
> (*Historia ecclesiastica* 5.12)³⁹

> We came to a valley of great width and depth, but of infinite length. Situated to our left, it revealed one side exceedingly terrible with blazing flames, the other no less intolerable for its raging hail and the cold of snow blowing and driving across all things. Both sides were full of human souls, which appeared to be hurled back and forth from one side to the other as though by the force of the gale. For when they were unable to tolerate the force of the immense heat, the wretched souls leapt into the midst of the violent cold; and when they were unable to find any rest there either, they jumped back into the midst of the inextinguishable flames to be burned.

---

[36] Gustav Neckel, ed., *Edda: Die Lieder des Codex Regius nebst verwandten Denkmälern*, vol. 1, *Text*, 5th ed., rev. Hans Kuhn (Heidelberg: Winter, 1983), 1–16; for the dating, see Ursula Dronke, 'Art and Tradition in *Skírnismál*', in *English and Medieval Studies: Presented to J. R. R. Tolkien on the Occasion of his Seventieth Birthday*, ed. Norman Davis and C. L. Wrenn (London: Allen / Unwin, 1962), 2:63.
[37] 'Munu ósánir acrar vaxa' (*Vǫluspá*, st. 62).
[38] Silverstein, *Visio Sancti Pauli*, 199 (Oxford, Bodley, MS Rawlinson C 108, fols 79r–81v).
[39] Colgrave and Mynors, *Ecclesiastical History*, 490.

The motif of an infernal punishment consisting in an alternation between hot and cold in fact occurs in texts across the medieval Christian world,[40] but it enjoyed a marked popularity in the North Atlantic region.[41] A scene similar to that in Dryhthelm's vision is found in the Hiberno-Latin *Visio Tnugdali*. In this text, the group of souls subjected to seasonality is that of the highwaymen and traitors, who are made to walk a path with a dark, sulphurous fire along one side, while the other side is plagued by snow and hail. Unlike in the vision of Dryhthelm, where it seems to be the souls' own desperate volition that drives them to alternate between the two, the *Visio Tnugdali* speaks of demons using pitchforks to seize the souls by the throat and cast them back and forth between hot and cold.[42] Although the *Visio Tnugdali* is too late to have influenced Anglo-Saxon literature, it was read in Iceland, as its thirteenth-century[43] Old Norse translation demonstrates. It renders the relevant passage as follows:

> Sidan geingu þau leid sina til eins undarliga mikils fialz audnar og ognar. Fiall þetta gaf þraungan ueg ollum um forundum. Enn þeim megin fiallsins sem uegrin uar þa uall enn fulazsti daun og brenusteins logi myrkur sem kolreykur. Enn odrum megin j mot uar is frosin snær og hiner huosuztu uindar med hinum meinsomuzstum hoglum. Þetta fiall uar buit huarum tuegia megin med salna fiollda[44] fullt af leidiligum dioflum er yfer uoro þeim pislum sua at eingi uar þar uegur oruggur yfer at fara. Enn allir dioflar er uoro j þeim pislum hofdu þrikuislada liostra og skutu j gegnum þær salr er þar uilldu um fara og geingu suo til pislar. (*Duggals leiðsla*, 27–8)[45]

> They then went on their way until they came to a wondrously large mountain of desolation and terror. The mountain offered a narrow path to all travellers. But on the side of the mountain where the path was, there rose up the foulest stench and a fire of brimstone, dark as coal fumes. But opposite, on the other side, was ice, frozen snow, and the sharpest winds with the most harmful hailstorms. This mountain was

---

[40] Apart from the *Visio Pauli*, it is found in the apocryphal 2 Enoch, extant in medieval Slavonic and fragmentarily in Coptic (ch. 10: Charles, *The Book of the Secrets of Enoch*, 9–11), and in numerous Western texts, including Haymo of Halberstadt's ninth-century *Expositio in Apocalypsin* (*Patrologia Latina*, 117:1155a) and the early-twelfth-century *Chronicon* of Hugo of Flavigny (ch. 10): Georgius Heinricus Pertz, ed., *Chronicon Hugonis monachi Virdunensis et Divionensis, abbatis Flaviniacensis*, Monumenta Germaniae Historica, Scriptores 8 (Hannover: Hahn, 1848), 343.

[41] Some Insular examples are referenced in Charles D. Wright, *The Irish Tradition in Old English Literature*, Cambridge Studies in Anglo-Saxon England 6 (Cambridge: Cambridge University Press, 1993), 131, n. 102. Wright's inference that the northern popularity of this motif is a response to northern climates seems unwarranted.

[42] Wagner, *Visio Tnugdali*, 14.

[43] Cahill dates *Duggals leiðsla* to 1217 x 1263, the reign of Hákon Hákonarson of Norway: Paul Cahill, ed., *Duggals leiðsla* (Reykjavik: Stofnun Árna Magnússonar, 1983), xlix–lviii; see further Kirsten Wolf, 'Visio Tnugdali', in *Medieval Scandinavia: An Encyclopedia*, ed. Phillip Pulsiano (New York and London: Garland, 1993), 705–6.

[44] The Latin source has 'ad puniendum animas' ('for the souls to be punished'): Wagner, *Visio Tnugdali*, 14.

[45] Cahill, *Duggals leiðsla*; cf. the Latin text in Wagner, *Visio Tnugdali*, 14.

equipped on either side with a multitude of souls, full of hideous devils who were in charge of those torments so that there was no path by which it was safe to travel. And all the devils that were at those torments had three-pronged spears and poked against the souls that wanted to cross there, and in this way they proceeded to torment.

The thirteenth-century Icelandic poetic vision known as *Sólarljóð*[46] shows a reliance on the same tradition in its description of the punishment of two specific wicked souls:

> Munað þau drýgðu   á marga vegu
> ok höfðu gull fyrir gaman;
> nú er þeim goldit,   er þau ganga skulu
> meðal frosts ok funa.   (st. 18)[47]

> They practised lust in many ways and had gold for their enjoyment. Now it is repaid them, since they have to walk between frost and fire.

The punitive use of hot and cold likewise occurs in biblical retellings, as when Satan in the Old English poem *Christ and Satan* observes that 'her hat and ceald hwilum mencgað' ('at times hot and cold mingle here', 131) and *Genesis A* describes hell as 'geondfolen fyre and færcyle' ('filled with fire and terrible cold', 43).[48] *Genesis B*, however, uses the extremes of hot and cold in a cycle more reminiscent of earthly climate, assigning heat to the evenings and cold to the early mornings:

> Þær hæbbað heo on æfyn   ungemet lange,
> ealra feonda gehwilc,   fyr edneowe,
> þonne cymð on uhtan   easterne wind,
> forst fyrnum cald.   Symble fyr oððe gar,
> sum heard gewrinc   habban sceoldon.   (lines 313–17)

> There they, all the fiends, suffer fire anew for an immeasurably long time in the evening; then, in the last part of the night, there comes an east wind, a terribly cold frost. They must always suffer some severe torment, fire or cold.[49]

---

[46] Carolyne Larrington and Peter Robinson, eds and trans., 'Anonymous: *Sólarljóð*', in *Poetry on Christian Subjects*, ed. Margaret Clunies Ross, vol. 1, Skaldic Poetry of the Scandinavian Middle Ages 7 (Turnhout: Brepols, 2007), 287–357. For a discussion of its date, see pp. 287–8 of the edition.

[47] For full context, see also stanzas 16–17.

[48] An analogous description has often, and with some plausibility, been proposed for Vercelli Homily 9, but considerable emendation is there required to read 'frea' and 'forclas' ('lord' and '?little forks') as 'fyre' and 'forcilas' ('fire' and 'extreme chillings'): Donald Scragg, ed., *The Vercelli Homilies*, EETS, os 300 (Oxford: Oxford University Press, 1992), 170; *DOE*, s.v. '? *for-cyle, ? *forcel': Angus Cameron, Ashley Crandell Amos, Antonette diPaolo Healey, et al., eds, *Dictionary of Old English: A to G* (Toronto: Dictionary of Old English Project, 2007), accessed 15 March 2015, http://doe.utoronto.ca/ (hereafter cited as *DOE*).

[49] The literal translation of 'fyr oððe gar' is 'fire or spear.' In view of the contrast between hot and cold just described, however, many critics have understood *gar* as the metaphorical sting of cold. Frederick Klaeber, 'Notizen zur jüngeren *Genesis*', *Anglia* 37 (n.s. 25) (1913): 539; Krapp, *Junius*, 165; cf. *DOE*, s.v. 'gār', sense 1.a.ii.

The Hiberno-Latin *Navigatio Sancti Brendani* similarly tells of cold and heat by regular alternation when it describes Judas as normally punished by fire, but exposed to the cold of the elements on Sundays and feast days (ch. 25).[50] This text is exceptional in depicting the cold as a relief from the infernal fires, while also selecting a milder form of cold, namely exposure to the surf with no mention of snow or ice. By contrast, the twelfth-century Dutch verse rendering of this text has Judas undergo simultaneous burning and freezing on different sides of his body as a Sunday relief from weekday punishments (*De reis van Sente Brandane* 1321–1448).[51] This indeed is the more typical configuration, resembling the visions of Dryhthelm and Tnugdalus. Unlike *Genesis B* and the Latin *Navigatio Brendani*, most literary depictions of hell employ a seasonal contrast in a radical, compressed form, an image that seems to underline once again the belief that the seasonal extremes, and by implication all seasonal variation, are to be explained as punishment.

THE SEASONS IN SCANDINAVIAN MYTH

A straightforward Scandinavian aetiology of the seasons survives in the eddic poem *Vafþrúðnismál*,[52] a wisdom debate commonly dated to the tenth century:[53]

> Óðinn qvað:
>
>> Segðu þat iþ fiórða,   allz þic fróðan qveða
>>   oc þú, Vafðrúðnir, vitir,
>> hvaðan vetr um kom   eða varmt sumar
>>   fyrst með fróð regin.
>
> Vafðrúðnir qvað:
>
>> Vindsvalr heitir; hann er Vetrar faðir,
>>   enn Svásuðr Sumars.   (st. 26–7)

Óðinn said, 'Tell me this fourthly – everyone says you are wise and you know this, Vafþrúðnir: whence did Winter and warm Summer first come among the wise deities?'

Vafþrúðnir said, 'One is called Vindsvalr ['Wind-cool']; he is Winter's father, and Svásuðr ['Pleasant'] is Summer's father'.

---

[50] Carl Selmer, ed., *Navigatio Sancti Brendani abbatis: From Early Latin Manuscripts* (Notre Dame, IN: University of Notre Dame Press, 1959), 65–70.

[51] W. G. Brill, ed., *Van Sinte Brandane*, Bibliotheek van Middelnederlandsche letterkunde 6 (Groningen: Wolters, 1971).

[52] Neckel, *Edda*, 45–55.

[53] See Tim William Machan, ed., *Vafþrúðnismál*, 2nd ed., Durham Medieval and Renaissance Texts 1 (Durham: Centre for Medieval and Renaissance Studies, Durham University, 2008), 6–8 and the literature there cited.

It is apparent in Vafþrúðnir's response that Vetr and Sumar are here personifications of the two seasons of the year; by implication, these gods govern seasonally, thus giving rise to the extremes within the climate system. The rooting of the seasons in a genealogy does not provide a purpose for their existence, but it does imply a divine aetiology and thus answers the question.

In his prose reworking of the passage, Snorri Sturluson appears to express a degree of dissatisfaction with the genealogical justification of the seasons, as he modifies the question to ask specifically for an explanation of seasonal extremes: 'Why is there such a great difference that summer has to be hot but winter cold?' (*Gylfaginning*, ch. 19).[54] His version of the response differs subtly but tellingly from that in *Vafþrúðnismál*. Apart from slight modifications to the genealogy, Snorri explains that Sumar's father led such a pleasant life that the term *svásligr* ('pleasant') derives from his name, but Vetr comes from a family of grim and cold-hearted men. Not only does Snorri here bring out more explicitly the preference for summer found implicit in the name *Svásuðr*, he also explains the existence of the seasons by the inherited personalities of individual deities. Like the more orthodox texts discussed above, Snorri roots seasonality in a spiritual dimension. By associating summer with mildness of character and winter with harsh personality, however, he understands summer and winter as benevolent and malevolent. As was seen, the Church Fathers employ a similar contrast with regard to light and dark, but they describe all macroseasonal variation as a curse. The two systems of interpretation may thus be combined as long as they operate on different levels, but a text that uses the expulsion from Eden as a cultural reference point is more likely to condemn seasonal variation on the basis of its absence from paradise. Snorri here departs markedly from that orthodox course, as indeed he means to, since his aim is to describe a system of belief that is essentially other.

The second noteworthy seasonal reference in eddic mythology concerns the *fimbulvetr*. Translating as 'great winter' or 'terrible winter', this concept is presented as a life-devastating event to take place at the end of an era. *Vafþrúðnismál* introduces the concept as follows:

> Óðinn qvað:
>
> > Fiolð ec fór,   fiolð ec freistaðac,
> >   fiolð ec reynda regin:
> > hvat lifir manna,   þá er inn mæra líðr
> >   fimbulvetr með firom?

---

[54] 'Hví skilr svá mikit at sumar skal vera heitt en vetr kaldr?' Anthony Faulkes, ed., *Snorri Sturluson: 'Edda'*, 4 vols (London: Viking Society for Northern Research / University College London, 1988–99), 1:21.

Vafðrúðnir qvað:

> Líf oc Lífðrasir,   enn þau leynaz muno
>   í holti Hoddmimis;
> morgindǫggvar   þau sér at mat hafa,
> þaðan af aldir alaz.   (st. 44–5)

Óðinn said, 'I have travelled a great deal, I have tried a great deal, I have put many deities to the test. What human being will live when the famous great winter comes over the people?'

Vafþrúðnir said, 'Líf ["Life"] and Lífðrasir ["Life-persister"], but they will hide in Hoddmimir's forest; they will have the morning dew for food. Mankind will spring from them'.

The passage implies a winter obliterating an entire population with the exception of a single couple. The remainder of the poem makes clear that this survival is part of a global rebirth when it describes a new sun and a new dynasty of Æsir following a world conflagration (*Vafþrúðnismál*, sts 46–7, 50–1; cf. *Vǫluspá*, sts 59–65). The co-occurrence of winter and fire is reminiscent of Christian traditions of hell discussed above, raising the question whether the two traditions share a genetic connection. Eddic eschatology on the whole certainly seems to reflect Christian tradition.[55] However, winter is no traditional element in Christian accounts of latter-day events. The *fimbulvetr* is therefore best understood as an independent construct, a conflation of Christian accounts of hell and latter days, or a mix of Nordic and Latinate traditions.

The eschatological element of winter weather reported in *Vafþrúðnismál* has a parallel in *Hyndluljóð* (composed before 1225):[56]

> Haf gengr hríðom   við himin sjálfan,
> líðr lǫnd yfir,   enn lopt bilar;
> þaðan koma snióvar   oc snarir vindar;
> þá er í ráði,   at regn um þrióti.   (st. 42)

The sea will go against heaven itself with gusts, it will flood the lands, and the sky will give way. Snows and strong winds will follow. Then the rain is meant to cease.

Here too, the most elaborate depiction of this development is given by Snorri, who combines material from the two abovementioned poems in his account of Ragnarǫk. Asked about this event, his character Hár begins his response as follows:

---

[55] See, for example, John McKinnell, '*Vǫluspá* and the Feast of Easter', *Alvíssmál* 12 (2008): 3–28.

[56] Neckel, *Edda*, 288–96. For the dating, see Klaus von See *et al.*, eds, *Kommentar zu den Liedern der 'Edda'* (Heidelberg: Winter, 1993–), 3:689.

> Mikil tíðindi eru þaðan at segja ok mǫrg. Þau in fyrstu at vetr sá kemr er kallaðr er fimbulvetr. Þá drífr snær ór ǫllum áttum. Frost eru þá mikil ok vindar hvassir. Ekki nýtr sólar. Þeir vetr fara þrír saman ok ekki sumar milli. En áðr ganga svá aðrir þrír vetr at þá er um alla verǫld orrostur miklar. (*Gylfaginning*, ch. 51)[57]

> There are many extraordinary things to be said about that. Firstly, the so-called 'terrible winter' will come. At that time, snow will drive from all directions; there will be great frosts and sharp winds. The sun will be of no use. Three such winters will come in succession with no summer in between. But first three other years will precede them in such a way that there will then be great battles across the entire world.

The succession of warfare and winter is attained by combining the accounts of *Vǫluspá* and *Vafþrúðnismál*; the numerals are almost certainly Snorri's own contribution. The parallelism of three *vetr* of winter weather and three *vetr* of war requires some explanation. The former are contrasted with *sumur* and are thus meteorological winters that continue for three full astronomical years. The usual season for warfare is the summer, however, so that *vetr* in the second instance is used synecdochically and should be translated 'years', with the understanding that these are three continuous solar years of warfare not punctuated by winter quarters.[58]

Further relevant seasonality may with varying degrees of plausibility be extrapolated from less overtly seasonal material in the eddic poetry. The only such reading worthy of consideration is a widespread interpretation of *Skírnismál*, a late[59] eddic poem exploring the theme of love between members of different social groups (Vanir and giants). The text's potential for seasonality lies in the associations of its protagonists. The lover in question is Freyr, identified as an agricultural fertility god in texts of the thirteenth and perhaps the fourteenth century.[60] The object of his affection is a giantess called Gerðr

---

[57] Faulkes, *Edda*, 1:49.

[58] Cf. with the *fimbulvetr* an episode in *Jómsvíkinga saga*. In ch. 3 of that work, a prophetic dream is elicited by sleeping alone in a particular house during the three Winter Nights. The resulting dream is interpreted as signalling, among other things, the coming of three snowy winters causing all the crops in Denmark to fail, followed by three severe winters but with little snow, and finally three famine-plagued winters so severe that no one will remember their like. N. F. Blake, ed. and trans., *Jómsvíkinga saga* (London: Nelson, 1962), 3–4.

[59] *Skírnismál* may have been composed in the twelfth or thirteenth century (Paul Bibire, 'Freyr and Gerðr: The Story and its Myths', in Rudolf Simek, Jónas Kristjánsson, and Hans Bekker-Nielsen, *Sagnaskemmtun*, 19–21; von See *et al.*, *Kommentar*, 2:64–5). At any rate it was composed prior to the Prose *Edda* (*c*. 1220), which quotes from it (*Gylfaginning*, ch. 37: Faulkes, *Edda*, 1:31).

[60] Esp. in Snorri: *Gylfaginning*, ch. 24: ibid., 1:24; *Skáldskaparmál*, ch. 7: ibid., 2:18; cf. *Ynglinga saga*, ch. 10: Bjarni Aðalbjarnarson, ed., *Heimskringla*, 3 vols, Íslenzk fornrit, 26–8 (Reykjavik: Hið íslenzka fornritafélag, 1941–51), 1:23–5. The thirteenth- or fourteenth-century *Ǫgmundar þáttr dytts* connects Freyr with a wagon procession intended to attain improvement of the year's yields (*árbót*; for a discussion of the dates of composition of the tale's two parts, see Ian Wyatt and Jessie Cook, eds, *Two Tales of Icelanders: Ögmundar þáttr dytts og Gunnars helmings, Ǫlkofra þáttr*, Durham Medieval Texts 10 (Durham: Durham Medieval Texts, Department of English, 1993), xxix–xxxiv). This episode, set in Sweden, survives in the late-thirteenth- or early-fourteenth-century *Óláfs saga Tryggvasonar en mesta* (Ólafur Halldórsson, ed., *Óláfs saga Tryggvasonar en mesta*, 3 vols,

(possibly 'enclosed [field]', though the form is not far off from meaning simply 'girded'),[61] who is approached through the mediation of Skírnir ('shining one'). Accordingly, the text has been thought to symbolize the sun turning its radiance to the soil in spring, believed by some to reflect an annual spring ritual.[62] Readings of this sort demand extreme caution, and some indeed have questioned the interpretation, but their criticism is as yet not fully developed.[63] The seasonal reading is backed by considerable circumstantial evidence, including Freyr's filial relationship to Njǫrðr,[64] whose name is cognate with Nerthus, the *terra mater* or mother earth mentioned in Tacitus's *Germania* (ch. 40) who shares with Freyr the attribute of a procession by wagon.[65] The implications of this particular connection are difficult to assess in view of the long interim between its classical and Norse nodes, however, and can be done no justice here.[66] The Icelandic evidence is more straightforward, establishing that there existed a literary understanding of an agricultural fertility cult of Freyr by the thirteenth century with explicit reference to Swedish practice. Since these ideas circulated not long after *Skírnismál* was composed, it may indeed be the case that its author intended the poem to evoke agricultural processes associated with spring.[67]

A further branch of seasonal mythology is found in a small group of texts describing an eastern Scandinavian dynasty headed by an individual named Fornjótr. The earliest of these seems to be the opening episode to *Orkneyinga saga* (c. 1200),[68] known separately as

Editiones arnamagnæanæ A, 1–3 (Copenhagen: Munksgaard, 1958–2000), 2:13–18; for the dating, see Sveinbjörn Rafnsson, *Ólafs sögur Tryggvasonar: Um gerðir þeirra, heimildir og höfunda* (Reykjavik: Háskólaútgáfan, 2005), 82) and in a compressed form in the late-fourteenth-century Vatnshyrna-redaction of *Víga-Glúms saga* (Jónas Kristjánsson, ed., *Eyfirðinga sǫgur*, Íslenzk fornrit 9 (Reykjavik: Hið íslenzka fornritafélag, 1956), 99–115; discussion and dating at liii–lxiv).

[61] Bibire, 'Freyr and Gerðr', 22–3.

[62] Magnus Olsen, 'Fra gammelnorsk myte og kultus', *Maal og minne* 1 (1909): 17–36; Eyvind Flejd Halvorsen, 'Freyr', *KLNM* 4 (1959): 618–20; Dronke, 'Art and Tradition'; Ursula Dronke, ed., *The Poetic Edda*, 3 vols (Oxford: Clarendon, 1969–2011), 2:396–400; Richard North, ed., *Heathen Gods in Old English Literature*, Cambridge Studies in Anglo-Saxon England 22 (Cambridge: Cambridge University Press, 1997), 19–25; Terry Gunnell, 'Viking Religion: Old Norse Mythology', in *'Beowulf' and Other Stories: A New Introduction to Old English, Old Icelandic and Anglo-Norman Literatures*, 2nd ed., ed. Richard North and Joe Allard (Harlow: Pearson Education, 2011), 362–3.

[63] Von See *et al.*, *Kommentar*, 2:51; John McKinnell, *Meeting the Other in Norse Myth and Legend* (Cambridge: Brewer, 2005), 65.

[64] *Skírnismál*, prose introduction: Neckel, *Edda*, 69–77; *Gylfaginning*, ch. 24: Faulkes, *Edda*, 1:24; *Skáldskaparmál*, ch. 7: ibid., 2:18; *Ynglinga saga*, ch. 10: Bjarni Aðalbjarnarson, *Heimskringla*, 1:23–5.

[65] Lund, *Germania*, 100; Olsen, 'Fra gammelnorsk myte og kultus', 21; North, *Heathen Gods*, 19–25; cf. Jan de Vries, ed., *Altnordisches etymologisches Wörterbuch* (Leiden: Brill, 1962), s.v. 'Njǫrðr'.

[66] Roman and Gallic parallels are noted in North, *Heathen Gods*, 19–25.

[67] Cf. Bibire, 'Freyr and Gerðr', 31.

[68] On the text's date of composition, see Sigurður Nordal, ed., *Orkneyinga sǫgur* (Copenhagen: Møller, 1913–16), i–v; Finnbogi Guðmundsson, ed., *Orkneyinga saga*, Íslenzk fornrit 34 (Reykjavik: Hið íslenzka fornritafélag, 1965), vii–ix; Preben Meulengracht Sørensen, 'The Sea, the Flame, and the Wind: The Legendary Ancestors of the Earls of Orkney', in *At fortælle Historien: Studier i den gamle nordiske litteratur*, ed. Michael Dallapiazza, Olaf Hansen, and Gerd Wolfgang Weber, Hesperides 16 (Trieste: Parnaso, 2001), 227.

Fundinn Noregr,⁶⁹ which probably served as a model for the very similar thirteenth-century⁷⁰ *Hversu Noregr byggðisk*.⁷¹ The seasonal value of both texts lies in the high concentration of unusual names with winter references among Fornjótr's descendants. His own three sons are Hlér or Ægir ('sea'), Logi ('flame'), and Kári ('wind'). In *Hversu Noregr byggðisk*, these men are said to have ruled the forces of nature referred to in their names, but this idea is not made explicit in the earlier *Fundinn Noregr*. Kári is father to Frosti ('frost', *Fundinn Noregr*) or Jǫkull ('icicle', *Hversu Noregr byggðisk*), who had as his son King Snær ('snow'). Snær again has one son, Þorri (the name of a late-winter month on the Icelandic calendar), or, in the later *Hversu Noregr byggðisk*, four sons, namely Þorri, Fǫnn ('snow[drift]'),⁷² Drífa ('driving snow, snowstorm, hailstorm'),⁷³ and Mjǫll ('fresh powdery snow').⁷⁴ The last three, however, play no further role in the narrative, since the line continues with Þorri's descendants; the extra characters seem to have been added merely to continue the trend of winter names. Þorri's children are three, sons Nórr and Górr (names without evident meanings) and daughter Gói (the winter month immediately following Þorri). In both accounts, genealogy now gives way to narrative.

It is in the narrative that the mythological value of the dynasty is played out, as it takes the form of an origin myth. Fornjótr's kingdom is situated east of the Gulf of Bothnia, i.e. in present-day Finnish Lapland.⁷⁵ King Þorri's

---

⁶⁹ Finnbogi Guðmundsson, *Orkneyinga saga*, 3–7.

⁷⁰ The text has not been persuasively dated with any great precision. See Gudbrand Vigfusson [Guðbrandur Vigfússon], ed., *Icelandic Sagas and Other Historical Documents Relating to the Settlement and Descents of the Northmen on the British Isles*, vol. 1 (London: H. M. Stationary Office, 1887), x; Finnur Jónsson, *Den oldnorske og oldislandske litteraturs historie*, 2nd ed., vol. 2 (Copenhagen: Gad, 1923), 646–53 for 653–9; Finnbogi Guðmundsson, *Orkneyinga saga*, ix–xi; Margaret Clunies Ross, 'Snorri Sturluson's Use of the Norse Origin-Legend of the Sons of Fornjótr in his *Edda*', *Arkiv för nordisk filologi* 98 (1983): 55; Elizabeth Ashman Rowe, 'Origin Legends and Foundation Myths in Flateyjarbók', in *Old Norse Myths, Literature and Society*, ed. Margaret Clunies Ross (Odense: University Press of Southern Denmark, 2003), 199–200 with notes 5 and 6.

⁷¹ Guðni Jónsson and Bjarni Vilhjálmsson, eds, *Fornaldarsögur norðurlanda*, 3 vols (Reykjavik: Bókaútgáfan forni, 1943–4), 2:137–48. On the relationship between these texts, see Sigurður Nordal, *Orkneyinga sǫgur*, i–v; Rowe, 'Origin Legends'.

⁷² Johan Fritzner, *Ordbog over det gamle norske Sprog* (Kristiania [Oslo]: Den norske Forlagsforening, 1883–96; hereafter cited as Fritzner), s.v.; Richard Cleasby and Gudbrand Vigfusson [Guðbrandur Vigfússon], eds, *An Icelandic-English Dictionary*, 2nd ed., with a supplement by William A. Craigie (Oxford: Clarendon, 1957; hereafter cited as CV), s.v.; see further Sveinbjörn Egilsson and Finnur Jónsson, eds, *Lexicon poeticum antiquæ linguæ septentrionalis / Ordbog over det norsk-islandske skjaldesprog*, 2nd ed. (Copenhagen: Møller, 1931), s.v.

⁷³ Fritzner, s.v.; *A Dictionary of Old Norse Prose*, s.v.: Helle Degnboll et al., eds, *Ordbog over det norrøne prosasprog / A Dictionary of Old Norse Prose* (Copenhagen: Den arnemagnæanske kommission, 1989–), accessed 15 March 2015, http://onp.ku.dk; see further *Lexicon Poeticum*, 2nd ed., s.v.

⁷⁴ Fritzner, s.v.; CV, s.v.; see further *Lexicon Poeticum*, 2nd ed., s.v.

⁷⁵ 'Hann réð fyrir því landi [*var*. Jótlandi], er kallat [er] Finnland ok Kvenland; þat liggr fyrir austan hafsbotn þann, er gengr til móts við Gandvík; þat kǫllu vér Helsingjabotn' ('he governed the land that is called *Finnland* and *Kvenland*, which lies east of the gulf that stretches towards the White Sea; we call it [i.e. the gulf] *Helsingjabotn*', Finnbogi Guðmundsson, *Orkneyinga saga*, 3).

daughter Gói disappears during her father's annual sacrificial feast, which comes to be named Þorrablót after him (a word not elsewhere recorded until early-modern times).[76] Hoping to get her back, Þorri performs his sacrificial rites again the next month, and this event provides the aetiology for Góiblót (a Swedish rite confirmed by Snorri).[77] His sons then set out to find her, conquering Norway and its archipelagos in the process. In the course of time, these regions are distributed among their descendants, who constitute the dynasties of Norway and Orkney.[78]

In view of this foundational function of the dynasty, Meulengracht Sørensen has proposed that the author of the narrative set out to write an indigenous origin myth to rival the Trojan migration that formed the paradigm for foundation myths in this period and was used by Snorri, among others.[79] Although it cannot be verified whether the author's aim was quite so deliberate, conceived with a rival narrative in mind, the episode's position at the start of *Orkneyinga saga* makes clear that it was intended as an origin myth for the ruling class featuring in the remainder of the work. The author's decision to root the Norwegian and Orcadian ruling houses in the very essence of winter (*frosti, snær, þorri*) also positions winter at the heart of their culture, suggesting that he believed there could be something noble or desirable to this affiliation.

The authors of *Orkneyinga saga* and the episode's retelling in *Hversu Noregr byggðisk* were not, in fact, alone in these opinions. Regardless of the Trojan ancestry that Snorri assigns the Æsir in the frame narrative of his *Prologue*,[80] the core content of *Snorra Edda* responds to and amplifies a very different origin myth, similarly rooted in winter. Pre-existing eddic poetry associates the giants with winter, among other things through their description as *hrímþursar* ('rime giants').[81] Snorri strengthened this association in his version of the myth, in which the world's first giant is formed out of melting rime. In addition, however, he gave giants and Æsir a shared origin, as in his account the first god is freed from a block of rime by a cow similarly grown from drops of melting rime, and the tribe of Æsir results from his son's marriage with the daughter of a giant.[82] This association between gods and giants is not dissimilar to the

---

[76] Árni Björnsson, *Saga daganna*, 434–5; Árni Björnsson, *Þorrablót* (Reykjavik: Mál og menning, 2008), 9–11.

[77] *Óláfs saga helga*, ch. 77: Bjarni Aðalbjarnarson, *Heimskringla*, 2:109.

[78] *Fundinn Noregr*, chs 1–3: Finnbogi Guðmundsson, *Orkneyinga saga*, 3–7; *Hversu Noregr byggðisk*, ch. 1: Guðni Jónsson and Bjarni Vilhjálmsson, *Fornaldarsögur*, 2:137–44. See also Meulengracht Sørensen, 'The Sea'; Margaret Clunies Ross, 'Two Old Icelandic Theories of Ritual', in Clunies Ross, *Old Norse Myths, Literature and Society*, 279–99; Rowe, 'Origin Legends'.

[79] Meulengracht Sørensen, 'The Sea', 229. Snorri employs the paradigm in the Prologue to his *Edda* (Faulkes, *Edda*, 1:4–5) as well as in *Ynglinga saga*, chs 2–5: Bjarni Aðalbjarnarson, *Heimskringla*, 1:11–16.

[80] Faulkes, *Edda*, 1:3–6.

[81] See below, pp. 101–6.

[82] *Gylfaginning*, chs 5–6: Faulkes, *Edda*, 1:9–11.

Fornjótr material. Since the northern regions governed by Fornjótr and his descendants are typically associated with the dangerous supernatural,[83] *Fundinn Noregr* and its cognates similarly imply that the North Germanic peoples derive from supernatural winter stock. Even if the Fornjótr legend seems at first sight quite distinct from the eddic material, then, the two have a great deal in common, and the former may be far more canonical in outline than Meulengracht Sørensen suggests.

Snorri also relays the Fornjótr dynasty and adds a pair of names not found in other texts of the tradition. His *Ynglinga saga* is based on *Ynglingatal*,[84] which has been dated as far back as the ninth century[85] and is an enumeration of the royal Swedish descendants of Freyr. Although the poem uses numerous transparent names, it is only in the prose reworking that winter names are introduced, largely derived from the Fornjótr material which Snorri echoes elsewhere as well.[86] In accordance with the now Swedish perspective, however, they are here all names of neighbouring rulers and antagonists. Snjár *inn gamli*, for instance, is identified as a king of Finnland. King Vanlandi of Sweden meets him on his eastern exploits and marries Snjár's daughter Drífa.[87] Frosti, too, is mentioned, and called the chieftain of the Finnar; King Agni of the Swedes defeats him in battle.[88] In addition to these now canonical names, however, Snorri adds two new ones that are equally connected with winter. These are the sons of King Vísburr of Sweden and the daughter of Auði *inn auðgi*, whose region of origin is not specified. Their sons are Gísl ('hostage', but here probably to be understood as *geisl* ['ski stick'])[89] and Qndurr ('snowshoe'). Vísburr leaves his wife for another woman, evidently taking back his lavish wedding gifts. When Gísl and Qndurr are adolescents, they raise an army and burn down their father's house after he refuses to hand over their mother's wedding gifts.[90] Nowhere in *Ynglinga saga* does Snorri acknowledge the Finnar as the ancestors of the North Germanic peoples, however, so that he cannot be considered a proponent of this origin myth. On the other hand, he does reiterate a widespread tradition associating the Finnar with winter.[91]

---

[83] See below, pp. 106–10.
[84] Finnur Jónsson, ed., *Den norsk-islandske skjaldedigtning*, 4 vols (Copenhagen: Villadsen / Christensen, 1912–15; Copenhagen: Rosenkilde and Bagger, 1967), A1:7–15.
[85] Finnur Jónsson, *Skjaldedigtning*, B1:7–9; Hallvard Magerøy, 'Ynglingatal', KLNM 20 (1976): 362–4.
[86] *Skáldskaparmál* 29–30: Faulkes, *Edda*, 2:39–40.
[87] *Ynglinga saga*, ch. 13: Bjarni Aðalbjarnarson, *Heimskringla*, 1:28–9; cf. *Ynglingatal* 3; *Fundinn Noregr*, ch. 1: Finnbogi Guðmundsson, *Orkneyinga saga*, 3; *Hversu Noregr byggðisk*, ch. 1: Guðni Jónsson and Bjarni Vilhjálmsson, *Fornaldarsögur*, 2:137.
[88] *Ynglinga saga*, ch. 19: Bjarni Aðalbjarnarson, *Heimskringla*, 1:37–9; cf. *Ynglingatal* 9; *Fundinn Noregr*, ch. 1: Finnbogi Guðmundsson, *Orkneyinga saga*, 3.
[89] McKinnell, *Meeting the Other*, 71.
[90] *Ynglinga saga*, ch. 14: Bjarni Aðalbjarnarson, *Heimskringla*, 1:30–1; cf. *Ynglingatal* 4.
[91] See below, pp. 106–10.

A crucial difference between the Christian and the alternative Scandinavian mythology of the seasons consists in their respective attitudes towards seasonal extremes. In Christian tradition, all seasonal variation is a curse, both directly through exposure to heat and cold and indirectly through the consequent introduction of agricultural toil. In the golden age of Eden as in the heavenly Jerusalem to come, neither of these exists. Eddic tradition likewise looks forward to a world without seasons (whether or not under Christian influence), but it also acknowledges a debt of Æsir and giants alike to an origin in the elements of winter. The Fornjótr material does the same for the human population of Scandinavia, suggesting that associations between winter, Scandinavia, and its inhabitants were a common mythological theme. Rather than implying that the Icelanders looked especially kindly on the winter season, this theme may be indicative of Scandinavians' attempts to reconcile themselves with the realities of the harsh climate of their habitat by taking pride in their hardiness and recognizing the challenges of daily life as part of their identity.[92]

Performing the Seasons

In agricultural societies, the timing of the larger festive, religious, and in some cases political gatherings tends to be influenced significantly by the economic calendar. Resource-intensive gatherings require a critical mass of leisure and provisions, but acts of thanksgiving and prayers for divine intervention also frequently concern a specific agricultural process bound to a particular season.[93] A culture's social cycle is thus likely to follow the economic year in general outline, which in turn binds it to the solar year. In societies with strongly heterogeneous economic seasons, the ritual year could therefore show marked seasonal identities. As will be seen below, patterns of this sort play a distinct role in Scandinavian texts, while traces of seasonal identities in Anglo-Saxon culture are largely restricted to liturgical evidence.

The Christian ritual year enacted in medieval England and Iceland was itself informed by seasonal patterns, but the seasons in question had mostly been transplanted from southern economies. For instance, the Pentateuch explicitly relates the three annual Pilgrimage Festivals of Judaic tradition to Israel's grain and fruit harvests.[94] Two of these festivals, Passover and Shavuot, found Christian counterparts in Easter and Pentecost. The seven

---

[92] Cf. present-day Finnish pride in the purportedly national characteristic of *sisu* (approximately 'grit'), frequently adduced in connection with winter.

[93] Grottanelli, 'Agriculture', 186–92.

[94] Ex 23:14–19, 34:18–26; Dt 16:1–8; Jan A. Wagenaar, *Origin and Transformation of the Ancient Israelite Festival Calendar*, Beihefte zur Zeitschrift für altorientalische und biblische Rechtsgeschichte 6 (Wiesbaden: Harrassowitz, 2005), 7–9.

weeks between the two corresponded to the grain harvest in Israel, Pentecost coinciding with the post-harvest celebration. The start of the grain harvest ushered in the region's long harvest season, which ended with the olive harvest in November.[95] The Jewish ecclesiastical year follows this pattern: it begins with the spring month of Nisan,[96] just after the vernal equinox. Originally, this month was called *Aviv* ('[fresh] barley') for the time of its harvest.[97]

The Church Fathers favoured a similar calendar, but they did so on astronomical and allegorical grounds: light and darkness are separated at the equinox as at creation, and the liturgical chronology of the passion forms a parallel with the sequence of creation.[98] Although spring is a time of floral and faunal renewal in Europe as well, it coincides rather with the sowing season and lacks the strong agricultural connotations associated with this season in the Fertile Crescent. Since spring marks the return of Europe's all-important grazing season, however, it nevertheless signals the defeat of winter hardship, which may help explain why Easter grew into such an important festival in Europe.

The other great feast of the Church, Christmas, was by the fourth century purported to have been instituted in late December because a pagan festival of sun worship celebrated about the time of the winter solstice was drawing Christian interest. An influence of that celebration on the date of Christmas cannot be proved, though the balance of evidence suggests it.[99] At any rate, the coincidence of these and other feasts shows that winter was a popular time for celebrations. In imperial Rome, late December was marked by the Saturnalia and the New Year, both festive occasions, while rumours of sun festivals about the time of the Nativity recurred on a few occasions.[100] The first lengthening of the days may indeed have inspired cultures to celebrate, but the leisure and provisions afforded by the agricultural quiet of winter should be acknowledged as a loosely necessary condition for the proliferation of festivities at this time of year.[101]

---

[95] Oded Borowski, *Agriculture in Iron Age Israel* (Winona Lake, IN: Eisenbrauns, 1987), 31–44.

[96] Cf. Ex 12:2. The civil year is dated instead from Rosh Hashana, which takes place six months later, about the autumnal equinox. Early rabbinic authorities argued for the primacy of either date on the basis of the flora and fauna described in Genesis. Babylonian Talmud: Rosh hashana, ch. 1: Michael Levi Rodkinson, ed. and trans., *The Babylonian Talmud*, 2nd ed., 18 vols (New York: New Talmud Publishing Company, 1918), 4:16–17.

[97] Wagenaar, *Festival Calendar*, 8.

[98] See, for example, Ambrose, *Hexaemeron* 1.4.13: Carolus [Karl] Schenkl, ed., *S. Ambrosii opera*, vol. 1, Corpus Scriptorum Ecclesiasticorum Latinorum (Vienna: Tempsky, 1897), 11; Bede, *De temporum ratione*, ch. 6: Jones, *De temporum ratione*, 290–3; Faith Wallis, trans., *Bede: 'The Reckoning of Time'*, Translated Texts for Historians 29 (Liverpool: Liverpool University Press, 1999), 273–4.

[99] Susan K. Roll, *Toward the Origins of Christmas* (Kampen: Kok Pharos, 1995), 107–64.

[100] Ibid., 152–7.

[101] Martin P. Nilsson, 'Folkfesternas samband med år och arbetsliv', in *Årets högtider*, ed. Martin P. Nilsson, Nordisk kultur 22 (Stockholm: Bonniers, 1938), 2–4. That a seasonally induced surplus of provisions is not strictly required is demonstrated by the two largest Christian festivals, each of which was preceded by a fast that would have served, among other things, to store up food for the feast.

Knowledge of much of Europe's preexisting ritual was lost in the wake of its Christianization. This is especially true of Anglo-Saxon England, where writing was largely the privilege of a clergy at pains to suppress heathen ritual. Nevertheless, emphases in the English liturgy may be used alongside the Anglo-Saxon month names to form a rough impression of a ritual cycle partly predating the Conversion and partly overlaid onto the new ritual tradition. Scandinavian tradition proved more resilient to the cultural assimilation that came with Christianity; moreover, Christian Icelanders did not hesitate to describe what they believed pagan practice had looked like. Thus both Anglo-Saxon and Icelandic culture reveal something of a festive cycle distinct from Christian liturgy.

Classical authors offer the earliest evidence of Germanic ritual, but this is limited in both extent and reliability. Although Tacitus's discussion of the earth goddess Nerthus is suggestive of fertility (*Germania*, ch. 40),[102] he does not describe the seasonality of Germanic religion other than by stating that worship took place 'certis diebus' ('on specific days', ch. 9)[103] or 'stato tempore' ('at a fixed time', ch. 39).[104] Events in his *Annales* may be dated with greater precision, but they do not explain what little ritual they mention.[105] Accordingly, our knowledge of Germanic ritual is largely based on accounts by Germanic authors and what clues survive in their lexica.

ANGLO-SAXON RITUAL

Little evidence is to be had of pre- or sub-Christian ritual in Anglo-Saxon England, but the basic facts of one or more harvest ceremonies, an autumnal slaughtering event, and wintertime gatherings may be gleaned from the Old English month names supplemented with comparative evidence. Although Bede's interpretations of the month names read like guesswork and deserve little credence,[106] the names themselves are well established, and several have transparent meanings. *Haligmonaþ* ('holy month'), for instance, is identified with September by Bede and a number of independent witnesses.[107]

---

[102] Lund, *Germania*, 100.

[103] Ibid., 76.

[104] Ibid., 100.

[105] For example 1.49–51: Furneaux, *Annali*, 69–71; cf. 1, 16–30 for the timing: ibid., 53–60.

[106] Cf. Karl Weinhold, ed., *Die deutschen Monatnamen* (Halle: Waisenhaus, 1869), 4–5; Tille, *Yule and Christmas*, 138–57; R. I. Page, 'Anglo-Saxon Paganism: The Evidence of Bede', in *Pagans and Christians*, ed. T. Hofstra, L. A. J. R. Houwen, and A. A. MacDonald, Germania Latina 2 (Groningen: Forsten, 1995), 99–129; Andreas Nordberg, ed., *Jul, disting och förkyrklig tideräkning: Kalendrar och kalendariska riter i det förkristna Norden*, Acta academiae Regiae Gustavi Adolphi 91 (Uppsala: Kungliga Gustav Adolfs Akademien för svensk folkkultur, 2006), 60–1; Marilyn Dunn, *The Christianization of the Anglo-Saxons c. 597–c. 700: Discourses of Life, Death and Afterlife* (London: Continuum, 2009), 62–3.

[107] Bede, *De temporum ratione*, ch. 15: Jones, *De temporum ratione*, 330; *Menologium* 164; *Martyrology* §171b: Christine Rauer, ed., *The Old English Martyrology: Edition, Translation and Commentary* (Cambridge: Brewer, 2013), 172; Byrhtferth, *Manual* 1.2: Peter S. Baker and Michael

What evidence can be gleaned from the month's name therefore suggests that an Anglo-Saxon unit of time overlapping with the Julian month of September was associated with worship. Economically, this time of year was overwhelmingly associated with the harvest. That explains the alternative month name *hærfestmonaþ*,[108] but it also suggests that the religious referent of *haligmonaþ* had some association with that process. That the harvest had a religious dimension in Anglo-Saxon England is apparent from Lammas, celebrated on the first of August and thus prior to *haligmonaþ*. This festival was concerned with the consecration of bread from the first grain harvest,[109] a ritual hinted at in the word's Old English form, *hlafmæsse* ('bread-mass'). The festival thus gave expression to the same impulse of thanksgiving also found in the Jewish festival of Passover. The Old English calender poem *Menologium* indicates that *hærfest*, whether the harvest itself or its season, arrived one week after Lammas (136–43).

Blodmonaþ ('blood-month', sometimes written *blotmonaþ* 'sacrificial month'), overlapping with November according to the Julian sources,[110] was almost certainly named after the annual slaughter of livestock. The name has analogues in Old Norse *gormánuðr*, Welsh *Mis Tachwedd*, and the archaic modern forms *slachtmaand* (Dutch), *slaktmånad* (Swedish), and *slagtemaaned* (Danish). The first of these unambiguously means 'blood-month', the others 'slaughter-month'.[111] Whether the slaughter was accompanied by a celebration, and whether such a celebration would have been secular or religious, is not known, although a twelfth-century[112] reader of Bede gave the month name the explanation 'because this is when they offered the cattle to be killed to their gods' (*Notes 4.6*).[113] Whether this should be read

Lapidge, eds, *Byrhtferth's 'Enchiridion'*, EETS, ss 15 (Oxford: Oxford University Press, 1995), 24; *Notes 4.1, 4.2, 4.3*: Francis Wormald, ed., *English Kalendars before AD 1100* (London: Henry Bradshaw Society, 1934), 136, 164, 262; *Notes 4.4*: Baker and Lapidge, *Enchiridion*, 409; *Notes 4.6* (Oxford, St. John's College, MS 17, fol. 76v); Meritt glosses 63: H. D. Meritt, ed., *Old English Glosses: A Collection* (New York: Modern Language Association of America, 1945), 56.

[108] Ælfric's *Grammar*, ch. 18: Julius Zupitza, ed., *Aelfrics 'Grammatik' und 'Glossar'* (Berlin: Weidmann, 1880), 43.

[109] N. R. Ker, *Catalogue of Manuscripts Containing Anglo-Saxon* (Oxford: Clarendon, 1957), no. 224, item q; *Oxford English Dictionary* s.v. 'Lammas'.

[110] Bede, *De temporum ratione*, ch. 15: Jones, *De temporum ratione*, 330; *Menologium* 193–8; Byrhtferth, *Manual* 1.2: Baker and Lapidge, *Enchiridion*, 24.

[111] *Bókarbót*: Beckman and Kålund, *Alfræði íslenzk II*, 78; Weinhold, *Die deutschen Monatnamen*, 18–23; Fritzner, s.v. 'gormánáðr'; Thomas Gwynn Jones, *Welsh Folklore and Folk-Custom* (Cambridge: Brewer, 1930), 146; Verner Dahlerup and Lis Jacobsen, *Ordbog over det danske Sprog: Historisk ordbog 1700–1950*, 28 vols (Copenhagen: Det danske sprog- og litteraturselskab, 1918–56), s.v. 'Slagte-maaned', accessed 15 March 2015, http://ordnet.dk/ods/; R. J. Thomas, G. A. Bevan, and J Gareth Thomas, *Geiriadur Prifysgol Cymru*, 61 vols (Cardiff: Gwasg Prifysgol Cymru, 1950–2002), s.v. 'tachwedd'; Ton der Boon and Dirk Geeraerts, eds, *Van Dale Groot woordenboek der Nederlandse taal*, 14th ed., CD-ROM ('s-Hertogenbosch: C-Content, 2005), s.v. 'slachtmaand'; Anki Mattisson, *Ordbok över svenska språket* (Stockholm: Svenska Akademien, 1898–), s.v. 'slakt-månad', accessed 15 March 2015, http://www.saob.se/.

[112] Ker, *Catalogue*, no. 360.

[113] 'Quia in eo pecora quae occisuri erant diis suis uouerent' (Oxford, St John's College, MS

as speculation or report, it is certain that the necessary conditions for a gathering, secular or religious, were in place at this time of year.

Finally, the well-attested *geola* months, overlapping with December and January, may be suspected of festive or ritual associations both by Bede's testimony to a *modraniht* coinciding with Christmas Eve and by analogy with the Scandinavian cognate *jól* ('Yule').[114] The meaning of Bede's 'night of mothers', however, is impossible to divine.

Although Bede claims that *hreþmonaþ* (approximately March) and *eastermonaþ* (approximately April) were named after goddesses,[115] this cannot be confirmed.[116] In the historical Old English period, *hreþ* meant 'glory';[117] it could thus refer to a victory of light over dark, or summer over winter, which would likely have a festive and thus a ritual dimension. However, it could just as well refer to the start of the military season, in which case it need not have had a religious dimension, even if it coincided with the month of Mars. Jacob Grimm claimed that the worship of a goddess Eostre is confirmed by the name's survival in *Easter* and German *Ostern*,[118] but all this demonstrates is that the unidentified concept behind the word *eostre* was associated with this time of year. On the other hand, recent defences of Bede's claim adduce Continental votive inscriptions predating the Migration Period dedicated to the *matronae Austriahenae*.[119] While this is a noteworthy discovery that permits the conjecture of a cult associated with deities involving the Germanic root *austra*, the evidence remains too thin to demonstrate the existence of a seasonal cult in Anglo-Saxon England.

Clerical injunctions against pagan practice have little to add to this index: specific practices are condemned, but they are not associated with particular times of year.[120] Between Lammas, *modraniht*, the etymology of *haligmonaþ*, the North Germanic analogue to *geola*, and the ceremonial potential of *blodmonaþ*, therefore, the hypothesis may be posited that there were religious harvest events in August and September, and further social events with festive or religious potential from November to January. Additional traditions of seasonal ritual or worship must be supposed, but they are difficult either to substantiate or to identify.

17, fol. 76vb).
[114] Bede, *De temporum ratione*, ch. 15: Jones, *De temporum ratione*, 330–1; Byrhtferth, *Manual* 1.2: Baker and Lapidge, *Enchiridion*, 24; *Martyrology* §§8a, 233b: Rauer, *The Old English Martyrology*, 42, 222; *Menologium* 218–21.
[115] Bede, *De temporum ratione*, ch. 15: Jones, *De temporum ratione*, 330–1.
[116] Cf. Page, 'Anglo-Saxon Paganism'.
[117] Grimm, *Deutsche Mythologie*, 1:240 for 267; Joseph Bosworth, ed., *An Anglo-Saxon Dictionary, Revised by T. Northcote Toller* (Oxford: Oxford University Press, 1898), s.v. 'hréð'.
[118] Grimm, *Deutsche Mythologie*, 1:241 for 268.
[119] For example Philip A. Shaw, *Pagan Goddesses in the Early Germanic World: Eostre, Hreda and the Cult of Matrons*, Studies in Early Medieval History (London: Bristol Classical Press, 2011).
[120] For example *Poenitentiale pseudo-Egberti* § 4.12–16: Josef Raith, ed., *Die altenglische Version des halitgar'schen Bussbuches* (Hamburg: Grand, 1933; Darmstadt: Wissenschaftliche Buchgesellschaft, 1964), 53–5; *II Cnut* §§ 5–5.1: Liebermann, *Gesetze*, 1:312; *Norðhymbra preosta lagu* §§ 48–53: ibid., 1:383.

SCANDINAVIAN RITUAL

If evidence of Scandinavian seasonal ritual can also be elusive, at least there is a larger body of material to go by.[121] Firstly, there is Procopius's sixth-century account of a Nordic festive welcoming of the sun following the winter darkness. According to this work, the residents of the northern island of Thule send scouts up to a mountain top in January to watch for the return of the sun following its forty-day absence in winter. When the scouts return with the good news, a celebration is held.[122] This early account, however, is difficult to place in a continuous tradition, not only because the identity of the island Thule is uncertain but also because the next earliest evidence of a similar custom is so recent it involves the consumption of coffee to celebrate the first day of the year when direct sunlight reaches into the Icelandic valleys.[123]

The eleventh-century historiographers Thietmar of Merseburg and Adam of Bremen describe a Scandinavian sacrificial festival taking place once every nine years. A scholium attached to Adam's account fixes this event to a time about the spring equinox.[124] Since the festival is purportedly not annual, however, its seasonal character would have been less striking than that of a yearly celebration of the type described by Procopius.

Greater detail is to be had from Scandinavian sources, beginning with the Norwegian *Ágrip* (c. 1190).[125] This is the first of a number of texts describing pre-Conversion ritual in the context of its subsequent Christian reinterpretation:

> Á þeim fimm vetrum, er hann [Óláfr Tryggvason] bar konungs nafn í Nóregi, kristnaði hann fimm lǫnd: Nóreg ok Ísland ok Hjaltland, Orkneyingar ok it fimmta Færeyjar, ok reisti fyrst kirkjur á sjálfs síns hǫfuðbólum ok felldi blót ok blótdrykkjur ok lét í stað koma í vild við lýðinn hátíðadrykkjur jól ok páskar, Jóansmessu mungát ok haustöl að Mikjálsmessu.   (*Ágrip*, ch. 19)[126]
>
> During the five years in which he [i.e. Óláfr Tryggvason] bore the title of king in Norway, he converted five countries to Christianity: Norway, Iceland, Shetland, Orkney, and fifthly the Faroe Islands. He first erected churches by his own residences, and he did away with sacrifice and

---

[121] The traditions mentioned in this paragraph are discussed at greater length in Terry Gunnell, 'The Season of the *dísir*: The Winter Nights and the *dísablót* in Early Medieval Scandinavian Belief', *Cosmos* 16, no. 2 (2000): 117–49; Nordberg, *Jul, disting och förkyrklig tideräkning*.

[122] *History of the Wars* 6.15: H. B. Dewing, ed. and trans., *Procopius: 'History of the Wars'*, 3 vols (London: Heinemann, 1914–19), 3:414–18.

[123] Árni Björnsson, *Saga daganna*, 431–2.

[124] *Gesta Hammaburgensis ecclesiae pontificum*, ch. 27 and scholium 141: Bernhard Schmeidler, ed., *Adam von Bremen: Hamburgische Kirchengeschichte*, 3rd ed., Scriptores rerum germanicarum 2 (Hannover: Hahn, 1917), 260.

[125] Bjarni Einarsson, ed., *Ágrip af Noregskonunga sögum*, Íslenzk fornrit 29 (Reykjavik: Hið íslenzka fornritafélag, 1984), x–xi.

[126] Ibid., 22.

sacrificial toasts, substituting the festive toasts of Christmas and Easter, St John's Mass brew and the autumn ale at Michaelmas as a favour to the people.

It should be noted that the text does not strictly state that these four Christian feasts were instituted to replace the same number of festivals taking place about the same time of year; indeed, they could conceivably constitute a representative sample of Christian feast days. If that were the case, however, it would be remarkable for the author to have chosen St John's Day and Michaelmas alongside the religion's main festivals of Christmas and Easter, favouring an even seasonal distribution over a listing of Western Christendom's most important celebrations, which would certainly have included Pentecost. Instead, the text seems to suggest that each of these Christian feasts was indeed designed to replace a specific pagan festival not too distant in time from the named feasts, thereby to ease the transition to the new religion.[127]

Snorri largely confirms the evidence from *Ágrip*, filling in the nature and timing of the pre-Conversion festivals there implied. He repeats his information at various points in his compendium of kings' sagas, leaving little doubt as to his understanding of the ritual tradition. In *Ynglinga saga*, he states that a euhemerized Óðinn instituted three annual sacrifices, namely for a successful year at the start of winter, for the growth of crops at midwinter, and for military victory at the start of summer (ch. 8).[128] Sacrifices at all these points in time are twice recorded in Snorri's *Óláfs saga ins helga* (chs 109, 117),[129] while individual confirmations occur repeatedly across *Heimskringla*.[130] What is more, Snorri states specifically that a pre-Conversion Yule was assimilated into Christmas (*Hákonar saga góða*, ch. 13)[131] and that a Swedish feast in late winter, originally sacrificial, was absorbed by Candlemas (*Óláfs saga helga*, ch. 77),[132] thus further strengthening the idea implied in *Ágrip* that seasonal Christian feasts were deliberately selected to replace pre-Conversion ritual events taking place about the same time of year.

A few of these festivities are described in greater detail in the sagas. To begin with, the narrative sources amply attest to the pre-Conversion existence of a festive Winter Nights celebration at the start of winter,[133]

---

[127] Gunnell, 'The Season of the *dísir*'.
[128] Bjarni Aðalbjarnarson, *Heimskringla*, 1:20–1.
[129] Ibid., 2:180, 194.
[130] For example *Hákonar saga góða*, chs 13, 17: ibid., 1:166–7, 171; *Óláfs saga helga*, chs 77, 108: ibid., 2:109, 178.
[131] Ibid., 1:166–7.
[132] Ibid., 2:109.
[133] For example *Gísla saga*, chs 10, 15: Björn K. Þórólfsson and Guðni Jónsson, *Vestfirðinga sǫgur*, 36, 50–1; *Víga-Glúms saga*, ch. 6: Jónas Kristjánsson, *Eyfirðinga sǫgur*, 17; *Eyrbyggja saga*, ch. 37: Einar Ólafur Sveinsson and Matthías Þórðarson, *Eyrbyggja saga*, 98; *Laxdœla saga*, ch. 46: Einar Ólafur Sveinsson, ed., *Laxdœla saga*, Íslenzk fornrit 5 (Reykjavík: Hið íslenzka fornritafélag, 1934),

which can therefore hardly be doubted. Similarly beyond doubt on account of widespread report is a propensity for celebrating weddings during the Winter Nights.[134] More caution is in order when religious aspects to the celebration are described, as such ritual had been banned from the public view for over two centuries when the first surviving sagas were written.[135] Accordingly, there is some variation between accounts of this type. *Gísla saga*, of doubtful reliability in these affairs since it describes one or two purported heathen practices not recorded elsewhere,[136] states that the Winter Nights involved sacrificing to Freyr;[137] *Víga-Glúms saga* speaks of a *dísablót* ('sacrifice to the *dísir* or goddesses') taking place at this time (ch. 6),[138] a ritual similarly situated in autumn in *Egils saga* (chs 42–4).[139] Other texts speak simply of sacrifice without specifying an object of worship.[140] In view of the large body of references and the fact that the Winter Nights were close in time to the annual slaughter, it may be accepted that religious sacrifice of livestock took place at this time, but references to this feast provide no firm evidence for the seasonal worship of any particular deity or group of deities.[141]

The sagas describe the winter feast of Yule in considerable detail and with great frequency, although it is often difficult to distinguish between its Christian and purported pre-Conversion forms. As with the Winter Nights,

---

139; *Vápnfirðinga saga*, ch. 4: Jón Jóhannesson, *Austfirðinga sǫgur*, 29; *Vatnsdœla saga*, ch. 46: Einar Ólafur Sveinsson, ed., *Vatnsdœla saga*, Íslenzk fornrit 8 (Reykjavík: Hið íslenzka fornritafélag, 1939), 124–5; cf. *Egils saga*, chs 2, 86: Bjarni Einarsson, *Egils saga*, 2, 176.

[134] *Gunnars saga Keldugnúpsfífls*, ch. 10: Jóhannes Halldórsson, ed., *Kjalnesinga saga*, Íslenzk fornrit 14 (Reykjavík: Hið íslenzka fornritafélag, 1959), 377; *Gunnlaugs saga ormstungu*, ch. 9: Sigurður Nordal and Guðni Jónsson, *Borgfirðinga sǫgur*, 82; *Valla-Ljóts saga*, ch. 1: Jónas Kristjánsson, *Eyfirðinga sǫgur*, 235; *Laxdœla saga*, ch. 43: Einar Ólafur Sveinsson, *Laxdœla saga*, 130; *Vatnsdœla saga*, chs 32, 44: Einar Ólafur Sveinsson, *Vatnsdœla saga*, 85–6, 116; *Víglundar saga*, ch. 6: Jóhannes Halldórsson, *Kjalnesinga saga*, 72. Several further episodes do not mention the festival itself but situate weddings more loosely in the autumn; thus *Eyrbyggja saga*, ch. 28: Einar Ólafur Sveinsson and Matthías Þórðarson, *Eyrbyggja saga*, 75; *Víga-Glúms saga*, ch. 11: Jónas Kristjánsson, *Eyfirðinga sǫgur*, 38; *Heiðarvíga saga*, ch. 42: Sigurður Nordal and Guðni Jónsson, *Borgfirðinga sǫgur*, 326; *Laxdœla saga*, ch. 7: Einar Ólafur Sveinsson, *Laxdœla saga*, 11.

[135] *Íslendingabók*, ch. 7: Jakob Benediktsson, *Íslendingabók, Landnámabók*, 17.

[136] Notably the *helskór* in ch. 14: Björn K. Þórólfsson and Guðni Jónsson, *Vestfirðinga sǫgur*, 45–6; cf. Hermann Pálsson, 'Odinic Echoes in *Gísla saga*', in *Gudar på jorden: Festskrift till Lars Lönnroth*, ed. Stina Hansson and Mats Malm (Stockholm and Stehag: Brutus Östling, 2000), 99.

[137] *Gísla saga*, ch. 15: Björn K. Þórólfsson and Guðni Jónsson, *Vestfirðinga sǫgur*, 50.

[138] Jónas Kristjánsson, *Eyfirðinga sǫgur*, 17.

[139] Bjarni Einarsson, *Egils saga*, 56–8; see further Gunnell, 'The Season of the *dísir*'.

[140] For example *Egils saga*, ch. 2: Bjarni Einarsson, *Egils saga*, 2; *Vatnsdœla saga*, ch. 46: Einar Ólafur Sveinsson, *Vatnsdœla saga*, 124–5; *Vápnfirðinga saga*, ch. 4: Jón Jóhannesson, *Austfirðinga sǫgur*, 29.

[141] Contrast Gunnell, 'The Season of the *dísir*'. Although two autumnal references to a *dísablót* are found in the sagas of Icelanders, the general absence of the *dísir* from Icelandic sources suggests that their default scholarly interpretation as a specific class of deities may be unwarranted in an Icelandic context. There is no evidence to suggest that *dís* had a reference more specific than 'goddess' to Icelandic saga authors. Contrast Folke Ström, 'Diser', *KLNM* 3 (1958): 101–3; and again Gunnell, 'The Season of the *dísir*'.

Saga Age authors thought of Yule as a social gathering[142] including a banquet.[143] The attestation across a variety of sagas of the words *jóladrykkja* ('Yule drink') and *jólaǫl* ('Yule ale') confirms the evidence from the Norwegian *Gulaþingslǫg* that the Christian celebration involved a toast.[144] Since the toast is also a consistent element in *Ágrip*'s descriptions of pre-Christian festivals quoted above, the Norwegian legal requirement to brew ale for the Christian festival may well date back to the older feast.[145] According to Snorri, the festivities of pre-Christian Yule lasted for three days, like the Winter Nights, and overlapped with Epiphany.[146] Little more can be said with any certainty about the early feast, and indeed all that has been listed so far was recorded by a culture deeply entrenched in Christian tradition, rendering even this tentative.

As far as non-Christian annual festivities in medieval Iceland are concerned, the two abovementioned traditions of Winter Nights and Yule are the only ones to make frequent appearances in narrative literature. Granted, Snorri claims that Óðinn instituted a sacrifice for military victory at the start of the summer half-year, while *Ágrip* suggests that Easter replaced a pagan libation about the same time of year. The *Ágrip* passage, however, composed in Norway, does not distinguish between King Óláfr's various North Atlantic holdings, and Snorri's reference is to Sweden. It is indeed in Sweden that evidence of a spring festival is best attested, primarily in the form of the *dísablót* that is thought to have taken place at that time of year.[147] *Egils saga* suggests there was an annual spring sacrifice in the Norwegian area of Gaular as well (ch. 49).[148] Since the Swedish *dísablót* is explicitly linked with religious sacrifices, this seems the most unambiguous case of a religious festival aimed at influencing the quality of the season to come. However, there is little evidence of its popularity in Iceland. Instead, the authors of the sagas of Icelanders treat the regional assemblies as the only spring gatherings worthy of report. It is only in the contemporary sagas and other texts dealing with post-Conversion Iceland that the ritual

---

[142] For example *Víga-Glúms saga*, ch. 1: Jónas Kristjánsson, *Eyfirðinga sǫgur*, 4–5; *Haralds saga hárfagra*, ch. 25: Bjarni Aðalbjarnarson, *Heimskringla*, 1:125.

[143] For example *Hálfdanar þáttr svarta*, ch. 8: ibid., 1:91–2.

[144] *Gulaþingslǫg*, ch. 7: R. Keyser and P. A. Munch, eds, *Norges gamle love indtil 1387* (Christiania [Oslo]: Grøndahl, 1846–95), 1:6; *Bjarnar saga Hítdœlakappa*, ch. 27: Sigurður Nordal and Guðni Jónsson, *Borgfirðinga sǫgur*, 180; *Eyrbyggja saga*, ch. 54: Einar Ólafur Sveinsson and Matthías Þórðarson, *Eyrbyggja saga*, 148; *Fóstbrœðra saga*, ch. 22: Björn K. Þórólfsson and Guðni Jónsson, *Vestfirðinga sǫgur*, 226–7; *Hákonar saga herðibreiðs*, ch. 15: Bjarni Aðalbjarnarson, *Heimskringla*, 3:365; *Laxdœla saga*, ch. 74: Einar Ólafur Sveinsson, *Laxdœla saga*, 217.

[145] So also Andr Seierstad, 'Jul', *KLNM* 8 (1963): 7–8.

[146] *Hákonar saga góða*, ch. 13: Bjarni Aðalbjarnarson, *Heimskringla*, 1:166.

[147] *Óláfs saga helga*, ch. 77: Bjarni Aðalbjarnarson, *Heimskringla*, 2:109; *Gesta Hammaburgensis ecclesiae pontificum*, ch. 27 and scholium 141: Schmeidler, *Kirchengeschichte*, 260; John Granlund, 'Veckoräkning och veckoår', *ARV* 11 (1955): 1–37; Ström, 'Diser'; Gunnell, 'The Season of the *dísir'*; Nordberg, *Jul, disting och förkyrklig tideräkning*, 107–12.

[148] Bjarni Einarsson, *Egils saga*, 69.

significance of spring plays a role in the guise of the moveable feasts of Christian tradition.

The situation is much the same for midsummer festivals. Here too, *Ágrip* suggests the season accommodated a major celebration prior to the Conversion. Some additional support for such an event comes from the fact that *miðsumar* is attested as a point on the calendar, in mid-July.[149] On the other hand, a midsummer celebration is conspicuously absent from Snorri's canon of three pre-Christian festivals. Moreover, the sagas of Icelanders, which deal extensively with pre-Conversion times, do not mention it, although the term *miðsumarshelgr* ('midsummer feast') makes an appearance in *Þorgils saga skarða* (ch. 40), which forms part of the contemporary saga collection *Sturlunga saga* set and composed in the thirteenth century, where the date is used as a setting for an *ad hoc* political gathering.[150] Fritzner understood this term to refer to the Nativity of John the Baptist on 24 June, but it probably refers to the pre-Christian *miðsumar* in mid-July given the chronology of developments surrounding its mention.[151] The occurrence is remarkable in a text as firmly embedded in the Church calendar as *Sturlunga saga*, and hints at a continued familiarity with this feast day. Since the family sagas and Snorri's historiographical works make no mention of it, however, it cannot have been considered a major festival.

The Nativity of John the Baptist has long been the second-most important festival in mainland Scandinavia, eclipsed only by Christmas.[152] It is attested as a major festival in medieval Norway as well as in the Icelandic contemporary sagas.[153] The silence on annual summer festivals in the sagas of Icelanders suggests that the festival in July lost much of what ritual importance it had as the feast of John the Baptist took its place, but survived as a more muted calendrical presence. Accordingly, the pre-Conversion celebration is likely to have assumed a modest place in the ritual year to begin with, since the sagas make no effort to suppress the importance of the analogous festivals of Yule and the Winter Nights. Although the sagas of Icelanders should not be read as straightforward accounts of pre-Christian ritual given the Christian culture in which they were written down, their lack of interest in a midsummer festival surely reflects the relative insignificance of such a festival at least by the thirteenth and fourteenth centuries, and probably before.

---

[149] *Rím I*, ch. 26: Beckman and Kålund, *Alfræði íslenzk II*, 22; *Rím II*, chs 3, 113, 171: ibid., 83–4, 138, 172–3; *Grágás*, ch. 78: Vilhjálmur Finsen, *Grágás*, 1:129; John Granlund, 'Midsommar', *KLNM* 11 (1966): 612–14; Kirsten Hastrup, 'Temporal Categories', in *Culture and History in Medieval Iceland* (Oxford: Clarendon, 1985), 28–9.

[150] Jón Jóhannesson, Magnús Finnbogason, and Kristján Eldjárn, *Sturlunga saga*, 2:166.

[151] Fritzner, s.v.; Jón Jóhannesson, Magnús Finnbogason, and Kristján Eldjárn, *Sturlunga saga*, 2:306, n. 40.1.

[152] Nilsson, 'År och arbetsliv', 8.

[153] See the passages referenced for the majority of words beginning in *jóns-* in Fritzner.

A greater discrepancy between the historical calendar and that found in the sagas of Icelanders may be recognized in the narrative emphases during autumn and spring. Although a cursory reading of these texts may suggest otherwise, regional assemblies in Iceland gathered not just in spring but in autumn as well. In the sagas, however, the autumn *þing* receives only a fraction of the attention of the Winter Nights taking place in the same season. In the concordance to the *Íslendingasögur* by Bragi Halldórsson et al. (working from a collection of popular editions with modernized spelling),[154] the term *haustþing* ('autumn assembly') has only six occurrences, half of which are found in *Droplaugarsona saga*, while *vorþing* ('spring assembly') occurs thirty times across nineteen sagas or major saga redactions; *veturnætur* and its compounds occur forty times across twenty texts. Thus if this genre were to be used as a guide to the social and political year, one might be led to believe that autumn was defined by its festive character and had no political significance. Conversely, spring and summer in these texts are usually the setting of political events. There is some limited evidence of entertainment at the *alþingi*,[155] but that aspect of the meeting is usually left unmentioned in the family sagas. These texts thus present autumn and winter as times for feasting, while spring and summer are depicted as the seasons for political activity.

Some aspects of this literary calendar do follow historical patterns and may be explained by conditions resulting from the economic cycle. Firstly, there is the suitability for feasting during both the post-harvest agricultural lull and the time of the annual slaughter. Secondly, the timing of the *alþingi* to a time of midnight sun and a minimum of snow was only practical, as attendees camped out in booths and many had to travel across the mountainous interior to reach the assembly grounds. Of the summer months, moreover, June was agriculturally the least intensive,[156] so that the farmwork of this period could be carried out by a smaller work force. Finally, the agricultural quiet of winter combines with the ready availability of food stocks and the necessity of spending time indoors to explain the relative prominence of midwinter feasting.[157] Accordingly, some argue that Christmas has held greater significance in northern Europe than in the Mediterranean,[158] where milder winters with more sun hours did not result in the same level of confinement. Moreover, northern countries emphasized further liturgical dates at this time of year and gave them a symbolism

---

[154] Bragi Halldórsson et al., eds, *Íslendinga sögur: Orðstöðulykill og texti*, 2nd ed., CD-ROM (Reykjavík: Mál og menning, 1998).

[155] *Þorsteins þáttr sǫgufróða*, for instance, suggests there was storytelling (Jón Jóhannesson, *Austfirðinga sǫgur*, 336).

[156] Nilsson, 'År och arbetsliv', 8; cf. Granlund, 'Midsommar', 613.

[157] Nilsson, 'År och arbetsliv', 2–4.

[158] Ronald Hutton, *The Stations of the Sun: A History of the Ritual Year in Britain* (Oxford: Oxford University Press, 1996), 3–4; Gopnik, *Winter*, 98–9.

of light amidst the dark of winter. Within the Christian framework this is most striking in the Scandinavian observance of Lucia (13 December, corresponding to the solstice in the later Middle Ages)[159] and the northern popularity of Candlemas (2 February).[160]

The existence of all these celebrations could be taken to suggest that there was a demand for a ritual marking of the passing of winter darkness. However, that is not the most obvious explanation. For one thing, this reading does not explain why there would be less occasion for celebration in summer. Indeed, the conditions that make June an appropriate setting for political gatherings also make it an attractive time for festivals, as the post-Conversion Scandinavian popularity of Midsummer Night testifies. Above all, however, the festive identity of the start and midway points of the winter half-year in the sagas of Icelanders should not be considered without taking into account that this was a time of greater leisure, less travel, and more time spent indoors in the possession of substantial provisions.

The tendency in these texts to concentrate on the festive potential of autumn and winter against the political functions of spring and summer also translates into convenient narrative functions. Prominent among these is the development of discord at winter feasts, followed by attempts at pacification at the spring and summer assemblies. In *Gísla saga*, for instance, the 'doomed quartet' at the heart of the story attempt to establish a political league at the spring assembly in order to pre-empt the internal strife that has been prophesied for them. They experience a falling out all the same, and of the four consequential killings, as Hermann Pálsson observes, three take place during the Winter Nights, and it is one of these deaths that inspires the killing of the fourth member, Þorkell, at a spring assembly. The first three killings are embedded in the early-winter season on a meteorological level as well, as Vésteinn's takes place during a severe rainstorm, while the valley is covered with snow and hoarfrost respectively during the killings of Þorgrímr and Gísli.[161] In *Laxdœla saga*, tensions arise over two valuable items that are stolen at two autumn feasts taking place in the same year shortly before and during the Winter Nights. These tensions escalate into feuding over the course of the winter, followed by peace talks finalized at the spring assembly.[162] The feud does not end there, and hostilities follow in various seasons; but the autumn feasts provide a first opportunity for tensions to surface.

The tensions in *Njáls saga* between Bergþóra and Hallgerðr escalate during successive general assemblies in June, but here too the first offence

---

[159] Hilding Celander and Kustaa Vilkuna, 'Lucia', KLNM 10 (1965): 704–10; Árni Björnsson, *Saga daganna*, 297–301.

[160] Hutton, *Stations*, 139–41; Árni Björnsson, *Saga daganna*, 491–5.

[161] *Gísla saga*, chs 5–6, 10–17, 28, 34–6: Björn K. Þórólfsson and Guðni Jónsson, *Vestfirðinga sǫgur*, 17–24, 34–56, 89–91, 109–16; *Eyrbyggja saga*, ch. 12: Einar Ólafur Sveinsson and Matthías Þórðarson, *Eyrbyggja saga*, 20; Hermann Pálsson, 'Odinic Echoes', 113.

[162] *Laxdœla saga*, chs 46–51: Einar Ólafur Sveinsson, *Laxdœla saga*, 139–59.

Myth and Ritual 59

is given at a winter feast. When Gunnarr and Hallgerðr attend Njáll's feast, Hallgerðr gets into an argument over the seating arrangement with the hostess, and an unpleasant exchange ensues (ch. 35).[163] This initial wintertime strife sets the stage for mortal feuding between the two households in the summers that follow (chs 36–42).[164]

This last example raises the question whether women played any special part in wintertime strife. After all, the sagas of Icelanders and other Old Norse texts frequently portray women as a source of conflict, both through envy amongst themselves and through their insistence on the male obligation of vengeance.[165] Moreover, it has been proposed that winter was the social domain of women: in summer, many texts concentrate on male action, not seldom out of doors or abroad. In winter, however, Icelanders spent more time indoors, where women enjoyed greater power and influence.[166] It might thus be expected that tensions often escalate as a consequence of female wintertime rivalry and goading, whether at feasts or on other occasions when time is spent indoors.

This potential is not exploited as often as conditions might suggest, however. A rare episode of female troublemaking in winter occurs in *Grœnlendinga saga* when Freydís Eiríksdóttir first deceives her trading partners, then antagonizes them by refusing them access to her brother's house in Vínland, forcing them to build their own. In the course of the winter, discord arises between the two houses until contact ceases altogether. Eventually, Freydís contrives to have everyone in her partners' company killed (ch. 7).[167] Female envy is likewise a factor in the episode with the stolen valuables in *Laxdæla saga*, but Guðrún Ósvífrsdóttir is at the root of most conflicts in that saga, regardless of season.

When tensions do escalate at winter feasts, it is more commonly men and alcohol that are to blame. Thus Egill Skalla-Grímsson famously makes trouble at an autumnal feast on Atley, eventually killing his host Bárðr after the latter tries to poison him (*Egils saga*, ch. 44).[168] Perhaps the tensest of wintertime confrontations is that between Þorgeirr and Grettir in *Grettis saga* (written about the first quarter of the fourteenth century),[169] or Þorgeirr and Butraldi in *Fóstbrœðra saga*, each of which tells how two troublemakers are

---

[163] Einar Ólafur Sveinsson, ed., *Brennu-Njáls saga*, Íslenzk fornrit 12 (Reykjavik: Hið íslenzka fornritafélag, 1954), 90–2.
[164] Ibid., 92–109.
[165] Judith Jesch, *Women in the Viking Age* (Woodbridge: Boydell, 1991), 182–202.
[166] Ibid., 187; Terry Gunnell, 'Ritual Space. Ritual Year. Ritual Gender: A View of the Old Norse and New Icelandic Ritual Year', in *First International Conference of the SIEF Working Group on the Ritual Year: Proceedings*, Malta, March 20–4, 2005, ed. George Mifsud-Chircop (San Gwann, Malta: Publishers Enterprises Group, 2005), esp. 292–5.
[167] Einar Ólafur Sveinsson and Matthías Þórðarson, *Eyrbyggja saga*, 264–7.
[168] Bjarni Einarsson, *Egils saga*, 58–60.
[169] Guðni Jónsson, ed., *Grettis saga Ásmundarsonar, Bandamanna saga, Odds þáttr Ófeigssonar*, Íslenzk fornrit 7 (Reykjavik: Hið íslenzka fornritafélag, 1936), lxviii–lxx.

forced to spend the night (in *Grettis saga* the winter) under the same roof.[170] Not a single woman features in either of these accounts; in *Fóstbrœðra saga*, even the food is served by the farmer himself.[171]

In the legendary sagas, perhaps in imitation of Continental texts,[172] some female characters meddle with the drinks they serve at feasts whose season is not always specified,[173] but here too there are examples of revelry escalated by male action.[174] In both legendary and family sagas, sports are another aspect of male recreational activity, often situated in winter or autumn, that tends to escalate without interference from women; an index of such escalations is given below (p. 152, n. 179). These examples are largely representative of configurations of gender, winter, and violence in the sagas of Icelanders, which do not reserve a special place for female troublemakers in this respect.

Perhaps the most extended episode of female goading in the sagas of Icelanders is the rivalry in *Njáls saga* mentioned above between Bergþóra and Hallgerðr, which takes place during the *alþingi* in summer, when the men are away (chs 36–42).[175] That rivalry between these women first arises at a winter feast (ch. 35)[176] demonstrates not so much a connection between season and gender but rather the general tendency for winter to serve as a breeding ground for strife in the sagas.

Apart from the social confrontations inherent in festive occasions, the tradition of taking vows during toasts and celebrations (*heitstrenging*,[177] sometimes presented as a drink-induced game[178]) is a second source of conflict, this one exclusively male. Since feasts in the sagas most commonly take place in the winter half-year, the tradition of vows is likewise associated with winter feasts.[179] It is at a feast in autumn or winter that Hersteinn vows to marry no one but Helga in *Flóamanna saga*, but Helga's brother Ingólfr

---

[170] See further below, p. 139.

[171] *Grettis saga*, ch. 50: Guðni Jónsson, *Grettis saga*, 159–63; *Fóstbrœðra saga*, ch. 6 Björn K. Þórólfsson and Guðni Jónsson, *Vestfirðinga sǫgur*, 142–7.

[172] The love potion is central to the Tristan material, while potions of various kinds are a common element in Old French romance generally. They are typically prepared by women. Cf. Sylvia Huot, 'A Tale Much Told: The Status of the Love Philtre in the Old French Tristan Texts', *Zeitschrift für deutsche Philologie* 124, Sonderheft (2005): 82–95; Edward J. Gallagher, trans., *The Lays of Marie de France* (Indianapolis, IN: Hackett, 2010), 98–9.

[173] *Vǫlsunga saga*, chs 10 (an autumn funerary feast), 28, 32: R. G. Finch, ed. and trans., *Vǫlsunga saga / The Saga of the Volsungs*, Icelandic Texts (London: Nelson, 1965), 18, 47, 62.

[174] For example *Vǫlsunga saga*, ch. 3: ibid., 4–5; *Hervarar saga*, ch. 5: Gabriel Turville-Petre, ed., *Hervarar saga ok Heiðreks* (London: Viking Society for Northern Research / University College London, 1976), 24–5.

[175] Einar Ólafur Sveinsson, *Brennu-Njáls saga*, 92–109.

[176] Ibid., 90–2.

[177] Fritzner, s.v.

[178] *Jómsvíkinga saga*, ch. 26: Blake, *Jómsvíkinga saga*, 28–9.

[179] Cf. Inger M. Boberg, *Motif-Index of Early Icelandic Literature*, Bibliotheca Arnamagnaeana 27 (Copenhagen: Munksgaard, 1966), 191 (motif M119.3), where it is asserted that the motif is primarily associated with Yule.

promptly vows to marry her to none other than his foster-brother Leifr, thus setting the stage for hostilities between the foster-brothers and Hersteinn, who receives the aid of his own brothers (chs 2–3).[180] *Hœnsa-Þóris saga* tells of vows taken at a feast in winter to the effect that certain guilty parties will be outlawed before the year's *alþingi* is over (ch. 12).[181] Drinking vows also lead to larger-scale conflicts, as with the vows of the *Jómsvíkingar* at a funerary toast at the time of the Winter Nights to drive away or kill Athelstan of England and Hákon of Norway (*Jómsvíkinga saga*, ch. 26), the latter of which undertakings proves fatal to the brotherhood (chs 27–37).[182] Similarly, in the AM 291-redaction of the same saga, Emperor Otto of Saxony vows, at Christmas, to convert Denmark within three years or die in the attempt (ch. 6).[183] In *Eiríks saga víðfǫrla*, the protagonist vows, on Christmas Eve, to find the earthly paradise.[184] All such traditions associated with wintertime feasting strengthen the social differentiation between the literary seasons, characterizing feasting as a winter activity but also setting the stage for conflict, which often plays out in the summer that follows.

Conclusions

The introduction to this volume established a paradigm of soft solar determinism: the more dependent a society is on seasonal parameters, the more its organization will follow the cycle of the seasons. This first chapter has extended this reasoning into the cultural domain by documenting the ways in which ritual too followed a seasonal rhythm in the cultures under study.

Of course, the degree of determinism involved should not be overstated. On the one hand, the seasonal cycle has profound and inevitable implications for the succession of agricultural labours, and the distribution of such labours in turn determines the general distribution of leisure across the year in labour-intensive agricultural societies. Recreational and religious activities thus receive a strong impetus to concentrate in seasonal economic calms, as do periodic political gatherings in societies without a professional administration. On the other hand, the only link in this chain quite beyond negotiation is the astronomical cycle of the solar year and the consequent earthly growth cycle. To varying degrees, organic societies are at liberty to adjust their diets by altering the balance between crop production and

---

[180] Þórhallur Vilmundarson and Bjarni Vilhjálmsson, eds, *Harðar saga*, Íslenzk fornrit 13 (Reykjavik: Hið íslenzka fornritafélag, 1991), 234–7.
[181] Sigurður Nordal and Guðni Jónsson, *Borgfirðinga sǫgur*, 33–4.
[182] Blake, *Jómsvíkinga saga*, 29–44.
[183] Ólafur Halldórsson, *Jómsvíkinga saga* (Reykjavik: Jón Helgason, 1969), 85.
[184] Helle Jensen, ed., *Eiríks saga víðfǫrla*, Editiones arnamagnæanæ B 29 (Copenhagen: Reitzel, 1983), 4.

fishery, for instance, two sectors with considerably divergent calendars. In the religious sphere, if a particular date or time of year becomes sufficiently important to a culture, people may choose to worship even if the time diverted from production translates into lower yields. On the whole, however, a society with a largely agricultural economy will mow and harvest in summer and autumn, but spend more time around the home in winter, engaged in indoor labour but conceivably also at leisure.

This chapter has also moved the discussion into the domain of narrative analysis to investigate the nature of seasonal mythology in medieval England and Scandinavia. A meaningful contrast was found between rivalling aetiologies of the seasons. If seasonal variation began as a curse on mankind, as is asserted in the patristic literature, then there is no inherent redeeming value to either summer or winter. If, as is suggested in several Scandinavian texts, humans and associated groups derive their existence from the elements of winter, then authors have a vested interest in finding something ennobling in the season.

These divergent interpretations of seasonality contrast also in the channels that advanced them: one Latinate, the other more Nordic in its interests. This disparate affiliation joins the contrast to another, namely the seasonal taxonomy addressed in the introduction. That contrast too has literary implications: reference to four seasons, namely two extremes and two periods of change, invites their use in images of progress and development, while the bipartite calendar is more suitable for the expression of contrasts. The chapters that follow will show that the narrative literature of the medieval north primarily employs a bipartite scheme, setting up sharp contrasts between safe and dangerous settings. When using seasonal imagery with a view to such associations, authors conventionally do so without establishing a chronological progression. Instead, they evoke a physical winter setting (in Old English and Old Norse literature) or summer setting (in Middle English romance and vision literature) because it enhances, even enables, the otherness of the scene. The seasonal environment thus becomes an embodiment of danger and the unfamiliar, contrasting with the comfort and safety of human society.

~ 2 ~
Winter Mindscapes

Introduction

The study of the natural world in Old English literature is by no means new. Old Germanic philology came into its own against a background of national historicism and Romantic culture.[1] This intellectual environment also gave rise to a political brand of environmental determinism asserting that 'national character' was shaped by the geographical features accommodating a society.[2] Given this background and the continued interest in nation state and geography in the early-twentieth century,[3] it should come as no surprise not only that literary scholars of this period were interested in the natural world, but also that some continued to bring an ideological burden to bear on Anglo-Saxon depictions of weather and landscape. Frederic Moorman worked within this school of thought when he juxtaposed Homer and the *Beowulf* poet as 'the classic and the romantic',[4] grouping the Anglo-Saxon poet with Shakespeare, Wordsworth, and Shelley, poets who 'lived nearest to Nature'.[5] Scholars in this tradition held that Old English poets

---

[1] Anthony D. Smith, 'The Formation of Nationalist Movements', in *Nationalist Movements*, ed. Anthony D. Smith (London: Macmillan, 1976), 15–19; Anthony D. Smith, 'Neo-Classicist and Romantic Elements in the Emergence of Nationalist Conceptions', in Smith, *Nationalist Movements*, 74–87; Ulrich Hunger, 'Die altdeutsche Literatur und das Verlangen nach Wissenschaft: Schöpfungsakt und Fortschrittsglaube in der Frühgermanistik', in *Wissenschaftsgeschichte der Germanistik im 19. Jahrhundert*, ed. Jürgen Fohrmann and Wilhelm Voßkamp (Stuttgart and Weimar: Metzler, 1994), 239–40, 255–6; Katinka Netzer, *Wissenschaft aus nationaler Sehnsucht: Verhandlungen der Germanisten 1846 und 1847* (Heidelberg: Winter, 2006), 11–13.

[2] Herder was instrumental in the popularization of climate determinism as well as a nationalist interest in German culture, language, and history. See Bernhard Suphan, ed., 'Ueber den Fleiß in mehreren gelehrten Sprachen', in *Herders sämmtliche Werke*, vol. 1 (Berlin: Weidmann, 1877–13), 1–7; Eugen Kühnemann, ed., *J. G. Herders 'Ideen zur Philosophie der Geschichte der Menschheit'* (Berlin: Deutsche Bibliothek, 1914), 75–8; Carlton J. H. Hayes, 'Contributions of Herder to the Doctrine of Nationalism', *The American Historical Review* 32, no. 4, 723–7; Robert R. Ergang, *Herder and the Foundations of German Nationalism*, Studies in History, Economics and Public Law 341 (New York: Columbia University Press, 1931).

[3] Friedrich Ratzel, *Politische Geographie* (Munich and Leipzig: Oldenbourg, 1897); Ellen Churchill Semple, *Influences of Geographic Environment on the Basis of Ratzel's System of Anthropo-Geography* (New York: Holt / Rinehart / Winston, 1911); cf. Edmund Dale, *National Life and Character in the Mirror of Early English Literature* (Cambridge: Cambridge University Press, 1907), 51.

[4] Frederic W. Moorman, *Nature*, Quellen und Forschungen zur Sprach- und Culturgeschichte der germanischen Völker 95 (Strasbourg: Trübner, 1905), 15.

[5] Ibid., 4, 216–39.

were fascinated with the rougher manifestations of nature so prominent in northern Europe, but indifferent to its gentler side.[6] In his study of 'the Teuton' through Old English literature, Edmund Dale observed in 1907 that 'it is always the hardship of the life upon which he dwells, because he has mastered it, fighting his battle alone in the solitude of the sea'.[7] Although scholars today may cringe at this type of discourse and its ideas regarding 'primitive poetry',[8] 'the Teutonic mind',[9] and 'feeling for nature',[10] the paucity of summer landscapes in Old English poetry, though not absolute,[11] remains a remarkable fact contrasting with a considerable body of barren landscapes and winter scenes. This disparity continues to be observed by scholars today, though often in passing.[12]

While scholarship of the mid-twentieth century likewise took an interest in medieval nature imagery, it employed a different paradigm, based on the understanding that landscape descriptions in much of Western literature are highly conventional. At times, this approach was given so absolute a form that landscape was now understood as a self-contained tradition with little bearing on the world inhabited by the culture that described it. Instead, the emphasis came to rest on classical motifs, resulting in a series of studies tracing the depiction of such motifs from the classical to the medieval tradition.[13] This approach proved significantly more fruitful for Middle English than for Old English literature, so that publications of larger scope either treated pre-Conquest material briefly or passed it over altogether.[14]

Towards the close of the twentieth century, following the formal inception of ecocriticism,[15] a paradigm gained popularity in which literary uses of

---

[6] Richard Burton, 'Nature in Old English Poetry', *Atlantic Monthly* (1894): 476–7; Elizabeth Deering Hanscom, 'The Feeling for Nature in Old English Poetry', *Journal of English and Germanic Philology* 5 (1903–5): 440; Moorman, *Nature*, 8–15, 29–35, 39–40, and cf. 41–3.

[7] Dale, *National Life and Character in the Mirror of Early English Literature*, 13.

[8] Moorman, *Nature*, 22.

[9] Ibid., 40.

[10] Hanscom, 'The Feeling for Nature in Old English Poetry', 457 and title.

[11] On paradisal landscapes, see Hugh Magennis, *Images of Community in Old English Poetry*, Cambridge Studies in Anglo-Saxon England 18 (Cambridge: Cambridge University Press, 1996), 147–8; Kathleen Barrar, 'A Spacious, Green and Hospitable Land: Paradise in Old English Poetry', *Bulletin of the John Rylands University Library of Manchester* 86, no. 2 (2004), 105–25.

[12] This tendency is noted in Derek Pearsall and Elizabeth Salter, *Landscapes and Seasons of the Medieval World* (Toronto and Buffalo, NY: University of Toronto Press, 1973), 41–3; Anderson, 'The Seasons of the Year', 236–8; Jennifer Neville, 'The Seasons in Old English Poetry', in Carruthers, *La ronde des saisons*, 37–49; Anderson, *Folk-Taxonomies*, 219–66. Of these, only Neville is centrally interested in the pattern.

[13] Rosemond Tuve, *Seasons and Months: Studies in a Tradition of Middle English Poetry* (1933; Cambridge: Brewer, 1974); Enkvist, *The Seasons of the Year*; James J. Wilhelm, *The Cruelest Month: Spring, Nature, and Love in Classical and Medieval Lyrics* (New Haven, CT, and London: Yale University Press, 1965); B. K. Martin, 'Aspects of Winter in Latin and Old English Poetry', *Journal of English and Germanic Philology* 68, no. 3, 375–90; Pearsall and Salter, *Landscapes and Seasons*.

[14] Tuve, *Seasons and Months*; Pearsall and Salter, *Landscapes and Seasons*, 41–4.

[15] Cheryll Glotfelty, 'Literary Studies in an Age of Environmental Crisis', in *The Ecocriticism*

space and the natural world were once again understood to reflect the author's experience. This time, causality was understood to be the reverse of that assumed a century before: literary landscapes were now thought to bear an imprint of existing social and mental constructs rather than acknowledge a societal debt to the natural world. In his 1996 *Images of Community in Old English Poetry*, Hugh Magennis expends several chapters on natural environments and their social functions.[16] Jennifer Neville pushes the same paradigm in her 1999 book on Old English poetic representations of the natural world, identifying definitions-by-delineation of human society and individual heroes engaging with the extrasocietal sphere.[17] More recently still, Fabienne Michelet devoted a monograph to the spatial organization of Old English prose and verse narrative, reflecting on the core-and-periphery thinking underlying Old English literary representations of society in its landscape.[18] These studies are indicative of a belief that the systemic relationships between literary characters and their physical surroundings reflect on a culture's conceptual world at various levels of deliberation and consciousness.

The argument developed in the following chapters proceeds from the recognition that each of these three paradigms, which may be called environmental determinism, literary autonomy, and environmental projection, outlines a valid motivation behind literary scenery. To the Romantics it must be conceded that the arts, like humankind itself, developed in, and by the grace of, a material ecosystem, which accordingly has some claim to having inspired their products. A degree of continuity in literary conventions is likewise beyond dispute. Most of all, however, this study relies on the more recent projection paradigm for its recognition that the extrasocietal other is defined in contrast with the psychological and societal self, and vice versa. What these chapters contribute to that school of thought is a seasonal dimension hitherto left out of consideration in the juxtaposition of self and other.

If seasonality has received recurring but cursory attention in Anglo-Saxon studies, it has been prominently on everyone's mind in the study of Middle English verse. Spring and the month of May are so ubiquitous in Middle English lyric, romance, and dreams, and above all in Chaucer, that their thematic associations will have escaped no one's attention.[19] This

---

Reader: Landmarks in Literary Ecology, ed. Cheryll Glotfelty and Harold Fromm (Athens, GA, and London: The University of Georgia Press, 1996), xv–xxxvii; Michael P. Branch and Scott Slovic, 'Surveying the Emergence of Ecocriticism', in *The ISLE Reader: Ecocriticism, 1993–2003*, ed. Michael P. Branch and Scott Slovic (Athens, GA, and London: University of Georgia Press, 2003), xiii–xxiii.

[16] Magennis, *Images of Community*, 121–88.

[17] Jennifer Neville, *Representations of the Natural World in Old English Poetry*, Cambridge Studies in Anglo-Saxon England 27 (Cambridge: Cambridge University Press, 1999).

[18] Fabienne Michelet, *Creation, Migration, and Conquest: Imaginary Geography and Sense of Space in Old English Literature* (Oxford: Oxford University Press, 2006).

[19] A foundational study is Pearsall and Salter, *Landscapes and Seasons*; for more recent work,

emphasis forms a strong contrast with the more hibernal interests of the Old English poetic corpus, inviting comparative analysis. As will be proposed in the following section, the theoretical basis for such an investigation stands to benefit especially from an adaptation of the Bakhtinian chronotope.

Unlike medieval English literature, the Old Norse tradition has rarely been studied for its use of the natural environment. In large part this is because Old Norse prose in particular expends few words on the matter, while the poetry largely limits environmental imagery to circumlocutions for various literary demographics.[20] Whereas Old English literature makes extensive use of parallels between the microcosm of the mind and the natural environment as macrocosm,[21] landscape in the sagas is generally acknowledged to be important only insofar as it affects the social action of the narrative.[22] Apart from Schach's unpublished 1949 dissertation, little work has been done on the natural world in Old Norse literature. Such landscape studies as have been written strongly tend to leave seasonality out of the equation. An exception is formed by the Fornjótr narrative introduced in the previous chapter, which sets up a legendary ancestry for the Norwegian and Orcadian aristocracy. This material has drawn the attention of Margaret Clunies Ross and Preben Meulengracht Sørensen for the high concentration of transparent winter names applied to the first generations of this line.[23] While the Fornjótr material certainly contains the most striking concentration of winter names in the Old Norse corpus, similar motifs are widespread but have been overlooked as a result of their subtle and organic inclusion in the narrative structure. It is, of course, precisely such common and well-integrated seasonal themes that shed light on perceptions of seasonality fundamental to Saga Age culture.

The argument of the remaining chapters proceeds thematically from winter to summer. This chapter and the next concentrate on Old English and

---

see Carruthers, *La ronde des saisons*.

[20] For kennings using landscape features, see the indices in Rudolf Meissner, *Die Kenningar der Skalden: Ein Beitrag zur skaldischen Poetik*, Rheinische Beiträge und Hülfsbücher zur germanischen Philologie und Volkskunde 1 (Bonn and Leipzig: Schroeder, 1921), for example 110–24, 256–7.

[21] Robert B. Burlin, 'Inner Weather and Interlace: A Note on the Semantic Value of Structure in *Beowulf*', in *Old English Studies in Honour of John C. Pope*, ed. Robert B. Burlin and Edward B. Irving Jr (Toronto: University of Toronto Press, 1974), 81–9; Stanley B. Greenfield, '*Sylf*, Seasons, Structure and Genre in The Seafarer', *Anglo-Saxon England* 9 (1981): 208–9; Anderson, 'The Seasons of the Year', 256–8; Neville, 'The Seasons', 43–8.

[22] Paul Schach, 'The Anticipatory Literary Setting in the Old Icelandic Family Sagas', *Scandinavian Studies* 27, no. 1, 1–13; Peter Hallberg, *The Icelandic Saga*, trans. Paul Schach (Lincoln, NE: University of Nebraska Press, 1962), 71; Pearsall and Salter, *Landscapes and Seasons*, 45; Heather O'Donoghue, *Old Norse–Icelandic Literature: A Short Introduction* (Oxford: Blackwell, 2004), 59–60; cf. Finn Hansen, 'Naturbeskrivende indslag i *Gísla saga Súrssonar*', *Scripta Islandica* 29 (1978): 45–9. A more comprehensive study is Schach, 'Scenery', which acknowledges other uses of landscape but asserts that 'the most unique and characteristic use of scenery in the Sagas of Icelanders is the anticipatory or expository setting, consisting in the depiction of such features of the natural suroundings as are necessary for an understanding of the following action' (1).

[23] Clunies Ross, 'Sons of Fornjótr'; Meulengracht Sørensen, 'The Sea'.

Old Norse literature because these corpora show a marked interest in winter themes. Chapter 4 is largely dedicated to Middle English verse in view of its strong focus on spring and summer motifs. But if winter environments are commonly evoked in Old English and Old Norse literature, not all authors meant thereby to imply that the narrative subsequently passes into spring or summer. Instead, aspects of winter are often introduced for conceptual-associative purposes, without cyclical intent. In order to award associative and cyclical depictions each their due attention, the latter subject is deferred to the next chapter. The present chapter deals instead with winter as an unchanging environment. It demonstrates that winter settings in Old English and Old Norse literature are commonly evoked for reasons of contrast with society, whether by posing a threat to communities or by accentuating the solitary's deprivation of community. Both corpora reveal the antagonistic functions of winter landscapes through the inclusion of these environments in a dark domain accommodating hostile social categories, thus revealing assumptions of who belongs where in the landscape.

Mind, Space, and Season

Since the 1950s, the term *psycho-geography* has been used to describe theories and practices of diverse form and varying academic value. When coined by artist Guy-Ernest Debord, it referred to the subconscious influences of urban planning and architecture on the route and subjective experience of the pedestrian.[24] In the 1980s, however, the term was co-opted by psychoanalyst Howard Stein, who used it to describe the reciprocal influence between identity and topography in a Freudian view of the self: we impose our own psychological structure onto geographic space, but also distill meaning from topography to make sense of who we are.[25] Neither the artistic nor the Freudian framework will here be adopted. However, both partake of the valuable recognition that we invest our physical surroundings with subjective meaning (psycho-geographical projection), while those surroundings in turn inform our psyche and culture (psycho-geographical injection). Since literature is a potent carrier of psychological and cultural content, it is also a natural data type to subject to psycho-geographical analysis.

Of the concept's two directions of influence, psycho-geographical

---

[24] Guy-Ernest Debord, 'Introduction à une critique de la géographie urbaine', *Les lèvres nues* 6 (September 1955): 11, reprinted in *Les lèvres nues: Collection complète* (1954–8), Paris: Plasma, 1978; cf. Simon Ford, *The Situationist International: A User's Guide* (London: Black Dog, 2005), 33–6; Merlin Coverley, *Psychogeography* (Harpenden: Pocket Essentials, 2006), 81–110.

[25] Howard F. Stein, *Developmental Time, Cultural Space: Studies in Psychogeography* (Norman, OK, and London: University of Oklahoma Press, 1987), 3, 15–16.

projection is most usefully considered at literature's extradiegetic level to interpret the geographical framework fed into the text by its author and culture. Taking a cue from the field of human geography, literary landscape may be understood as 'physical extent fused through with cultural intent'.[26] By contrast, psycho-geographical injection becomes relevant at the diegetic level to explain the geographical distribution of social groups within the confines of the narrative. In the present chapter, for instance, monstrous categories will be seen to inhabit areas shunned by human agents on account of the fear these regions impart to ordinary individuals. At the diegetic level, the landscape supplements and complements the horror instilled by the monsters themselves because the landscape is antagonistic to mankind: the monsters inhabit these regions because their nature is in agreement with the environment. At the extradiegetic level, the monsters are part of a hostile landscape projected onto the narrative universe because the author's culture does not engage with this landscape category to a sufficient degree to render it familiar and perceive it as safe. But the psycho-geographical dynamic is also a positive feedback loop: the demons projected onto reality become part of the intersubjective map of the environment, amplifying the unease experienced when the unfamiliar territory is traversed. The more an author draws on existing, widespread fears in her depiction of a landscape, the more effective will this narrative of fear become among her audience when it is confronted with the landscape category in question.

A second theoretical construct of relevance to seasonal time and space is that which seeks to define the connection between temporal and spatial dimensions: the Bakhtinian chronotope. With this concept, Bakhtin sought to document the incorporation of the historical convergence of time and space into narrative literature. This unrealistic ambition to root literary setting in historical actuality is at once the central weakness in Bakhtin's discourse. The concept's most valuable contribution, by contrast, is the recognition that a literary genre comes equipped with conventions concerning the spatiotemporal configuration appropriate to certain types of plot development. In Bakhtin's analysis, for instance, the spatial code in Greek or medieval romance prescribes that the adventure-time separating the work's conclusion from its opening be rife with spatial removes. The temporal dimension has adventure-time rely heavily on contingency, since adventure depends centrally on chance encounters, whether looked for (as

---

[26] Modelled after Neil Smith's phrase 'physical extent fused through with social intent': Neil Smith, *Uneven Development*, 3rd ed. (Athens, GA: University of Georgia Press, 2008), 214; see further Derek Gregory, *Geographical Imaginations* (Cambridge, MA, and Oxford: Blackwell, 1994); Ernest W. B. Hess-Lüttich, 'Text Space: Holistic Texts?', in *Signs & Space: An International Conference on the Semiotics of Space and Culture in Amsterdam*, ed. Ernest W. B. Hess-Lüttich, Jürgen E. Müller, and Aart van Zoest, Kodikas/Code, supplement 23 (Tübingen: Narr, 1998), 342–3; Joël Bonnemaison, *Culture and Space: Conceiving a New Cultural Geography*, trans. Josée Pénot-Demetry (London and New York: Tauris, 2005).

is common in medieval romance) or not (as in Greek romance).[27]

Since Bakhtin's discussion is aimed at abstraction and generalization across the history of Western literature, his concept of the chronotope is best applied to more specific traditions through the identification of more concrete settings. This holds true for the spatial element: in medieval romance, for instance, the spatial removes of adventure-space tend to be represented by forests, while narratives typically begin and end in court settings.[28] Narrative time may likewise be more closely identified, but Bakhtin's interest in the perceived pace of time's passing will here be replaced by a mapping of events to the seasons of the year. The forest expeditions of medieval romance, for instance, are strongly tied to the summer half-year. This detheorized, seasonal application of chronotopicity, in which it is reduced to the identification of the landscape and season of the narrative action, will be a central tool of this study. Because landscapes connotative of particular seasons may be found in isolation from, or even in conflict with, the narrative time of year, however, the remainder of this chapter will consider seasonal landscape in isolation from the annual cycle, deferring the study of narrative time to the next.

Anglo-Saxon Elegy

ELEGIAC SETTING

While the dominant theology of weather and season in north-western European literature was clearly inspired by foreign models, their concrete literary depictions seem to rely more immediately on vernacular traditions. In Anglo-Saxon England, such depictions are particularly prevalent in elegiac poetry. Elegy as a narrative mode is not, however, limited to the body of poems traditionally discussed under that heading.[29] One relevant passage normally excluded from this corpus has already been discussed: Adam's lament near the end of *Genesis B*[30] seems to draw on Saxon rather than biblical tradition when it uses environmental conditions to heighten

---

[27] M. M. Bakhtin, 'Forms of Time and of the Chronotope in the Novel: Notes towards a Historical Poetics', in *The Dialogic Imagination: Four Essays*, ed. Michael Holquist, trans. Caryl Emerson and Michael Holquist (Austin, TX: University of Texas Press), esp. 84–110, 151–5. Gurevich revisited the concept in 1995, proposing that medieval narratives are characterized by chronotopes that cannot be dissociated from the individual characters central to the action. Aaron J. Gurevich, 'Medieval Chronotope', *Theoretische geschiedenis* 22, no. 3 (1995): 225–40.

[28] Ad Putter, *'Sir Gawain and the Green Knight' and French Arthurian Romance* (Oxford: Clarendon, 1995), 10–50.

[29] For a traditional discussion of the genre, see Anne L. Klinck, ed., *The Old English Elegies: A Critical Edition and Genre Study* (Montreal: McGill-Queen's University Press, 1992); for a recent reclassification and repositioning of Old English elegiac texts in a European literary context, see Andy Orchard, 'Not what it was: The World of Old English Elegy', in *The Oxford Handbook of the Elegy*, ed. Karen Weisman (Oxford: Oxford University Press, 2010), 101–17.

[30] Lines 790–820, quoted in part above, p. 34.

the sorrow associated with the fall from grace. Adam cites not only the dark and fiery landscape of hell, but also the worldly afflictions of tempest and precipitation, summer heat and winter cold as external attestations of the first couple's newfound misery. This is a particularly clear example of horror instilled in the protagonist's mind by his physical environment with an explicit recognition of the roles of seasonal extremes. In fact, such treatment is no exclusive prerogative of vernacular poetry, as even Bede employs the motif in his Latin prose account of the conversion of Edwin, as will be seen below. Nevertheless, elegiac associations of mind and environment remain most prevalent in the texts traditionally referred to as the Old English elegies.

Although Anglo-Saxon elegiac texts and passages make use of seasonal themes to varying degrees, each sets up a pivotal connection between sterile landscape and the elegiac mode, investing the protagonist's immediate environment with a burden of melancholy and solitude. Within this function, it is important to recognize the relevance of real experiential responses to barren landscape, an intersubjective cultural reflex that enables the author to immerse his audience more fully into the protagonist's world than could be accomplished by a reliance on mere intellectual metaphor or pathetic fallacy.[31]

Settings typical of Old English elegy are found in *The Wife's Lament*.[32] The narrator of this lyric inhabits an *eorþscræf* ('underground cave') in a wooded area surrounded by dark valleys. A reference to thorny plant life recalls mankind's exile from Eden to a land filled with thorns and thistles (lines 27–11; cf. Gn 3:18). This physical setting for the narrator's bitter complaint provides an excellent example of mind engaging environment, here in apparent pathetic fallacy, a subtype of psycho-geographical projection as defined above. Given the content of Adam's lament in *Genesis B*, this situation may seem to call for another seasonal reference, but a real seasonal connection is never made. Although the narrator does qualify her day as *sumerlang* ('summer-long', 37), this adjective serves merely to indicate that her solitary days seem as long to her as the days surrounding the summer solstice.[33]

In the narrator's curse or imagination,[34] however, the imagined landscape of her *freond* is plagued by winter weather:

---

[31] Contrast Stanley B. Greenfield, 'The Old English Elegies', in *Continuations and Beginnings: Studies in Old English Literature*, ed. E. G. Stanley (London: Nelson, 1966), 142–75, which emphasizes the metaphorical quality of winter imagery as well as other conventional Old English poetic content (148).

[32] Krapp and Dobbie, *Exeter Book*, 210–11.

[33] So also Bosworth and Toller, *An Anglo-Saxon Dictionary*, s.v. 'sumer-lang'; Frederick Klaeber, 'Zur jüngeren *Genesis*', *Anglia* 49 (n.s. 37) (1925): 364; Klinck, *The Old English Elegies*, 185.

[34] This problem is addressed in John D. Niles, 'The Problem of the Ending of *The Wife's Lament*', *Speculum* 78, no. 4 (2003): 1107–50, which makes a cogent case for the reading of this passage as a curse. My translation follows this interpretation.

> Sy æt him sylfum gelong
> eal his worulde wyn,   sy ful wide fah
> feorres folclondes,   þæt min freond siteð
> under stanhliþe   storme behrimed,
> wine werigmod,   wætre beflowen
> on dreorsele.   (lines 45–50)
>
> May all his joy in the world depend on himself; may he be outlawed far from his distant holdings, so that my friend sits below a rocky slope, covered with hoarfrost by the storm, my companion sits sad, surrounded with water in a dreary hall.

As he sits below a cliff, this young man (42) is covered in hoarfrost by the storm while water flows about him. No doubt is left as to the associations of this environment: the narrator imagines that the man 'very often recalls a more pleasant place' (50–1).[35] The landscape of cold and wet accommodating the narrator's beloved is *wynna leas* ('joyless', 32) like her own,[36] and winter combines with water, rainstorm, and rocky landscape to convey this mood to the immediate victim as well as to narrator and audience. The isolation of both these characters is particularly stark because it is juxtaposed with their previous union (21–3) as well as with the social pleasures of other *frynd on eorþan* ('lovers on earth', 33–41), and the landscape setting of each serves to underline this contrast. This text thus relies extensively on the psycho-geographical influence of unpleasant landscapes, and one of the instruments by which it achieves this effect is a winter landscape far removed from human settlement.

Seasonal imagery plays a comparable role in the elegiac descriptions of abandoned human habitations found in *The Ruin*[37] and *The Wanderer*.[38] The former, describing an ancient bathing site in ruins, speaks of hoarfrost on the limestone ('hrim on lime', 4) of a building with collapsed roof. This cold present condition of a building unprotected against the winter weather contrasts with a past when a hot stream fed into its baths (38–46). Although there is no reason to assume that the hot spring has since ceased, all the verbs in this passage are in the preterite, setting up a contrast between the past, when the warmer aspects of the natural world were channelled to improve living conditions, and the narrative present, in which the natural world in its winter guise has free rein to penetrate a roofless structure.

A similar picture is drawn in *The Wanderer*, lines 73–110, which express horror at the prospect of a future in which the remains of man-made constructions will have outlived their makers. Already now, the poet points

---

[35] 'Gemon to oft / wynlicran wic.'
[36] Alaric Hall, 'The Images and Structure of *The Wife's Lament*', *Leeds Studies in English* 33 (2002): 6–7 notes the phrase's poetic resonance in view of analogous occurrences describing Grendel's abode in *Beowulf* 821 and the postlapsarian world in *Genesis A* 928.
[37] Krapp and Dobbie, *Exeter Book*, 227–9.
[38] Ibid., 134–7.

out, such scenes may be witnessed:

> Swa nu missenlice geond þisne middangeard
> winde biwaune weallas stondaþ,
> hrime bihrorene, hryðge þa ederas. (lines 75–7)

Just as in various places throughout this world walls now stand assailed by the wind, covered by hoarfrost, the enclosures stand storm-beaten.

The role of winter in this scene is further brought out:

> Ond þas stanhleoþu stormas cnyssað,
> hrið hreosende hrusan bindeð,
> wintres woma; þonne won cymeð,
> nipeð nihtscua, norþan onsendeð
> hreo hæglfare hæleþum on andan. (lines 101–5)

And storms beat down upon these rocky slopes; the raging tempest, blast of winter, binds the earth; when the darkness comes, when the shade of night grows dark, it angrily sends a savage cargo of hail to men from the north.

It is unlikely that *The Ruin* and *The Wanderer* share the same aim in describing ruins as winter-afflicted.[39] The ultimate end advertised in the latter poem is the personal attainment of lasting fulfilment, in which the transience of earthly glory serves to contrast with the eternal comforts of the Christian faith (114–15). No such contrast is suggested in *The Ruin*, which instead follows up its description of crumbled buildings with a celebration of the glory that was. In the traditional reading, the poem concludes with that description: the last legible clause is *þæt is cynelic þing* (48; conventionally 'that is a kingly thing'). Since the manuscript leaves no space for further lines,[40] the Exeter Book text could have had no conclusion other than the depiction of past glory.[41] A superior reading was

---

[39] Differences in mood between *The Ruin* on the one hand and *The Wanderer* and other Old English elegies on the other are emphasized in R. F. Leslie, ed., *Three Old Englies Elegies: 'The Wife's Lament', 'The Husband's Message', 'The Ruin'* (Manchester: Manchester University Press, 1961), 30; Greenfield, 'The Old English Elegies', 143–6; Kathryn Hume, 'The "Ruin Motif" in Old English Poetry', *Anglia* 94 (1976): 349; Arnold V. Talentino, 'Moral Irony in *The Ruin*', *Papers on Language & Literature* 14, no. 1 (Winter): 3; Alain Renoir, 'The Old English *Ruin*: Contrastive Structure and Affective Impact', in *The Old English Elegies: New Essays in Criticism and Research*, ed. Martin Green (Rutherford, NJ: Fairleigh Dickinson University Press, 1983), 149–55; Roy Liuzza, 'The Tower of Babel: *The Wanderer* and the Ruins of History', *Studies in the Literary Imagination* 36, no. 1 (Spring 2003): 9–10. With reference to patterns of alliteration, rhyme, and diction shared between these poems, however, it has been suggested that they share a tradition (Leslie, *Three Old Englies Elegies*, 30) and that the author of *The Wanderer* may have been familiar with *The Ruin*: Andy Orchard, 'Reconstructing *The Ruin*', in *Intertexts: Studies in Anglo-Saxon Culture Presented to Paul E. Szarmach*, ed. Virginia Blanton and Helene Scheck, Medieval and Renaissance Texts and Studies 334; Arizona Studies in the Middle Ages and the Renaissance 24 (Tempe, AZ: Arizona Center for Medieval and Renaissance Studies / Brepols, 2008), 59–60.

[40] Exeter, Exeter Cathedral Library, MS 3501 fol. 124b.

[41] Greenfield, 'The Old English Elegies', 143–4; Klinck, *The Old English Elegies*, 63.

suggested to me by Ian McDougall, however, who proposes to read *cynelic* as a cognate of Old Norse *kynligr* to mean 'strange, wondrous'.[42] Given that the incomplete sentence at the end of the text begins *þæt is cynelic þing, hu*, this reading brings the poem in connection with the corpus of Old English riddles, which contains several sentences analogous in sense and syntax.[43] In this interpretation as in the traditional reading, however, the final sentiment is unlikely to turn to such heavenly contemplation as is found in *The Wanderer*.

What the two poems certainly have in common is an interest in the role of buildings in the contrast between worldly glory and worldly decay.[44] Winter imagery is particularly well suited to this literary device because, together with storms,[45] winter weather is what buildings in this part of the world were erected to withstand. Thus not only do these poems evoke melancholy by reference to uncomfortable weather conditions, they further reinforce this mood by drawing attention to the fact that the structures described are now governed by the elements they were designed to keep at bay. This convergence of winter weather and social space conveys a mood of desolation and decay: this is a society overcome by its perpetual assailant,[46] whose hostile character is thus asserted.[47]

Bede's uncharacteristic foray into the elegiac associations of landscape occurs in his celebrated account of the conversion of King Edwin of Deira. Although the sparrow simile offered to the king by one of his counsellors is today popularly recounted and referenced in diverse contexts,[48] it is not

---

[42] An Old English intensive prefix **cyne-* cognate with Old Norse *kyn-* was proposed in Sophus Bugge, 'Studien über das Beowulfepos', *Beiträge zur Geschichte der deutschen Sprache und Literatur* 12 (1887): 122, where Falk is credited with having reached the same conclusion.

[43] 'Wrætlic me þinceð, hu' (*Riddle 31* 18–19: Krapp and Dobbie, *Exeter Book*, 196); 'þæt is wundres dæl [...] hu' (*Riddle 60* 10: ibid., 225). Ian McDougall, personal communication, 30 March 2012.

[44] Contrast Renoir, 'The Old English *Ruin*', which contends that *The Ruin* is unique in its emphasis on contrast where other poems focus on either past glory or present decay (155).

[45] *Ruin* 11; *Wanderer* 76, 101–2.

[46] Battle imagery of this sort is in fact used in *Andreas* 1257–8: Kenneth R. Brooks, ed., *'Andreas' and 'The Fates of the Apostles'* (Oxford: Clarendon, 1961), 1–55, which speaks of 'hrim ond forst, / hare hildstapan' ('rime and frost, grey warriors'; cf. *Menologium* 202–7).

[47] At the same time, of course, the structures, though imperfect, have withstood time and outlasted their builders and one-time residents. This aspect of their existence is apparent in their designation as *enta geweorc* (line 2). See further P. J. Frankis, 'The Thematic Significance of "enta geweorc" and Related Imagery in *The Wanderer*', *Anglo-Saxon England* 2 (1973): 253–69.

[48] For example Mary Faith Schuster, 'Bede and the Sparrow Simile', *The American Benedictine Review* 8, no. 1 (1957): 47–50; Calvin B. Kendall, 'Imitation and the Venerable Bede's *Historia Ecclesiastica*', in *Saints, Scholars, and Heroes: Studies in Medieval Culture in Honour of Charles W. Jones*, ed. Margot H. King and Wesley M. Stevens, vol. 1 (Collegeville, MN: Hill Monastic Manuscript Library, 1979), 178–9; M. L. Cameron, *Anglo-Saxon Medicine*, Cambridge Studies in Anglo-Saxon England 7 (Cambridge: Cambridge University Press, 1993), 5–6; Neville, *The Natural World*, 24–5; Éamonn Ó Carragáin and Richard North, '*The Dream of the Rood* and Anglo-Saxon Northumbria', in North and Allard, *'Beowulf' and Other Stories*, 175. The passage is studied for its own sake in Donald K. Fry, 'The Art of Bede: Edwin's Council', in King and Stevens, *Saints, Scholars, and Heroes*, 1:191–207; M. J. Toswell, 'Bede's Sparrow and the Psalter in England', *ANQ* 13, no. 1 (2000): 7–12;

generally observed that this supposedly 'heartrendingly simple'[49] figure of speech seems at first sight somewhat imprecise in terms of correspondence between symbol and referent:

> 'Talis' inquiens 'mihi uidetur, rex, uita hominum praesens in terris, ad conparationem eius quod nobis incertum est temporis, quale cum te residente ad caenam cum ducibus ac ministris tuis tempore brumali, accenso quidem foco in medio et calido effecto cenaculo, furentibus autem foris per omnia turbinibus hiemalium pluuiarum uel niuium, adueniens unus passerum domum citissime peruolauerit; qui cum per unum ostium ingrediens mox per aliud exierit, ipso quidem tempore quo intus est hiemis tempestate non tangitur, sed tamen paruissimo spatio serenitatis ad momentum excurso, mox de hieme in hiemem regrediens tuis oculis elabitur. Ita haec uita hominum ad modicum apparet; quid autem sequatur, quidue praecesserit, prorsus ignoramus. Vnde, si haec noua doctrina certius aliquid attulit, merito esse sequenda uidetur.' (Historia ecclesiastica 2.13)[50]

> 'Such seems to me the life of men on earth, my King', he said, 'compared to the time that is uncertain to us, as though while you are seated at a banquet with your nobles and officials in wintertime, with a fire burning in the centre and the dining room heated, but with storms of winter rain or snow raging mercilessly outside, a passing sparrow were to fly through the hall very rapidly. Coming in at one entrance, it soon goes out through the other. In the time when it is inside, it is untouched by the winter storm; but when that very brief moment of peace has run out, it soon escapes your sight going from winter back into winter. So also this life of men appears for a short time; but of what follows after, or of what came before, we are wholly ignorant. Therefore, if this new teaching brings anything of greater certainty, it seems right to follow it.'

The advisor's stated point is that life on earth is both preceded and followed by uncertainty; whatever religion provides the most reliable knowledge on these matters is to be adopted. Strictly speaking, then, all that the audience is to gather from the image is the darkness of the outside world and the brightness of the hall, representing ignorance and knowledge respectively. Nevertheless, the natural world is described in such detail as to invite the objection that the parable offers sufficient information regarding the world outside to invalidate the counsellor's argument. An unpleasant world awaits outside, and if the bird may yet encounter other halls in its path, none will be categorically better than the

---

Fred C. Robinson, 'Possible Biblical Resonances in Bede's Presentation of the Conversion of the English', in *Text and Language in Medieval English Prose: A Festschrift for Tadao Kubouchi*, ed. Jacek Fisiak and John Scahill, Studies in English Medieval Language and Literature 12 (Frankfurt: Peter Lang, 2005), 207–13; Tristan Major, '1 Corinthians 15:52 as a Source for the Old English Version of Bede's Simile of the Sparrow', *Notes & Queries* 54, no. 1 (2007): 11–16.

[49] Toswell, 'Bede's Sparrow and the Psalter in England', 7.
[50] Colgrave and Mynors, *Ecclesiastical History*, 182–4.

present hall, whatever the counsellor's new religion may proclaim. This, of course, is not the response Bede's unnamed speaker was intended to elicit, either from the king or from Bede's audience. The conclusion must instead be that the details of interior and exterior environments, strictly redundant to the image, are all to be understood as contributing to the opposition between security and uncertainty, and the passage's winter weather is representative of the latter.

While this understanding of the sparrow simile supports the spatial dynamics of society and its environment described by Magennis,[51] Neville,[52] and Michelet,[53] it also illustrates the need for a psycho-geographical approach to the material with a seasonal focus. The author of the image has chosen to make winter its expressed seasonal context because this allows him to draw on a range of social and experiential connotations. Firstly, winter represents a spatial restriction of society, as the human domain is limited to a smaller area; this aspect of the image emphasizes the short duration (*parvissimum spatium*) of life on earth. Next, it is because of society's spatially reduced engagement with the natural world at this time of year, as well as in consequence of the season's darkness, that natural and supernatural outside threats of various levels of articulation seem to encroach upon society;[54] it is this hibernal unease that permits the natural world of the simile to represent uncertainty. By the same token, the confined space of the hall is never so emphatically conceived of as a safe haven as it is in winter, when the conceptual boundary between inside and out holds the greatest significance.[55] This aspect receives expression in the fire, providing heat and light, and the meal, an element not traditionally given a place in vernacular poetry[56] but representative of the ample provisions stored up during the annual harvest and slaughter. The full import of the image with all its detail pivots on the cultural experience of winter within and without the human domain, thus relying on psycho-geographical dynamics for effect.

Although the scene of indoor comfort has more in common with late-medieval calendar conventions than with what survives of Anglo-Saxon cultural expression, the detail here provided on the natural world is primarily reminiscent of the Old English elegies.[57] Bede's narrative shares

---

[51] *Images of Community*; the sparrow episode is accordingly discussed on pp. 129–30.
[52] *The Natural World*; the sparrow episode is discussed on pp. 24–5.
[53] *Creation, Migration, and Conquest*.
[54] See ch. 3 below.
[55] On the significance of spatial boundaries in Old English literature, see Michelet, *Creation, Migration, and Conquest*.
[56] Hugh Magennis, *Anglo-Saxon Appetites: Food and Drink and their Consumption in Old English and Related Literature* (Dublin: Four Courts, 1999), 28–34.
[57] The episode's use of Anglo-Saxon hall and winter imagery is noted also in Maria José Mora, 'Un invierno entre los hielos: Los paisajes de la poesía anglosajona', *Cuadernos del CEMYR* 7 (1999): 237–8.

the motif of winter storm and winter precipitation with such texts as *The Wife's Lament, The Wanderer,* and *The Seafarer,* and it may be presumed that the simile was so embellished in order to elicit the same connotations of winter weather as those texts, depicting the pagan cosmos as a place of melancholy and loneliness graced only by a brief moment of warmth and communion. Conversely, however, the sparrow narrative also illuminates the connotative significance of winter weather in the more obviously elegiac texts. Bede's use of a winter environment as an expression of uncertainty has a counterpart in *The Wanderer* and *The Seafarer*,[58] which convey the sentiments 'all this world's constitution will become empty' (*Wanderer* 110)[59] and 'I do not believe that worldly goods remain forever for him [who lives this dead life]' (*Seafarer* 66–7).[60] Just as the sparrow's brief spell in the hall of heat and brightness is followed by a return into winter weather, so also the worldly glories of the hall give way to hoarfrost and hailstorm in *The Ruin* and *The Wanderer*, while the narrator of *The Seafarer* flees the pleasantries of spring on land for the sober relativism of the wintry sea. Although the coming of winter is thus an inevitable chronological reality, all these texts employ winter *environments* as representatives of uncertainty and mutability. A notable distinction is that the elegiac poems express uncertainty regarding the present life only, whereas Bede's counsellor as yet holds that the present is man's only a priori certainty. In his understanding, Christianity must be embraced to roll back the winter of uncertainty covering the soul's past and future.[61] Once that is achieved, he will be ready for the paradigm shift signalled by *The Wanderer*'s defeat of heroic convention at the hands of Christian stoicism.[62]

---

[58] Krapp and Dobbie, *Exeter Book*, 143–7.

[59] 'Eal þis eorþan gesteal idel weorþeð.'

[60] 'Ic gelyfe no / þæt him eorðwelan ece stondað.' See Krapp and Dobbie, *Exeter Book*, 296, commentary to line 67, for this understanding of 'him'.

[61] Cf. Bede's interpretation in his *In Cantica canticorum allegorica expositio* of a reference to rain and winter (Ct 2:11) as a time of apostasy. Bede uses the phrase *hiems longae infidelitatis* ('winter of long faithlessness') and associates this environment also with the dark of night: D. Hurst, ed., 'In Cantica canticorum', in *In Tobiam, In Proverbia, In Cantica canticorum*, Bedae venerabilis opera 2; Corpus Christianorum, Series Latina, 119B (Turnhout: Brepols, 1983), 181.

[62] In an interesting parallel to the storm imagery (though not the seasonality) of all these texts as well as the bird simile of Edwin's council, the Boethius translator introduces the image of an eagle soaring above the clouds to escape their storms, representing Wisdom soaring with her servants (or qualities) learning, skills, and true riches. Prose *Consolation of Philosophy*, ch. 7, lines 100–3: Malcolm Godden and Susan Irvine, eds, *Boethius: An Edition of the Old English Versions of Boethius's 'De Consolatione Philosophiae'*, 2 vols (Oxford: Oxford University Press, 2009), 1:254. The parallel confirms the popularity of storms as an image of sublunary mutability while demonstrating the suitability of bird imagery for storm metaphors. For discussions of how the Anglo-Saxon translator may have arrived at his innovation, see Bately, 'Time', 41–2; Godden and Irvine, *Boethius*, 2:281, commentary to 7.100–3.

WINTER AND THE SEA: *THE WANDERER* AND *THE SEAFARER*

The above discussion demonstrates that *The Wanderer*, like the other elegies, emphasizes barren landscape categories. In so doing, it describes winter weather on land in some detail, but it is cold conditions at sea that form the poem's most immediate setting. In fact, the strongest connections between landscape, weather, season, and the elegiac mode are to be found in *The Wanderer* and *The Seafarer*, but the setting that takes centre stage in both poems is the open sea.

In its opening lines, *The Wanderer* establishes a connection between two of the poem's central themes: the search for spiritual fulfilment and the harsh physical realities of the present world. The visualization of the latter, however, suggests that the considerations to follow are written specifically with seafaring exiles in mind:

> Oft him anhaga are gebideð,
> metudes miltse, þeah þe he modcearig
> geond lagulade longe sceolde
> hreran mid hondum hrimcealde sæ,
> wadan wræclastas. (lines 1–5)
>
> The solitary often experiences grace, the Lord's mercy, even if sad across the waterways he has to stir the rime-cold sea with his hands for a long time, travel the paths of exile.

This focus is confirmed at a later point in the poem, where the narrator tells of a solitary sea voyage during which the exile is alone with sea, birds, and winter precipitation:

> Gesihð him biforan fealwe wegas,
> baþian brimfuglas, brædan feþra,
> hreosan hrim ond snaw, hagle gemenged.
> [. . .]
>   Cearo bið geniwad
> þam þe sendan sceal swiþe geneahhe
> ofer waþema gebind werigne sefan. (lines 46–8, 55–7)
>
> Before him he sees the pale waves, sea-birds bathing, spreading their wings, hoarfrost and snow falling, mingled with hail. [. . .] Sorrow is renewed for him who very often has to send his weary mind across the bond of the waves.

Combined with the transience of earthly glory, seafaring hardships provide a background for the poem's central argument. This is summed up in the concluding lines: 'it will be well for him who seeks grace, comfort from the father in heaven, where resides all that is lasting for us'.[63] This advice forms an envelope pattern with the poem's opening lines (1–2), which

---

[63] 'Wel bið þam þe him are seceð, / frofre to fæder on heofonum, þær us eal seo fæstnung stondeð' (*Wanderer* 114–15).

express a similar sentiment. The material that separates the two statements demonstrates that there is no worldly alternative to religious devotion, as the heroic code leads the individual to misery both physical and emotional, while none of the achievements it offers is lasting.[64] In this context, the function of the tactile and visual representatives of winter (*snaw, hrim, hægl,* and *hrimcealdu sæ*) is to remind the audience of the physical discomforts characteristic of this life in general and heroic society in particular. Rather than depict both seasonal extremes as afflictions within the context of their alternation, as is commonly done in visions of hell, *The Wanderer* situates life on earth in a winter environment that does not pass into spring until the heavenly harbour is reached.

The perspective of *The Seafarer* differs from that of *The Wanderer* primarily in the contrast it sets up between life on land and at sea. Here too, the protagonist, now the narrator, is based at sea, beset by cold weather and 'hot' (i.e. intense)[65] sorrows:

> Calde geþrungen
> wæron mine fet, forste gebunden,
> caldum clommum, þær þa ceare seofedun
> hat ymb heortan. (lines 8–11)

> My feet were pinched with cold, bound with frost, with cold bonds, while hot sorrows grieved around the heart.

The conditions here described, however, are known only to the experienced sailor:

> Þæt se mon ne wat
> þe him on foldan fægrost limpeð,
> hu ic earmcearig iscealdne sæ
> winter wunade, wræccan lastum
> winemægum bidroren,
> bihongen hrimgicelum; hægl scurum fleag.
> Þær ic ne gehyrde butan hlimman sæ,
> iscealdne wæg. (lines 12–19)

> He whose life on land passes most pleasantly does not know how, sorrowful at my wretched condition, I spent the winter on the ice-cold sea, on the exile's path, deprived of friends and kinsmen, weighed down with icicles; hail came flying down in showers. I heard nothing there but the sea roaring, the ice-cold wave.

---

[64] So also W. F. Klein, 'Purpose and the "Poetics" of *The Wanderer* and *The Seafarer*', in *Anglo-Saxon Poetry: Essays in Appreciation; for John McGalliard*, ed. Lewis E. Nicholson and Dolores Warwick Frese (Notre Dame and London: University of Notre Dame Press, 1975), 212.

[65] See Leslie Lockett, *Anglo-Saxon Psychologies in the Vernacular and Latin Traditions* (Toronto: University of Toronto Press, 2011), 54–109.

> þæt se beorn ne wat,
> esteadig secg, hwæt þa sume dreogað
> þe þa wræclastas widost lecgað. (lines 55–7)

The fellow, the man blessed with bounty, does not know what some then suffer who travel the paths of exile most widely.

The natural world of dry land is described in a general way only, in what is a rare depiction of pleasant landscape in the Old English elegies:

> Bearwas blostmum nimað, byrig fægriað,
> wongas wlitigiað, woruld onetteð. (lines 48–9)

The groves blossom, the towns grow fair, the fields grow beautiful, the world hastens onwards.

Its function, however, is not to attract but to usher out: the spring renewal of the natural world, epitomized by the cuckoo's call (53–5), is the starting signal for the seafaring season, sending the narrator back into the cold and barren seascape of exile. It is for this reason that the cuckoo is perceived as singing with a sad voice ('geomran reorde', 53).[66]

This role of the cuckoo as a herald of hardship is traditional: it fulfils the same function in the Latin *Conflictus veris et hiemis*[67] attributed to Alcuin, in which a personified Winter regards the cuckoo as the starting signal for hardship and war on land and sea following the comforts of winter (13–15, 19–21, 25–7). Even in the Old English *Husband's Message*,[68] where the start of the seafaring season has clear positive connotations as a time of spousal reunion, the cuckoo that heralds it is portrayed as a sad bird:

> Heht nu sylfa þe
> lustum læran, þæt þu lagu drefde,
> siþþan þu gehyrde on hliþes oran
> galan geomorne geac on bearwe. (lines 20–3)

He [your husband] himself has now ordered that you joyfully be instructed to sail the water once you have heard the sad cuckoo calling in the hillside grove.

Despite this connotation, the prospect of a warmer time of year here unambiguously signals an improvement in fortunes. In its focus on the joy of a spring reunion, *The Husband's Message* represents a complete reversal of the argument in *The Wife's Lament*, which expresses the emotional anguish

---

[66] Cf. E. C. Knowlton, 'Nature in Older Irish', *Publications of the Modern Language Association of America* 44, no. 1 (1929): 100–1; J. E. Caerwyn Williams, 'The Nature Prologue in Welsh Court Poetry', *Studia Celtica* 24–5 (1989–90): 77, 86; Klinck, *The Old English Elegies*, 137, n. to *The Seafarer* 53–5a; Marie-Françoise Alamichel, '*Sumer is icumen in*: Chants et saisons dans la Grande-Bretagne médiévale', in Carruthers, *La ronde des saisons*, 54–5; Dubois, 'Le rondeau du coucou'.

[67] Peter Godman, ed., *Poetry of the Carolingian Renaissance* (London: Duckworth, 1985), 144–9.

[68] Krapp and Dobbie, *Exeter Book*, 225–7.

of its protagonists' isolation with reference to barren landscapes and winter weather. In its connotative use of spring, however, *The Husband's Message* is a reversal rather of *The Seafarer*, whose seemingly appreciative depiction of the season in fact serves to underline the discomfort of life at sea – but this discomfort is expressed with reference to a winter seascape.

As in *The Wanderer*, the point that *The Seafarer* was intended to get across is that the only lasting fulfilment is to be had through religious devotion.[69] Despite the contrast drawn between life at sea and on land, the narrator makes clear that earthly joys do not last. Following the account of his hardships, he states

> Forþon me hatran sind
> dryhtnes dreamas   þonne þis deade lif,
> læne on londe.   Ic gelyfe no
> þæt him eorðwelan   ece stondað.   (lines 64–7)
>
> Therefore the joys of the Lord are hotter to me than this dead, transitory life on land. I do not believe that its earthly riches remain for ever.

Hat ('hot') is here used in a sense of intense emotion similar to that expressed by the 'hot sorrows' of line 11,[70] although the feeling is now triggered by desire rather than the oppression of worldly cares.[71] Here too, a contrast of temperatures may have been intended in view of the winter imagery employed elsewhere in the poem. The description of the eternal joys of heaven as 'hotter' or 'exciting more fervent emotion' than the foregoing recalls earlier complaints of the cold seafaring existence, ensuring that these discomforts are fresh in the audience's mind when the heavenly alternative is brought forward. The remainder of the poem makes repeated and explicit reference to God, stressing the importance of loving and fearing him (for example 103, 106, 121). Again, then, the winter seascape painted in *The Seafarer* should be understood as an argument against worldly fulfilment, accentuating the fragility of the strawman of earthly joys. In so doing, both this poem and *The Wanderer* characterize the sea as a cold and hostile environment suitable for the expression of elegy when contrasted with human society.

Cold Water

The poetic association between seascapes and winter is not limited to the elegies. Though no other Old English text foregrounds this combination

---

[69] So also Klein, 'Purpose and the "Poetics" of *The Wanderer* and *The Seafarer*', 218.

[70] Hill, 'Heat and Cold Imagery', 531; cf. *Oxford English Dictionary Online* (Oxford: Oxford University Press), s.v. 'hot, adj. and n.1' sense A.II.8.a. Accessed 15 March 2015, http://www.oed.com/.

[71] For a fuller discussion of heat as a descriptor of emotions, see Lockett, *Anglo-Saxon Psychologies*, 54–109.

of environmental features as prominently as *The Seafarer* or *The Wanderer*, a considerable number of texts refer to bodies of water as cold, thereby strengthening the identification of seascapes with winter settings. In *Beowulf*, for instance, Grendel's mother is banished to 'cealde streamas' ('cold currents') following Cain's crime (1258–63). Moreover, Beowulf's swimming contest with Breca is explicitly set in winter: the poem states that 'the ocean was surging with waves, winter's billows',[72] and we hear that the match takes place in the coldest of weathers ('wedera cealdost', 546). The poem's three instances of *warm* water are explained by their context. Thus the dragon's flames heat (or are the metaphorical referent of) the stream that runs from the dragon's mound (2542–9), and the water of the monsters' pool is on two occasions described as contaminated with blood in a set collocation *hat heolfre* ('hot with gore', 847–9, 1422–3).[73] Where such circumstances are not adduced, the water of *Beowulf*'s monsters and dangerous undertakings is cold.

Scenes at sea in Old English poetry repeatedly favour the descriptor *ceald* in stressed position. Although the word frequently alliterates with *ceol* ('ship') and once with *clif* as a circumlocution for wave, its inability to alliterate with straightforward words for water suggests that its frequent application to such words should be explained by conceptual association rather than reduced to alliterative expediency. The combination occurs, for instance, in all of the following lines from *Andreas*:

>   ofer cald wæter   cuðe sindon   (201)
>   ceol gestigan,   ond on cald wæter   (222)
>   on cald wæter   ceolum lacað   (253)
>   ofer cald cleofu   ceoles neosan   (310)

No reference to cold water appears in the Greek and Latin versions of this episode.[74] Despite the alliterative advantages of *ceald*, the threefold repetition of the phrase *ceald wæter* within fifty-three lines, augmented with the wave-metaphor *ceald clifu* ('cold cliffs') shortly after, cannot fail to draw attention to the uncomfortable quality of the water, and hence to its perceived danger. In the first instance, this connotation fits the context particularly well: ordered by God to travel to Mermedonia, Andrew objects that both the people and the customs of that land across the water are unknown to him (171–201). By specifying the uncomfortable temperature of the water, he groups the setting of the voyage with the environment of his destination as alien and dangerous, thereby heightening the heroic challenge of traversing

---

[72] 'Geofon yðum weol, / wintrys wylmum' (515–16).
[73] Cf. *Andreas* 1240–1, 1275–7.
[74] The passage corresponds to chs 3–6 in the Πράξεις Ανδρέου and *Acta Andreae* (Casanatensis-redaction) as edited in Franz Blatt, ed., *Die lateinischen Bearbeitungen der 'Acta Andreae et Matthiae apud anthropophagos'* (Gießen: Töpelmann, 1930), 34–45.

it.⁷⁵ The fourth reference to the cold sea, the circumlocution of line 310, is similarly effective: here, Christ tests Andrew's resolve by asking him his purpose in seeking out the discomforts of the sea (305–14), recalling the contrast between life on land and at sea expressed in *The Seafarer*. The remaining two lines on cold water form part of God's insistence that Andrew should undertake the journey (203–24) and an account of God and his angels sailing into the harbour to take Andrew on board (244–53). All four descriptions taken together emphasize the seafaring feat that takes Andrew to Mermedonia, suggesting that it represents the first of three tests, a natural threat preceding the disciple's human and demonic challenges. The perceived hostility of the sea is confirmed elsewhere in the poem, which twice refers to it using the compound *wæteregesa* ('water-terror'; 375, 435), once extending the concept into a battle image in which the waves are recast as warriors: 'the water-terror rose up with hosts of troops'.⁷⁶ The only other occurrence of the term *wæteregesa* is in *Beowulf*, where a direct connection is made between cold water and perceived hostility: this is the passage mentioned above in which Grendel's mother is banished to 'the terror of water [. . .], the cold currents'.⁷⁷

The references in *Andreas* to the cold of the water to be traversed are paralleled in *Christ B*,⁷⁸ which allegorizes life on earth as a sea voyage:

>   Nu is þon gelicost   swa we on laguflode
>   ofer cald wæter   ceolum liðan,
>   geond sidne sæ   sundhengestum,
>   flodwudu fergen.   Is þæt frecne stream
>   yða ofermæta   þe we her on lacað
>   geond þas wacan woruld,   windge holmas
>   ofer deop gelad.   Wæs se drohtað strong
>   ærþon we to londe   geliden hæfdon
>   ofer hreone hrycg.   Þa us help bicwom,
>   þæt us to hælo   hyþe gelædde
>   godes gæstsunu   ond us giefe sealde

---

⁷⁵ Cf. Martin, 'Aspects of Winter', 377, which suggests that the winter passage in *Andreas* 1255–65 emphasizes the saint's fortitude. Cf. also *Sir Gawain and the Green Knight* 713–32, in which Gawain is described as less bothered by the enmity of his various supernatural enemies than by the winter weather encountered on his journey: J. R. R. Tolkien and E. V. Gordon, eds, *Sir Gawain and the Green Knight*, 2nd ed., rev. Norman Davis (Oxford: Clarendon, 1967). On the heroism of travel, see Paul Battles, '*Genesis A* and the Anglo-Saxon "Migration Myth"', *Anglo-Saxon England* 29 (2000): 59; Michelet, *Creation, Migration, and Conquest*, 176–87, 201–2; cf. Neville, *The Natural World*, 89–138. On the hostility of the sea, see Stopford A. Brooke, *The History of Early English Literature: Being the History of English Poetry from its Beginnings to the Accession of King Ælfred* (New York and London: Macmillan, 1892), 162–88; Magennis, *Images of Community*, 126–7; cf. E. G. Stanley, 'Old English Poetic Diction and the Interpretation of *The Wanderer*, *The Seafarer* and *The Penitent's Prayer*', *Anglia* 73.4 (n.s. 61.4) (1956): 436–7. On the heroism of saints, see Rosemary Woolf, 'Saints' Lives', in Stanley, *Continuations and Beginnings*, 50–3.
⁷⁶ 'Wæteregsa stod / þreata þryðum' (*Andreas* 375–6).
⁷⁷ 'Wæteregesan [. . .], cealde streamas' (*Beowulf* 1260–1).
⁷⁸ Krapp and Dobbie, *Exeter Book*, 15–27.

> þæt we oncnawan magun   ofer ceoles bord
> hwær we sælan sceolon   sundhengestas,
> ealde yðmearas,   ancrum fæste.   (lines 850–63)

> The present time is most like the way we travel on the ocean, by ship across cold water, with swimming-horses across the wide sea, journey by water-wood. The perilous stream of the waves on which we bob here throughout this insubstantial world is beyond measure; the waves are windy over the deep way. The conditions were rough before we made it to land across the stormy ridge. Then help came to us, so that God's spirit-son led us into the safe harbour and gave us his gift, that we might know where firmly to moor our swimming-horses, the old wave-mares, with the anchor over the ship's board.

Here too, the water is referred to as *ceald* as part of the overall imagery representing the various afflictions of life. Such detail is not provided in the Latin source, which limits seafaring imagery to a single metaphor portraying hope as the mind's anchor:

> Quamuis adhuc rerum perturbationibus animus fluctuet, iam tamen spei uestrae ancoram in aeternam patriam figite, intentionem mentis in uera luce solidate.   (Gregory the Great, *Homiliae in evangelia* 29, 254)[79]

> Even though your mind now surges with unrest, nevertheless fix the anchor of your hope in the eternal homeland, fasten your resolve in the true light.

The Anglo-Saxon poet saw here the potential for an extended simile, but in its creation it seems he made use of an existing Anglo-Saxon tradition of voyaging descriptions, which he employed to outline the dangers of life at sea.[80] As a simile, the resulting passage draws attention to the inhospitable qualities of life on earth. The image used, however, emphasizes the cold of the sea.

The collocation *ceald wæter* also makes an appearance in *The Battle of Maldon*[81] during the parley across the River Pante between Byrhtnoth and the foreign raiders: 'Byrhthelm's son then began to call out across the cold water' (91–2).[82] It has been suggested that the description could have no

---

[79] Raymond Étaix, ed., *Gregorius Magnus: 'Homiliae in evangelia'*, Corpus Christianorum, Series Latina, 141 (Turnhout: Brepols, 1999), 244–55. Cf. also the figure used in the Old English *Soliloquies*, book 1, 22.11–25: W. Endter, ed., *König Alfreds des Grossen Bearbeitung der 'Soliloquien' des Augustinus*, Bibliothek der angelsächsischen Prosa 11 (Hamburg: Grand, 1922), 22, alongside a redaction of its Latin source, and the figurative uses of *hyþ* ('harbour') cited in *DOE*, s.v. 'hȳþ' (forthcoming), sense 3.

[80] The passage's reliance on traditional Old English poetic diction is demonstrated in Andy Orchard, 'The Word Made Flesh: Christianity and Oral Culture in Anglo-Saxon Verse', *Oral Tradition* 24, no. 2 (2009): 302–3, 317–18. See also Stanley, 'Poetic Diction', 436–7; Magennis, *Images of Community*, 126–7; Thomas D. Hill, 'The Anchor of Hope and the Sea of this World: Christ II, 850–66', *English Studies* 75, no. 4 (1994): 289–92.

[81] Donald Scragg, ed., *The Battle of Maldon* (Manchester: Manchester University Press, 1981).

[82] 'Ongan ceallian þa ofer cald wæter / Byrhtelmes bearn.'

literal implications here: after all, the battle was fought in August.[83] This is armchair reasoning, of course: for English tidal waters to be cold at any time of year should come as no surprise. In the same way, the *Death of Edward*[84] poet cannot be faulted for lack of realism when he observes of the subject of his elegy,

> Weold wel geþungen Walum and Scottum
> and Bryttum eac, byre Æðelredes,
> Englum and Sexum, oretmægcum,
> swa ymbclyppað cealde brymmas. (lines 9–12)

The excellent son of Æðelred governed well the Welsh and Scots, and the British too, the Angles and the Saxons, the warriors as the cold waves surround them.

But even if British waters are cold, that does not mean that the *Edward* poet did not intend to heighten the heroic style of his eulogy by describing them as such in implication of their hostility, amplifying Edward's achievement by the suggestion that he faced external threats alongside the eleventh-century challenges of internal unity, whether from the sea itself or from the enemies it brought to English shores. Similarly, the *Maldon* poet must have intended to evoke a mood by his reference to cold water, as so much of poetic content serves the shaping of a mood.[85] Although nothing precludes the poet's contemporaneity with the actual battle,[86] whether he had been present to test the waters is anyone's guess. More to the point, his diction must have been informed by a combination of traditional poetic environmental depiction, alliterative requirement, and the knowledge that his collocation would do no unacceptable injustice to the historical record of East Saxon water temperatures.

An aspect of the poetic tradition that seems to have played a role in *Maldon*'s reference to cold water is the hostility of the natural world, which brings out the heroism as well as the drama of the action to which it forms the backdrop in much the same way as is done in *Andreas*. A starker example of this is found in the verse *Exodus*, whose author had considerably less oceanographical justification to refer to the Red Sea as *sinceald* ('perpetually cold', 472,[87] with a possible pun on the Egyptian *synn* ('sin') that occasions the massacre), though he may not have known that the

---

[83] Vivian Salmon, 'Some Connotations of *cold* in Old and Middle English', *Modern Language Notes* 74, no. 4 (1959): 314; cf. E. V. Gordon, ed., *The Battle of Maldon* (London: Methuen, 1937), 49, n. 91, which assigns the description both a literal and a figurative value.

[84] Dobbie, *Minor Poems*, 25–6.

[85] This understanding differs from Greenfield's statement that 'much [...] Old English poetic diction [is] best taken metaphorically' (Greenfield, 'The Old English Elegies', 148), a view that undervalues a text's rootedness in the world of sensory experience.

[86] Donald Scragg, ed., '*The Battle of Maldon*', in *The Battle of Maldon: 991 AD*, ed. Donald Scragg (Oxford: Blackwell, 1991), 32.

[87] This line is numbered 473 in Krapp's edition (Krapp, *Junius*, 89–107).

sea he was describing is among the warmest bodies of salt water on earth. Although his choice of words is again favoured by alliteration (the full line is 'sincalda sæ, sealtum yðum'), its natural contextual explanation is that the sea represented a hostile landscape category, first obstructing the Judaic refugees and then, in the passage containing the description in question, annihilating the Egyptian army.[88] Whether or not the episode reminded the poet of the continued threat of the sea to those who ventured out for trade, travel, or fishery,[89] his general understanding of the sea was such that he considered the adjective *sinceald* a fitting description for a particularly treacherous sea which he himself was unlikely ever to have visited.[90]

Occasional exceptions may be found to the negative connotations of cold water, but the temperature association persists. *The Phoenix* stands out in Old English poetry for its interest in the paradisal *locus amoenus*, here inhabited by the mythical bird that gave the poem its name. The poet uses the physical setting to represent paradise earthly and terrestrial (424–42, 575–88). The natural world surrounding the phoenix is universally pleasant, devoid of seasonality, precipitation, and rugged landscapes (1–84), but the poet nevertheless speaks of cold water:

> Foldan leccaþ
> wæter wynsumu   of þæs wuda midle;
> þa monþa gehwam   of þære moldan tyrf
> brimcald brecað.[91]   (lines 64–7)

Pleasant streams irrigate the land from the midst of the forest; cold as the sea, every month they burst forth from the turf of the earth.

> Swa se æþela fugel   æt þam æspringe
> wlitigfæst wunað   wyllestreamas,
> þær se tireadga   twelf siþum hine
> bibaþað in þam burnan   ær þæs beacnes cyme,
> sweglcondelle,   ond symle swa oft
> of þam wilsuman   wyllgespryngum
> brimcald beorgeð   æt baða gehwylcum.[92]   (lines 104–10)

Where the noble and beautiful bird inhabits the running waters by the source of the river, there the glorious one bathes itself in the stream twelve

---

[88] Cf. Salmon, 'Connotations of *cold*', 319.

[89] Cf. Nicholas Howe, *Migration and Mythmaking in Anglo-Saxon England* (New Haven, CT: Yale University Press, 1989); Battles, '*Genesis A* and the Anglo-Saxon "Migration Myth"'.

[90] Cf. Jacques le Goff, 'Discorso di chiusura', in *Popoli e paesi nella cultura altomedievale: 23–29 aprile 1981*, Settimane di studio del centro Italiano di studi sull'alto medioevo 29, ed. not given (Spoleto: Presso la sede del Centro, 1983), 821–2.

[91] Cf. Lactantius, *De ave phoenice* 25–6: 'fons in medio [est], quem "Vivum" nomine dicunt, / perspicuus, lenis, dulcibus uber aquis' ('there is a spring in the centre which is called Vivum ["Life"], clear, calm, and abundant with sweet water').

[92] Cf. ibid., line 38: 'ter quater e Vivo gurgite libat aquam' ('three times four it tastes water from the stream Vivum').

times before the coming of the beacon, the sky-candle, and always equally
often it tastes of the pleasant source, cold as the sea, at each bathing.

Here, water for irrigation, bathing, and drinking is cold, even in a land where nothing of an unpleasant nature is permitted (14–84), and in contrast with a Latin source that does not so qualify the water. In the *Metres of Boethius*[93] likewise, the ideal age is portrayed as a time when people drank cold water, again unprompted by the Latin:

> Ac hi simle him
> eallum tidum   ute slepon
> under beamsceade,   druncon burnan wæter,
> calde wyllan.   (*The Metres of Boethius* 8, lines 26–9)[94]

But they always slept out under the shade of trees at all times, they drank water from a stream, a cold spring.

The poetry, then, looks favourably on cold water for personal use. This water is cold because it is fresh from the spring, suggesting purity and potability.[95] All the same, *The Phoenix* compares its temperature to that of the sea in the adjective *brimceald*,[96] thereby confirming the association of seascapes with cold, while both *The Phoenix* and the *Metres* extend this association to freshwater.

The widespread poetic convention of describing waterscapes as cold, aided by water's association with winter weather in *The Wanderer*, *The Seafarer*, *The Wife's Lament*, and *Beowulf*, leads to an understanding of the sea as a setting of permanent winter. This association is less pronounced in the prose corpus, where water is described as cold only in imitation of Latin models.[97] This difference may be explained in part by the recognition

---

[93] Godden and Irvine, *Boethius*.

[94] Cf. Boethius, *De consolatione philosophiae* 2m5, lines 10–12: 'somnos dabat herba salubres, / potum quoque lubricus amnis, / umbras altissima pinus' ('the grass provided wholesome sleep, a quick-flowing river drink, and the tallest pines shade'). Claudio Moreschini, ed., *Boethius: 'De consolatione philosophiae', Opuscula theologica*, 2nd ed. (Munich and Leipzig: Saur, 2005).

[95] Cf. Paolo Squatriti, *Water and Society in Early Medieval Italy, AD 400–1000* (Cambridge: Cambridge University Press, 1998), 37–8.

[96] *Brimceald* has alternatively been read as *brim ceald* ('cold waters') (M. Trautmann, 'Beiträge zu einem künftigen Sprachschatz der altenglischen Dichter', *Anglia* 33 (1910): 279–80), but since *brim* typically denotes seawater and the passage in *The Phoenix* unambiguously describes a stream, this reading is unlikely. Cf. Ernst A. Kock, *Jubilee Jaunts and Jottings: 250 Contributions to the Interpretation and Prosody of Old West Teutonic Alliterative Poetry*, Lunds Universitets Årsskrift, n.s. section 1 14.26 (Lund: Gleerup, 1918), 59–60; *DOE*, s.v.

[97] Cold water as a landscape feature occurs in Ælfric's *Forty Soldiers*, lines 142–217: Walter W. Skeat, ed., *Ælfric's Lives of Saints: Being a Set of Sermons on Saints' Days Formerly Observed by the English Church*, 4 vols, EETS, os 76, 82, 94, 114 (London: Oxford University Press, 1881–1900; reprinted in two volumes 1966), 1:238–60; cf. *Acta XL martyrum Sebastenae*, ch. 2: Joannes [Jean] Bolland et al., eds, *Acta sanctorum quotquot toto orbe coluntur, vel a catholicis scriptoribus celebrantur*, 68 vols (Paris and Rome: Palmé, 1643–1940), 10 March, p. 19; the Old English *Orosius* 3, ch. 9: Janet Bately, ed., *The Old English 'Orosius'*, EETS, ss 6 (London: Oxford University Press, 1980), 68; cf. Orosius, *Historiae adversum paganos* 3.16: Carolus [Karl] Zangemeister, ed., *Paulus Orosius:*

that prose translation tends to leave less room for innovation than poetic paraphrase, let alone original verse composition. It furthermore underscores the creative input required by poetic form. However, it may also be taken to reflect on the nature of the narrative mode of verse. Evidently, Old English poetic narratives are set in a diegetic world that answers to certain environmental expectations. Actual Anglo-Saxon perceptions of the sea may have differed, but the poetry describes it as a cold and hostile environment.

Despite these observations, it should be pointed out that the cold water topos is by no means mandatory in poetic passages describing the sea. *Genesis A*, for instance, makes no use of it even in its account of the flood, whose waters it calls *hreoh* ('rough', 1325), *sweart* ('black', 1326), *deop* ('deep', 1331; cf. 1451), and *famig* ('foamy', 1452), never *ceald*.[98] Nevertheless, the original collocation of *ceald* with words for water and sea across some ten

---

'Historiarum adversum paganos libri VII', accedit eiusdem 'Liber apologeticus' (Hildesheim: Olms, 1967), 173; the Old English *Dialogues* of Gregory the Great 2.1: Hans Hecht, ed., *Übersetzung der 'Dialoge' Gregors des Grossen über das Leben und die Wundertaten italienischer Väter und über die Unsterblichkeit der Seelen*, 2 vols (1900–7; Darmstadt: Wissenschaftliche Buchgesellschaft, 1966), 1:98; cf. Gregory the Great, *Dialogi* 2.1.3: De Vogüé and Antin, *Dialogues*, 2:130; and by simile in Ælfric's *Passion of Saint Cecilia*, lines 345–8: Skeat, *Ælfric's Lives of Saints*, 2:376; cf. the Latin source in Boninus Mombritius [Bonino Mombrizio], ed., *Sanctuarium seu Vitae sanctorum*, 2 vols (Paris: Fontemoing, 1910; Hildesheim and New York: Olms, 1978), 1:341. Whereas the passages in *Forty Soldiers* and the Old English *Orosius* employ the cold water as an affliction, *Cecilia* instead uses cold water as a simile representing divine protection from the flames of torture. The episode in the Old English *Dialogues* of Gregory the Great seems to take a favourable view of the river in question, as its waters are 'perspicuas' or 'swiðe hluttre' ('very clear'), but the water is mentioned only as an explanation of the place name *Sublacus*, playing no further role in the narrative. As a drink (disregarding medical texts, which make frequent mention of beverages both hot and cold), cold water occurs in Assmann Homily 11, lines 81–5: B. Assmann, ed., *Angelsächsische Homilien und Heiligenleben*, Bibliothek der angelsächsischen Prosa 3 (Kassel: Wigand, 1889; reprinted with an introduction by Peter Clemoes, Darmstadt: Wissenschaftliche Buchgesellschaft, 1964), 141; the Old English Gospel of Matthew 10.42: Walter W. Skeat, ed., *The Gospel According to Saint Matthew* (Cambridge: Cambridge University Press, 1887; Darmstadt: Wissenschaftliche Buchgesellschaft, 1970), 88; cf. Mt; *Pastoral Care*, ch. 58: Henry Sweet, ed., *King Alfred's West-Saxon Version of Gregory's 'Pastoral Care'*, 2 vols, EETS, os 45, 50 (London: Oxford University Press, 1871), 445–7; cf. Gregory the Great, *Regula pastoralis* 3.34: Floribert Rommel and Charles Morel, eds, *Grégoire le Grand: 'Règle pastorale'*, 2 vols, Sources chrétiennes 381 (Paris: Cerf, 1992), 1:510; Ælfric, *Catholic Homilies I*, 38, lines 105–7: Peter Clemoes, ed., *Ælfric's Catholic Homilies: The First Series*, EETS, ss 17 (Oxford: Oxford University Press, 1997), 510; and Ælfric, Additional Homilies 17, lines 194–8: John C. Pope, ed., *Homilies of Ælfric: A Supplementary Collection*, 2 vols, EETS, os 259–60 (London: Oxford University press, 1967–8), 2:555. The majority of these derive from the New Testament promise of a reward for those who provide Christ's 'little ones' with cold water (Mt 10:42; cf. Mc 9:40). In the original geographical context of this anecdote, of course, cold was intended as a favourable property for a beverage (cf. Squatriti, *Water and Society*, 38). Interesting in this respect is the Assmann 11 homilist's attempt to explain the specification as a way of pre-empting the excuse of not having a vessel in which to heat the water one is expected to give. The homilist here betrays his difficulty in understanding why cold water would be a desirable drink. Less cultural disagreement may have existed regarding the undesirability of tepid drinks, as both the Latin and the Old English version of the *Pastoral Care* echo this biblical sentiment (cf. Apc 3:15–16). On the other hand, the definite context provided with this image in the Apocalypse rendered it difficult to misinterpret.

[98] Moorman, comparing the episode to the nature descriptions of *Beowulf*, *Exodus*, and the riddles, remarked that 'what we miss is the passion, the breathlessness, the fine frenzy of the more primitive poetry' (Moorman, *Nature*, 22).

poetic texts, combined with further associations between water and winter in *Beowulf*, *The Wife's Lament*, *The Wanderer*, and *The Seafarer*, is sufficient to conclude that water described in the poetic mode was widely expected to be cold, and that water landscapes in the poetry tend to connote winter and winter weather regardless of the season on land.[99]

The association here described is not limited to narrative literature. The combination of cold and water is frequently encountered in the Old English names of streams and springs,[100] which may be taken as a reminder that a literary topos based on a concept as tactile as 'cold water' is unlikely to develop in isolation from everyday experience. Likewise based on experience is the learned Latinate doctrine of the four elements and qualities. Relayed in Anglo-Saxon England by Bede, Byrhtferth, and Ælfric, mostly in imitation of Isidore of Seville,[101] this system groups winter and water as sharing the same qualities. In Byrhtferth's words,

> Hiemps ys winter; he byð ceald and wæt. Wæter ys ceald and wæt; swa byð se ealda man ceald ⁊ snoflig.   (*Manual* 1.1)[102]
>
> *Hiemps* is winter; it is cold and wet. Water is cold and wet; the old man likewise is cold and sniffly.

It is unlikely that this particular detail of the learned tradition of the four elements, not taken over into Old English narrative prose except in *The Consolation of Philosophy* (ch. 33),[103] should have been picked up by the poetic tradition in order to describe sea journeys. Rather, it seems, the association was arrived at independently by two distinct traditions. Once in place, the learned and poetic views of winter could certainly reinforce each other in the mind of an Anglo-Saxon poet. This could only go so far, however, since the cold of water did not contrast with land temperature in the scholarly tradition:

> Wæter and eorðe   wæstmas brengað.
> Þa sint on gecynde   cealda ba twa:
> wæter wæt and ceald   (wangas ymbelicgað);
> eorðe ælgreno,   eac hwæðre ceald.
>   (*The Metres of Boethius* 20, lines 75–8)[104]

---

[99] A poetic connection between the sea, cold, winter, and misery has previously been discussed by Stanley, 'Poetic Diction', 436–7; cf. Bately, 'Time', 4–8.

[100] A. H. Smith, ed., *English Place-Name Elements*, 2 vols (Cambridge: Cambridge University Press, 1970), s.v. 'cald'.

[101] Isidore of Seville, *De natura rerum* 11: Fontaine, *Traité de la nature*, 213–17; Bede, *De temporum ratione*, ch. 35: Jones, *De temporum ratione*, 391–5; Byrhtferth, *Manual* 1.1: Baker and Lapidge, *Enchiridion*, 10–14; Ælfric, *De temporibus anni*, lines 385–400.

[102] Baker and Lapidge, *Enchiridion*, 12.

[103] Godden and Irvine, *Boethius*, 1:315.

[104] This 281-line metre is an extensive elaboration of a 38-line Latin original which mentions the elements and their qualities, if more briefly (Boethius, *De consolatione philisophiae* 3m9, esp. lines 10–12; see further the commentary in Godden and Irvine, *Boethius*, 2:510–12).

Water and earth produce fruits. They are both of a cold nature: water is wet and cold (it surrounds the fields); the earth is very green, but nevertheless also cold.

Sites of Fear and Mourning in *Beowulf*

It has become clear from the preceding section that some of the passages collocating *ceald* and *wæter* assign the adjective *ceald* a non-literal value centrally concerned with danger and hostility. For instance, it was observed that there was no oceanological justification for the *Exodus* poet to refer to the water of the Red Sea as *sinceald*. Salmon has written at some length about this phenomenon, proposing that Old English *ceald*, like Old Norse *kaldr*, bore 'implications of "hostility"[,] "treachery" or "ill-omen"'.[105] She speaks of 'connotations' and 'implications' rather than a distinct lexical sense, a distinction resting on the question whether the word occurs without a literal referent, as Old Norse *kaldr* does in the combinations *kǫld rǫdd* ('a cold [i.e. hostile] voice') and *kalt ráð* ('cold [i.e. cold-hearted] counsel').[106] A cognate of the former collocation occurs once also in the Old English *Soul and Body I*[107] ('cealdan reorde', 15) with a disputable but certainly figurative sense,[108] while a related form of the latter occurs repeatedly in Middle English, suggesting it existed at least in Anglo-Scandinavian England.[109] The unquestionably figurative adjective *cealdheort* ('cold-hearted')[110] is found in

---

[105] Salmon, 'Connotations of *cold*', 321 and passim.

[106] *Kǫld rǫdd* occurs in *Atlakviða*, st. 2: Neckel, *Edda*, 240–7. *Kalt ráð*, best known for its occurrence in the expression *kǫld eru kvenna ráð* ('women's counsels are cold'), is found in several texts, including *Lokasenna*, st. 51: ibid., 96–110; *Vǫlundarkviða*, st. 31: ibid., 116–23; *Óláfs saga helga*, ch. 131: Bjarni Aðalbjarnarson, *Heimskringla*, 2:226; *Njáls saga*, ch. 116: Einar Ólafur Sveinsson, *Brennu-Njáls saga*, 292; *Gísla saga*, ch. 19: Björn K. Þórólfsson and Guðni Jónsson, *Vestfirðinga sǫgur*, 61. Cf. the adjective *kaldráðr* ('cold-counselled', *Sturlu saga*, ch. 34: Jón Jóhannesson, Magnús Finnbogason, and Kristján Eldjárn, *Sturlunga saga*, 1:112) and similar metaphorical compounds listed in CV.

[107] George Philip Krapp, ed., *The Vercelli Book*, Anglo-Saxon Poetic Records 2 (New York: Columbia University Press, 1932), 54–9.

[108] Spinner and Salmon understood it as 'hostile': Katharina Spinner, 'Die Ausdrücke für Sinnesempfindungen in der angelsächsischen Poesie verglichen mit den Bezeichnungen für Sinnesempfindungen in der altnordischen, altächsischen und althochdeutschen Dichtung' (unpublished doctoral thesis, University of Halle, 1924), 105; Salmon, 'Connotations of *cold*', 318; DOE includes it under 'ceald' sense 6c, 'chilling, dolorous'. What precise sense the poet intended is impossible to ascertain.

[109] For example *Proverbs of Alfred*, 444: O. Arngart, ed., *The Proverbs of Alfred*, vol. 2: *The Texts Edited with Introduction, Notes and Glossary* (Lund: Gleerup, 1955), 118; Robert of Gloucester's *Metrical Chronicle*, MS A, 2775: William Aldis Wright, ed., *The Metrical Chronicle of Robert of Gloucester*, 2 vols, Rerum Britannicarum medii ævi scriptores 86 (London: Her Majesty's Stationery Office, 1887; New York: Kraus, 1965), 198; *Nun's Priest's Tale* 3256 (=B2 4446; Benson, *The Riverside Chaucer*, 253–61); see further Hans Kurath et al., eds, *Middle English Dictionary* (Ann Arbor, MI: University of Michigan Press, 1956–2007), s.v. 'cōld', sense 6a, accessed 15 March 2015, http://quod.lib.umich.edu/m/med/; Salmon, 'Connotations of *cold*', 318–21; Magennis, *Images of Community*, 176, esp. n. 54.

[110] It has been observed that this word could alternatively be taken as an adverb *cealdheorte* (Brooks, *'Andreas' and 'The Fates of the Apostles'*, 68, commentary to line 138 and glossary, s.v. 'cald-

Andreas, line 138. It serves to secure the sympathies of the audience against the Mermedonian cannibals, arguably carrying a sense like 'heartless'.[111] A different figurative use of heat and cold is found in *Judgement Day I*, which asserts that the defendants at that event will confess 'all, hot and cold, good or evil, that has happened below the heavens' (106–7),[112] aligning these ranges of heat and ethics. Finally, several English place names have been found in which the initial element *ceald-* (though in many cases indistinguishable from Old Norse *kald-*) seems to be used figuratively, for example Catcherside ('cold cheer hill').[113] A non-literal lexical sense is thus warranted for Old English *ceald* with a semantic range from 'inhospitable' to 'hostile, treacherous'. On either end of the spectrum, the concept is wired to unsettle.

If *ceald* had an unsettling figurative sense, the ocean it so often describes was no less associated with danger. As Sebastian Sobecki points out, water was the world's placeholder prior to creation; it thus represents primeval chaos, and is often associated with Satan as well as with the wicked world in patristics and medieval writings.[114] The ocean is governed by the whale, a creature identified as a representation of Satan in the *Physiologus* tradition.[115] Water is the one earthly domain not cleansed by the flood.[116] Accordingly, nearly all the monsters of *Beowulf* are associated with this environment, further confirming the hostility implied in the widespread union of winter and water.

The triad of water, winter, and monsters in *Beowulf* becomes especially clear in the swimming contest. Following Unferth's brief account, which introduces the hibernal conditions of the contest ('the ocean was surging with waves, winter's billows', 515–16),[117] the monsters are introduced in Beowulf's own words:

> Hæfdon swurd nacod, þa wit on sund reon,
> heard on handa; wit unc wið hronfixas
> werian þohton.

heort'; *DOE*, s.v. 'ceald-heort').

[111] Others have proposed sinfulness: Bugge, 'Studien über das Beowulfepos', 13; Hill, 'Heat and Cold Imagery', 531–2. No equivalent term is found in the Greek and Latin analogues in Blatt, *Acta Andreae et Matthiae*, 36–7.

[112] 'Eal swylce under heofonum gewearð hates ond cealdes, / godes oþþe yfles.' Krapp and Dobbie, *Exeter Book*, 212–15.

[113] Smith, *English Place-Name Elements*, s.v. 'cald'.

[114] Sebastian I. Sobecki, *The Sea and Medieval English Literature*, Studies in Medieval Romance 5 (Cambridge: Brewer, 2008), 34–41.

[115] *The Whale*: Ann Squires, ed., *The Old English 'Physiologus'*, Durham Medieval Texts 5 (Durham: Durham Medieval Texts, 1988), 41–5; see further Frederick S. Holton, 'Old English Sea Imagery and the Interpretation of *The Seafarer*', *The Yearbook of English Studies* 12 (1982): 212, and the literature there cited.

[116] Augustine, *De civitate Dei* 15.27: Dombart and Kalb, *De civitate Dei*, 2:496; P. S. Langeslag, 'Monstrous Landscape in *Beowulf*', *English Studies* 96, no. 2 (2015): 119–38.

[117] 'Geofon yþum weol, / wintrys wylmum.'

[...]
Ða wit ætsomne   on sæ wæron
fif nihta fyrst,   oþþæt unc flod todraf,
wado weallende,   wedera cealdost,
nipende niht,   ond norþanwind
heaðogrim ondhwearf;   hreo wæron yþa.
Wæs merefixa   mod onhrered;
þær me wið laðum   licsyrce min,
heard, hondlocen,   helpe gefremede,
beadohrægl broden   on breostum læg
golde gegyrwed.   Me to grunde teah
fah feondscaða,   fæste hæfde
grim on grape;   hwæþre me gyfeþe wearð
þæt ic aglæcan   orde geræhte,
hildebille;   heaþoræs fornam
mihtig meredeor   þurh mine hand.
Swa mec gelome   laðgeteonan
þreatedon þearle.   Ic him þenode
deoran sweorde,   swa hit gedefe wæs.
Næs hie ðære fylle   gefean hæfdon,
manfordædlan,   þæt hie me þegon,
symbel ymbsæton   sægrunde neah;
ac on mergenne   mecum wunde
be yðlafe   uppe lægon,
sweordum aswefede,   þæt syðþan na
ymb brontne ford   brimliðende
lade ne letton.   Leoht eastan com,
beorht beacen godes;   brimu swaþredon,
þæt ic sænæssas   geseon mihte,
windige weallas.   Wyrd oft nereð
unfægne eorl,   þonne his ellen deah.
Hwæþere me gesælde   þæt ic mid sweorde ofsloh
niceras nigene.   No ic on niht gefrægn
under heofones hwealf   heardran feohtan.   (lines 539–41, 544–76)

We had strong bare swords in our hands when we swam out paddling; we intended to defend ourselves against sea-fish. [...] Then we were together at sea for a period of five nights, until the tidal current drove us apart, the surging waters, the coldest of weathers, the darkening night, and the battle-grim north wind turned against us; the waves were rough. The hearts of the sea-fish were stirred up; my strong, handmade byrnie gave me aid against the hostile ones there, the woven battle-garment lay on my chest, adorned with gold. A hostile enemy dragged me to the bottom, the grim one had me firmly in his grip. Nevertheless it was given to me that I reached my fierce opponent with the tip of my blade, with my battle-sword; the battle-attack took off the mighty sea-beast by my hand. In this way the evildoers frequently beset me closely. I served them with my formidable sword, as was fitting. They did not have the pleasure of their fill, the criminal destroyers, that they should eat me, sit at banquet near the bottom of the sea; instead, by the morning they lay up with the jetsam, wounded by blades, put to sleep with swords, so that they would no longer obstruct the passage of sea-travellers in the deep crossing. Light came from the east, God's bright beacon; the waves calmed down, so that I was able to see headlands, windy cliffs. Fate often saves the undoomed man if his courage holds. Nevertheless it was given to me that I killed nine sea-monsters with the sword. I have not heard of a harder fight in the nighttime below the arch of heaven.

The account is quoted at length because it outlines a number of relevant details. To begin with, the setting is described not only in terms of winter – 'wedera cealdost' ('coldest of weathers', 546) and 'wintrys wylmum' ('winter's billows', 516) – but also as nighttime: the poet mentions the 'nipende niht' ('darkening night', 547) and specifies that the battle with the water-monsters takes place 'on niht' ('in the nighttime', 575). Victory becomes apparent 'on mergenne' ('in the morning', 565), when 'leoht eastan com' ('light came from the east', 569); the poet thus draws on the powerful associations of light and dark with their moral as well as seasonal connotations. The environment is further rendered inhospitable by a storm and strong waves (545–8). The monsters themselves are first introduced through anticipation, as the swimmers arm themselves against just such an encounter (539–41). It is suggested that the creatures belong near the bottom of the sea, as this is where Beowulf is taken (553–4) and where the banqueting imagery is brought in (562–4). They are described as *hronfixas* and *merefixas* ('sea-fish', 540, 549), *laþgeteonan* ('evildoers', 559), *manfordædlan* ('criminal destroyers', 563), and *niceras* ('sea-monsters', 575), who habitually waylay sea-travellers (565–9); one of them is individually described as a *feondscaþa* ('enemy', 554), *aglæca* ('fierce opponent', 556), and *meredeor* ('sea-beast', 558). In short, the episode represents a confrontation with all that is most daunting to mankind, for which nighttime, the sea, and winter weather form the setting.

Hostile creatures are likewise associated with water and night in the poem's central narrative.[118] The element of water is most obvious in the case of Grendel's mother,

> se þe wæteregesan   wunian scolde,
> cealde streamas,   siþðan Cain wearð
> to ecgbanan   angan breþer,
> fæderenmæge;   he þa fag gewat,
> morþre gemearcod,   mandream fleon,
> westen warode.   Þanon woc fela
> geosceaftgasta;   wæs þæra Grendel sum,
> heorowearh hetelic.   (lines 1260–7)

She[119] who had to inhabit the terror of water, the cold currents, after

---

[118] Langeslag, 'Monstrous Landscape'.
[119] Lit. 'he'. On the gender transgression of Grendel's mother, see William Witherle Lawrence, *'Beowulf' and Epic Tradition* (Cambridge, MA: Harvard University Press, 1928), 181–2; C. L. Wrenn, ed., *Beowulf: With the 'Finnesburg Fragment'* (Boston, MA, and London: Heath / Harrap, 1953), 209;

Cain became the killer by the sword of his only brother, his father's son. Then, doomed and marked with murder, he fled human society and occupied the wilderness. From there, many ancient fated spirits arose; Grendel was one of them, the hateful, savage villain.

On the evidence of this passage, the *wæteregesa* ('terror of water') may be understood as a subtype of the *westen* ('wilderness'). As descendants of Cain, after all, both Grendel and his mother are banished to the same wilderness as their forefather. In *Beowulf*, however, they are associated with three distinct landscape categories: water, marshland, and coastal highland. Moreover, only Grendel's mother is explicitly characterized as a water creature using such terms as *brimwylf* ('sea-wolf', 1599),[120] *merewif* ('water-woman', 1519), and *grundwyrgen* ('accursed creature of the deep', 1518).[121] Descriptions of Grendel's movements, as well as descriptions applying to both creatures, pivot on the terms *fenn* ('marsh') and *mor* ('mountain', but sometimes 'marsh'),[122] with further interest in *næss* ('promontory') and *hliþ* ('slope'). Although it has been observed that 'factually [. . .] the combination of fenland and mountains, of wind-swept headlands and woods overhanging the pool is not possible',[123] the poem does indeed associate both adversaries of the first half of the poem with all these landscapes:

>   Hie dygel lond
> warigeað, wulfhleoþu, windige næssas,
> frecne fengelad,   ðær fyrgenstream
> under næssa genipu niþer gewiteð,
> flod under foldan.   (lines 1357–61)

They occupy a hidden land, wolf-slopes, windy headlands, a perilous fen-passage, where a mighty stream goes down below the shadows of headlands, water below the land.

Despite this confusion of categories, the pool occupies a central position in the landscape of both monsters. Grendel's association with his mother's underwater cave is suggested not only by the fact that this is where he flees when wounded, but also by Hrothgar's focus on the pool in his description

---

Margaret E. Goldsmith, *The Mode and Meaning of 'Beowulf'* (London: Athlone, 1970), 104; Fulk, Bjork, and Niles, *Beowulf*, commentary to lines 1260 f.

[120] The term is applied to Grendel's mother a second time by emendation, where the manuscript reads *brimwyl*; the water element is thus at any rate secure (British Library, MS Cotton Vespasian A. XV, fol. 163r).

[121] *Grundwyrgen* could alternatively be read as 'accursed creature of the abyss', i.e. of hell.

[122] Associations with *fenn* are made in lines 104, 764, 820, 851, 1295, and 1359; *mor* occurs in lines 103, 162, 450, 710, 1348, and 1405. For the meaning of *mor* in *Beowulf*, see Langeslag, 'Monstrous Landscape', 122–3.

[123] Stanley, 'Poetic Diction', 441; cf. William Witherle Lawrence, 'The Haunted Mere in *Beowulf*', *Publications of the Modern Language Association of America* 27, no. 2 (1912): 208–45.

of both monsters' habitat (1357–76).[124] Additional evidence for Grendel's association with the cave lies in the runic sword-hilt found there. The hilt narrates the flood with an emphasis on the destruction of giants, but it is found in a dry cave that is home to Cain's monstrous relations. This reminds the reader that Grendel's ancestors must themselves have survived the flood in one way or another, a puzzle to which the dry underwater cave presents itself as a natural (if physically implausible) answer.[125] That the cave is dry does not stop the poet from referring to Grendel's mother in the marine terms listed above, so that the other straightforward explanation of flood survival, namely as a marine species, is likewise represented in the text, and specifically in lines 1260–2 quoted above.[126] Instead of providing a detailed and unambiguous account, the poet touches on multiple solutions and leaves his audience to draw their own conclusions. In either reading, however, the pool plays a pivotal role in the survival of Grendel's line, giving him a strong connection with water.

In Hrothgar's description, the pool is situated in a hibernal environment by its proximity to 'hrinde bearwas' ('frosted groves'):

> Nis þæt feor heonon
> milgemearces   þæt se mere standeð;
> ofer þæm hongiað   hrinde bearwas,
> wudu wyrtum fæst   wæter oferhelmað.   (lines 1361–4)

> It is not far from here in measure of miles that the pool is located; frosted groves hang over it, a wood firm in its roots overhangs the water.

Here too the winter imagery is strictly detached from the seasonal cycle, as Hrothgar is not describing the scene as he witnessed it recently but rather reporting a folk-tradition of a more or less timeless character among his subjects (1345–76). The passage closely resembles a description of hell in Blickling Homily 16,[127] in which St Paul has a vision of trees alternately

---

[124] The landscapes of Grendel and his mother have been described in the contrasting terms of fen and water in Ruth Mellinkoff, 'Cain's Monstrous Progeny in *Beowulf*, Part I: Noachic Tradition', *Anglo-Saxon England* 8 (1979): 151–2; Michelet, *Creation, Migration, and Conquest*, 50; the opposition is one of hall and water in Larry Dean Benson, 'The Originality of *Beowulf*', in *The Interpretation of Narrative: Theory and Practice*, ed. Morton W. Bloomfield, vol. 1, Harvard English Studies (Cambridge, MA: Harvard University Press, 1970), 30.

[125] Langeslag, 'Monstrous Landscape', 125–8.

[126] Cf. Ruth Mellinkoff, 'Cain's Monstrous Progeny in *Beowulf*, Part II: Post-Diluvian Survival', *Anglo-Saxon England* 9 (1980): 186–7, which discusses the possibility of marine survival of giants with reference to a specific Talmudic tradition, and David Williams, *Cain and Beowulf: A Study in Secular Allegory* (Toronto: University of Toronto Press, 1982), 34–5, which suggests that the coming of the flood may have necessitated the underground dwelling of Grendel's line but never explains how, instead turning to the tradition that has Cain's sinfulness transferred onto Ham (52–3). A straightforward understanding of marine survival is suggested in Andy Orchard, *A Critical Companion to 'Beowulf'* (Cambridge: Brewer, 2003), 139.

[127] R. Morris, ed., *The Blickling Homilies*, 3 vols, EETS, os 58, 63, 73 (London: Trübner, 1874–80; reprinted in one volume 1967), 197–211 (there numbered XVII). A detailed comparison between these texts as well as the *Visio Pauli* may be found in Wright, *The Irish Tradition*, 116–36.

described as 'hrimige bearwas' ('rimy groves') and 'isige bearwas' ('icy groves') overhanging the waters of hell from a cliff twelve miles high. Here, the *nicoras* inhabiting the water are demons, eager to snap up the black souls dangling from the trees whenever a branch gives way.[128] Scholars have sought to read the frost in one or other of these texts tropologically or broadly symbolically, reflecting either the moral depravity of the lost souls or the surreal quality of the visionary experience.[129] The former reading certainly agrees well with the visionary tradition, which makes frequent use of punitive images of hot and cold. However, the shared material also partakes of a vernacular tradition of the monstrous, which seeks a more visceral response through the psycho-geographical association between winter landscapes and the dangerous supernatural.

Like the sea-monsters of the swimming contest, Grendel and his mother move at night only. Grendel is characterized as a *deorc deaþscua* ('dark death-shadow', 160), *sceadugenga* ('shadow-walker', 703), and *nihtbealwa mæst* ('the greatest of nightly torments', 193). Being *æfengrom* ('evening-angry'), he comes out 'syððan heofones gim / glad ofer grundas' ('when heaven's gem has passed over the lands', 2072–3), operates 'deorcum nihtum' ('in dark nights', 275; cf. 'sinnihte' ('in the perpetual night', 161)) and concludes his attack before dawn (126). His mother follows the same pattern, attacking at night (1251–1306). As well as implying that winter should be these creatures' prime season, this association draws them further into traditional hostile environments, suggesting similar associations for their underwater habitat.

The pool in *Beowulf* is surrounded by a further category of hostile beings, all associated with water. These are described when Beowulf and his followers arrive at the pool:

>   Gesawon ða æfter wætere   wyrmcynnes fela,
>   sellice sædracan   sund cunnian,
>   swylce on næshleoðum   nicras licgean,
>   ða on undernmæl   oft bewitigað
>   sorhfulne sið   on seglrade,
>   wyrmas ond wildeor.   Hie on weg hruron,
>   bitere ond gebolgne;   bearhtm ongeaton,
>   guðhorn galan.   Sumne Geata leod
>   of flanbogan   feores getwæfde,
>   yðgewinnes,   þæt him on aldre stod
>   herestræl hearda;   he on holme wæs
>   sundes þe sænra   ðe hyne swylt fornam.
>   Hræþe wearð on yðum   mid eoferspreotum

---

[128] Morris, *The Blickling Homilies*, 209–11.
[129] D. W. Robertson Jr, 'The Doctrine of Charity in Mediaeval Literary Gardens: A Topical Approach through Symbolism and Allegory', *Speculum* 26, no. 1 (January 1951): 33; Richard Butts, 'The Analogical Mere: Landscape and Terror in *Beowulf*', *English Studies* 68, no. 2 (1987): 115–16; Fulk, Bjork, and Niles, *Beowulf*, 201, commentary to line 1363.

> heorohocyhtum   hearde genearwod,
> niða genæged,   ond on næs togen,
> wundorlic wægbora;   weras sceawedon
> gryrelicne gist.   (lines 1425-41)

> Then they saw many serpents in the water, strange sea-dragons exploring the pool, as well as water-monsters lying on the outlying headlands, such as often watch a sorrowful journey on a sailing route in the morning, serpents and wild beasts. They sank away, bitter and angry; they heard a noise, the battle-horn calling. The Geatas deprived one of its life and its swimming with a bow, so that a rigid army-arrow stuck in his vitals; he was slower swimming in the water when death took him. Soon the wondrous wave-bearer was hard pressed among the waves with sword-barbed boar-spears, attacked with hostilities, and drawn onto the headland; the men looked at the hideous stranger.

These *sædracan* ('sea-dragons') and *nicoras* ('water-monsters') are further confirmation that water environments are the primary domain of monsters in *Beowulf*. If the latter group are seen to attack sailors by day rather than night, this may be explained by a common-sense association of routine seafaring with daytime.[130]

The final monster in *Beowulf*, the dragon, is the only one with no more than a tenuous connection to water landscapes. It lives in an underground space (*eorþsele*, 2232, 2215; *eorþscræf*, 3046) prepared for human burial below a rocky elevation (*stanbeorg steap*, 2213) most likely representing a neolithic barrow,[131] located on a plain (*wong*, 2242). The barrow is situated in the vicinity of a headland jutting out into the sea (2242-3). Although a stream flows out from the mountain occupied by the monster, its flow is not of the kind that can be grouped with the cold of winter:

> Wæs þære burnan wælm
> heaðofyrum hat,   ne meahte horde neah
> unbyrnende   ænige hwile
> deop gedygan   for dracan lege.   (lines 2546-9)

> The surge of that stream was hot with battle-fires; he [Beowulf] could not hold out deep inside near the hoard for any length of time without burning on account of the dragon's flame.

Evidently, the dragon inhabits an environment differing in a few critical respects from those of the other monsters. Nevertheless, there remains a considerable body of environmental overlap between the various monsters of *Beowulf*. Like Grendel and his mother, the dragon stirs only at night, returning

---

[130] In reality, longer voyages on the open seas could involve around-the-clock sailing, whether to increase efficiency or simply as necessitated by the width of a body of water (McCormick, *Origins*, 491-500).

[131] On the presentation of the dragon's abode see Gale R. Owen-Crocker, *The Four Funerals in 'Beowulf' and the Structure of the Poem* (Manchester and New York: Manchester University Press, 2000), 61-4; cf. *Beowulf* 2717, 2774 *enta geweorc*.

from its attacks before daybreak;[132] like all monsters in this poem, its habitat is a landscape peripheral to the human domain, in this case a rocky elevation near the sea. All these are hostile categories, and the cold associations of the water combine well with the creatures' other environmental properties.

All the monster habitats of *Beowulf* thus converge in their participation in nighttime and the peripheral, environments distancing both the landscapes and their inhabitants from the human. Although cyclical seasonality is largely absent from *Beowulf*, the cold of water is repeatedly mentioned in connection with dangerous undertakings and feuds taking place in this landscape category, suggesting that the hibernal quality of the water accords with the terror effected by the species inhabiting it. While readings of these monsters as seasonal personifications of the natural world are strictly unwarranted,[133] it is fair to assume that there were overlaps between the effects of the creatures and their environments on the society that imagined them. Thus if the monsters of *Beowulf* conveyed horror to the poem's audience, winter and water landscapes must have had potential for horror. This evidence through association of winter's hostile connotations confirms the season's more directly apparent role in setting the moods of such poems as *The Ruin*, *The Wanderer*, and *The Seafarer*, as well as its function as an affliction in *Andreas*, lines 1255–65, discussed in the next chapter.

A final image to discuss under the heading of *Beowulf*'s non-transient winter imagery is found in line 33. In the context of Scyld's funeral, we read:

   Þær æt hyðe stod hringedstefna,
   isig ond utfus, æþelinges fær.   (lines 32-3)

   There by the harbour stood the ship with the ringed prow, icy and eager
   for the voyage, the prince's vessel.

The adjective *isig* ('icy') has triggered substantial debate.[134] This was

---

[132] *Beowulf* 2211, 2270-4, 2302-20.

[133] The best-known instance of such an approach is Karl Müllenhoff, 'Der Mythus von Beóvulf', *Zeitschrift für deutsches Altertum* 7 (1849): 419–41, which reads Grendel as a literary representation of spring flooding, his mother as a personification of the sea, and the dragon attacks as autumn storms, despite the near-total absence of seasonal references in the poem's main narrative (on which see below, pp. 128–41).

[134] Moritz Trautmann, 'Berichtigungen, Vermutungen und Erklärungen zum *Beowulf*: Erste Hälfte', *Bonner Beiträge zur Anglistik* 2 (1899): 127; Eduard Sievers, 'Lückenbüsser', *Beiträge zur Geschichte der deutschen Sprache und Literatur* 27 (1902): 572; Moritz Trautmann, 'Auch zum *Beowulf*: Ein Gruß an Herrn Eduard Sievers', *Bonner Beiträge zur Anglistik* 17 (1905): 143–74; Theodor von Grienberger, 'Bemerkungen zum *Beowulf*', *Beiträge zur Geschichte der deutschen Sprache und Literatur* 36 (1910): 77–101; Eduard Sievers, 'Gegenbemerkungen zum *Beowulf*', *Beiträge zur Geschichte der deutschen Sprache und Literatur* 36 (1910): 397–434; L. M. Hollander, '*Beowulf* 33', *Modern Language Notes* 32, no. 4 (April 1917): 246–7; Willy Krogmann, 'Ae. īsig', *Anglia*, n.s., 44 = 56 (1932): 438–9; Stanley, 'Poetic Diction'; W. P. Lehmann, '*Beowulf* 33, isig', *Modern Language Notes* 74, no. 7 (November 1959): 577–8; Else von Schaubert, ed., *Heyne-Schückings 'Beowulf'*, 17th ed. (Paderborn: Schöningh, 1961); Ernst A. Ebbinghaus, review of *Heyne-Schückings 'Beowulf'*, *Journal of English and Germanic Philology* 62 (1963): 676–8; Dieter Bähr, 'Altenglisch īsig (Beowulf, Zeile 33)', *Zeitschrift für Anglistik und Amerikanistik* 19 (1971): 409–12; G. Mazzuoli Porru, '*Beowulf*, v. 33: īsig ond ūtfūs', in

occasioned partly by puzzlement over the seasonal reference[135] and partly by a sense that 'isig ond utfus' in the sense translated above does not form an acceptable appositive pair, as members of such pairs are often similar in meaning.[136] A third objection was that the intensified form *eallisig* in the prose and verse of the Old English *Consolation of Philosophy* seemed to translate a concept other than 'covered with ice',[137] but that argument has since been refuted.[138]

Since the apparent sense of the form *īsig* ('covered with ice') yields no unacceptable image, we may pass over the proposed emendations[139] and consider instead what literary functions ice might have here.[140] Kemble's early reading 'shining like ice'[141] is too liberal, even if 'shining *with* ice' is at least conceivable as one intended effect of the image. A purely figurative image of ice is used for its reflective qualities, and perhaps for the temperature of the metal, in Old Norse sword-kennings;[142] to see it used of a ship whose core is wood is unlikely, whatever the reference of the ring(s) in *hringedstefna*.

Other figurative readings have been proposed. Eric Stanley dismisses literal significance too summarily when he asserts that *isig* may be 'no more than [. . .] a word evocative of sorrow: the factual meaning does not matter'.[143] This position has proved an easy target for Anatoly Liberman, who counters rather categorically that words in *Beowulf* always have a literal referent in addition to any figurative associations.[144] Just because Stanley overstates his case, of course, does not mean his point is invalid: an image of ice in a setting of mourning is probably intended to evoke a mood.

Studi linguistici e filologici per Carlo Alberto Mastrelli, ed. Luciano Agostiniani, Vittoria Grazi, and Alberto Nocentini (Pisa: Pacini, 1985), 263–74; Anatoly Liberman, 'The "Icy" Ship of Scyld Scefing: *Beowulf* 33', in *Bright is the Ring of Words: Festschrift für Horst Weinstock zum 65. Geburtstag*, ed. Clausdirk Pollner, Helmut Rohlfing, and Frank-Rutger Hausmann (Bonn: Romanistischer Verlag, 1996), 183–203; Fulk, Bjork, and Niles, *Beowulf*, commentary to line 33.

[135] Ferdinand Holthausen, 'Zum *Beowulf* (v. 33)', *Beiblatt zur 'Anglia'* 14 (1903): 82; Trautmann, 'Auch zum *Beowulf*', 151; Hollander, '*Beowulf* 33', 577; Krogmann, 'Ae. *īsig*', 438; Stanley, 'Poetic Diction', 440.

[136] Holthausen, 'Zum *Beowulf* (v. 33)', 82; Trautmann, 'Auch zum *Beowulf*', 151; Krogmann, 'Ae. *īsig*', 184; Liberman, 'The "Icy" Ship'.

[137] Schaubert, *Heyne–Schückings 'Beowulf'*, 2:20; Liberman, 'The "Icy" Ship', 184–5.

[138] Bähr, 'Altenglisch *īsig*'.

[139] Emendations are put forward in Trautmann, 'Zum *Beowulf*', 127; Holthausen, 'Zum *Beowulf* (v. 33)'; Trautmann, 'Auch zum *Beowulf*'; Grienberger, 'Bemerkungen'; Hollander, '*Beowulf* 33'; Krogmann, 'Ae. *īsig*'; Liberman, 'The "Icy" Ship'.

[140] Of the icefree readings, only the observation that words for ice and iron are frequently confused in the Germanic languages is worth mentioning (Liberman, 'The "Icy" Ship', 191–2), but the convergence was not so strong in Old English that the poet or scribe would not have used *isern* if he had meant to.

[141] John M. Kemble, ed., *The Anglo-Saxon Poems of 'Beowulf', 'The Travellers Song' and 'The Battle of Finnesburh'*, 2nd ed., 2 vols (London: Pickering, 1835–7), 2:2.

[142] Meissner, *Kenningar*, 151–2.

[143] Stanley, 'Poetic Diction', 440–1.

[144] Liberman, 'The "Icy" Ship', 186–7.

Lehmann too claims that ice connoted death and mourning in early Anglo-Saxon England. Since his evidence relies on some of Wolfgang Krause's more dubious runological investigations, however, it does not hold up to scrutiny. Krause, having studied the inscription on the Niezdrowice urn, identifies a single vertical stroke as the ice-rune ⎮ and a series of ladder-like symbols as elaborate forms of the hail-rune ᚻ. With reference to the hostile connotations of these concepts in the Icelandic *Rune Poem* and the funerary function of the urn in question, Krause concludes that they served to curse anyone disturbing the grave, but above all to prevent the dead from returning as revenants.[145] Indeed, he speculates elsewhere that the ice-rune 'is probably the rune of Hel, the cold goddess of the dead'.[146] Lehmann's contribution has been to adduce these conjectures in the context of Scyld's funeral and propose for *isig* the reading 'dedicated through appropriate rites for its funeral function'.[147]

The problems with the Krause–Lehmann reading should be apparent. It is doubtful whether the Niezdrowice inscription contains any runes at all;[148] in such a context, a single upright stroke could mean anything or nothing. The association with Hel is not explained. However, it must depend on an understanding of stanza 9 of the Icelandic *Rune Poem*,[149] which may here briefly be examined for its winter imagery. The stanza in question reads as follows:

> ⎮ er árbörkr   ok unnar þak
> ok feigra manna fár.   (st. 9)

Ice is river's bark and wave's roof and a danger to doomed men.

The first two of these three definitions are neutral comparative descriptions of what ice is like. The third too is an objective observation, but it furthermore serves to associate ice with treachery and death. As will be seen in the following chapter, these are common saga associations of winter in general and ice in particular. Krause invests the description with cultic meaning, however, when he adds to its common-sense instrumental reading (ice is a means of death) an attributive understanding: ice *belongs* to death and thus to Hel. One could make a case for this reading if one chose to read the last word of the above stanza with a short vowel (which Krause does not),

---

[145] Wolfgang Krause, 'Die Inschrift auf der Urne von Niesdrowitz', *Altschlesien* 6 (1936): 239–53.

[146] 'Sie ist wohl die Rune der kalten Totengöttin Hel'; Wolfgang Krause, *Runeninschriften im älteren Futhark*, Schriften der Königsberger Gelehrten Gesellschaft, Geisteswissenschaftliche Klasse 13.4 (Halle: Niemeyer, 1937), 498.

[147] Lehmann, '*Beowulf* 33'.

[148] R. I. Page, 'The Use of Double Runes in Old English Inscriptions', in *Runes and Runic Inscriptions: Collected Essays on Anglo-Saxon and Viking Runes* (1962; Woodbridge: Boydell, 1995), 96.

[149] R. I. Page, ed., *The Icelandic Rune-Poem* (London: Viking Society for Northern Research / University College London, 1999).

yielding 'ice is the path of doomed men',[150] which could be understood to refer to the road to hell. Long vowel or short, however, it remains far more in the spirit of the *Rune Poem* to accept the assertion's more obvious sense only: ice is a treacherous surface on which to walk. Such mythological and ritual meaning as Krause and Lehmann add to this understanding is unwarranted.

The sensible majority view therefore remains that *isig* should be read as 'covered with ice'. Although scholars may have felt confirmed in their emendations by the paucity of attestations for *isig*, existing parallels make a strong case not only for understanding the word in this sense, but also for understanding the seasonality of the passage as the static type. The only other simplex occurrence of *isig* is found in the passage from Blickling Homily 16 referred to above. As noted, this vision of hell describes a scene of *hrimige bearwas* ('rimy groves'), subsequently called *isige bearwas* ('icy groves'), overhanging a cliff; sinners are suspended from these trees. The alternation between *hrimig* and *isig* strongly suggests that the trees should be understood as covered with either rime or ice, not just cold or gleaming as some have understood *isig* in the context of Scyld's funeral. At the same time, the fact that these trees have a penitentiary function makes clear that the element of winter is not just there because St Paul experiences his vision at the wrong time of year. Instead, this is a timeless environment of punitive winter. The corresponding passage in *Beowulf*, Hrothgar's description of the pool of monsters, is of the same nature. The king describes the pool in its unchanging form, overhung by *hrinde bearwas* ('rimy groves'). Both in the homily and in the poem, the wintry aspect of the setting contributes to the mood of the place, a mood of terror. Winter is a universal trigger, hardwired into our associative taxonomy because its survival requires vigilance. Authors of infernal visions such as the Blickling homily knew to tap this connection, and the *Beowulf* poet recognized its potential for his monstrous landscapes. He uses similar imagery for Scyld's funeral because winter imagery is equally appropriate to mourning, as its role in the elegies makes clear. The image does not serve a seasonal plot structure; though strictly literal, its real value lies in its associations.

Hostile Categories in Old Norse Literature

As has been observed, saga authors were little given to the description of landscape except where it affects the action, for instance as the setting of a battle.[151] On the other hand, myth and legend firmly associate winter with real and imagined social groups peripheral to society, specifically the giants

---

[150] Ibid., 28, n. to stanza 9.
[151] See Schach, 'The Anticipatory Literary Setting in the Old Icelandic Family Sagas', and the cursory observations in Hallberg, *The Icelandic Saga*, 71; Pearsall and Salter, *Landscapes and Seasons*, 45; O'Donoghue, *Old Norse–Icelandic Literature*, 59–60.

and the Finnar or Sami. These categories may be found in a few genres and are firmly associated with definite landscape categories or geographical locales. Giants were thought to inhabit the mountains, a landscape of perpetual or near-perpetual winter, while their mythological associations are likewise strongly hibernal. Meanwhile, the Sami were mapped to the plains and fells of northern and north-eastern Scandinavia and associated with sorcery and winter. Thus Old Norse literature reveals a grouping of hostile categories much like that of the Old English poetic tradition, but allocating dangerous creatures to the mountains and the hibernal north-east rather than the sea and the marsh.

GIANTS

Jǫtnar and other categories of giant[152] are widely represented in early Scandinavian narrative. It is difficult to establish their representation in carved illustrations of the preliterary period,[153] but they are attested in literature from the earliest datable texts to stories from modern times.[154] A taxonomy of giant categories will not be attempted here, but it may be noted that traits applied with considerable consistency include large body height and consequent intimidation.[155] The most consistent quality accompanying giants in the literature, however, may be the dysfunctionality between them and the society, human or superhuman, central to a narrative.[156]

Associations of *jǫtnar*, *þursar*, and *risar* with winter are most consistent in the eddic sources, although the poetry never explains the connection. The term *hrímþurs* ('rime giant') is the clearest indication of its existence, occurring in four of the mythological poems. In its account of first things, *Vafþrúðnismál* identifies Aurgelmir, patriarch of the *jǫtnar*, as a *hrímþurs* and a *jǫtunn*:[157]

---

[152] In Scandinavian studies, the word *giant* hides a plurality of overlapping terms and concepts. See especially Katja Schulz, *Riesen: Von Wissenshütern und Wildnisbewohnern in Edda und Saga* (Heidelberg: Winter, 2004), for example the unnumbered tables on pp. 39, 51–2. For present purposes, the terminology of the texts will be followed where any consistency is found, but the term *giant* will likewise be employed as an inclusive label.

[153] Signe Horn Fuglesang, 'Iconographic Traditions and Models in Scandinavian Imagery', lecture presented at the 13th International Saga Conference, Durham and York, 6–12 August 2006, accessed 15 March 2015, http://web.archive.org/web/20080227124110/http:/www.dur.ac.uk/medieval.www/sagaconf/fuglesangekphrasis.pdf; cf. Preben Meulengracht Sørensen, 'Thor's Fishing Expedition: Towards a Dialogue between Archaeology and History of Religion', in *Words and Objects*, ed. Gro Steinsland (Oslo: Norwegian University Press, 1986), 257–78.

[154] Schulz, *Riesen*.

[155] Ibid., 62–4, 141–6.

[156] Cf. ibid., 58–9, 156–8, 173–9.

[157] Snorri understood Aurgelmir to be the name given to Ymir by the *hrímþursar* (Faulkes, *Edda*, 1:10). Cf. *Vafþrúðnismál*, st. 28, which precedes the passage here cited: 'segðu [. . .] hverr ása elztr eða Ymis niðia / yrði í árdaga' ('tell me [. . .] who among the Æsir, or among Ymir's descendants, became the eldest in days of old'). If *Ymis niðjar* is to be read as a circumlocution for *jǫtnar* or *hrímþursar*, the inference is plausible that Ymir is indeed the eldest and therefore identical with Aurgelmir.

Óðinn qvað:

> Segðu þat iþ siauanda, allz þic svinnan qveða
> oc þú, Vafðrúðnir, vitir,
> hvé sá born gat, inn baldni iotunn,
> er hann hafðit gýgiar gaman.

Vafðrúðnir qvað:

> Undir hendi vaxa qváðo hrímþursi
> mey oc mǫg saman;
> fótr við fœti gat ins fróða iotuns
> sexhǫfðaðan son. (st. 32–3)

Óðinn said, 'Tell me this seventhly – everyone says you are wise and you know, Vafþrúðnir: how did the mighty *jǫtunn* beget children, since he had no pleasure of a giantess?'

Vafþrúðnir said, 'They said that a girl and a boy grew together below the *hrímþurs*'s arms; one foot of the wise *jǫtunn* begot a six-headed son on the other'.

This suggests that all *jǫtnar* may likewise be understood to be *hrímþursar*. The difficulty with this reading is that the latter term is virtually absent from non-eddic texts,[158] leading Cleasby and Vigfusson to conclude that the *hrímþursar* are the primeval counterpart to the *jǫtnar*.[159] Such a conclusion cannot be reached on the basis of the eddic evidence itself, however, which extends the description at least to *jǫtnar* of the narrative present. Indeed, the interchangeability of the terms *hrímþurs* and *jǫtunn* is twice suggested in *Skírnismál* (sts 30, 34) and again in *Hávamál* (sts 108–9). *Jǫtnar* are further described with the adjective *hrímkaldr* ('rime-cold') in two eddic poems,[160] while the *jǫtunn* Hymnir is said to have a frozen beard (*Hymiskviða*, st. 10).

The cosmological significance of the *hrímþursar* is suggested in *Grímnismál*.[161] This text, composed before 1220,[162] distinguishes three roots below the cosmic tree Yggdrasill, each of which covers a world:

> Hel býr undir einni, annarri hrímþursar,
> þriðio mennzcir menn. (st. 31)

Hel lives below one, the *hrímþursar* below the second, humans below the third.

---

[158] An exception is found in a curse in ch. 5 of *Bósa saga* invoking several supernatural categories (Guðni Jónsson and Bjarni Vilhjálmsson, *Fornaldarsögur*, 2:474).

[159] CV, s.v. 'hrím-þursar'.

[160] *Vafþrúðnismál*, st. 21; *Fáfnismál*, st. 38: Neckel, *Edda*, 180–8. Loki's son Nari is called *hrímkaldr* in *Lokasenna* 49, 50, implying that he too counts as a *jǫtunn* (cf. *Gylfaginning*, ch. 34: Faulkes, *Edda*, 1:27).

[161] Neckel, *Edda*, 57–68.

[162] The work is extensively (and explicitly) cited in the Prose *Edda*, for example in *Gylfaginning*, chs 21, 36, 40: Faulkes, *Edda*, 1:22, 30, 33.

While it seems clear that the roots of Yggdrasill were not intended to correspond to a full survey of mythological species, the realm of the *hrímþursar* is here on equal footing with the world of humans and that of the dead, indicating a high centrality of this class within the mythological framework, much like the centrality of *jǫtnar* in the legendary sagas, *þættir*, and some further texts. Although the position in Cleasby and Vigfusson that the term refers specifically to the *jǫtnar* of an earlier era cannot be strictly proved or disproved, it is clear that all *jǫtnar* in the eddic poetry are associated with winter through their description as *hrímkaldir* and their identification with *hrímþursar*.

A second element linking the giants of the eddic material with winter receives even less clarification than the term *hrímþursar*. In *Hymiskviða*, the gods, insisting that Ægir should host their next party, are told to fetch him a large cauldron. Þórr's companion[163] offers a solution to this problem in the following words:

> Býr fyr austan Élivága
> hundvíss Hymir, at himins enda;
> á minn faðir móðugr ketil,
> rúmbrugðinn hver, rastar diúpan. (st. 5)

> East of Élivágar lives the very wise Hymir, at the end of heaven; my bold father has a kettle, an enormous cauldron, a mile deep.

Hymir is expressly identified as a *jǫtunn*.[164] His association with winter in this passage resides in his residence 'fyr austan Élivága'. The compound noun *élivágar*, which likewise occurs in stanza 31 of *Vafþrúðnismál*, Snorri's derivative episode, and an *Íslendingaþáttr*,[165] translates as 'snowstorm bays' or 'hailstorm bays'.[166] Finnur Jónsson proposed reading it as a reference to the Arctic Ocean.[167] Whether or not it was so intended, there is no doubt that the term evokes a hibernal environment.

Beyond the transparent name, however, winter associations do not recur in the poetic context of the *Élivágar* reference. *Vafþrúðnismál* describes the body of water as poisonous rather than cold. Asked about Aurgelmir's origins, Vafþrúðnir responds,

---

[163] Described as 'týr' in the preceding stanza, the speaker has traditionally been identified as the mythological character Týr, although it has been more plausibly proposed in view of context and intertextual correspondences that this is the common noun meaning 'god', here referring to Loki: Marteinn Helgi Sigurðsson, 'Þórr's Travel Companion in *Hymiskviða*', *Gripla* 16 (2005): 197–208; Andy Orchard, trans., *The Elder Edda: A Book of Viking Lore* (London: Penguin, 2011), 293.
[164] *Hymiskviða*, sts 13, 14, 15, 25, 28, 30.
[165] *Bergbúa þáttr* (Þórhallur Vilmundarson and Bjarni Vilhjálmsson, *Harðar saga*, 447).
[166] Von See *et al.*, *Kommentar*, 2:288.
[167] *Lexicon Poeticum*, 2nd ed., s.v. 'Élivágar'; contrast Sveinbjörn Egilsson, ed., *Lexicon poeticum antiquæ linguæ septentrionalis* (Copenhagen: Det kongelige nordiske oldskriftselskab, 1860).

> Ór Élivágom   stucco eitrdropar,
> svá óx, unz varð ór iotunn.
> Þar órar ættir   kómo allar saman,
> því er þat æ alt til atalt.   (st. 31)

Drops of poison were sent flying from Élivágar; so it grew, until a *jǫtunn* came out of it. All our lineages met there; that is why all of it [our species] is perpetually hostile.

As in the case of the creatures' identification as *hrímþursar*, then, an association with winter weather is suggested by the word's transparent meaning but left unexplained in the texts. Although one can guess at underlying motifs and narratives, the poets who gave the eddic poetry its surviving form either did not know these or saw no reason to expound on them.

The silences in eddic cosmology seem to have been equally problematic to Snorri Sturluson when he set out to retell the myths in his thirteenth-century reference work. Time and again the Prose *Edda* gives the impression of piecing together a mythological universe from sources whose references were no clearer to Snorri than they are to modern scholars.[168] Snorri's creative influence is no less transformative where the origins of the giants are concerned. Against the cryptic creation account in *Vafþrúðnismál* presented above, Snorri placed the following explanation, following his invented account of the fiery land of Muspellsheimr:

> Gangleri mælir: 'Hversu skipaðisk áðr en ættirnar yrði eða aukaðisk mannfólkit?'
>
> Þá mælti Hár: 'Ár þær er kallaðar eru Élivágar, þá er þær váru svá langt komnar frá uppsprettunni at eitrkvikja sú er þar fylgði harðnaði svá sem sindr þat er renn ór eldinum, þá varð þat íss, ok þá er sá íss gaf staðar ok rann eigi, þá heldi yfir þannig úr þat er af stóð eitrinu ok fraus at hrími, ok jók hrímit hvert yfir annat allt í Ginnungagap'.
>
> Þá mælti Jafnhár: 'Ginnungagap, þat er vissi til norðrs ættar, fyltisk með þunga ok hǫfugleik íss ok hríms ok inn í frá úr ok gustr. En hinn syðri hlutr Ginnungagaps léttisk móti gneistum ok síum þeim er flugu ór Muspellsheimi.'
>
> Þá mælti Þriði: 'Svá sem kalt stóð af Niflheimi ok allir hlutir grimmir, svá var þat er vissi námunda Muspelli heitt ok ljóst, en Ginnungagap var svá hlætt sem lopt vindlaust. Ok þá er mœttisk hrímin ok blær hitans svá at bráðnaði ok draup, ok af þeim kvikudropum kviknaði með krapti þess er til sendi hitann, ok varð manns líkandi, ok var sá nefndr Ymir. En hrímþursar kalla hann Aurgelmi, ok eru þaðan komnar ættir hrímþursa, svá sem segir í Vǫluspá hinni skǫmmu.'   (*Gylfaginning*, ch. 5)[169]

Gangleri said, 'How was mankind created and how did they increase their numbers before the blood lines came about?'

---

[168] Cf. Faulkes, *Edda*, 1:xxvi–xxiii.
[169] Ibid., 1:9–10.

Then Hár said, 'When the rivers that are called the *Élivágar* had come so far from their source that the poisonous foam that accompanied them solidified like slag flying from a fire, they turned to ice. When the ice settled in one place and did not flow, the poison that came from it kept going across it in the same direction and froze into rime, and the rime accumulated all across Ginnungagap, one layer over another.'

Then Jafnhár said, 'Ginnungagap, the part that faces north, was filled with the weight and heaviness of ice and rime, and a drizzling rain and wind came into it. But the southern part of Ginnungagap was brightened by the sparks and molten particles that came flying from Muspellsheimr.'

Then said Þriði, 'Just as cold and all fierce things proceeded from Niflheimr, so the side that was near Muspell was hot and bright, but Ginnungagap was as mild as a windless sky. And then the rime and the warm breeze met so that it melted and dripped; and something took on life from those drops of foam through the power that the heat gave it, and it took on the likeness of a man, and he was called Ymir. But the *hrímþursar* call him Aurgelmir, and all the lines of the *hrímþursar* are descended from him, as it says in the shorter *Vǫluspá*.'

The transformation of the myth, for which Snorri cites only *Vafþrúðnismál*, st. 31 (quoted above) as a source, is considerable. Firstly, Snorri identifies Élivágar as a group of rivers rather than an open body of water, a reinterpretation suggested to him by the plural form of the name. More significantly, he sets up a geographical system of climate zones reminiscent of that found in the learned culture of medieval Europe.[170] In the south, he locates a land of fire called Muspellsheimr, somewhat like the equatorial belt that was considered impassable for its great heat. This land has no topographical precedent in eddic mythology and seems to derive only from the eddic character Muspellr conflated with Surtr and his flaming sword.[171] In the north, Snorri situates a land of frost named Niflheimr,[172] similar to the polar belt of learned tradition. In between, the two extremes mingle, resulting in a temperate climate thay may be compared to the conventional northern temperate zone that included Europe.[173] Significantly, however, while Snorri retains the poisonous drops of *Vafþrúðnismál*, st. 31, he includes them as a detail in an origin myth that has a definite focus on a polar climate. Although both heat and cold participate in the formation of the *hrímþursar*, heat is presented as a facilitator and the origin of life, while the actual substance from which the first man is formed is poisonous

---

[170] For a discussion of this tradition from a Scandinavian perspective, see Rudolf Simek, *Altnordische Kosmographie: Studien und Quellen zu Weltbild und Weltbeschreibung in Norwegen und Island vom 12. bis zum 14. Jahrhundert*, Ergänzungsbände zum Reallexikon der Germanischen Altertumskunde 4 (Berlin and New York: De Gruyter, 1990), 131–43.

[171] See *Vǫluspá*, sts 51, 52; cf. *Lokasenna*, st. 42.

[172] With this name cf. *Niflhel* in *Vafþrúðnismál*, st. 43 and *Baldrs draumar*, st. 2: Neckel, *Edda*, 277–9.

[173] Isidore of Seville, *De natura rerum* 10: Fontaine, *Traité de la nature*, 209–13; Bede, *De temporum ratione*, ch. 34: Jones, *De temporum ratione*, 386–91.

rime: 'something took on life from those drops of foam through the power that the heat gave it'.[174]

Although the possibility cannot strictly be excluded that Snorri drew on non-extant sources, written or oral, in addition to the known poetry, comparison between *Gylfaginning* and the surviving poetry suggests that very little such external borrowing took place in the creation of this work.[175] His handling of the *hrímþurs* material strengthens this hypothesis. Firstly, the origin of the *hrímþursar* from actual *hrím* ('rime') forms a convenient explanation of their name, suggesting that either Snorri or his source considered their designation as such aetiological. Such a conclusion seems natural if no other sources were consulted. Secondly, Snorri seems to have thought that the water from the Élivágar had to freeze once it was sufficiently far removed from the source that set it in motion. This suggests, again, that either he or his source was led by the transparent name to give the rivers a hibernal setting. Thus although the prose version of this origin myth has a far greater reliance on winter imagery than the succinct account in *Vafþrúðnismál*, all these winter elements are to some extent implicit in the poetry. Accordingly, winter was considered a crucial aspect of the giants of eddic tradition both when the eddic poetry was written and in the early-thirteenth-century context in which Snorri wrote his Prose *Edda*. Their mythological origin seems to have played a role in this connection.

The giants' intrinsic association with winter is compounded by their mountain habitat, a landscape itself connotative of winter by virtue of its high altitude. Kennings for giant affirm this connection through such forms as *bergbúi* ('mountain-dweller'), *bergstjóri* ('mountain-ruler'), and *bjargálfr* ('mountain-elf'),[176] making clear that the association was understood to be part of the conceptual world of poetry. A number of prose texts likewise make this connection.[177] These characteristic antagonists of Old Norse literature thus connote a hostile domain associated with winter both because they inhabit the frozen summits and because they seem to originate from an environment of rime and ice.

SAMI

If social categories thus far have been delineated exclusively on the evidence of narrative literature, the Finnar ('Sami', occasionally hard to distinguish from Finnar, 'Finns')[178] make the occasional appearance in legal texts. Rather

---

[174] 'Af þeim kvikudropum kviknaði með krapti þess er til sendi hitann' (11).
[175] Cf. Sigurður Nordal, *Snorri Sturluson* (Helgafell: Víkingsprent, 1973), 90–8.
[176] For an index, see Meissner, *Kenningar*, 256–8.
[177] For example *Gylfaginning* (Faulkes, *Edda*, 1:39); *Fljótsdœla saga*, ch. 5: Jón Jóhannesson, *Austfirðinga sǫgur*, 225–6.
[178] For the historical distinction, see Clive Tolley, *Shamanism in Norse Myth and Magic*, 2 vols, Folklore Fellows' Communications, 296–7 (Helsinki: Suomalainen tiedeakatemia, 2009), 1:39–43.

than prescribe their role in legal dealings, however, law codes mention the Sami only for their association with the winter activity of skiing. In the Icelandic law code known as *Grágás*, the context is an oath pronounced by a court official to confirm a truce between two parties. The text is particularly concerned with the prevention of future hostilities between the parties involved, and it warns that any further disagreements must be settled with compensation rather than armed conflict. It then adds the following:

> En sa yckaʀ er gengr a gørvar sáttir eða vegr aveíttar trygðir, þa scal hann sva viða vargr rækr oc rekiɴ sem menn viðazt varga reka, cristnir menn kirkior søkia, heiðnir menn hof blóta, elldr upp breɴʀ, iorð grør, mögr moðor callar, oc moþir mög föðir, alldir ellda kyɴda, scip scriðr, scildir blícia, sol scíɴ, snæ leɢr, fiðr scríðr, fura vex, valr flygr várlangan dag (stendr honom byʀ beiɴ undir báða vængi), himiɴ huerfr, heimr er bygðr, vindr þytr, vötn til sævar falla, karlar korne sá; hann scal fiʀaz kirkior oc cristna menn, Guðs hus oc guma, heim huern nema hælvite.   (*Grágás*, ch. 115)[179]

> But he among you who breaks the settlement or fights in breach of the truce will be outlawed and driven away as far as men will drive outlaws, as Christians attend church, as heathens bring sacrifices, as fire burns, as the earth grows, as a boy calls for his mother and a mother raises her son, as men light fires, as the ship glides, as shields gleam, as the sun shines, as the snow falls, as the Sami skis, as the pine grows, as the hawk flies the spring-long day (a direct wind stands below both wings), as the heavens turn, as the world is inhabited, as the wind whistles, as the waters fall into the sea, as men sow grain; he will be deprived of church and Christians, of the house of God and of men, of every home with the exception of hell.

The formula was intended to express the universally binding nature of the agreement, much like the eternity oaths known from Old Frisian law codes.[180] For this purpose, it employs a wide range of truisms representing basic facts of life. Many of these describe the primary associations of everyday concepts: although Christians may do more than attend church, what sets them apart from non-Christians is that they do; and the characterization of such concepts as mothers, ships, hawks, and the sun follows the same logic. The Sami are identified as part of the same conceptual world as the other elements here listed, and skiing (or 'gliding', like the ship) is their identifying characteristic. The fact that this association is cited as a truism in legal formulas suggests that this connection was uncontroversial, as the sagas suggest that procedural error was as eagerly exploited in medieval Iceland as it is in many present-day legal systems.[181] The formula

---

[179] Vilhjálmur Finsen, *Grágás*, 1:206.
[180] See Oebele Vries, 'De âldfryske ivichheidsformule', in *Miscellanea Frisica: A New Collection of Frisian Studies*, ed. N. R. Århammar *et al.*, Fryske Akademy 634 (Assen: Van Gorcum, 1984), 89–96.
[181] For example *Njáls saga*, chs 141–4: Einar Ólafur Sveinsson, *Brennu-Njáls saga*, 374–401.

recurs in much the same form in the Staðarhóll-manuscript of *Grágás* (chs 387–8).[182] A similar formula is found in the Norwegian *Gulaþingslǫg* in fragmentary form, but the surviving lines do not contain the reference to the Sami, and the extant items in the list are different from those found in Iceland.[183] The Icelandic form of the oath, however, also appears in narrative literature: *Grettis saga* and *Heiðarvíga saga* preserve versions of the oath that are virtually identical to its form in *Grágás*.[184] The uniformity of this oath surviving in such various contexts indicates that its form was carefully preserved, while its alliterative qualities suggest that this preservation was not limited to the written medium.

Suggestions that skiing and snowshoeing are the Sami's preferred modes of transportation are similarly found in non-formulaic narratives. In *Fundinn Noregr*, for instance, discussed in Chapter 1 above (pp. 43–6), Nórr, prince of 'Finnland ok Kvenland', waits for good snow before setting out on skis to rescue his sister.[185] The related *Hversu Noregr byggðisk* tells how Nórr's father Þorri, king of Gottland, Könland, and Finnland, brings sacrifices in hopes of good skiing weather.[186] The protagonists of these texts are never identified as ethnic Sami, but their geographical associations, not to mention their governance of these regions, would have sufficed for an Icelandic audience to make this identification.[187] Expert skill at skiing is noted alongside the other accomplishments of two individual Sami in a narrative in *Haralds saga ins hárfagra* (ch. 32)[188] that is picked up again in *Óláfs saga Tryggvasonar en mesta* (ch. 3),[189] and the Sami protagonists of the prose introduction to *Vǫlundarkviða* use the same mode of transportation. The concept of Sami on skis evidently spread further south as well, as forms like *Skritfinni* and *Scridefinnas* ('gliding *or* skiing Sami') are attested in a range of non-Icelandic sources from Procopius to King Alfred and

---

[182] Vilhjálmur Finsen, ed., *Grágás: Efter det Arnamagnæanske haandskrift nr. 334 fol., Staðarhólsbók* (Copenhagen: Gyldendal, 1879), 406–7.

[183] *Gulaþingslǫg*, ch. 320: Keyser and Munch, *Norges gamle love*, 1:110.

[184] *Grettis saga*, ch. 72: Guðni Jónsson, *Grettis saga*, 231–3; *Heiðarvíga saga*, ch. 33: Sigurður Nordal and Guðni Jónsson, *Borgfirðinga sǫgur*, 312–13. All these occurrences are noted in Else Mundal, 'Coexistence of Saami and Norse Culture: Reflected in and Interpreted by Old Norse Myths', in *Old Norse Myths, Literature and Society: Proceedings of the 11th International Saga Conference, 2–7 July 2000, University of Sydney*, ed. Geraldine Barnes and Margaret Clunies Ross (Sydney: Centre for Medieval Studies, 2000), 347–8.

[185] 'Norr [. . .] beið þess, er snjó lagði á heiðar ok skíðfœri gerði gott' (ch. 1: Finnbogi Guðmundsson, *Orkneyinga saga*, 3–4).

[186] 'Hann blótuðu Kænir til þess, at snjóva gerði ok væri skíðfæri gott' (ch. 1: Guðni Jónsson and Bjarni Vilhjálmsson, *Fornaldarsögur*, 2:137).

[187] Similar implications are present in other texts. In *Ketils saga hœngs*, for instance, Brúni and his daughter Hrafnhildr are residents of Finnmǫrk, but neither is explicitly identified as a Sami. However, Hrafnhildr's appearance is large and grotesque; her father has dealings with Sami, whom he calls his friends; and Brúni's brother turns out to be Gusir, king of the Sami (ch. 3: ibid., 1:251–5).

[188] Bjarni Aðalbjarnarson, *Heimskringla*, 1:135.

[189] Ólafur Halldórsson, *Óláfs saga en mesta*, 1:8–9.

Saxo Grammaticus.[190] Needless to say, not all these authors would have understood the etymology of the word they used to refer to this northern people.[191] Its spread, however, bears witness to the enduring popularity of the term among North Germanic speakers. The identification of the Sami by their method of transportation in winter thus must have been impressively widespread and longstanding.

A second, equally persistent association of the Sami endows them with supernatural properties, particularly prophecy and sorcery.[192] Although these skills occasionally benefit a non-Sami protagonist, they are commonly condemned in one way or another. In Oddr Snorrason's *Óláfs saga Tryggvasonar*, the proto-Christian protagonist is hesitant to enlist the services of a foresighted Sami, and the unease is mutual. Óláfr's precise objections remain unexpressed as he states that seeking out people of that sort and putting one's trust in them is displeasing to him and that he disapproves of it;[193] the Sami provides more insight into the reciprocal unease with reference to the bright spirits that accompany Óláfr and the new faith that he is to introduce (ch. 19).[194] In *Vatnsdœla saga*, a Sami prophetess provides the entertainment at a party, but the scene's protagonists sit off by themselves and express no interest in her. When she offers Ingimundr an unsolicited prophecy concerning his settlement of Iceland which the saga audience will recognize as accurate, Ingimundr asserts that he wishes to learn about future events only by their coming to pass, and that he has no intention of ever visiting Iceland. A heated exchange ensues, making clear that Ingimundr will have nothing to do with the seeress (ch. 10).[195] Active sorcery is suggested in the same story when the prophetess conjures Ingimundr's talisman from Norway to the site of his future settlement (chs 10, 15).[196] She is also called *fjǫlkunnig* ('skilled in magic') outright (ch. 10),[197] an adjective similarly applied to a Sami in the poetry of *Ketils saga*

---

[190] *History of the Wars* 6.15 (Dewing 3:418–19); *Gesta Danorum* 0.2.9 (Karsten Friis-Jensen and Peter Zeeberg, eds. and trans., *Saxo Grammaticus: Gesta Danorum / Danmarkshistorien*, 2 vols. (Copenhagen: Gad, 2005), 1:82; *Widsith* 79: Krapp and Dobbie, *Exeter Book*, 149–53; the Old English *Orosius* 1.1: Bately, *Orosius*, 13; and see further the citations and discussions in R. W. Chambers, ed., *Widsith: A Study in Old English Heroic Legend* (Cambridge: Cambridge University Press, 1912), 213, commentary to line 79, and esp. Ian Whitaker, '"Scridefinnas" in *Widsið*', *Neophilologus* 66, no. 4 (October 1982): 602–8; Ian Whitaker, 'Late Classical and Early Mediaeval Accounts of the Lapps (Sami)', *Classica et mediaevalia* 34 (1983): 283–303.

[191] Certainly Paul the Deacon provides a fairly accurate etymology: L. Bethmann and Georg Waitz, eds, 'Pauli Historia Langobardorum', in *Saec. VI–IX*, Monumenta Germaniae Historica, Scriptores rerum langobardicarum et italicarum 1 (Hannover: Hahn), 54–5.

[192] The authoritative study of this attribute is Tolley, *Shamanism*.

[193] 'Leitt er mer oc litit um at hitta þesskyns menn eða þeira traust at sòkia.' Finnur Jónsson, ed., *'Saga Óláfs Tryggvasonar' af Oddr Snorrason, munk* (Copenhagen: Gad, 1932), 67.

[194] Ibid., 68–9.

[195] Einar Ólafur Sveinsson, *Vatnsdœla saga*, 28–30; cf. *Landnámabók*, ch. S179: Jakob Benediktsson, *Íslendingabók, Landnámabók*, 217–19.

[196] Einar Ólafur Sveinsson, *Vatnsdœla saga*, 41–2.

[197] Ibid., 29.

hœngs (ch. 3).[198] In *Haralds saga ins hárfagra,* Gunnhildr learns *kunnusta* ('knowledge; witchcraft') from the same two Sami that were mentioned above as being experts at skiing; she tells Eiríkr's men of their skills, which include the superhuman ability to induce earthquakes and kill with a look (ch. 34).[199] Gunnhildr next conspires with the men to have the two Sami killed, suggesting that their superhuman properties are considered offensive, or at least dangerous in view of Gunnhildr's unwillingness to marry either of them. In short, associations of Sami with objectionable sorcery are numerous in Old Norse prose, suggesting that their winter connotations are part of the same dark domain of magic and danger.[200]

Conclusions

Literary encounters between humans and the inanimate environment provide ample opportunity to convey how a culture experiences the natural world. This chapter has demonstrated that the literature of medieval northwestern Europe commonly invokes winter landscapes and associated weather types to circumscribe human society by means of a hostile outside world. The starkest oppositions between winter and society in Anglo-Saxon literature are found in Old English elegiac and heroic poetry. While Adam's lament in *Genesis B* and the paradisal description of *The Phoenix* treat winter as only one among several afflictions affecting humankind after the fall, winter storms or their symbolic referents represent a clear threat to humans in the elegiac *Ruin, Wanderer, Seafarer,* and *Wife's Lament*, as well as in Bede's sparrow simile. Heroic narratives set off individual heroes against the cold sea they traverse: texts like *Andreas* and *Beowulf* make use of the hibernal connotations of water landscapes to bring out the heroism of sea voyages and other confrontations with bodies of water. In this application, the coldwater motif is divorced from the seasonal cycle, making the open sea a landscape of permanent winter evoked regardless of narrative seasonality.

That winter could take on the guise of a hostile literary environment rather than a recurring season is confirmed by its function as one association among several of aseasonal otherly categories. In *Beowulf*, this tendency is found above all in associations between monsters, winter, and water; in Scandinavian tradition, it may be recognized in the deep-rooted association of hostile giants and dangerous Sami sorcerers with permanent

---

[198] Guðni Jónsson and Bjarni Vilhjálmsson, *Fornaldarsögur,* 1:252.
[199] Bjarni Aðalbjarnarson, *Heimskringla,* 1:135.
[200] Further study on this assocation may be found in Hermann Pálsson, *Úr landnorðri: Samar og ystu rætur íslenskrar menningar,* Studia Islandica 54 (Reykjavik: Bókmenntafræðistofnun Háskóla Íslands, 1997), which, however, does not always distinguish clearly between Sami sorcery and generic witchcraft. An index of associations of Sami with magic may be found in Boberg, *Motif-Index,* 82 (motif D1711.10.1).

landscapes of winter. Accordingly, non-sentient and therefore normally neutral surroundings are enlisted as participants in a universal conflict, whether between good and evil, a central society and its surroundings, or both. In Christian as well as more indigenously inspired literature, winter landscapes consistently side with the enemy, and it frequently takes a saint or other hero to take them on successfully. As such, they provide inspiration not only for monster stories, but also for heroic tales and explorations of the exotic.

The antagonistic connotations of winter landscapes here described demonstrate the psycho-geographical dynamics at play in Anglo-Saxon and early Scandinavian communities. Geographical features peripheral to social space become distrusted in consequence of their unfamiliarity, instilling unease in their occasional visitor. Narrative literature responds by projecting this unease back onto the landscape in a more tangible form, whether by attention to the landscape's cold and stormy features or by the allocation to these regions of a supernatural counterpart embodying the danger associated with them. In both Anglo-Saxon and early Scandinavian literature, winter proves a potent conceptual field by which authors were able to give expression to such dangers.

Winter represents only one extreme of the seasonal cycle. However, the association of winter landscapes with the hostile and supernatural suggests that Old English and Old Norse chronological narratives should concentrate encounters with these categories in episodes set in winter. The following chapter will test this hypothesis, discussing seasonal patterns in narrative and instructional texts in order to confirm the thematic identity of the winter season.

– 3 –

Winter Institutions

It was shown in the previous chapter that Anglo-Saxon and early Icelandic authors commonly invoked elements of winter without chronological intent in order to attain certain associative effects. Specifically, winter in these corpora represents the antithesis of human society: it is an uncolonized space that harbours dangers. In Old English poetry, it is especially commonly introduced in order to accentuate personal deprivation. The present chapter will put these associations to the test. If supernatural threats and solitary affliction are indeed bound up with the winter season in these traditions, narratives that cycle through the seasons should reveal a higher concentration of such themes in the cold season than in summer, while Old English poetry should describe the afflictions of the season also when a cyclical timeframe is in place.

It will be seen that this hypothesis holds up remarkably well where Old Icelandic prose is concerned. Specifically, saga narratives that cycle through the seasons frequently present winter as a time of incursions into the human domain and increased access to the supernatural. In so doing, these texts reinforce the circumscription of society while recognizing that select individuals have the power to transcend this boundary. The supernatural aspect of this seasonal concentration is particularly evident in the sagas of Icelanders, which establish an almost exclusive connection of hauntings with winter, while prophecy likewise seems to have been associated with winter evenings. In addition, Old Norse prose commonly explores themes of hostility and treachery through scenes of winter conflict.

When Old English poems describe seasonal progress, they frequently use the image of nature being bound in winter (and, in some cases, released in spring) with a connotative range between hardship and indifference. However, an annual recurrence of personal deprivation is rarely found, as so little Old English poetry is seasonally structured. For the same reason, the annual oscillation of supernatural activity found in the Scandinavian material does not occur in *Beowulf*. Accordingly, there is no evidence that the hostile connotations of cold landscapes in Old English verse developed into an explicit seasonal concentration of the monstrous; instead, this association remains implicit in the creatures' reliance on the dark of night.

Hauntings

REVENANTS

The Glámr episode of *Grettis saga*[1] is a good illustration not only of the seasonal structure of the sagas of Icelanders in general, but also of the distribution of the supernatural within the cycle of the seasons. This part of the saga is subject to a strict chronology embedded in the narrative framework. The episode tells how a wealthy and reputable farmer named Þórhallr governs the Þórhallsstaðir estate in Forsœludalr, an inland valley in northern Iceland first settled by his great-grandfather. This valley, however, is plagued by hauntings posing such a danger to Þórhallr's shepherds that he has difficulty filling the winter position. Although Þórhallr has sought the counsels of many wise men, none has been able to advise him to satisfaction.

As soon as the scene is set, the episode provides its first seasonal marker in a structure built around midsummer, the Winter Nights, Christmas, and the bright days of spring. Þórhallr is accustomed to attend the *alþingi* or general assembly, which was held annually about the time of the feast of John the Baptist.[2] During one such assembly, he puts his problem to Skapti Þóroddsson, an experienced lawspeaker and legal reformer[3] who enjoys a reputation of wisdom in *Grettis saga*[4] and plays similar roles elsewhere.[5] Skapti sets Þórhallr up with a strongly built Swedish shepherd named Glámr. Glámr is a rather unpopular man whose services would not be considered desirable were it not for his strength and courage. Þórhallr and Glámr agree on a contract commencing at a second seminal point in time, the mid-October *vetrnætr* or Winter Nights. Glámr arrives, but while the author makes much of the shepherd's antipathy to Christian ritual and his inability to get along with the farm's other residents, there is no mention of supernatural phenomena until Christmas.

On the morning of Christmas Eve, Glámr has a disagreement with Þórhallr's unnamed wife, who denies him breakfast because it is a Christian fast-day. She serves him his meal eventually, but not before prophesying that it will go badly for him if he persists in his demand. By this time, the sky has gone dark and a storm has gathered, but Glámr nevertheless takes out his flock after breakfast. The gale turns into a drifting snowstorm in the afternoon, and Glámr does not come home that night. When a search

---

[1] Chs 32–5: Guðni Jónsson, *Grettis saga*, 107–23.
[2] *Íslendingabók*, ch. 7: Jakob Benediktsson, *Íslendingabók, Landnámabók*, 15; *Grágás*, chs 19, 23: Vilhjálmur Finsen, *Grágás*, 1:37, 43.
[3] *Íslendingabók*, ch. 8: Jakob Benediktsson, *Íslendingabók, Landnámabók*, 19; Jón Jóhannesson, *Íslendinga saga*, 70–4.
[4] For example, chs 27, 51, 54: Guðni Jónsson, *Grettis saga*, 93, 163–4, 177–8.
[5] *Njáls saga*, ch. 142: Einar Ólafur Sveinsson, *Brennu-Njáls saga*, 387–90; *Valla-Ljóts saga*, ch. 5: Jónas Kristjánsson, *Eyfirðinga sǫgur*, 247.

party is launched early the next morning, they find the livestock scattered and injured by the storm, and Glámr's black corpse near a trodden patch that looks as though it has been the scene of a severe struggle. After a few frustrated attempts to bring the body back to the church, Glámr is interred in a cairn out in the valley, but that does not put him to rest. He makes his first appearance as a revenant immediately after Christmas, which here means after Epiphany, as Glámr's burial does not take place until 27 December. The hauntings take place 'náliga nætr ok daga' ('virtually night and day'), with Glámr riding the buildings almost to their breaking point. Many flee the farm, and people avoid passing through the valley if they can. By the spring, however, the fear seems to have diminished:

> Um várit fekk Þórhallr sér hjón ok gerði bú á jǫrðu sinni; tók þá at minnka aptrgangr, meðan sólargangr var mestr; leið svá fram á miðsumar.   (*Grettis saga*, ch. 33)[6]
>
> In spring, Þórhallr hired servants and took up residence on his land. The revenant hauntings then began to grow less potent as the course of the sun was at its longest; so it continued until midsummer.

This brings the year full circle. Although Glámr's struggle with the harmful spirit seem to have put an end to the original problem, his own restlessness is equally undesirable, sending Þórhallr back to square one.

The second cycle follows much the same pattern, though told in less detail and with less condemning character description. After midsummer, Þórhallr learns of the arrival of another foreigner, Þorgautr, in need of a job. The two come to an agreement and Þorgautr takes up his new position at the Winter Nights. By this point in the narrative, Glámr's visitations are nightly, but Þorgautr appears in no way disturbed by them. On Christmas Eve, the shepherd again sets out with his flock, following another prophetic exchange with the farmer's wife, though there is now no expression of ill-will. It is an especially cold day and there is a severe snowstorm. By the time of the evening mass, Þorgautr has not returned, but the churchgoers refuse to carry out a search at night, since this is when malevolent beings control the valley. After breakfast the next day, the shepherd is found near Glámr's mound, his neck broken along with every bone in his body. They bury him in the churchyard, and he does not return. Glámr, by contrast, intensifies his hauntings after Christmas to such an extent that no animal is now able to cross the valley alive. By this time, everyone flees, including the farmer and his wife. Again, however, we are told that 'when spring came on and the course of the sun was at its longest, the revenant hauntings diminished considerably' (ch. 33),[7] allowing Þórhallr to return. A third cycle is signalled by the return

---

[6] Guðni Jónsson, *Grettis saga*, 113.
[7] 'Er váraði ok sólargangr var sem mestr, létti heldr aptrgǫngunum' (ibid., 115).

of hauntings in autumn, and this is where the narrative joins up with the saga's protagonist.

Many of the details of Grettir's encounter with Glámr need not be revisited here, but it is important to mention the chronological and seasonal aspects of the episode. This third iteration of the cycle omits the midsummer hire: instead, Grettir is visiting relatives in the region during the days leading up to the Winter Nights, and the nearby hauntings are the topic of constant discussion. The matter arouses Grettir's interest, and he resolves to go and see Glámr for himself. Thus Grettir arrives at Þórhallsstaðir around the time of the Winter Nights. To Grettir's disappointment, nothing happens the first night. When he stays for a second night, however, his horse is found dead and badly mauled in the morning. The third night satisfies Grettir's curiosity: Glámr arrives, rides the building for a long while and then enters it, triggering a fight with Grettir that recalls Beowulf's encounter with Grendel. Following the revenant's defeat, the question of further hauntings is not explicitly addressed, as the focus is now on Grettir's fame. Since the episode's conflict consists in the hauntings, however, and the Forsœludalr narrative is here brought to an end, Grettir's victory must represent its resolution.

The seasonal associations implicit in the narrative are clear. Although the valley is categorically described as haunted ('þar var reimt mjǫk', ch. 32),[8] supernatural events are reduced to a minimum in summer ('meðan sólargangr var mestr', ch. 33).[9] At this time of year, Þórhallr has no difficulty travelling and farming; this is also when he recruits new staff.[10] Even after the midwinter of the second cycle, when the hauntings reach their peak and all livestock in the valley dies off, the farmer evidently feels it is safe to return in the spring, even though he now has great difficulty hiring staff (ch. 33).[11] The story's basic arc of suspense thus runs from the Winter Nights, when the challenger arrives, to the coming of spring, when the intensity of the horror dissipates. In the first two cycles, a climax is reached on Christmas Eve, but no full denouement follows because the central conflict remains, and the hauntings intensify further after Christmastide. Grettir's visit breaks the pattern inasmuch as Grettir does not stay until Christmas but resolves the conflict immediately, around the Winter Nights, thereby cutting short the chronology set up by the two preliminary confrontations.

---

[8] 'The place was severely haunted' (ibid., 108).
[9] 'While the course of the sun was at its longest' (ibid., 113). Likewise on p. 115, 'er váraði ok sólargangr var sem mestr' ('when spring came on and the course of the sun was at its longest').
[10] The reference to the hiring of staff should be read in the context of the annual *fardagar* or Moving Days taking place in the seventh week of the summer half-year (i.e. around the beginning of June), when servants could seek new employment (*Grágás*, ch. 78: Vilhjálmur Finsen, *Grágás*, 1:128–9).
[11] Guðni Jónsson, *Grettis saga*, 115.

An analogous narrative in *Hávarðar saga Ísfirðings*, whose hauntings are not repeated in successive years, likewise has the struggle take place in autumn but without mention of the Winter Nights (ch. 2).[12] This text has been dated to the first half of the fourteenth century[13] and is thus contemporary with *Grettis saga*; similarities in plot suggest that the temporal setting may have been borrowed by the compiler of whichever text came last or assigned before the two known versions were written down. Given the traditional primacy of the Christmas setting, which also occurs in the first two cycles of the Glámr haunting, it may be tentatively supposed that the episode in *Hávarðar saga* is derivative of that in *Grettis saga*. Since a third full cycle survives in the analogous hauntings of *Grettis saga* (ch. 64) and in *Hrólfs saga kraka*, while cognate folktales recorded in modern times similarly resolve the conflict on Christmas Eve,[14] it may be assumed that the compiler of *Grettis saga* likewise was working with a pre-existing tale involving a third full cycle, which he redacted to accommodate the life and circumstances of Grettir. Even in the surviving narrative, however, winter is explicitly the season for hauntings, while summer represents a time of relief, recovery (expressed in the hiring of regular staff), and anticipation (signalled by the recruitment of sturdy shepherds for the winter season).

The related cycle of light and dark features just as prominently as that of summer and winter. After Þorgautr goes missing on Christmas Eve, churchgoers say they will not venture out into the dominion of evil powers at night,[15] but no such protest is reported when a search party sets out at daytime the next day. Although the previous year's refusal is decidedly less metaphysical when the snowstorm is cited alongside the dark of evening as a reason to postpone the search,[16] the decision nevertheless confirms a pattern in which people do not leave the farm grounds at night. Glámr's first postmortem appearances are likewise by night. They soon become a matter of 'virtually night and day' ('náliga nætr ok daga'),[17] but the adverb *náliga* still limits their spread in time, implying a concentration at night. In fact, daylight at this latitude is limited to four hours about the time of Epiphany (Julian or Gregorian),[18] so that the phrase *náliga nætr ok daga* applies equally well to the spread of darkness across the day as it does to the temporal extent of Glámr's hauntings. What is more, the haunted valley

---

[12] Björn K. Þórólfsson and Guðni Jónsson, *Vestfirðinga sǫgur*, 297–9.
[13] Ibid., lxxxix–xc.
[14] See below, pp. 123–5.
[15] 'Tíðamenn [. . .] sǫgðusk eigi mundu hætta sér út í trollahendr um nætr' (Guðni Jónsson, *Grettis saga*, 114).
[16] Ibid., 111–12.
[17] Ibid., 113.
[18] At 65°17', the approximate northern latitude of Þórhallsstaðir: Guðni Jónsson, *Grettis saga*, map 'Húnavatnsþing', facing p. 408; Jonathan Scott, 'EarthTools', August 2005, accessed 15 March 2015, http://www.earthtools.org.

goes by the name *Forsœludalr* ('shaded valley')[19] in recognition of the fact that its winters are particularly dark on account of the hills surrounding it to the east, west, and south: the sun, which at this latitude barely skims across the horizon in winter even in the absence of mountains, is here out of sight for several months of the year.[20] The supernatural potential of such valleys is demonstrated by the analogous usage of this type of location in the folktale *Gullbrá og Skeggi*, where just such a setting becomes the chosen residence of the witch Gullbrá.[21] On the whole, however, nighttime remains the time of Glámr's activity both in the Þorgautr cycle and during Grettir's visit. The dark is thus Glámr's exclusive domain, and it seems likely that its prevalence in winter and relative absence in summer go some length towards explaining his seasonal conduct.

The Christmas hauntings in the Glámr episode of *Grettis saga* have a counterpart in the Sandhaugar episode of chapters 64 to 66, a subplot again containing distinct parallels to the central narrative of *Beowulf*. Although this section does not trace supernatural developments through the various times of year, nocturnal winter hauntings are again manifested in three successive years, now consistently on Christmas Eve. Further parallels with the Glámr episode may be found in Grettir's active seeking out of the confrontation (ch. 64) and in details of the fight, such as the phrase 'allt þat, sem fyrir þeim varð, brutu þau'[22] and the progression from indoors to outdoors (ch. 65). While there is thus little doubt that the two episodes within *Grettis saga* derive from a common source, the repeated concentration of the motif around Christmas Eve makes clear that it concerns a deliberate association with this point on the calendar. A third episode highlighting Grettir's interest in supernatural confrontations is chapter 18 on the revenant of Kárr *inn gamli*,[23] an episode that shares some characteristics with the Sandhaugar narrative as well as with Beowulf's confrontation with Grendel's mother.[24] This part of the saga does not place the same emphasis on seasonal patterns as the other episodes, but it is made clear at the end of the chapter that the confrontation must have taken place in winter, before Christmas.[25] Here too, night is governed by the revenant, while daytime

---

[19] Kristian Kålund, *Bidrag til en historisk-topografisk Beskrivelse af Island*, 2 vols (Copenhagen: Gyldendal, 1877–82), 2:42; Fritzner, s.v. 'forsœla'.

[20] Kålund, *Beskrivelse af Island*, 2:42; cf. Guðni Jónsson, *Grettis saga*, map 'Húnavatnsþing', facing p. 408. Regarding the experiential implications of such extended darkness, see Procopius's *History of the Wars* 6.15 (Dewing 3.414–18); Árni Björnsson, *Saga daganna*, 431–2.

[21] Jón Árnason, ed., *Íslenzkar þjóðsögur og ævintýri*, 2nd ed., rev. Árni Böðvarsson and Bjarni Vilhjálmsson, 6 vols (Reykjavik: Bókaútgáfan þjóðsaga, 1954–61), 1:142.

[22] 'They broke all that was in their way' (Guðni Jónsson, *Grettis saga*, 212); cf. ch. 35, 'allt brotnaði, þat sem fyrir varð' ('all broke that was in their way', 120).

[23] Ibid., 56–61.

[24] A. R. Taylor, 'Two Notes on *Beowulf*', *Leeds Studies in English* 7–8 (1052): 13–14; R. McConchie, 'Grettir Ásmundarson's Fight with Kárr the Old: A Neglected *Beowulf* Analogue', *English Studies* 63, no. 6 (1982): 481–6.

[25] Guðni Jónsson, *Grettis saga*, 61.

is the human domain: although Grettir first observes the hauntings late at night, he waits until the morning before investigating the grave-mound.[26] Further Christmas conflicts in *Grettis saga* consist in his fight with a bear (ch. 21)[27] and an attack by twelve berserks (ch. 19).[28] In short, *Grettis saga* presents winter in general and Christmas in particular as a time of hostile incursions into the human domain.

The seasonal pattern of these episodes from *Grettis saga* is found again in *Eyrbyggja saga*. Chapter 34 of this work tells how Þórólfr *bægifótr*, who has died and been firmly (*rammlega*) interred in a cairn in the previous chapter, will not lie still.[29] It is again specifically after sunset that one cannot venture outside in safety. Livestock and a shepherd roaming too close to the cairn do not survive; when the shepherd's body is found, it is black like Glámr's corpse and all its bones are broken, as with Glámr's victims. The seasonal sequence commences with autumn, which is announced just as the shepherd goes missing. At this point in the narrative, noises are heard and the buildings are frequently ridden at night. When winter sets in, Þórólfr begins to appear in person to residents of the farm, causing injuries, nervous breakdowns, and deaths. As in the Glámr episode of *Grettis saga*, the hauntings intensify in the course of the winter, leading to the evacuation of all the farms in the valley, while those who are killed join in the hauntings. In spring, however, Þórólfr's body is dug up and moved out of the valley to a distant headland, where he causes no further trouble. Although this measure could not have been undertaken any earlier, since the ground had been frozen, there is again a contrast between winter, when hauntings cause the valley to be abandoned altogether, and spring, when nothing prevents the farmers from returning and digging up the culprit's body.

Somewhat further on in *Eyrbyggja saga* (chs 51–5),[30] another set of supernatural phenomena is described. These begin with a rain of blood one late afternoon during the haymaking season, after which a woman named Þórgunna falls sick, leading to her death a few days later. Hauntings begin when the execution of certain stipulations in her will is either hindered or neglected. Her first appearance takes place during the transportation

---

[26] Ibid., 57. The grave robberies in *Bárðar saga* and *Harðar saga* follow a similar pattern both in time of day and on the seasonal level: although in both texts the plan of the raid is first announced during Christmas Eve feasting, it is not carried out until the spring, and at daytime (*Bárðar saga Snæfellsáss*, chs 18–21: Þórhallur Vilmundarson and Bjarni Vilhjálmsson, *Harðar saga*, 160–70; *Harðar saga*, chs 14–15: ibid., 38–44). In *Hervarar saga ok Heiðreks*, by contrast, a burial mound is raided at nighttime (ch. 4: Turville-Petre, *Hervarar saga ok Heiðreks*, 13–22); so also *Hrómundar saga Gripssonar*, ch. 4: Guðni Jónsson and Bjarni Vilhjálmsson, *Fornaldarsögur*, 2:276; *Gull-Þóris saga*, ch. 3: Þórhallur Vilmundarson and Bjarni Vilhjálmsson, *Harðar saga*, 183–6; Saxo Grammaticus, *Gesta Danorum*, 3.3.8: Friis-Jensen and Zeeberg, *Gesta Danorum*, 1:204.

[27] Guðni Jónsson, *Grettis saga*, 73–8. The Christmas reference is present in the majority of manuscripts but lacking in the authoritative AM 551 A, 4to. See n. 3 on p. 75 of the edition.

[28] Ibid., 61–71.

[29] Einar Ólafur Sveinsson and Matthías Þórðarson, *Eyrbyggja saga*, 92–5.

[30] Ibid., 139–52.

of her corpse and seems intended to facilitate its removal to Skálaholt in accordance with her will. Afterwards, however, mysterious events take place at Fróðá where Þórgunna had lived. A shepherd comes home distraught and dies two weeks into the winter half-year, after which he takes up haunting, and several further members of the household die, at least one of which joins the shepherd on his nightly visits. Furthermore, supernatural seals appear and consume the farm's store of stockfish (ch. 53).[31] Þóroddr *skattkaupandi*, the Fróðá farmer, dies in a shipwreck with his men and all take up haunting at Fróðá. The timing of this event must be close to Christmas, because Christmas ale is served at the men's memorial service at which their revenants make their first appearance. Although the narrator remarks that attending one's own memorial service was considered a favourable omen in these early days of Christianity, the remaining residents become uneasy about the men's nightly visits, particularly when they continue beyond the duration of the funerary feast. Indeed, they persist throughout the Christmas season, and there is report of more deaths and additional supernatural phenomena, as well as an intensification of the pantry hauntings (ch. 54).[32] As with the hauntings in *Grettis saga*, there is a climax at Christmas and a further intensification around the time of the traditional midwinter, just after Epiphany. This time, the resolution occurs on Candlemas Eve (1 February). A priest oversees a tripartite purging, consisting in a legal element (a door-summonsing of the dead), a hygienic element (the burning of their possessions), and religious measures (singing mass and taking confessions). This puts an end to all trouble. The episode concludes with a final seasonal reference when Kjartan Þóroddsson, owner of the farm after his father's death, hires new staff in spring. No further hauntings are mentioned, and Kjartan lives at Fróðá for a long time afterwards (ch. 55).[33]

The connection thus established between hauntings and winter is sufficiently common in the sagas of Icelanders to be considered a literary topos within the genre;[34] in fact, it is so strong that it has potential for reverse application, wintertime connoting hauntings and the supernatural. Not all hauntings occur at this time of year, of course, and not all are given a seasonal chronology at all. In *Laxdœla saga*, for instance, Guðrún Ósvífrsdóttir encounters her dead husband Þorkell Eyjólfsson in Holy Week, on the day of his drowning. This episode employs another motif,

---

[31] Ibid., 146–7.
[32] Ibid., 148–50.
[33] Ibid., 152.
[34] See also Mary Danielli, 'Initiation Ceremonial from Norse Literature', *Folk-Lore* 56, no. 2 (1945): 29–41; Richard Neal Coffin, '*Beowulf* and its Relationship to Norse and Finno-Ugric Beliefs and Narratives' (unpublished doctoral thesis, Boston University, 1962), 147–8; Andy Orchard, *Pride and Prodigies: Studies in the Monsters of the 'Beowulf'-Manuscript*, rev. ed. (Toronto: University of Toronto Press, 2003), 153–4.

that of the instant or near-instant supernatural notification of the death of a loved one or relative.[35] Naturally, the timing of such notifications depends on the time of death, so there is no occasion for seasonal motifs beyond the seasonal distribution of death. However, the pattern associating hauntings with winter is remarkably consistent. Another episode in *Laxdœla saga* relates the hauntings of Víga-Hrappr Sumarliðason, without reference to the seasons at first (ch. 17),[36] but his final appearance and disposal take place one evening in winter (ch. 24).[37] In *Flóamanna saga*, a revenant haunts a farm 'um veturinn' ('in winter') and is neutralized through decapitation 'eina nótt' ('one night') in the same season in chapter 13.[38] Chapter 22 of this work tells how Þorgils Þórðarson and his men are shipwrecked off Greenland because Þorgils refuses to serve Þórr following his conversion. The Greenlandic episode begins a week before the start of winter and describes hauntings commencing on Christmas Day and deaths related to these hauntings taking place between 26 December and mid-Gói (early March in the Julian year).[39] Another Greenlandic narrative, this one in *Eiríks saga rauða*, tells of a foreboding vision and subsequent deaths and revenant hauntings following an epidemic in early winter (ch. 6).[40] In the Bǫðvarr section of *Hrólfs saga kraka*, a beast assails Hrólfr's court annually on Christmas Eve (ch. 23).[41] *Egils saga einhenda* has a vulture carry off the king's daughter on Christmas Day (ch. 2).[42] Attacks on the human domain thus frequently take place in winter, and especially at Christmas.

Episode		Timing
Egils saga einhenda, ch. 2:	vulture	Christmas Day
Eiríks saga rauða, ch. 6:	epidemic	Winter
Eyrbyggja saga, ch. 34:	Þórólfr *bægifótr*	Autumn to spring
Eyrbyggja saga, chs 51–5:	Fróðá	Haymaking/start of winter to Candlemas
Flóamanna saga, ch. 13:	revenant	Autumn(?) to winter
Flóamanna saga, ch. 22:	marooning	Start of winter to mid-Gói
Grettis saga, ch. 18:	Kárr *inn gamli*	Before Christmas

---

[35] Cf., for example, *Gunnlaugs saga*, ch. 13: Sigurður Nordal and Guðni Jónsson, *Borgfirðinga sǫgur*, 104–5. For a discussion of this and related motifs, see Georgia Dunham Kelchner, *Dreams in Old Norse Literature and their Affinities in Folklore* (Cambridge: Cambridge University Press, 1935), 62–72; for an index of motifs of divination, see Boberg, *Motif-Index*, 83–6 (motifs D1810–25).
[36] Einar Ólafur Sveinsson, *Laxdœla saga*, 39–40.
[37] Ibid., 68–9.
[38] Þórhallur Vilmundarson and Bjarni Vilhjálmsson, *Harðar saga*, 255–6.
[39] Ibid., 282–5.
[40] Einar Ólafur Sveinsson and Matthías Þórðarson, *Eyrbyggja saga*, 214–17.
[41] D. Slay, ed., *Hrólfs saga kraka*, Editiones Arnamagnæanæ B 1 (Copenhagen: Munksgaard, 1960), 78.
[42] Åke Lagerholm, ed., *Drei 'lygisǫgur': 'Egils saga einhenda ok Ásmundar berserkjabana', 'Ála flekks saga', 'Flóres saga konungs ok sona hans'* (Halle: Niemeyer, 1927), 7–9; see also 9, commentary to §§1–4.

Grettis saga, ch. 19:	twelve berserks	Christmas Eve
Grettis saga, ch. 21:	bear	Early winter to Christmas
Grettis saga, chs 32–5:	Glámr	Christmas Eve/Winter Nights to spring
Grettis saga, chs 64–6:	Sandhaugar	Christmas Eve
Hávarðar saga Ísfirðings, ch. 2:	Þórmóðr	Autumn
Hrólfs saga kraka, ch. 23:	beast	Christmas Eve
Laxdœla saga, chs 17–24:	Víga-Hrappr	Winter (final haunting and resolution)

Table 1: The seasonality of extrasocietal threats in Old Icelandic narrative prose.

The episode in *Egils saga einhenda* is the only one in this list containing no suggestion that the confrontation takes place at nighttime or in the dark; all the other texts bear out such an association, rarely awarding daytime hauntings a subsidiary role. This element is certainly not unique to Icelandic tradition, as most European ghosts are likewise nightbound,[43] as are the monsters of *Beowulf* and the majority of post-Conquest English revenants according to Walter Map[44] and William of Newburgh.[45] Indeed, angels,[46] demons,[47] and the blessed departed[48] in England and elsewhere likewise tend to concentrate their appearances in the nighttime. In part, no doubt, this statistic results from an association between visions and dreams.[49] Likewise responsible, however, is the fear and heightened subjectivity associated with nighttime owing to the increased uncertainty that comes

---

[43] Jean-Claude Schmidt, *Ghosts in the Middle Ages: The Living and the Dead in Medieval Society*, trans. Teresa Lavender Fagan (Chicago: University of Chicago Press, 1998), 177–8.

[44] *De nugis curialium* 2.27, 4.10: Montague Rhodes James, C. N. L. Brooke, and R. A. B. Mynors, eds and trans., *Walter Map: De nugis curialium / Courtiers' Trifles* (Oxford: Clarendon, 1983), 202, 348–50; an exception is 2.28 (p. 204).

[45] *Historia rerum Anglicarum* 5.23, 5.24: Hans Claude Hamilton, ed., *'Historia rerum Anglicarum' Willelmi Parvi, Ordinis Sancti Augustini canonici regularis in Cœnobio beatæ Mariæ de Newburgh in agro Eboracensi*, 2 vols (London: [English Historical] Society, 1856), 2:184–90; it is presented as an extreme case that another initially nocturnal revenant eventually walks the earth by day as well as by night in 5.22 (pp. 182–4).

[46] For example, Bede, *Historia ecclesiastica* 4.24: Colgrave and Mynors, *Ecclesiastical History*, 416; *Vita Oswaldi*, ch. 2: Andrew J. Turner and Bernard J. Muir, eds and trans., *Eadmer of Canterbury: Lives and Miracles of Saints Oda, Dunstan, and Oswald* (Oxford: Clarendon, 2006), 52.

[47] For example Felix's *Vita Guthlaci*, ch. 31: Bertram Colgrave, ed. and trans., *Felix's 'Life of Guthlac'* (Cambridge: Cambridge University Press, 1956), 100–6; *Vita Oswaldi*, ch. 8: Turner and Muir, *Lives and Miracles*, 82; see further Nancy Caciola, 'Wraiths, Revenants and Ritual in Medieval Culture', *Past & Present* 152, no. 1 (August 1996): 10–14.

[48] For example *Vita Oswaldi*, ch. 16: Turner and Muir, *Lives and Miracles*, 76.

[49] On the distinction in Macrobius and elsewhere, see Hans Joachim Kamphausen, *Traum und Vision in der lateinischen Poesie der Karolingerzeit*, Lateinische Sprache und Literatur des Mittelalters 4 (Frankfurt: Peter Lang, 1975), esp. 9–58; Peter Dinzelbacher, *Vision und Visionsliteratur im Mittelalter*, Monographien zur Geschichte des Mittelalters 23 (Stuttgart: Hiersemann, 1981), 28–55; Gwenfair Walters Adams, *Visions in Late Medieval England: Lay Spirituality and Sacred Glimpses of the Hidden Worlds of Faith*, Studies in the History of Christian Traditions 130 (Leiden: Brill, 2007), 175–6.

with the loss of vision.[50] Although this association of the supernatural with the dark of night suggests that winter should be the most haunted season, such a pattern is nowhere made as explicit as in Scandinavia.

CHRISTMAS VISITORS

The Scandinavian popularity and spread of the motif of winter hauntings is confirmed by more recent folktale evidence. In part, this is found in a large body of disparate local revenant tales. Not all of these employ seasonality, but winter, Christmas, and the start of the winter half-year are common contexts, while nearly all stories take place at night.[51] However, there is also a more unified folk-tradition known as the Christmas Visitors.[52] In this tale, which has been widely recorded in Norway and Iceland, elves or *huldufólk* ('hidden people') pay an annual visit to a particular farmhouse on or around Christmas Eve to feast there, while its human residents are either gone to mass or spend the night away from home on account of the supernatural invasion of their home.[53] Inasmuch as the narrative always centres on the visit's final iteration, in which the supernatural visitors are scared off for good by an obscure farmhand (not unlike Glámr) or visiting stranger (like Grettir), it is tempting to see here a continuity between the various hauntings in *Grettis saga* and the more recent folktales.[54] Indeed, the large number of occurrences of this literary pattern in both medieval and modern times renders its uninterrupted popularity more likely than a modern revitalization of a once-popular medieval tradition. Accordingly, the medieval uses of seasonality and darkness here studied appear to have had a lasting impact on narrative conventions at least in local traditions.[55]

---

[50] Jean Verdon, *Night in the Middle Ages*, trans. George Holoch (Notre Dame: University of Notre Dame Press, 2002), 7. For discussions of the evolutionary psychology of fear, see Charles Darwin, 'A Biographical Sketch of an Infant', *Mind* 2, no. 7 (July 1877): 288; Paul Diel, *Fear and Anxiety: Primary Triggers of Survival and Evolution*, trans. Brigitte Donvez (Claremont, CA: Hunter House, 1989); David M. Buss, *Evolutionary Psychology: The New Science of the Mind*, 3rd ed. (Boston: Pearson, 2008), 92–8.

[51] Jón Árnason, *Íslenzkar þjóðsögur og ævintýri*, 1:222–317; Sigurður Nordal, ed., *Þjóðsagnabókin: Sýnisbók íslenzkra þjóðsagnasafna*, 3 vols (Reykjavik: Almenna bókafélágið, 1971–3), 2:1–101.

[52] Catalogued as ML 6015 in Reidar Th. Christiansen, *The Migratory Legends: A Proposed List of Types with a Systematic Catalogue of the Norwegian Variants* (Helsinki: Suomalainen tiedeakatemia, 1958), 144–56; cf. ML 6015A (pp. 156–8).

[53] Reidar Th. Christiansen, *The Dead and the Living*, Studia Norvegica 2 (Oslo: Aschehoug, 1946), 70–83; Christiansen, *The Migratory Legends*, 144–56; Reidar Th. Christiansen, *Folktales of Norway*, trans. Pat Shaw Iversen (Chicago: University of Chicago Press, 1964), 121–4; Jacqueline Simpson, ed. and trans., *Icelandic Folktales and Legends* (Berkeley and Los Angeles: University of California Press, 1972), 52–5; Terry Gunnell, 'The Coming of the Christmas Visitors... Folk Legends Concerning the Attacks on Icelandic Farmhouses Made by Spirits at Christmas', *Northern Studies* 38 (2004): 51–75.

[54] Gunnell, 'Christmas Visitors', 60–1.

[55] Cf. Theodore M. Andersson, 'The Discovery of Darkness in Northern Literature', in Burlin and Irving, *Old English Studies in Honour of John C. Pope*, 1–14.

Even today, traditions current throughout Iceland have it that disobedient children are devoured by a troll-woman at Christmas,[56] while a child that does not receive new clothes to wear on Christmas Eve runs the risk of being snatched away by a large cat.[57]

One permutation of the Christmas Visitors motif is worth mentioning in the form of the episode known as *Þiðranda þáttr ok Þórhalls* contained in several redactions of the early-fourteenth-century *Óláfs saga Tryggvasonar en mesta*.[58] An important divergence from the mean, medieval and modern, is the timing, as it centres around the Winter Nights celebrated in mid-October. In this text, a man named Þórhallr who is gifted with foresight grows silent as the summer draws to a close because he foresees that one gifted with foresight will be killed during the autumn celebration. During the Winter Nights, the weather turns rough; Þórhallr advises that no one venture out of the house because he foresees great harm if anyone does. In the middle of the night, a young man named Þiðrandi hears a knocking at the door and goes out to find nine armed women in black riding from the north, and nine women in white from the south, but the women in black get to him first and attack him. He is found wounded in the frosty, moonlit morning, and he dies that day. Þórhallr now prophesies the coming of a new religion (to be understood as Christianity) and explains the dark women as Þiðrandi's pagan *fylgjur* or accompanying spirits, who knew they would lose Þiðrandi to the new religion should they leave him alive; the women in white were representatives of the new religion, meaning to save him.

Although the haunting in *Þiðranda þáttr* has been fitted with a religious motivation, it has considerable overlap with the various other Old Norse apparitions described above. The timing is different from most parallels, but it may be remembered that the final iteration of the Glámr-haunting in *Grettis saga* likewise takes place during the Winter Nights, while *Hávarðar saga Ísfirðings* speaks of autumn. That this time of year is conceptually associated with the winter season becomes clear from the details in *Þiðranda þáttr*: the storm, the frost, and the moonlit morning all connote winter, even if the festive correspondences between Christmas and the Winter Nights are overlooked.[59] Þórhallr's ominous silence at the approach of the feast is mirrored in *Hrólfs saga kraka*, in which the whole court falls quiet at the approach of Yule because the courtiers know of the creature that annually attacks the hall at this time of year (ch. 23).[60] If anything, therefore, the

---

[56] Árni Björnsson, *Saga daganna*, 338–40; Gunnell, 'The Season of the *dísir*', 136–8; Terry Gunnell, 'Grýla, *grýlur*, *grøleks* and *skeklers*: Medieval Disguise Traditions in the Early Middle Ages?', *ARV* 57 (2001): 33–54.

[57] Árni Björnsson, *Saga daganna*, 368–70.

[58] Ch. 215: Ólafur Halldórsson, *Óláfs saga en mesta*, 2:145–50.

[59] The reference to moonlight likewise recalls Grettir's encounter with Glámr, which either suggests that the (full) moon had an association with the supernatural (see *Grettis saga*, ch. 35: Guðni Jónsson, *Grettis saga*, 121) or simply testifies to its atmospheric potential.

[60] Slay, *Hrólfs saga kraka*, 78.

application of the haunting-motif to both Christmas and the Winter Nights demonstrates the conceptual unity in Icelandic tradition between the times of year corresponding to the Julian autumn and winter, or at least between the feasts that assume such prominent positions in the literary identities of these seasons.

ACCOUNTING FOR WINTER HAUNTINGS

That the dangerous supernatural in medieval Scandinavia had an annual cycle extending to more social categories than revenants and *fylgjur* becomes clear in the legendary saga *Ketils saga hængs*. This text shows considerable interest in the Finnar or Sami, whose associations with winter and dangerous sorcery have been outlined in the previous chapter. In *Ketils saga*, the same connections are given a place in the cycle of the seasons. Staying with Bruni in Finnmǫrk, Ketill intends to go on his way after *jól*, but Bruni declares that to be impossible, as he says, 'on account of the winter severity and the bad weather; and Gusir, king of the Finnar, is lurking in the shadows'.[61] When spring arrives, Ketill and Bruni are both able to set out (ch. 3).[62]

Significantly, this episode adduces the superhuman threat of the Sami in one breath with the natural annual prevalence of storms, suggesting some degree of mythologization of natural threats. It is the same association between natural and supernatural winter threats that brings Ketill to the supernaturally charged region of Finnmǫrk in the first place, as he is shipwrecked there after disregarding a specific injunction not to sail out as late as the Winter Nights.[63] Indeed, the Glámr episode of *Grettis saga* makes a similar connection when it has the supernatural deaths of its winter shepherds coincide with the natural event of a winter storm.

This tendency to explain the physical implications of winter in supernatural terms may likewise be found in the Greenlandic hauntings of *Eiríks saga rauða*. Specifically, this text may shed light on the Scandinavian popularity of hibernal revenant hauntings. The narrator suggests that the dead return in consequence of negligent burial rites, as one deceased person returns to the living specifically to denounce Greenlandic burial customs on God's behalf. The saga goes into some detail regarding these rites:

> Sá hafði háttr verit á Grœnlandi, síðan kristni kom þangat, at menn váru grafnir á bœjum, þar sem ǫnduðusk, í óvígðri moldu. Skyldi setja staur upp af brjósti inum dauða, en síðan, er kennimenn kómu til, þá skyldi

---

[61] 'Fyrir vetrarríki ok illum veðrum; en Gusir Finna konungr liggr úti á mörkum.'
[62] Guðni Jónsson and Bjarni Vilhjálmsson, *Fornaldarsögur*, 1:252.
[63] Ibid., 1:251. Cf. *Eyrbyggja saga*, ch. 16, in which it is observed that many sea spirits are about in early winter. Gunnlaugr ventures out at night regardless and is mysteriously killed; the consensus is that it was magic (Einar Ólafur Sveinsson and Matthías Þórðarson, *Eyrbyggja saga*, 28–9).

upp kippa staurinum ok hella þar í vígðu vatni ok veita þar yfirsǫngva, þótt þat væri miklu síðar.   (Eiríks saga rauða, ch. 6)⁶⁴

It had been the custom in Greenland since Christianity had arrived there that people were interred on the farm where they had died, in unconsecrated soil. A stake had to be set up, rising from the chest of the deceased. Later, when the clergy arrived, the stake had to be pulled out and holy water poured down [the resulting channel] and a funeral service held there, even if that was much later.

Missing from the account is the key piece of information that inhumation was and remains a complicated affair in Greenland. Even in locations where soil is plentiful, snow and frozen topsoil hinder the digging of graves in winter, while permafrost in many places precludes the creation of graves more than a few feet deep even in summer,⁶⁵ at least since the late-medieval cooling set in.⁶⁶ Accordingly, arctic cultures have traditionally disposed of the bodies of the dead above ground,⁶⁷ while various cultures situated in the north, including northern communities in Western cultures, postpone burial until the spring thaw even today.⁶⁸ There are also present-day Greenlandic parallels to the saga account of burial beside one's own house;⁶⁹ this is commonly done in winter. The same practice has also been recorded for

---

⁶⁴ Einar Ólafur Sveinsson and Matthías Þórðarson, *Eyrbyggja saga*, 217; cf. Niels Lynnerup, *The Greenland Norse: A Biological-Anthropological Study*, Meddelelser om Grønland: Man and Society 24 (Copenhagen: Commission for Scientific Research in Greenland, 1998), 51–2.

⁶⁵ During the 1921 excavation at Herjolfsnes in southern Greenland, only the topmost 70–80 cm of soil was seen to thaw in summer. The deepest archaeological finds were discovered in the permafrost at 135 cm below the twentieth-century surface level, or at least 105–10 cm below the estimated medieval surface level: Poul Nørlund, *Buried Norsemen at Herjolfsnes: An Archaeological and Historical Study*, Meddelelser om Grønland 67.1 (Copenhagen: Rietzel, 1924), 241–2, 262–7; for the estimate of soil rise since the time of the settlement, see Nørlund, *Buried Norsemen*, 239; Poul Nørlund, 'Kirkegaarden paa Herjolfsnæs: Et bidrag til diskussionen om klimateorien', *Historisk tidsskrift* 27 (1927): 386–8. See further Edward Moffat Weyer Jr, *The Eskimos: Their Environment and Folkways* (New Haven: Yale University Press, 1932), 263; Seaver, *Frozen Echo*, 9, 117–18.

⁶⁶ Nørlund, *Buried Norsemen*, 228–44; cf. Nørlund, 'Kirkegaarden'; Lamb, *Climate*, 2:438.

⁶⁷ Weyer, *The Eskimos*, 263–6; Kaj Birket-Smith, *The Eskimos*, enlarged and rev. ed., trans. W. E. Calvert and C. Daryll Forde (London: Methuen, 1959), 158–9; Jane M Hughes, *An Eskimo Village in the Modern World* (Ithaca, NY: Cornell University Press, 1960), 66; Robert Petersen, 'Burial-Forms and Death Cult among the Eskimos', *Folk* 8–9 (1966–7): 259–80; cf. Nørlund, *Buried Norsemen*, 238, n. 1.

⁶⁸ For example among the Finnish Skolt Sami (Nils Storå, *Burial Customs of the Skolt Lapps*, Folklore Fellows' Communications 210 (Helsinki: Suomalainen tiedeakatemia, 1971), 98–103) and the general population of upstate New York (Donna Liquori, 'Where Death Comes in Winter, and Burial in the Spring', *New York Times* (1 May 2005): Late Edition, East Coast, Section 1, p. 41). It is worth pointing out that certain Sami cultures, like medieval Norse culture, require burial rites to be carried out in meticulous compliance with a normative custom to prevent the dead returning from their graves (Storå, *Burial Customs*, 260–1). Cf. Birket-Smith, *The Eskimos*, 158–9 for similar requirements among the arctic peoples of North America, and D. Jenness, *The Life of the Copper Eskimos: Southern Party, 1913–16*, Report of the Canadian Arctic Expedition 1913–18 12 (Ottawa: Acland, 1922), 171–8 for revenants and resurrections in the same region.

⁶⁹ Witness, for instance, the numerous domestic graves in the village of Kulusuk, off eastern Greenland, in spite of the fact that there is also a cemetery a short way outside the village.

Iceland in a later period.[70] The saga description of a stake placed over the corpse closely follows the procedure outlined in the Norwegian *Gulaþingslǫg* to be followed if the priest is absent, but the law code specifies that the stake is to be inserted only after the priest arrives (ch. 23).[71] The Greenlandic variant, to drive in the stake immediately upon burial, may be understood not just as a way of creating a channel for the holy water, but also as a means of locating the body below the cover of the snow. Meanwhile, the fact that delayed burial rites were legislated as an exception in Norway but are presented as the default procedure in Greenland reflects complicated Greenlandic logistics, which would have been at their worst in winter. In short, the practices denounced by the revenant in *Eiríks saga* seem to have followed from the difficulty in subarctic climates of complying with Christian burial rites developed in warmer regions, especially in winter. This socioreligious concern may be understood as a practical inspiration for narratives of winter hauntings and a legislative impulse to the productive range of seasonal-chronotopical motifs.[72]

If bad living and bad dying are widespread causes of medieval revenant hauntings,[73] a poor disposal of the dead and their possessions is at least as common a cause in the Icelandic material, and rectifying such a mistake typically ends the hauntings.[74] Both these patterns may be recognized in *Grettis saga*, where Glámr, not buried in the manner stipulated in Christian law, takes up haunting, whereas Þorgautr, killed under very similar circumstances but given a lawful burial, does not. These men's lifestyles and religious commitments are surely a decisive factor in their posthumous behaviour, but the consequent ritual difference seems equally significant. While the climate of most of Iceland was far milder than that of the Greenlandic settlements, sagas set in Iceland also make reference to snow and frozen ground as obstructions to burial and reburial.[75] The concern over burial protocol expressed in *Eiríks saga* would have received considerable impetus from the strict procedures outlined in the law codes, which prescribe severe monetary and personal penalties for ritual neglect.[76] Thus it is likely that the introduction of

---

[70] Poul Nørlund, *Viking Settlers in Greenland*, trans. W. E. Calvert (London and Copenhagen: Cambridge University Press / Gad, 1936), 44–6.

[71] Keyser and Munch, *Norges gamle love*, 1:14.

[72] Cf. Paul Barber, *Vampires, Burial, and Death: Folklore and Reality* (New Haven, CT: Yale University Press, 1988), esp. 166–77.

[73] Caciola, 'Wraiths, Revenants and Ritual in Medieval Culture', 27–9.

[74] Thus, for example, *Flóamanna saga*, chs 13, 22: Þórhallur Vilmundarson and Bjarni Vilhjálmsson, *Harðar saga*, 255–6, 285; *Eiríks saga rauða*, ch. 6: Einar Ólafur Sveinsson and Matthías Þórðarson, *Eyrbyggja saga*, 216–17; *Eyrbyggja saga*, ch. 55: ibid., 150–2. The connection between improper burial and postmortem activity is likewise stressed in Barber, *Vampires*, for example 37–8.

[75] For example *Heiðarvíga saga*, ch. 9: Sigurður Nordal and Guðni Jónsson, *Borgfirðinga sǫgur*, 232–5; *Eyrbyggja saga*, ch. 34: Einar Ólafur Sveinsson and Matthías Þórðarson, *Eyrbyggja saga*, 94.

[76] *Grágás*, ch. 2: Vilhjálmur Finsen, *Grágás*, 1:7–12; *Gulaþingslǫg*, ch. 23: Keyser and Munch, *Norges gamle love*, 1:13–15.

Christian burial law gave a considerable boost to revenant traditions and strengthened any association they may already have had with the winter season.

The Grendel Season

As was observed earlier, a number of encounters with the extrasocietal in *Grettis saga* are widely held to correspond to the attacks on Heorot in the first two thousand lines of *Beowulf*. The strongest echoes of what can only be a shared tradition[77] surface in the *draugr* of Kárr *inn gamli* on Háramarsey (ch. 18);[78] a rampant bear in Hálogaland (ch. 21);[79] Glámr's part in the Forsœludalr-hauntings (chs 32–5);[80] and the two *troll* around Sandhaugar (chs 64–7).[81] Apart from their interest in incursions into the human domain, what unites these episodes is that they all take place in winter, while the last three centre around Christmas. The saga compiler clearly intended to associate this point on the calendar with outside threats to human society, as yet another episode set on Christmas Eve has Grettir ward off an attack on a farm by twelve berserks (ch. 19).[82] Finally, Grettir's death, brought about by the liminal force of witchcraft, likewise takes place in winter (chs 79–82).[83]

---

[77] This point of widespread consensus has occasionally been challenged, most elaborately in Magnús Fjalldal, *The Long Arm of Coincidence: The Frustrated Connection between 'Beowulf' and 'Grettis saga'* (Toronto: University of Toronto Press, 1998). Although the precise nature of the relationship between these texts has been variously understood over the years (as documented in Anatoly Liberman, 'Beowulf – Grettir', in *Germanic Dialects: Linguistic and Philological Investigations*, ed. Bela Brogyanyi and Thomas Krömmelbein, Amsterdam Studies in the Theory and History of Linguistic Science 4 (Amsterdam and Philadelphia, PA: Benjamins, 1986), 353–401), the analogues outlined below are too close and too many to ascribe to coincidence. See, for example, R. W. Chambers, *Beowulf: An Introduction to the Study of the Poem with a Discussion of the Stories of Offa and Finn*, 3rd ed., with a supplement by C. L. Wrenn (Cambridge: Cambridge University Press, 1959); Orchard, *Pride and Prodigies*, 140–68.

[78] Guðni Jónsson, *Grettis saga*, 56–61. See Taylor, 'Two Notes on *Beowulf*', 13–14; McConchie, 'Grettir Ásmundarson's Fight with Kárr the Old'; Orchard, *Pride and Prodigies*, 152–60.

[79] Guðni Jónsson, *Grettis saga*, 73–8. See Danielli, 'Initiation Ceremonial from Norse Literature', 231; Arthur A. Wachsler, 'Grettir's Fight with a Bear: Another Neglected Analogue of *Beowulf* in the *Grettis sage Asmundarsonar*', *English Studies* 66, no. 5 (1985): 381–90; Orchard, *Pride and Prodigies*, 52.

[80] Guðni Jónsson, *Grettis saga*, 107–23. The scholarship on this episode and that at Sandhaugar is extensive. The main studies on these chapters and on the connection between *Beowulf* and *Grettis saga* in general are listed in Liberman, 'Beowulf – Grettir' and Magnús Fjalldal, *The Long Arm of Coincidence*. Some of the most persuasive evidence of a relationship between the two is brought together in Orchard, *Pride and Prodigies*, 140–68.

[81] Guðni Jónsson, *Grettis saga*, 209–19.

[82] Ibid., 62–71. For further proposed parallels, see Douglas Stedman, 'Some Points of Resemblance between *Beowulf* and the *Grettla* (or *Grettis saga*)', *Saga-Book* 8 (1913–14): 25; Benson, 'The Originality of *Beowulf*', 20–30; Richard L. Harris, 'The Deaths of Grettir and Grendel: A New Parallel', *Scripta Islandica* 24 (1973): 25–53; Orchard, *Pride and Prodigies*, 140–68.

[83] Guðni Jónsson, *Grettis saga*, 249–64.

Certain motifs found in *Beowulf* and *Grettis saga* are believed to surface again in a range of further Scandinavian texts.[84] The closest of these is the story of Bǫðvarr *bjarki*, surviving in Saxo Grammaticus's *Gesta Danorum* and the legendary *Hrólfs saga kraka*. The latter tells of a dragon attacking Hrólfr's court annually during the night of Christmas Eve, thus making the same unambiguous association also found in *Grettis saga* between this time of year and outside threats (ch. 23).[85] The episode in *Gesta Danorum*, by contrast, survives without any reference to the passing of the seasons,[86] which is largely true of *Beowulf* as well. The precise relationship between these various texts remains a matter of debate, but the seasonal development may be assumed to answer to one of two possibilities. The first is that the Scandinavians transformed a pre-existing aseasonal tradition into a haunting taking place annually around Christmas. The other possibility places seasonality at the heart of the underlying narrative, deriving even the Grendel episode of *Beowulf* from a winter tale. If the former scenario could be proved correct, this stemma would be further testimony to a Scandinavian association between hauntings and winter. If the latter, this would provide the attacks on Heorot with a firmer traditional context than they have hitherto enjoyed. Since either outcome would shed light on literary uses of winter in the cultures under investigation, it is worth briefly considering the relationship between *Beowulf* and its various Scandinavian analogues. To avoid losing sight of the subject under investigation, however, the entire debate will not be rehearsed here.[87]

THE CAVE EPISODE

Key to an understanding of the connections between *Beowulf*, *Grettis saga*, and analogues is the recognition that the material under consideration divides into two distinct episodes: the defence of the hall and the fight in the cave.[88] The Scandinavian material, although centuries younger than the Nowell codex containing *Beowulf*,[89] let alone the poem's inception,

---

[84] Chambers, *Beowulf*, esp. 54–61, 451–503; J. Michael. Stitt, *'Beowulf' and the Bear's Son: Epic, Saga, and Fairytale in Northern Germanic Tradition*, Albert Bates Studies in Oral Tradition 8 (New York and London: Garland, 1992).
[85] Slay, *Hrólfs saga kraka*, 78.
[86] Saxo Grammaticus, *Gesta Danorum*, 2.6.11 (Friis-Jensen and Zeeberg 1:168).
[87] Scandinavian analogues to *Beowulf* have been the subject of numerous studies, the more seminal of which include Lawrence, *'Beowulf' and Epic Tradition*; R. W. Chambers, 'Beowulf's Fight with Grendel, and its Scandinavian Parallels', *English Studies* 11 (1929): 81–100; R. W. Chambers, *Beowulf*; G. N. Garmonsway and Jacqueline Simpson, trans., *'Beowulf' and its Analogues* (London and New York: Dent / Dutton, 1968); Liberman, 'Beowulf – Grettir'; Stitt, *'Beowulf' and the Bear's Son*.
[88] R. Mark Scowcroft, 'The Irish Analogues to *Beowulf*', *Speculum* 74, no. 1 (January 1999): 25.
[89] British Library, MS Cotton Vespasian A. XV has been loosely dated to the first decade of the eleventh century (Fulk, Bjork, and Niles, *Beowulf*, xxvii), while *Grettis saga* was written no earlier than about 1300 (Guðni Jónsson, *Grettis saga*, lxviii–lxx).

may be considered particularly authoritative for the reconstruction of the underlying cave episode, since it appears to explain a number of blind motifs in *Beowulf*. The first of these, and probably the most extensively studied, is the poem's ambiguity regarding the geography of the cave. In two extended descriptions (1357–76, 1402–41), the reader learns that the monsters' habitat is centrally characterized by a pool; however, the image is somewhat confused by the lines

> ðær fyrgenstream
> under næssa genipu niþer gewiteð,
> flod under foldan.   (lines 1359–61)

where a mighty stream goes down below the shadows of headlands, water below the land.

The image of a large river[90] disappearing underground is hard to reconcile with that of a static pool, while the presence of steep headlands further complicates the geography. Beowulf now enters the water and swims to the bottom, where he is pulled into a dry cave by Grendel's mother (1492–1517). This passage is subject to further confusion, as the hero is first dragged in 'so that he could not wield his weapon, no matter how brave he was' (1508–9),[91] but as soon as he is in the cave, he sees Grendel's mother as though for the first time and is able to attack her using the sword Hrunting (1512–22). A third element in the passage that may be reinterpreted on the basis of Scandinavian material is the light that follows on the hero's victory. After Beowulf defeats Grendel's mother, the poem tells of a mysterious shining:

> Lixte se leoma,   leoht inne stod,
> efne swa of hefene   hadre scineð,
> rodores candel.[92]   (lines 1570–2)

The shining gleamed, a light shone within, just as heaven's candle shines brightly from heaven.

The hero now turns his attention to Grendel's corpse, which he decapitates in revenge for the slaughter the monster has inflicted among the Danes (1572–90). The function of the light is unclear. While it could be conceived as a divine celebration of the hero's victory, this reading casts a dubious light on Beowulf's subsequent attack on Grendel, as though this part of the episode is not worthy of the same praise. At best, it would therefore be a qualified approval of Beowulf's deeds.

---

[90] The term *fyrgenstream* has also been understood as a circumlocution for the ocean, but that reading makes the lines even harder to understand. See the discussion in Martin Puhvel, *'Beowulf' and the Celtic Tradition* (Waterloo, ON: Wilfrid Laurier University Press, 1979), 105–12; *DOE*, s.v. 'fyrgen-strēam'.

[91] 'Swa he ne mihte – no he þæs modig wæs – / wæpna gewealdan.'

[92] The demonstrative pronoun *se* suggests that the light has been mentioned before and is identical with that mentioned at Beowulf's entrance into the cave, *Beowulf* 1512–17.

With the help of a group of Scandinavian narratives including not only *Grettis saga* but also *Orms þáttr Stórólfssonar*, *Harðar saga ok Hólmverjar*, *Samsons saga fagra*, and *Gull-Þóris saga*, as well as the folktale *Gullbrá og Skeggi* recorded in modern times, Chambers has demonstrated, following Lawrence's lead, that valid explanations for all these obscure motifs are readily available in Scandinavian parallels. Firstly, several of these texts describe a fight in a cave behind a waterfall, a setting that explains how a pool combines with a descent of water; how an underwater cave can be dry; and also how blood from a fight in a dry cave may end up on the water surface.[93] Indeed, the quoted description from *Beowulf* of a stream disappearing below the shadow of the headlands becomes entirely transparent once it is understood as a waterfall. Several of the analogues furthermore tell of a bright light or other supernatural intervention that weakens the opponent, puts him to sleep, or turns her to stone,[94] while in *Gull-Þóris saga* it may furthermore be understood to highlight the swords with which the cave-dwellers may be defeated (ch. 4).[95] The sword motif likewise occurs in *Beowulf*. In the hero's retelling of his fight to Hrothgar, he makes no mention of the light, but he attributes his victory to God's intervention in showing him a sword on the wall by which he is able to overcome Grendel's mother (1659–66; cf. 1557–69). With the help of the Scandinavian analogues, a plausible reconstruction of these elements may be achieved: it is by way of the radiant light that God helps the hero overcome the monster, in illuminating the sword and perhaps also in the monster's incapacitation.[96] Finally, Chambers proposed that *Beowulf* has incorporated two different versions of the hero's entrance, one forced and one by his own power. The former tradition is represented by *Samsons saga*, the latter by *Grettis saga*, *Gull-Þóris saga*, and *Gullbrá og Skeggi*.[97] In view of such repeated and plausible illumination of *Beowulf* by its Scandinavian analogues, it seems that the underlying narrative of the cave episode was better preserved in Scandinavia than in England.

THE DEFENCE OF THE HALL

Although variants of the cave fight may thus shed light on the spread and development of the larger shared narrative, seasonality in *Grettis saga* and *Hrólfs saga* finds its most regular expression in the motif of the haunted hall.

---

[93] See *Beowulf* 1591–9. For this argument, see Lawrence, 'The Haunted Mere in *Beowulf*', 231–45; Frederick Klaeber, ed., *'Beowulf' and 'The Fight at Finnsburg'*, 3rd ed. (Boston: Heath, 1950), 182–3, commentary to lines 1357 ff. Chambers, *Beowulf*, 52–3, 451–72.
[94] *Harðar saga*, ch. 15: Þórhallur Vilmundarson and Bjarni Vilhjálmsson, *Harðar saga*, 42; *Orms þáttr Stórólfssonar*, ch. 9: ibid., 417; *Gullbrá og Skeggi*: Jón Árnason, *Íslenzkar þjóðsögur og ævintýri*, 1:150.
[95] Þórhallur Vilmundarson and Bjarni Vilhjálmsson, *Harðar saga*, 187–8.
[96] Chambers, *Beowulf*, 466–8.
[97] Ibid., 470–2, 476.

As it happens, there seems to be nothing in *Beowulf*'s treatment of this motif that benefits from comparison with the Scandinavian material. One cannot therefore single out elements within this motif known only from Scandinavian sources and assume that the *Beowulf* poet was familiar with them.

Instead, the defence of Heorot resembles a folktale with an early Irish presence known as The Hand and the Child. This tale tells how a visiting hero defends a royal hall against a monster in the habit of stealing infants from this particular hall by sticking his arm through its chimney or window. The protagonist resists a spell of sleep and hacks or tears off the arm. The next day, he follows the trail of blood to the waterside dwelling of the kidnapper (who sometimes lives there with a female companion), kills him, and rescues the children.[98] Although the relevance of this tale as an analogue to the texts under study is not limited to the hall episode, the particular appeal of the Irish tale to readings of *Beowulf* consists in the same benefits of rational illumination outlined above for the Scandinavian counterparts to the cave episode. In *Beowulf*, there is no particular reason why the hero should wrench off the intruder's arm, nor is this an expected outcome of hand-to-hand combat. Less explicable still is the Geatas' apparent decision to sleep through their long-anticipated hall defence without so much as keeping a guard. Both these details are satisfactorily explained by certain versions of the folktale, as the arm is the only part of the kidnapper exposed to attack, and all the residents of the hall except one are overcome by sleep against their will, often through a magic spell.[99] Since there was a Scandinavian presence in both Ireland and England for the greater part of the ninth to eleventh centuries, moreover, the possibility of an Irish node in the Defence of the Hall tradition in no way challenges the connection found between *Beowulf* and Scandinavian texts.

When the Hand and Child narratives are studied for their structure, it quickly becomes clear that seasonality plays no significant role in the Irish tradition. The versions of the tale that contain both of the central elements, namely the hand and the child, tend strongly to situate the abduction on the day the child is born,[100] or sometimes around its first

---

[98] George Lyman Kittredge, 'Arthur and Gorlagon', *Harvard Studies and Notes in Philology and Literature* 8 (1903): 223–31; Scowcroft, 'The Irish Analogues to *Beowulf*', 23; for a detailed study, see R. Mark Scowcroft, 'The Hand and the Child: Studies of Celtic Tradition in European Literature' (unpublished doctoral dissertation, Cornell University, 1982).

[99] Gerard Murphy, ed., *Duanaire Finn / The Book of the Lays of Fionn*, vol. 3, Irish Texts Society 43 (Dublin: Irish Texts Society, 1953), 186; Scowcroft, 'The Irish Analogues to *Beowulf*', 23.

[100] Thus, for instance, the versions in D. MacInnes, ed. and trans., *Folk and Hero Tales*, Waifs and Strays of Celtic Tradition: Argyllshire Series 2 (London: Nutt, 1890), 32–67, at 58–67; John Gregorson Campbell, ed., *The Fians; Or, Stories, Poems, & Traditions of Fionn and his Warrior Band*, Waifs and Strays of Celtic Tradition: Argyllshire Series 4 (London: Nutt, 1891), 204–10; James MacDougall, ed. and trans., *Folk and Hero Tales*, Waifs and Strays of Celtic Tradition: Argyllshire series 3 (London: Nutt, 1891), 1–9; Jeremiah Curtin, trans., *Hero-Tales of Ireland* (London: MacMillan, 1894), 438–62; see further Kittredge, 'Arthur and Gorlagon', 224, 227.

birthday.[101] There is usually no explicit mention of the time of year, nor any evidence that the narrator considers this of any relevance to the tale. The fact that the protagonist usually arrives by ship and pokes himself with a hot iron to stay awake at night should thus not be taken to mean that the narrative is set at a time when the seafaring season and the period of active nighttime heating overlap, as these elements are not introduced for their seasonal value.

It should be noted that a Welsh version of the narrative exists that does rely on seasonal recurrence. In *Pwyll pendeuic Dyuet* (c. 1100),[102] we hear of a child disappearing only once, with inclusion of the sleep motif. However, the story goes on to tell how a mare gives birth annually during the night leading up to the first of May, but the foal is always stolen before anyone gets to it. On the first May Night after the newborn child goes missing, the mare's owner Teirnon stays up to guard his property. Following a successful foaling, he sees an arm enter through a window intending to steal the foal; Teirnon cuts it off using his sword. He now finds the lost infant, which by implication has likewise been carried off by the horse thief.[103] Here is thus an analogue to *Beowulf*'s hall episode that makes use of an annual pattern, like the similar episodes in *Grettis saga* and *Hrólfs saga kraka*, but centred around a different season. Since this version has considerably more plot complexity not paralleled in *Beowulf*, however, the Old English poem is more likely to rely on a variant closer to the surviving Irish analogues, and thus most likely without mention of seasons.

In the light of the Irish lack of seasonal motifs, it is significant that an Icelandic attestation of the Hand and Child tale makes full use of the supernatural connotations of Christmas Eve, exactly like the hauntings in the sagas: here, a king is robbed of one of his daughters every Christmas Eve.[104] In its larger structure, this narrative is a version of an internationally known tale referred to as Skilful Companions, in which the monster is overcome by a group of characters, each of which has one skill required for the operation.[105] None of the Irish witnesses to this configuration of the narrative makes reference to the seasons.[106] However, Skilful Companions has no witnesses predating the mid-thirteenth century,[107] while arguably analogous tales with neither children nor companions can be traced back

---

[101] For example Patrick Kennedy, ed., *Legendary Fictions of the Irish Celts*, 2nd ed. (London: MacMillan, 1891), 200–5.

[102] R. L. Thomson, ed., *Pwyll pendeuic Dyuet*, Mediaeval and Modern Welsh Series 1 (Dublin: Dublin Institute for Advanced Studies, 1957), xii–xvi.

[103] Ibid., 17–19. This analogue was pointed out to me by David Klausner (personal communication, 30 April 2012).

[104] Josef Calasanz Poestion, ed., *Isländische Märchen* (Vienna: Carl Gerold's Sohn, 1884), 285–9.

[105] Kittredge, 'Arthur and Gorlagon', 226–7; Scowcroft, 'The Irish Analogues to *Beowulf*', 23–5.

[106] Most of the versions cited above (n. 100) are representatives of Skilful Companions.

[107] James Carney, *Studies in Irish Literature and History* (Dublin: Dublin Institute for Advanced Studies, 1955), 374.

to the eighth century.[108] It thus seems that a Skilful Companions version of the Hand and Child tale made its way north to Iceland only after the Viking Age. The absence of a winter theme in the Irish variants suggests that it was in Iceland that the narrative became a Christmas tale. Since the Defence of the Hall motif is aseasonal both in *Beowulf* and in Irish folktales, the most natural explanation is that the hauntings of *Grettis saga* and related Scandinavian texts likewise received their seasonality in the Scandinavian branch only, while *Pwyll pendeuic Dyuet* developed a seasonal quality separately.[109] It may thus be assumed that the Scandinavian tradition is more authoritative for the cave episode of *Beowulf*'s ancestral tradition, while Irish tales preserve critical elements of an earlier stage of the defence of the hall, leaving *Beowulf* without a seasonally inflected model.

KEEPING QUIET

The Scandinavian tendency to invest hauntings with a winter setting is further confirmed by the Greenlandic marooning in *Flóamanna saga*. As will be seen, this episode resembles the Grendel narrative also in its suggestion that supernatural intruders may be drawn to the sounds of revelry.

In *Beowulf*, which lacks the child element of the Hand and Child tale, Grendel's motivation is reduced to anger at the sounds of merrymaking:

---

[108] Scowcroft, 'The Irish Analogues to *Beowulf*', 23–4.

[109] Contrast Leo Tepper, 'The Monster's Mother at Yuletide', in *Monsters and the Monstrous in Medieval Northwest Europe*, ed. by K. E. Olsen and L. A. J. R. Houwen (Leuven: Peeters, 2001), 93–102, which proposes that the material shared between *Beowulf* and *Grettis saga* derives from an Indo-European tradition surfacing also in the Iranian branch; the Yuletide chronology is central to Tepper's argument. In addition, it should be noted that a Welsh tale published in 1935 tells of a burglar of gigantic stature fleeing to a cave behind a waterfall after one of his victims wrenches off his arm; this episode takes place 'one winter's night when the snow was falling': Constance Davies, 'Beowulf's Fight with Grendel', *The Times* (9 November 1935): Literary Supplement, 722. Puhvel asserts that the existence of the Welsh tale 'has been noted since the seventeenth century', but he gives no source for this claim. Davies herself assumed the tale had undergone change over time, but she believed its landscape to be authentic. If the tale in question is to be considered a faithful retelling of a medieval folktale, its value as an analogue to the *Beowulf–Grettis saga* material can hardly be overstated. However, the fact that only a single witness to it has been recorded, and only several decades after the *Beowulf–Grettis saga* analogue was discovered, renders it probable that this tale is a modern retelling of the Sandhaugar narrative. Even if the tale represents a genuine medieval witness to the material, there is no reason to assume that the seasonal structure is cognate with that of *Grettis saga*. The resemblance is superficial: rather than establishing a cyclical seasonal pattern, the Welsh source makes reference to one winter's night only. Moreover, at an earlier point in the tale the robber is seen to enjoy the sun in the hills, contradicting both the Icelandic insistence on winter activity and the consistent reliance on the dark of night in the sagas as well as in *Beowulf*. Finally, snowy winter nights are more commonly used to determine the mood of modern than of medieval English stories, suggesting again that the seasonal reference is not medieval even if the tale itself is. Thus although there seems to be no way of proving that the seasonality of *Grettis saga* was not a feature of the source it shares with *Beowulf*, the most straightforward explanation is that the winter motif is a Scandinavian addition that did not make it to the British Isles until modern times.

> Ða se ellengæst   earfoðlice
> þrage geþolode,   se þe in þystrum bad,
> þæt he dogora gehwam   dream gehyrde
> hludne in healle.   (lines 86–9)
>
> Then the powerful spirit, he who waited in the dark, for a time endured with difficulty that he heard loud revelry in the hall every day.

This motivation is strongly reminiscent of Satan's envy of Adam following Lucifer's fall, expressed to great effect in *Genesis B* (lines 364–8). The *Beowulf* poet's efforts to strengthen this connection suggest that the resemblance is no accident. Satan's envy moves him to destroy the harmony of Eden just as Grendel destroys the harmony of Heorot, implicitly likened to Eden by the scop's song of creation at the hall's inauguration (*Genesis B* 395–762; *Beowulf* 86–98).[110] Indeed, the passage in *Beowulf* is so constructed that the joyous life and its disruption by *an feond on helle* ('a certain fiend in hell'), though strictly linked to the Danish setting by reference to Grendel, reads at first sight as a continuation of the creation account, describing the joys of Eden and their termination at Satan's hands (*Beowulf* 99–102).[111] Eden is only an archetype of the devil's envy, however; the notion that he envies human enjoyment in general[112] and is particularly averse to the joys of divine worship[113] was widespread in the Middle Ages. This theological tradition thus seems to have replaced the monster's folk-traditional motive for the invasion of the hall.

Supernatural agents' hatred of the sounds of hall revelry is likewise commonly found in Icelandic accounts of winter hauntings. The most detailed episode containing this motif is the Greenlandic marooning in *Flóamanna saga* (ch. 22).[114] Throughout this passage, Þorgils is contrasted with his fellow castaway Jósteinn. The shelter they build is partitioned in two, Þorgils commanding half the party and Jósteinn the other. The narrator dwells repeatedly on their contrast in governance, consistently portraying Þorgils as more industrious, judicious, and pious. Significantly, Þorgils tells his men to be quiet in the evenings, while Jósteinn spends the nights making merry with his men:

---

[110] Paul Beekman Taylor, 'Heorot, Earth, and Asgard: Christian Poetry and Pagan Myth', *Tennessee Studies in Literature* 11 (1966): 119–30; Alvin A. Lee, *The Guest-Hall of Eden: Four Essays on the Design of Old English Poetry* (New Haven and London: Yale University Press, 1972), 171–223; William Helder, 'The Song of Creation in *Beowulf* and the Interpretation of Heorot', *English Studies in Canada* 13, no. 3 (September 1987): 243–55.

[111] So also Malcolm Godden, 'Biblical Literature: The Old Testament', in *The Cambridge Companion to Old English Literature*, 2nd ed., ed. Malcolm Godden and Michael Lapidge (Cambridge: Cambridge University Press, 2013), 223–4.

[112] Oliver Farrar Emerson, 'Grendel's Motive in Attacking Heorot', *The Modern Language Review* 16, no. 2 (April 1921): 113–19.

[113] Magennis, *Images of Community*, 72.

[114] Þórhallur Vilmundarson and Bjarni Vilhjálmsson, *Harðar saga*, 282–6.

> Þorgils [. . .] bað sína menn vera hljóðláta ok siðsama á kveldum ok halda vel trú sína. [. . .] Þat er sagt, at Jósteinn ok hans menn gerðu mikit um sik ok höfðu náttleika með háreysti.
>
> Þorgils [. . .] asked his men to be quiet and well behaved in the evenings and keep their faith well. [. . .] It is said that Jósteinn and his men made a lot of noise and played loud games at night.

Þorgils specifically repeats his injunction as Christmas approaches, adding that they should go to bed early, and he warns his men a third time, after disease strikes. In the E-text, he uses the terms *hljóðlátr* ('quiet') and *siðsamr* ('well behaved') in all three instances, which occur in the space of thirty-five edited lines.[115] Religious piety also plays a significant role in the contrast. Although his recent conversion is described as personal conviction, contrasting especially with the attitudes of Jósteinn and his wife Þorgerðr, Þorgils takes firm pastoral command of his own men. This is apparent not only in the orders he gives his company in the evenings, but also in the determination with which he cuts all ties with Þórr, leading the renounced deity to cause their shipwrecking in the first place (chs 20–1).[116] Þorgils's choices ultimately pay off: as the winter hauntings commence, Jósteinn's men fall ill and die off one by one, returning as revenants, until by mid-Gói all the male members of his company are dead. None of Þorgils's men dies, and the hauntings concentrate in Jósteinn's half of the shelter, especially in the K-text. The E-version makes the same claim, but also states that the revenants all go after Þorgils for a time. In both versions, the protagonist's successful endurance of these afflictions gives the narrative a distinctly hagiographical flavour. Þorgils's success in warding off the revenants is naturally understood to be a consequence of his renunciation of Þórr and his sense of discipline, a quality befitting an abbot. When in the E-text the reverse happens, this makes him no less eligible for Christian celebration, as evil spirits will naturally attack God's favourites, as they did Guthlac; the distinguishing characteristic is that they do not succeed in breaking a saint's spirit.[117]

If Þorgils's plight is to be explained as the persecution of a holy man, this hagiographical convention does not explain why the same forces afflict his fellow-castaways who live irreverent lives and spend the nights making merry. Rather, the role of sound in the attraction of dangerous forces seems to play a role as well. While the *dream* ('merriment') that triggers Grendel's attacks in *Beowulf* is strongly religious in character, the pious thing to do in *Flóamanna saga* is evidently to engage in a more subdued expression of

---

[115] Ibid., 283–5; the E-text is found in the lower deck.
[116] Ibid., 274–81.
[117] See Colgrave, *Felix's 'Life of Guthlac'*, or the Old English verse *Guthlac A* and *B* in Krapp and Dobbie, *Exeter Book*, 49–88. On innocence, guilt, and demonic visitations, see Adams, *Visions in Late Medieval England*, 95–8.

piety in the evenings by keeping quiet and turning in early. In fact, keeping quiet and going to bed early are common measures against hauntings in Icelandic prose, including texts without explicit religious content. One or both of these motifs occur also in chapter 13 of *Flóamanna saga*[118] as well as in *Heiðarvíga saga* (ch. 9)[119] and *Hrólfs saga* (ch. 23).[120] All these episodes are explicitly situated in winter, and there is no evidence that they are modelled on the motif of diabolical envy as in *Beowulf*. Instead, they give expression to a tradition in which nighttime revelry attracts unwanted elements in a seasonal chronotope that concentrates hauntings in settled valleys during the winter.

Seasonal Progression in *Beowulf*

If *Beowulf* lacks an overarching seasonal structure, there is nevertheless occasional mention of seasonal progression. The only such passage to structure the action around the seasons is the Finnsburh episode. Following the battle at Finn's hall, a truce is established between Hengest, leader of the Danes, and Finn, who commands the Frisians in this episode and takes oaths of loyalty from Hengest. Finn's extended army, it seems, then disperses across Frisia to spend the winter in their own homes,[121] or perhaps warriors from both sides who are not part of either immediate retinue find winter quarters across the region.[122] Hengest and his retainers, however, have no choice but to spend the winter with their enemy Finn now that the seafaring season has ended:

> Gewiton him ða wigend   wica neosian
> freondum befeallen,   Frysland geseon,
> hamas ond heaburh.   Hengest ða gyt
> wælfagne winter   wunode mid Finne.
> He unhlitme   eard gemunde,
> þeah þe ne meahte   on mere drifan
> hringedstefnan   – holm storme weol,
> won wið winde;   winter yþe beleac

---

[118] Þórhallur Vilmundarson and Bjarni Vilhjálmsson, *Harðar saga*, 255.
[119] Sigurður Nordal and Guðni Jónsson, *Borgfirðinga sǫgur*, 233.
[120] Slay, *Hrólfs saga kraka*, 78.
[121] So, for example, Donald K. Fry, ed., *Finnsburh: Fragment and Episode* (London: Methuen, 1974), 42–3, commentary to line 1125; Fulk, Bjork, and Niles, *Beowulf*, 187, commentary to lines 1125 ff.
[122] Cf. the discussions on the identities of the *wigend* in R. A. Williams, *The Finn Episode in 'Beowulf': An Essay in Interpretation* (Cambridge: Cambridge University Press, 1924), 78–82; Ritchie Girvan, *Finnsburuh*, Sir Israel Gollancz Memorial Lecture (Oxford: Oxford University Press, 1941), 44; Kemp Malone, 'Hildeburh and Hengest', *ELH* 10, no. 4 (December 1943): 274–5 and n. 14; Kemp Malone, 'Finn's Stronghold', *Modern Philology* 43, no. 1 (August 1945): 83–4; J. R. R. Tolkien and Alan Bliss, eds, *Finn and Hengest: The 'Fragment' and the 'Episode'* (London: Allen & Unwin, 1982), 115–17.

> isgebinde –   oþ ðæt oþer com
> gear in geardas,   swa nu gyt deð,
> þa ðe syngales   sele bewitiað,
> wuldortorhtan weder.   Ða wæs winter scacen,
> fæger foldan bearm.   Fundode wrecca,
> gist of geardum.   He to gyrnwræce
> swiðor þohte   þonne to sælade,
> gif he torngemot   þurhteon mihte,
> þæt he Eotena bearn   inne gemunde
> – swa he ne forwyrnde   woroldrædenne –
> þonne him Hunlafing   hildeleoman,
> billa selest   on bearm dyde,
> þæs wæron mid Eotenum   ecge cuðe.
> Swylce ferhðfrecan   Fin eft begeat
> sweordbealo sliðen   æt his selfes ham,
> siþðan grimne gripe   Guðlaf ond Oslaf
> æfter sæsiðe   sorge mændon,
> ætwiton weana dæl;   ne meahte wæfre mod
> forhabban in hreþre.   Ða wæs heal roden
> feonda feorum,   swilce Fin slægen,
> cyning on corþre,   ond seo cwen numen.
> Sceotend Scyldinga   to scypon feredon
> eal ingesteald   eorðcyninges,
> swylce hie æt Finnes ham   findan meahton
> sigla searogimma.   Hie on sælade
> drihtlice wif   to Denum feredon,
> læddon to leodum.   (lines 1125–59)

Then warriors, bereft of friends, travelled through Frisia in search of lodgings, estates and the main town. Hengest then still dwelt with Finn for a bloodstained[123] winter. He keenly[124] remembered his homeland, although he could not sail his ship with the ringed prow on the sea – the ocean welled up with storm, strove against the wind; the winter locked up the waves with a bond of ice – until another summer[125] came to the dwelling-places, as it still does now, those gloriously bright weathers which perpetually observe their proper times. Then the winter was past, the bosom of the earth beautiful. The exile, the visitor was eager to leave that dwelling-place. He thought more keenly of avenging his injury than of a sea voyage, whether he would be able to bring about a hostile meeting, because inwardly he remembered the sons of the

---

[123] The sense of *wælfah* has been contested, suggestions ranging from 'bloodstained' (here adopted) to 'hostile to moving waters', i.e. 'cold'. The former sense is more straightforwardly suggested by the compound itself. While no blood is shed during the winter, the qualifier may serve to describe the mood during the winter as determined by the slaughter that preceded it. For an overview of readings of *wælfah*, see the commentary to line 1128 in Fulk, Bjork, and Niles, *Beowulf*, 187.

[124] I assume with Fulk, Bjork, and Niles, *Beowulf*, 187–8, that the adverb *unhlitme* could by this time be used without invoking its literal sense 'not assigned by lot, i.e. voluntarily' to mean 'keenly, eagerly'.

[125] For a discussion of Old English *gear* denoting the warm season in a two-season taxonomy, see Anderson, 'The Seasons of the Year', 238–9, 255–8.

> Jutes – since he had not refused rulership – when Hunlafing placed the battle-light in his lap, the best of swords, whose edges were known among the Jutes. So then cruel sword-harm came upon bold-spirited Finn in his own home, after Guðlaf and Oslaf lamented the grim attack, expressed their grief by the seaside, blamed him for their share of woes; the restless mind could not be restrained in the chest. Then the hall was reddened with enemy bodies, and Finn killed, the king among his retinue, and the queen taken. The Scylding-warriors carried all the king's hall-possessions to their ships, such precious gems of treasures as they were able to find at Finn's home. They took the royal lady on a sea voyage to the Danes, led her to their people.

The restrictions on travelling here posed by winter influence the social action of the narrative in a way most typical of Old Icelandic prose. Virtually all the sagas of Icelanders and contemporary sagas, as well as many legendary sagas, make use of such seasonal limitations to structure their narratives. The specific element of tensions during a winter stay is likewise mirrored in the sagas. In chapter 50 of *Grettis saga*, Grettir asks for winter lodging at Reykjahólar, where the foster-brothers Þorgeirr and Þormóðr are also staying. Although they try to avoid confrontation out of respect for the farmer, Þorgeirr and Grettir are engaged in constant rivalry during the winter, and only the farmer's interference keeps them from fighting it out to the death.[126] The same motif is explored with a different timeframe in *Fóstbrœðra saga* when the same Þorgeirr finds a single night's lodging on a farm where a vagrant named Butraldi is also staying. The narrator describes to great effect the tension between the two men as they share a meal, while similarly emphasizing the winter conditions that effectively lock them in. Here too the farmer, now portrayed as a cowardly miser, asks that they not make trouble while at his farm. Obliging, the two keep themselves in check until Butraldi leaves the next morning, at which point Þorgeirr intercepts and kills him (ch. 6).[127] The passage in *Beowulf*, though itself surely unrelated to these episodes, may reflect a cognate narrative tradition in its structural and social deployment of the winter season.

In its figurative and connotative uses of winter, however, *Beowulf* stands firmly in the Old English poetic tradition. The historical or legendary sources of the Finnsburh episode may well have contained the surviving seasonal structure from their inception, but *Beowulf* at least does not limit its relevance to practical considerations. The episode's rich non-literal burden has generally been interpreted in one of two ways. On the one hand, the 'binding' quality of winter (1132–3) has been thought to extend into the sphere of social action, as the truce is reached after the end of the seafaring

---

[126] Guðni Jónsson, *Grettis saga*, 159–63; cf. the brief account in the Hauksbók-redaction of *Fóstbrœðra saga*, ch. 13: Björn K. Þórólfsson and Guðni Jónsson, *Vestfirðinga sǫgur*, 191.

[127] Björn K. Þórólfsson and Guðni Jónsson, *Vestfirðinga sǫgur*, 142–7.

season and broken as soon as fair weather returns.[128] Conversely, the violent sea storm (1131–3) has frequently been understood to mirror Hengest's emotional state by way of pathetic fallacy during this winter that prevents him from seeking revenge.[129] These readings are not at odds, as long as it is agreed that the former pertains to action, the latter to psychological experience. However, the psychological reading relies on a liberal reading of the text, which does not strictly indicate that Hengest experiences vengeful emotions during the winter. Rather, it states that he is keen to go home when prevented by the season to do so (1129–33); it is only at the return of the nautical season that his desire for his homeland is surpassed by his thirst for revenge (1137–40). Thus, rather than projecting Hengest's anger, it may be proposed that the storm imagery cleverly taps into the winter seascape associated with exile (as in *The Wanderer* and *The Seafarer*), forcefully illustrating Hengest's longing for his native land without violence to the narrative fact of his winter marooning. It is with the onset of the spring thaw and the renewed viability of escape that social restraints give way, and only at this point is there reference to Hengest's thirst for blood.

Although the Finnsburh episode may seem to depart from the elegiac tradition in its favourable depiction of spring, the season is nevertheless charged with an ambiguity similar to that found in the elegiac poetry. It was seen in the previous chapter that the coming of spring in *The Seafarer* is depicted in a rare image of pleasant landscape that nevertheless carries negative associations for the narrator, who understands it as a call to the deprivations of seafaring exile. A strikingly similar expression of spring melancholy was found in the otherwise joyful prospect of spousal reunion in *The Husband's Message*. Although the *Beowulf* poet does not speak overtly of spring sadness in the Finnsburh episode, the bloody violence of the attack, the Danes' recollection of the previous year's afflictions, the dishonourable betrayal of Finn in his own hall, and the fate of his queen add up to a stark contrast with the 'wuldortorhtan weder' ('gloriously bright weathers', 1136) of early summer for both sides of the conflict. The passage thus adds to the evidence that Old English verse accommodates a tradition of ambivalence towards spring.

Such ambivalence is altogether absent from the poem's other reference to seasonal progression, which follows the defeat of Grendel's mother and the decapitation of her son. This passage takes the form of an extended simile and runs as follows:

---

[128] Burlin, 'Inner Weather and Interlace', 81–2; Anderson, 'The Seasons of the Year', 256–7.
[129] Williams, *The Finn Episode in 'Beowulf'*, 89–90; Tom Shippey, ed., *Old English Verse* (London: Hutchinson University Library, 1972), 23–4; Burlin, 'Inner Weather and Interlace', 81–2; Fry, *Finnsburh*, 23, 43–4, commentary to lines 1133–6; John F. Vickrey, 'The Narrative Structure of Hengest's Revenge in *Beowulf*', *Anglo-Saxon England* 6 (1977): 91–103; Anderson, 'The Seasons of the Year', 256–7.

> Þa þæt sweord ongan
> æfter heaþoswate   hildegicelum,
> wigbil wanian;   þæt wæs wundra sum
> þæt hit eal gemealt   ise gelicost,
> ðonne forstes bend   fæder onlæteð,
> onwindeð wælrapas,   se geweald hafað
> sæla ond mæla;   þæt is soð metod.   (lines 1605–11)

> Then the sword, the battle-blade, began to dissolve into battle-icicles on account of the battle-sweat. It was a marvel how the whole thing melted, most like ice when the father releases the bonds of frost, unbinds the gulf-fetters, he who has power over times and seasons; that is the true Lord.

In the lines that follow, the poet specifies that it is the temperature of Grendel's blood[130] that causes the blade to melt or indeed burn up ('forbarn brodenmæl', 1616,[131] confirmed in 1666–8), although the poisonous quality of its victim is given as an additional explanation (1615–17).[132] Whatever the role of the poison, iron is typically dissolved by heat, and the heat of the monster's blood certainly strengthens the analogy with the melting of ice in spring.

Although the poet does not here use a description like *wuldortorht weder* to express an affection for the spring season, the imagery of loosening still suggests that the passing of winter is thought of as a form of relief. Indeed, in view of the cold habitat of the monsters, the frosty landscape surrounding them, and the fact that their reign of terror has just ended, the spring simile may be understood to extend to the larger narrative. The winter of Grendel's supremacy that afflicted the Danes and 'bound' their hearts with fear has passed; a time of metaphorical spring has arrived. Of course, no worldly spring lasts indefinitely; accordingly, the poet announces future afflictions for the Danes through his hints at discord to come (81–5), a season-like pattern of feud and truce that recurs throughout the poem as one of its most persistent themes.

---

[130] The victim is identified only as 'ellorgæst se þær inne swealt' ('the alien spirit who died in there', 1617). Both Grendel and his mother die in the cave, of course. Although apparently dead by this time, Grendel is the sword's last victim, suggesting that the reference is to him, and this is the most commonly held view: for example Orchard, *Critical Companion*, 135; Daniel Anlezark, 'Poisoned Places: The Avernian Tradition in Old English Poetry', *Anglo-Saxon England* 36 (2007): 107–8; Fulk, Bjork, and Niles, *Beowulf*, 210, commentary to lines 1616b f. Contrast Johann Köberl, 'The Magic Sword in *Beowulf*', *Neophilologus* 71, no. 1 (January 1987): 125. Since Grendel and his mother are portrayed as the same category of being, however (for example 1345–61), the question is irrelevant: it is after Beowulf completes his feat by disposing of both monsters that the sword, having fulfilled its task, loses its functionality. Cf. S. Viswanathan, 'On the Melting of the Sword: *wæl-rāpas* and the Engraving on the Sword-Hilt in *Beowulf*', *Philological Quarterly* 58, no. 3 (summer 1979): 361.

[131] 'The pattern-welded sword burned up.'

[132] A parallel to poisonous monster blood melting iron is given in Orchard, *Critical Companion*, 135.

The Bonds of Winter

Both descriptions of the winter progression in *Beowulf* make use of an image of remarkable popularity in Old English poetry: the bonds of winter. This metaphor, which describes water or land as fettered by the winter weather, has been most fully explored by B. K. Martin, who demonstrated that the motif is not in fact exclusive to Old English poetry, as a range of classical and medieval Latin poetic and also prose texts employ strikingly similar images.[133] Many of these texts are known to have been available in Anglo-Saxon England. Thus even Isidore of Seville's influential *Etymologiae*[134] explain *gelu* ('frost, hoarfrost') by its binding powers ('because the earth is bound by it', 13.10.7),[135] and Alcuin likewise made use of the image.[136] This Latinate background adds pertinence to the question how this figure of speech relates to the Anglo-Saxon winter imagery described in the previous chapter.

Binding imagery has been studied most thoroughly for its applications in *The Wanderer*, which are not limited to the bonds of winter. The narrator of this poem repeatedly employs a binding metaphor with reference to the heroic virtue of reticence (11–14, 17–21), while those who are alone with their misery are portrayed as bound by exhaustion and grief (39–40).[137] Although *The Wanderer* thus seems at first sight to conceive of bonds as capable of both virtue and affliction, it quickly becomes clear that the narrator is hardly partial to the heroic ideal of restraint of one's thoughts and feelings, if only because he breaks this custom by uttering this confessional poetic monologue. In fact, although the poem lists several practical applications of wisdom in a heroic setting (65–72), its central argument seems to be that all worldly achievements are destined to end, while heavenly glories remain (114–15). Heroic values are thus drawn into question, so that the fetters they represent are reduced to a discomfort with little to redeem itself. When these bonds are juxtaposed with those of sorrow and exhaustion (39–40), it seems that the poem's extension of the binding imagery to winter must similarly connote its discomfort.

If the reference of the binding imagery thus far is unambiguous, critics have had more difficulty interpreting the phrase *waþema gebind* ('the bond

---

[133] Martin, 'Aspects of Winter'.

[134] W. M. Lindsay, ed., *Isidori Hispalensis episcopi 'Etymologiarum sive Originum libri XX'*, 2 vols (Oxford: Clarendon, 1911).

[135] 'Quod eo stringatur tellus.'

[136] W. Wilmanns, ed., 'Disputatio regalis et nobilissimi iuvenis Pippini cum Albino scholastico', *Zeitschrift für deutsches Alterthum* 14 (1869): quaestio 62 (538).

[137] The bonds of winter are discussed as one among several images of binding in *Wanderer* in James L. Rosier, 'The Literal-Figurative Identity of the Wanderer', *Publications of the Modern Language Association of America* 79, no. 1 (March 1964): 366–9; Lars Malmberg, 'The Wanderer: *waþema gebind*', *Neuphilologische Mitteilungen* 71 (1970): 96–9; Karen A. Mullen, 'The Wanderer: Considered Again', *Neophilologus* 58, no. 1 (January 1974): 79; Patrick Cook, '*Woriað þa winsalo*: The Bonds of Exile in *The Wanderer*', *Neophilologus* 80 (1996): esp. 130–1. The bonds of sorrow of *Wanderer* 39–40 have a parallel in *Genesis A* 2793–5.

of the waves'), which occurs twice in the course of *The Wanderer*. This description, otherwise unique in the corpus of Old English, is first applied to the waves of the sea when the death of his lord forces the narrator to set out by sea in search of a new employer:

> Ond ic hean þonan
> wod wintercearig   ofer waþema¹³⁸ gebind,
> sohte sele dreorig   sinces bryttan.   (lines 23–5)

> And abject I went from there, winter-sorrowful, across the bond of the waves; sad I sought the hall of a dispenser of treasure.

The noun phrase recurs in line 57, further demonstrating the poet's interest in this type of imagery. Several critics have understood the phrase as a circumlocution for ice or the freezing of the water traversed, thereby contributing to the winter imagery already in place.¹³⁹ Whether this is its intended reference, however, is doubtful. This reading may be inspired by the analogous 'winter yþe beleac / isgebinde'¹⁴⁰ of the Finnsburh episode (*Beowulf* 1132–3), but that compound specifies ice as the binding agent; the one in *The Wanderer* identifies none. Instead, we may compare Genesis 1:10, where the seas are called *congregationes aquarum* ('gatherings of waves'), an image recalled in *Andreas* 519, where God is 'se ðe brimu bindeð' ('he who binds the waters'). Leslie has accordingly understood *gebind* as 'expanse'.¹⁴¹ Analogy between the *Andreas* passage and *waþema gebind* in *The Wanderer* is encouraged by the observations that one cannot sail a frozen sea¹⁴² and birds cannot bathe in one,¹⁴³ though one could certainly imagine a body of water containing drift ice. But external analogues are not required to understand the noun phrase *waþema gebind*, which by itself suggests an interlocking of waves, and thus a body of water plain and simple.

The remaining occurrence of the binding motif in *The Wanderer* is unambiguously connected with winter, but not with the sea:

> Hrið hreosende   hrusan bindeð,
> wintres woma;   þonne won cymeð,

---

¹³⁸ MS 'waþena'; the emendation is justified by the phrase's recurrence in line 57 and the general prevalence of minim confusion.

¹³⁹ Rosier, 'The Literal-Figurative Identity of the Wanderer', 367–8; T. P. Dunning and A. J. Bliss, eds, *The Wanderer* (London: Methuen, 1960), 42; Malmberg, '*The Wanderer: waþema gebind*', 98; Cook, '*Woriað þa winsalo*', 130.

¹⁴⁰ 'Winter closed off the waves with a bond of ice.'

¹⁴¹ R. F. Leslie, ed., *The Wanderer* (Manchester: Manchester University Press, 1966), 70, commentary to line 24; cf. John C. Pope, ed., *Seven Old English Poems* (Indianapolis and New York: Bobbs-Merill, 1966), s.v. 'ġe-bind'.

¹⁴² Rosemary Greentree, 'The Wanderer's Horizon: A Note on *ofer waþema gebind*', *Neophilologus* 86 (2002): 308. The remark by the same author that waves cannot be frozen ignores the metonymic qualities of Old English verse.

¹⁴³ Leslie, *The Wanderer*, 70, n. to line 24; the birds in question occur in line 47.

> nipeð nihtscua, norþan onsendeð
> hreo hæglfare hælepum on andan. (lines 102–5)

The raging storm, blast of winter, binds the earth; when the darkness comes, when the shade of night grows dark, it angrily sends a savage cargo of hail to men from the north.

In this passage, it is the land that is bound, while the binding agent is the winter storm rather than the frost. *The Wanderer* is not alone in these details. *The Seafarer*, which shares many other particulars with *The Wanderer*,[144] contains a similar passage:

> Nap nihtscua, norþan sniwde,
> hrim hrusan bond; hægl feol on eorþan,
> corna caldast. (lines 31–3)

The shade of night grew dark, it snowed from the north, hoarfrost bound the earth; hail fell on the earth, the coldest of grains.[145]

Here hoarfrost is specified as the binding agent, although the motif occurs in between references to snow and hail. Since hoarfrost as well as snow can be thought of as visible evidence of frost, the passage need not be at variance with the Latin motif. *Andreas* too specifies precipitation, here snow, as the material with which the earth is bound: 'snaw eorðan band / wintergeworpum' ('snow bound the earth with winter showers', 1255–6). Indeed, snow binds the fruits of the earth in the verse *Solomon and Saturn II*:[146]

---

[144] See, for example, Stanley, 'Poetic Diction'; Daniel G. Calder, 'Setting and Mode in *The Seafarer* and *The Wanderer*', *Neuphilologische Mitteilungen* 72 (1971): 264–75; Martin Green, 'Man, Time, and Apocalypse in *The Wanderer*, *The Seafarer*, and *Beowulf*', *Journal of English and Germanic Philology* 74, no. 4 (1975): 502–18; Klein, 'Purpose and the "Poetics" of *The Wanderer* and *The Seafarer*'; Rosemary Woolf, '*The Wanderer*, *The Seafarer*, and the Genre of *planctus*', in Nicholson and Frese, *Anglo-Saxon Poetry*, 192–207; Muriel Cornell, 'Varieties of Repetition in Old English Poetry: Especially in *The Wanderer* and *The Seafarer*', *Neophilologus* 65, no. 2 (1981): 292–307; Andy Orchard, 'Re-reading *The Wanderer*: The Value of Cross-References', in *Via Crucis*: Essays on Early Medieval Sources and Ideas in Memory of J. E. Cross, ed. Thomas N. Hall (Morgantown: West Virginia University Press, 2002), 19–20.

[145] This description of hail is paralleled in Old Norse as well as elsewhere in Old English: cf. the Old English *Rune Poem* 25 'ᚻ byþ hwitust corna' ('hail is the whitest of grains'): Maureen Halsall, ed., *The Old English 'Rune Poem': A Critical Edition*, McMaster Old English Studies and Texts 2 (Toronto: University of Toronto Press, 1981); Norwegian *Rune Poem* 13 'ᚼ er kaldastr korna' ('hail is the coldest of grains'): Finnur Jónsson, *Skjaldedigtning*, A2:229–30; Icelandic *Rune Poem* 7 'ᚼ er kaldakorn' ('hail is a cold grain'): Page, *The Icelandic Rune-Poem*, 27–30, and cf. the transcriptions on pp. 7, 11, 17, 19, 22. The image transcended metaphorical status at least in Scandinavia, where Old Norse *haglkorn* (lit. 'hail-grain') and its modern forms are attested as the default terms for 'hailstone', *korn* thus coming to refer to grain-shaped or grain-sized particles much like modern English *grain*. Fritzner, s.v. 'haglkorn'; Dahlerup and Jacobsen, *Ordbog*, s.vv. 'hagl-korn', 'korn' sense 3; Mattisson, *Ordbok*, s.vv. 'hagel-korn', 'korn' sense 6; Mörður Árnason, ed., *Íslensk orðabók*, 4th ed. (Reykjavik: Edda, 2007), s.vv. 'korn' sense 2, 'snjókorn'; *DOE*, s.v. 'grain, n.1', senses under II.

[146] Daniel Anlezark, ed. and trans., *The Old English Dialogues of Solomon and Saturn* (Cambridge: Brewer, 2009), 78–95.

> Ac forhwon fealleð se snaw,   foldan behydeð,
> bewrihð wyrta cið,   wæstmas getigeð,
> geðyð hie and geðreatað,   ðæt hie ðrage beoð
> cealde geclungne?   (lines 124–7)

> But why does the snow fall, conceal the earth, cover the shoots of roots, bind plants, press and oppress them, so that for a time they are congealed[147] with cold?

Reading these passages in conjunction, it seems that they all present winter precipitation as the agent in the metaphor. To bind the earth or its fruits, then, here means to cover the earth and suppress its production of plant life, but a connection with the effects of frost is also made. Snow, hail, and hoarfrost are thus treated as visible manifestations of frost. They leave a trace on the land, not the sea, and so this tradition of winter binding-imagery does not apply to waterscapes unless they freeze over, as in the Finnsburh episode.

Winter binding metaphors in Old English are not limited to land and crops, however, as becomes clear when *The Seafarer* contributes the image of limbs gone numb with the bonds of frost:

> Calde geþrungen
> wæron mine fet,   forste gebunden,
> caldum clommum.   (lines 8–10)

> My feet were pinched with cold, bound with frost, with cold bonds.

The phrase *cealde clommas* ('cold bonds') is also found in *Andreas* 1212 and *Christ C* 1629,[148] where it refers to the literal bonds of St Andrew and the literal or figurative bonds of hell respectively. Clearly, then, the bonds of winter as found in the Old English poetic corpus do not all derive from Latin descriptions of frost's effects on land or sea. Instead, what characterizes the majority of Old English attestations is an association with personal deprivation and subjective experience, where the Latin metaphor is on the whole more disinterested.

Following its foreboding reference to *cealde clommas*, *Andreas* describes the application of these fetters in great detail, again in a context of personal suffering like that of *The Wanderer* or *The Seafarer*. Here, however, the

---

[147] Although the lexicographical consensus is to read *(ge-)clingan* in this passage as 'shrivelled' (Bosworth and Toller, *An Anglo-Saxon Dictionary*, s.v. 'ge-clungen'; J. R. Clark Hall, ed., *A Concise Anglo-Saxon Dictionary*, 4th ed., with a supplement by Herbert D. Meritt (Cambridge: Cambridge University Press, 1960), s.v. 'clingan'; *DOE*, s.v. 'clingan'; Anlezark, *Solomon and Saturn*, s.v. 'geclingan'), the reading 'congeal', which is the primary sense of *clingan* in Clark Hall and *DOE*, accords better with the parallel verb *getigan* ('bind') and represents more accurately the state of hibernating plant life at a time of snowfall. That the object of the verb is hibernating plant life in general rather than *wæstmas* in the precise sense 'fruits' is suggested by the adverbial *þrage* ('for a time'), suggesting ultimate recovery.

[148] Krapp and Dobbie, *Exeter Book*, 27–49.

afflictions of winter are used to increase the heroism of St Andrew, who withstands its onslaught unaffected:

> Þa se halga wæs   under heolstorscuwan,
> eorl ellenheard,   ondlange niht
> searoþancum beseted.   Snaw eorðan band
> wintergeworpum;   weder coledon
> heardum hægelscurum,   swylce hrim ond forst,
> hare hildstapan,   hæleða eðel
> lucon, leoda gesetu.   Land wæron freorig
> cealdum cylegicelum;   clang wæteres þrym
> ofer eastreamas;   is brycgade
> blæce brimrade.   Bliðheort wunode
> eorl unforcuð,   elnes gemyndig,
> þrist ond þroht   heardin þreanedum
> wintercealdan niht.   (lines 1253–65)

> Then the saint, the courageous man, was beset with schemes in the shadow of dark throughout the night. Snow bound the earth with winter showers. The weathers cooled down with harsh hailstorms as well as rime and frost, grey warriors; they closed off the homeland of men, the home of the people. The lands were freezing with cold icicles; the sound of water resounded over the river currents, ice bridged the dark riding of the waters. Joyful, the man remained unafraid, mindful of courage, confident and resistant to hardship in his afflictions throughout the winter-cold night.

This extended weather description, which has no parallel in the Greek and Latin analogues,[149] combines binding imagery with a personification of rime and frost, which may be compared with a personification in the *Menologium* discussed below as well as a parallel in the Old Norse *Fóstbrœðra saga*.[150] In terms of elegy, the *Andreas* passage not only invokes the binding image in a passage concerned with personal affliction, but the onslaught of winter mirroring the protagonist's condition similarly recalls a number of elegiac texts, particularly *The Wanderer* and *The Seafarer*. A crucial difference is that Andrew does not allow the external violence to weaken his spirit, and it is in this that his sainthood resides.[151]

Even the *Menologium*, a sober poem describing the course of the year with reference to the major feasts of the Church, admits a sense of loss, not to mention a high degree of poetic elaboration, when it speaks of seasonal binding:

---

[149] Brooks, '*Andreas*' and '*The Fates of the Apostles*', 107.
[150] In the Möðruvallabók-redaction of *Fóstbrœðra saga*, 'fjúk ok frost gekk alla nóttina' ('fog and frost went [strictly 'walked'] round all night', Björn K. Þórólfsson and Guðni Jónsson, *Vestfirðinga sǫgur*, 136). The image is even more elaborate in Hauksbók, which reads 'fjúk ok frost kveða helgaldra um húsþekjur ok sýna þeim, er út sjá, sinn snarpan leik með litilli mœði ok mikilli ógn' ('fog and frost sing a death-song around the roofs and show those looking out their rough game with little weariness and great terror', n. 1 in the same edition). The personification is striking in view of the fact that authors in this genre seldom deviate from a behaviourist style of narration.
[151] Cf. Mora, 'Un invierno entre los hielos', 236.

> Syþþan wintres dæg   wide gangeð
> on syx nihtum,   sigelbeortne genimð
> hærfest mid herige   hrimes and snawes,
> forste gefeterad,   be frean hæse,
> þæt us wunian ne moton   wangas grene,
> foldan freatuwe.   (lines 202–7)

> Then, six nights later, Winter's Night arrives far and wide. It captures sun-bright autumn with an army of rime and snow, fettered with frost by the Lord's command, so that green fields, the ornaments of the earth, cannot remain with us.

The metaphor here used is the most elaborate of binding images in Old English poetry, again containing a martial personification, now presenting autumn as a prisoner of war bound with a fetter of frost. The elegiac element expressed in this passage is far less personal in nature than that found in the other instances of the motif, consisting instead in a regret that the warmer season has passed, a sentiment not altogether widespread in Old English poetry.

If the regret commonly expressed at winter's binding of nature implies a matching sense of relief at the corresponding loosening in spring, such relief is rarely expressed. One text that makes mention of the unloosening is another text on gnomic truths, *Maxims I*. This wisdom poem contains a section describing the entire cycle of the year in similar imagery, interspersed with other facts of life:

> Forst sceal freosan,   fyr wudu meltan,
> eorþe growan,   is brycgian,
> wæter helm wegan,   wundrum lucan
> eorþan ciþas.   An sceal inbindan
> forstes fetre   felameahtig God;
> winter sceal geweorpan,   weder eft cuman,
> sumor swegle hat,   sund unstille.   (lines 71–7)

> Frost must freeze, fire melt wood, the earth grow, ice form bridges, water carry a covering,[152] wondrously close off the earth's saplings. One very powerful God must unbind the fetter of frost; winter must pass by, good weather return, the summer hot with the sun, the unquiet waters.

The description seems neutral in tone, unless it is maintained that metaphorical bonds must always be perceived as undesirable. A better case for relief at the unloosening in spring can be made with reference to the two instances of the motif in *Beowulf*. The image of the melting sword quoted above can be read in this way, although this still requires bold

---

[152] The verse may alternatively be read 'water wear a helmet'. However, martial imagery would here be less fitting than in the passages in *Andreas* and *Menologium*, where it is the time of year or the precipitation that is personified as the bringer of winter weather and not, as here, an impartial landscape.

interpretation. Much as in the *Maxims* passage, the *Beowulf* poet simply states that ice melts when God releases the bonds of frost (1608–10). He then follows up this observation with a brief glorification of God, but strictly in his capacity as governor of the seasons, not favouring spring over winter (1610–11). A subjective reading of the passage becomes viable if spring is read as a metaphor for the relief following the defeat of the episode's monsters.

The seasonal passage in the Finnsburh episode quoted above does offer unequivocal praise of spring. It makes reference to *wuldortorht weder* ('gloriously bright weathers', 1136) and calls the bosom of the earth in spring *fæger* ('beautiful', 1137). The only detraction from this explicit praise of the warm season consists in the bloody revenge that follows. Thus there is certainly irony in the juxtaposition of fair weathers and violent deeds, but this seems to affect the burden of the latter rather than the poet's appraisal of the former. This passage, of course, does not strictly refer to a release from bonds, but it may be said to imply as much given its earlier reference to the winter binding of the sea. In much the same way, an implicit relief may be understood to accompany the undoing of the bonds of winter in all texts describing those bonds as an affliction. Nevertheless, Old English poetry mentions winter more frequently than spring or summer, thus investing it more than the others with subjective experience and establishing a seasonal chronotope of oppression conjoining winter with open landscapes not populated unless by a solitary protagonist.

Winter Conflict

Even more so than in the Mediterranean, long-distance sea travel in medieval northern Europe was dangerous in winter and therefore seldom practised at that time of year, whether for economic or military purposes.[153] Land-based warfare was not restricted in the same way: if some routes were impassable in winter, others, especially fjords, lakes, and marshes, were easier to traverse when frozen, as is occasionally made clear in the sagas.[154] The strategic use of such seasonal infrastructure logically entailed the possibility of battles carried out on ice and in otherwise hibernal landscapes. Scenes of winter combat are indeed widely found in medieval Scandinavian

[153] *Konungs skuggsjá*, chs 22–3: Brenner, *Speculum regale*, 59–63; Jean-Michel Rat, 'Les activités maritimes du Haut Moyen Age en relation avec les saisons', in Carruthers, *La ronde des saisons*, 27–8. Although military expeditions were one of the main exceptions to the Mediterranean winter hiatus in sea travel, this practice has been explained as strategic: fleets would set out to surprise the enemy at a time of limited vigilance, thus confirming the overall trend (McCormick, *Origins*, 462–8).

[154] For example *Eyrbyggja saga*, chs 37, 45: Einar Ólafur Sveinsson and Matthías Þórðarson, *Eyrbyggja saga*, 99–100, 125–6; see further Schach, 'Scenery', 47–55. Naturally, weather extremes still negatively impacted land-based travel (see, for example, *Svínfellinga saga*, ch. 9: Jón Jóhannesson, Magnús Finnbogason, and Kristján Eldjárn, *Sturlunga saga*, 2:97).

literature. Such accounts cannot be used to quantify the historical reality of winter expeditions, though their large number leave little doubt that they were a reality. Their literary effect, however, is to associate winter with treachery and unpredictability, while celebrating those who turn the season's dangers to their advantage.

Among the episodes with some claim to historical credibility are the battles found in the kings' sagas, as these often imply larger armies and populations, enabling historiography through communal memory. Of course, a distinction should be made between events written down within a few generations of their occurrence and accounts of the earliest known Scandinavian kings, whose transmission has a strong mythological motivation. The first chapters of *Ynglinga saga* belong firmly in the latter category for their euhemerization of the Æsir. However, when chapter 29 describes a battle fought between Aðils and Áli on the ice of Lake Vænir,[155] now Vänern, Sweden's largest lake, the episode has sufficient realism to have its roots in a historical encounter. *Beowulf* furthermore references this battle as one of the Swedish conflicts that help sketch the Geatas' geopolitical situation. The conflict thus had a strong and widespread narrative presence, reinforcing the likelihood of a historical referent.

While *Beowulf* does not mention that the battle takes place on ice, it is within the poem's account of this event that the phrase 'cealdum cearsiþum' ('cold sorrow-journeys') is used (2391–6), leading Bugge to suppose a literal sense for the adjective *ceald* alongside its figurative sense in this passage.[156] This reading has found little resonance with later critics,[157] but it would not be beyond the associative style of Old English heroic narration to gesture towards a known story in this way, as one has only to glance at the concise references in *Deor*[158] or *Waldere B*[159] to acknowledge. Exclusively metaphorical uses of *ceald* do exist, as was noted above, but in a case like the *Beowulf* passage, where a winter setting is externally attested, to discount the suggestive connection between wording and context would be unduly to detract from the poet's command of his medium. It is the dynamic range of semantic reference in *cealde cearsiþas*, from the bitter feelings that motivated these expeditions[160] to their hibernal setting, that exemplifies the richness of Old English poetic expression.

---

[155] Bjarni Aðalbjarnarson, *Heimskringla*, 1:57.
[156] Bugge, 'Studien über das Beowulfepos', 13.
[157] A.J. Wyatt and R.W. Chambers, eds, *Beowulf: With the 'Finnsburg Fragment'* (Cambridge: Cambridge University Press, 1915), 120, n. to line 2396; Spinner, 'Sinnesempfindungen', 105; L. Whitbread, 'A Medieval English Metaphor', *Philological Quarterly* 17, no. 4 (October 1938): 366; Wrenn, *Beowulf*, s.v. 'ceald'; Stanley, 'Poetic Diction', 436; Salmon, 'Connotations of *cold*', 316; Fulk, Bjork, and Niles, *Beowulf*, 244, commentary to lines 2395b f. and glossary, s.v. 'ceald'; *DOE*, s.v. 'ceald adj.', sense 6c.
[158] Krapp and Dobbie, *Exeter Book*, 178–9.
[159] Dobbie, *Minor Poems*, 5–6.
[160] The plural, of course, resists explanation in the absence of a detailed historiography.

Winter battles are also found in the more contemporary kings' sagas, which are generally more firmly rooted in historical events. *Sverris saga*, commissioned by King Sverrir himself and thus contemporary with many of the events it describes,[161] depicts several winter campaigns. Chapter 163 recounts a sequence of winter encounters between the loyalist Birkibeinar and the Túnsbergsmenn opposing them. The season's effects on this campaign do not go unnoticed: the snow is mentioned as advantageous to the king's scouts who wear skis, but an obstacle to walking. Similarly, the final confrontation of the chapter takes place on ice, and this helps decide the battle in the king's favour, as his men wear crampons while the Túnsbergsmenn, who arrive by ship, do not.[162] Winter expeditions and the military challenges and advantages proper to them are recounted at various other turns in this text, making clear that the concept was not an alien one at least in narrative.[163] The most spectacular such episode is found in chapter 19, where Sverrir and his soldiers are caught in a snowstorm in which they lose over 120 horses and eat nothing but snow for eight days; the wind is so severe that a man is thrown to the ground and dies of a triple spine fracture by the force of the gale alone.[164] Though this account has no doubt been embellished, it must still be assumed that the campaign, reported so shortly after the event, did indeed take place in winter, and that the logistic difficulties following from the time of year were familiar ones.

An episode in Saxo Grammaticus's *Gesta Danorum* parallels the battle on ice in *Sverris saga*, though Saxo harms his historical credibility by surrounding the passage with romance features. Alf encounters a fleet of Blacmanni whose ships are trapped in ice, and orders his men to run across the ice 'caligatis vestigiis' ('with booted feet') rather than in their slippery standard issue, resulting in an easy victory.[165] Unsurprisingly, some translators have understood the boots to refer to spiked shoes,[166] but such a translation is not strictly warranted by the text. In either reading, however, it is appropriate equipment that proves decisive in winter battle, as in *Sverris saga*.

A more firmly legendary passage in the *Gesta Danorum* is Saxo's account of Ragnarr *loðbrók*. In the vernacular saga, this hero covers his woollen outfit in tar and sand to protect him against the serpent's poison (ch. 3).[167] In Saxo's rendering, by contrast, he dips himself in freezing water, woollen clothes

---

[161] Þorleifur Hauksson, ed., *Sverris saga*, Íslenzk fornrit 30 (Reykjavik: Hið íslenzka fornritafélag, 2007), xxii–xxiv.
[162] Ibid., 252–5.
[163] Esp. chs 12, 19, 160: ibid., 20, 32–4, 247.
[164] Ibid., 33.
[165] Saxo Grammaticus, *Gesta Danorum*, 7.6.5 (Friis-Jensen and Zeeberg 1:462).
[166] For example ibid., 1:463.
[167] Guðni Jónsson and Bjarni Vilhjálmsson, *Fornaldarsögur*, 1:100–2.

and all, to form armour out of ice, thus turning the season to his advantage.[168]

Hákonar saga herðibreiðs contains another winter campaign, and here too the winning party is the one that succeeds in making the season into an ally. Grégóríús Dagsson pursues Hákon and his army late during Christmastide, and catches up with him at a river. The ice separating the two armies has, however, been sabotaged by Hákon and covered up with snow; Grégóríús falls through the ice and is killed with an arrow (ch. 14).[169]

Despite widespread references to winter battles in the kings' sagas, the best known of such episodes from Scandinavia are doubtlessly those depicted in the sagas of Icelanders. *Njáls saga*, often cited in discussions of landscape for its unusual inclusion of a brief *locus amoenus* passage,[170] tells how Njáll's sons fall into disagreement with Þráinn Sigfússon over damages incurred in Norway (chs 88–91).[171] Three or four weeks into the winter, word reaches them that Þráinn is visiting a friend in the district, and the brothers decide to confront him. When they intercept him, the two groups of men are separated by the glacial river Markarfljót. The river is not fully frozen, and the nearest ford some distance away. However, Skarphéðinn comes in running and leaps across twelve ells of water to land on the ice sheet supporting his enemies, driving his axe into Þráinn's skull as he slides past him. If the remainder of the fight also takes place on the ice sheet, no further use is made of the landscape (ch. 92).[172]

Eyrbyggja saga tells of another ice battle, now on Vigrafjǫrðr, just north of Snæfellsnes. Here, Steinþórr and eight of his men come upon their enemies, the sons of Þorbrandr, in a group of six. It concerns a chance encounter: the season is conducive to it only inasmuch as Steinþórr has delayed an errand but wants it done before Christmas, while the sons of Þorbrandr are on their way to a Christmas celebration. The winter landscape here plays a critical role in the development of the battle. On first eye contact, the sons of Þorbrandr, being the smaller of the two groups, make a stand on a skerry surrounded by sloping ice floes resulting from the fjord's tidal

---

[168] Saxo Grammaticus, *Gesta Danorum*, 9.4.5–7 (Friis-Jensen and Zeeberg 1:588–90).

[169] Bjarni Aðalbjarnarson, *Heimskringla*, 3:363–4.

[170] The passage is Gunnarr's fatal resolution not to leave Iceland on account of his outlawry: 'fǫgr er hlíðin, svá at mér hefir hon aldri jafnfǫgr sýnzk, bleikir akrar ok slegin tún, ok mun ek ríða heim aptr ok fara hvergi' ('the slope is fair, it has never seemed as fair to me; the fields are white and the infield mowed, and I will ride home and go nowhere', ch. 75: Einar Ólafur Sveinsson, *Brennu-Njáls saga*, 182). It is invariably referenced as an exception where the genre's lack of nature description for its own sake is discussed: Hallberg, *The Icelandic Saga*, 71; Pearsall and Salter, *Landscapes and Seasons*, 45–6; O'Donoghue, *Old Norse–Icelandic Literature*, 59–60. It is not entirely unique, however: indeed, it has been proposed that Gunnar's phrase *bleikir akrar* came to the *Njála* compiler from having read it in a landscape description in *Alexanders saga*, itself based on the Latin *Alexandreis*. Einar Ólafur Sveinsson, *Brennu-Njáls saga*, xxxiv–xxxvii; Lars Lönnroth, *Njáls saga: A Critical Introduction* (Berkeley, Los Angeles, and London: University of California Press, 1976), 149–54.

[171] Einar Ólafur Sveinsson, *Brennu-Njáls saga*, 214–29.

[172] Ibid., 232–4; for further discussion of the episode, see Schach, 'The Anticipatory Literary Setting in the Old Icelandic Family Sagas', 2–3.

flow. This makes the company difficult to attack other than with arrows, and the episode describes an ultimately successful series of slippery attempts (ch. 45).[173]

Not on the ice but similarly concerned with winter landscape is the Butraldi episode of *Fóstbrœðra saga* mentioned earlier in this chapter. This episode tells how Butraldi and his men have difficulty climbing the slope out of Gervidalr on account of the firm snowdrift that has gathered there. Þorgeirr ascends the slope on the other side of the river where it is easier and reaches the top of the ridge when Butraldi is still making his way up the steep slope, cutting footholds with his axe. Þorgeirr then rides his spear down the snow bank, dealing Butraldi his death stroke with his axe in passing (ch. 6).[174] Further winter episodes in the sagas of Icelanders include an attempt to send Egill to his death in impenetrable snow in *Egils saga* (ch. 73);[175] the subsequent ambush of Egill's tax mission, where the winter landscape serves only to betray the assailants' tracks (chs 75–7);[176] the occasional wintertime outlaw hunt in *Gísla saga* (chs 20, 34)[177] and *Grettis saga* (ch. 59);[178] and various games of *knattleikr* on ice turned violent.[179]

A recurring element of strategic advantage in winter battles is access to crampons or spiked snowshoes. It was seen above that access to this equipment is decisive in the ice-based battle between the Birkibeinar and the Túnsbergsmenn depicted in *Sverris saga*, and that Alf's encounter with the fleet of Blacmanni is decided in his favour owing to a similar advantage. Likewise, during the abovementioned conflict in *Eyrbyggja saga*, Þorbrandr's foster-son Freysteinn wears crampons, which is apparently not to be taken for granted, as his opponent Steinþórr, at least, lacks this advantage (ch. 45).[180] It seems nevertheless to have been a fairly common type of equipment: in a wintertime conflict in *Íslendinga saga*, most members of a group confronted with a slippery passage are said to wear them (ch. 156).[181] Interestingly,

---

[173] Einar Ólafur Sveinsson and Matthías Þórðarson, *Eyrbyggja saga*, 125–30.
[174] Björn K. Þórólfsson and Guðni Jónsson, *Vestfirðinga sǫgur*, 145–7. Cf. the descent in *Þórðar saga hreðu*, ch. 9: Jóhannes Halldórsson, *Kjalnesinga saga*, 209–10.
[175] Bjarni Einarsson, *Egils saga*, 131–2.
[176] Ibid., 137–41.
[177] Björn K. Þórólfsson and Guðni Jónsson, *Vestfirðinga sǫgur*, 64–7, 109–16.
[178] Guðni Jónsson, *Grettis saga*, 188–94.
[179] *Knattleikr* was played both on land and on ice, but the sagas treat it as one and the same game, so that it is sometimes hard to see what surface is intended in a given passage. The game's narrative function is typically to cause or escalate tensions between men, as in *Egils saga*, ch. 40: Bjarni Einarsson, *Egils saga*, 53–5; *Gǫngu-Hrólfs saga*, ch. 9: Guðni Jónsson and Bjarni Vilhjálmsson, *Fornaldarsögur*, 2:379–81. Such escalations take place on ice in *Gísla saga*, ch. 15: Björn K. Þórólfsson and Guðni Jónsson, *Vestfirðinga sǫgur*, 49–50; *Grettis saga*, ch. 15: Guðni Jónsson, *Grettis saga*, 42–4; *Þórðar saga hreðu*, ch. 3: Jóhannes Halldórsson, *Kjalnesinga saga*, 177–8. They also take place in winter in *Egils saga*, ch. 40: Bjarni Einarsson, *Egils saga*, 53–5; *Harðar saga*, ch. 23: Þórhallur Vilmundarson and Bjarni Vilhjálmsson, *Harðar saga*, 61–2; *Gull-Þóris saga*, ch. 2: ibid., 181; and probably in *Þorsteins saga Víkingssonar*, ch. 10: Guðni Jónsson and Bjarni Vilhjálmsson, *Fornaldarsögur*, 203–4.
[180] Einar Ólafur Sveinsson and Matthías Þórðarson, *Eyrbyggja saga*, 125–30.
[181] Jón Jóhannesson, Magnús Finnbogason, and Kristján Eldjárn, *Sturlunga saga*, 1:463.

in both the accounts taking place in Iceland, this strategic difference between the two parties is cancelled out in one way or another by the skill or cunning of the disadvantaged party. In *Eyrbyggja saga*, Steinþórr kills Freysteinn despite the latter's stronger foothold (ch. 45).[182] The attacking force in the episode of *Íslendinga saga* is outwitted by the opposing party, whose foresight in watering the passage results in an ice sheet that proves treacherous even to a well-outfitted troop; moreover, the use of snowshoes necessitated by this situation means that no dense front can be formed (ch. 161).[183] In general, it may be said that crampons or skis in literary winter campaigns serve to accentuate the foresight of those wearing them; thus the author of *Sverris saga* sees to it that it is the king himself who recommends their use (ch. 163).[184] In the two Icelandic texts, however, the crampons emphasize the achievement of their owners' opponents in defeating those who have come better prepared.

Such literary effects of winter battles draw attention to the fact that however truthful an account may be, the season and its landscapes take on literary significance within each text as well. This may take the form of propaganda, as when King Sverrir has the foresight to bring skis and crampons, or it may serve narrative embellishment. The ice battle in *Sverris saga*, for instance, profits aesthetically when it states that 'ísinn gerðisk háll af blóði' ('the ice turned slippery with blood'),[185] making it not just a historical report but a story worth telling. The ice battle in *Njáls saga* draws attention to Skarphéðinn's prowess, since environmental interest ceases immediately following his feat; that of *Eyrbyggja saga*, by contrast, makes full use of the strategic implications of the frozen landscape. In the Butraldi episode of *Fóstbrœðra saga*, the winter landscape emphasizes the ignominy in the actions of Þorgeirr, who derives a tactical advantage from the same slope that renders his opponent defenceless. In spite of these individual aims, however, the common denominator between many of these episodes is the message that winter is a treacherous season for travel and combat, awarding victory to whichever party is best able to turn its threats and challenges to their advantage.

Winter motifs in the sagas are generally limited to episodic appearances. However, some texts employ winter imagery in ways that are both structural and consistent. It was seen already that *Grettis saga* consistently associates winter with dangerous outside forces. Another example of such usage is *Gísla saga*, whose interest in landscape and winter has been signalled by a number of scholars.[186] From the perspective of the present study, what

---

[182] Einar Ólafur Sveinsson and Matthías Þórðarson, *Eyrbyggja saga*, 128.
[183] Jón Jóhannesson, Magnús Finnbogason, and Kristján Eldjárn, *Sturlunga saga*, 1:463.
[184] Þorleifur Hauksson, *Sverris saga*, 252.
[185] Ibid., 255.
[186] Hansen, 'Naturbeskrivende indslag i *Gísla saga Súrssonar*'; Vésteinn Ólason, 'Introduction', in *'Gisli Sursson's Saga' and 'The Saga of the People of Eyri'*, trans. Judy Quinn and Martin S. Regal

characterizes the winter landscapes of *Gísla saga* is the danger they signal to human life. Gísli is careful not to leave any tracks in the snow when he sets out to kill Þorgrímr, yet is almost betrayed by the snow on his boots (chs 16–17).[187] Near the end of the saga, tracks in the hoarfrost are instrumental in revealing his whereabouts to Eyjólfr (ch. 34).[188] Snow is a means of malicious sorcery when the witch Auðbjǫrg causes an avalanche;[189] conversely, Freyr honours Þorgrímr posthumously by the absence of snow from the south-western face of his grave mound, indicating that there is no hostility between them (ch. 18).[190] Even in figurative usage, snow has connotations of danger: towards the end of his life as an outlaw, Gísli's lack of options is indicated with the expression 'it now seems to him that there is drift-snow in all his shelters' (ch. 23).[191] Finally, quiet cold spells and windless snowfalls serve to forebode violence at various turns in the saga (chs 15, 18, 34).[192] Although the use of winter landscapes as immediate settings for hostilities is limited in this text, all these references to winter landscapes and winter weather serve to signal violence and danger. The associations of winter in *Gísla saga* thus correspond closely to connections between winter and threats to the individual found more widely in Old Norse as well as Anglo-Saxon literature.

Prognostication and Prophecy

The Christmas season, which signalled the start of the year in early-medieval Insular cultures adhering to the Julian calendar,[193] was a time for resolutions in Old Norse culture. This is reflected in the sagas, which

---

(London: Penguin, 1997), xxii; Bernadine McCreesh, 'Good Weather, Bad Weather: The Use of the Natural World in *Gísla saga*', lecture presented at New Directions in Medieval Scandinavian Studies: The 30th Annual Conference of the Center for Medieval Studies, Fordham University, 28 March 2010.

[187] Björn K. Þórólfsson and Guðni Jónsson, *Vestfirðinga sǫgur*, 53–5. Cf. *Þiðreks saga*, in which Vǫlundr escapes suspicion of having killed the king's young sons by telling the boys to walk backwards to his smithy following a fresh fall of snow, making it look as though they survived the visit (chs 121–2): Henrik Bertelsen, ed., *Þiðriks saga af Bern*, 2 vols (Copenhagen: Møller, 1905–11), 1:116–18.

[188] Björn K. Þórólfsson and Guðni Jónsson, *Vestfirðinga sǫgur*, 109–11; see also Schach, 'Scenery', 40; Vésteinn Ólason, 'Introduction', xxii.

[189] Björn K. Þórólfsson and Guðni Jónsson, *Vestfirðinga sǫgur*, 59–60. Winter storms are likewise invoked in *Eyrbyggja saga*, ch. 40: Einar Ólafur Sveinsson and Matthías Þórðarson, *Eyrbyggja saga*, 109–10 and *Víglundar saga*, ch. 12: Jóhannes Halldórsson, *Kjalnesinga saga*, 83, but on the whole there is no distinct seasonal pattern to the malicious sorcery in the sagas as indexed in Boberg, *Motif-Index*, 89–91 (motifs D2050–99).

[190] Björn K. Þórólfsson and Guðni Jónsson, *Vestfirðinga sǫgur*, 57 and n. 2.

[191] 'Þykkir honum nú fokit vera í ǫll skjól' (ibid., 102).

[192] Ibid., 52, 59, 109. The noun *logn* ('calm') and its compounds mark the quiet and imply the bloodshed to come in all three passages. Vésteinn's murder is the exception: it takes place during a storm (ch. 13: ibid., 43–4). See further Hansen, 'Naturbeskrivende indslag i *Gísla saga Súrssonar*'.

[193] As noted in the introduction, 25 March was never New Year's Day in Anglo-Saxon England.

relay a tradition of Yuletide boasts to be fulfilled before the year is over.[194] The year's events were also determined by factors outside human control, however, and winter was a time of increased access to such information.

The surviving corpus of prognostics, which follows a Latin tradition,[195] provides some first evidence of the divining role of winter in England and Iceland. Most Latinate prognostics are atemporal or based around lunar cycles; only a modest few are tied to the solar year. Most of the latter group concern the start of the year. One such type, the brontology, interprets the year's fortunes on the basis of the weekday[196] or month[197] of the year's first thunderstorm. Since thunderstorms in this part of the world are characteristic of warm weather, this type of divination is tied loosely to spring, but the authors of the two surviving month brontologies in Anglo-Saxon manuscripts have dutifully listed out the months through to November or December.[198]

A more precisely defined annual prognostic is found in auguries attributed to Christmas Day, the twelve days of Christmas, or the kalends of January. In Anglo-Saxon England, the most widely attested genre of this type is the year prognosis, which predicts the year's outlook in terms of weather, farming, peace, and health on the basis of the weekday that marks the kalends of January or 25 December.[199] Often, the forecast was given for each of the year's four Julian seasons, in the format 'if the first day of the year falls on a Sunday, it will be a good winter, and a windy spring, a dry summer, a good autumn [or: harvest], and the sheep will breed, and there will be peace, and an abundance of fruits' (*Year Prognosis* 17/2).[200] Three Anglo-Saxon texts hold the entire Christmas season to be prophetic, taking either sunshine or wind on each of the twelve days as

---

Though this date was sometimes used in mainland Scandinavia in the thirteenth century, this is nowhere reflected in the prognostics, which hold rather to 25 December and the kalends of January: Finn Hødnebø, 'Juleskrå', *KLNM* 8 (1963): 19–20; Jansson, 'Nyår'; Árni Björnsson, *Saga daganna*, 393–4.

[194] See the index in Boberg, *Motif-Index*, 191 (motif M119.3) and above, pp. 60–1. If the tradition of boasts at Yule predates the Conversion, as the legendary sagas purport, the Midwinter festival was a time to deliberate on the year's plans even though it did not correspond to the start of the calendar in vernacular tradition. On the other hand, the association could be taken as evidence that Christmas boasts were introduced late.

[195] Hødnebø, 'Juleskrå'; Odd Nordland, 'Prognostica', *KLNM* 13 (1968): 496–8; László Sándor Chardonnens, ed., *Anglo-Saxon Prognostics, 900–1100: Study and Texts*, Brill's Studies in Intellectual History 153: Brill's Texts and Sources in Intellectual History 3 (Leiden: Brill, 2007), 2.

[196] For a discussion and edition of the Old English texts, see Chardonnens, *Prognostics*, 257–61.

[197] For a discussion and edition, see ibid., 262–5.

[198] Ibid., 265.

[199] For a discussion of the genre and for texts, see ibid., 491–500; for a discussion of its monastic popularity and an overview of textual witnesses, see Roy Liuzza, 'Anglo-Saxon Prognostics in Context: A Survey and Handlist of Manuscripts', *Anglo-Saxon England* 30 (2001): 181–230.

[200] 'Ðonne forme gearesdæig byð sunendæig: hit byð god winter, ꝼ windig lænctetid, dryge sumer, god hærfest, ꝼ scep tyðð‎rigeð, ꝼ hit byð grið, ꝼ wæstme manigfeald' (Chardonnens, *Prognostics*, 495).

indicative of the year's fortunes.²⁰¹ These texts employ a conceptual logic: the two closely related texts on sunshine predict more favourable outcomes than negative ones on sunny days, while predictions based on the wind are exclusively bad news.²⁰²

The reliance of these texts on the start of the Julian year indicates their embeddedness in this calendar system and the Latinate culture that brought it. At the same time, their association between winter and prophecy accords well with the Anglo-Saxon connection between the domain of winter and extrasocietal forces inasmuch as prophecy is a foreign power making itself available to human society at the darkest time of year.

A Latin version of the Pseudo-Bedan year prognosis also survives in several Scandinavian witnesses.²⁰³ Imported prognostic traditions thus contributed to the supernatural character of winter in medieval Scandinavia as in Anglo-Saxon England.

The literary motif of the travelling prophetess, or *vǫlva*,²⁰⁴ shows a pronounced seasonal identity in Icelandic prognostication. The feast in *Vatnsdœla saga* mentioned in the previous chapter centres on a Sami prophetess and takes place in winter (ch. 10).²⁰⁵ That this timing is no coincidence is suggested by the Greenlandic episode on Þorbjǫrg *lítilvǫlva* ('little prophetess') in *Eiríks saga rauða*, which makes the winter connection explicit when it states that 'in winter, it was Þorbjǫrg's custom to attend feasts, and those who were curious to hear their destiny or the year prognosis invited her into their homes most' (ch. 4).²⁰⁶ Like the Sami prophetess, Þorbjǫrg performs her craft in the winter evenings: 'she arrived in the evening [. . .]. When the day was drawing to a close, she was given the equipment she needed to carry out her witchcraft.'²⁰⁷ Depending on the textual interpretation, it may likewise be in winter that a travelling prophetess attends a feast in *Hrólfs saga kraka* (ch. 3).²⁰⁸ Regardless of the

---

²⁰¹ Ibid., 483–5, 489–90.

²⁰² Cf. ibid., 489.

²⁰³ For example in Hauksbók p. 468. Finnur Jónsson, ed., *Hauksbók* (Copenhagen: Thiele, 1892–6); discussion on pp. cxxvii–cxxviii, where other witnesses are also listed. See further Hødnebø, 'Juleskrå'; Jansson, 'Nyår'.

²⁰⁴ This is the second sense of the word by the definition in Eyvind Flejd Halvorsen, 'Vǫlva', *KLNM* 20 (1976): 355–7, contrasting with the witch who, often living within or in the margins of a sedentary society, uses sorcery to affect the lives of others.

²⁰⁵ Einar Ólafur Sveinsson, *Vatnsdœla saga*, 28–31.

²⁰⁶ 'Þat var háttr Þorbjargar um vetrum, at hon fór at veizlum, ok buðu þeir menn henni mest heim, er forvitni var á at vita forlǫg sín eða árferð' (Einar Ólafur Sveinsson and Matthías Þórðarson, *Eyrbyggja saga*, 206).

²⁰⁷ 'Hon kom um kveldit [. . .]. At áliðnum degi var henni veittr sá umbúningr sem hon þurfti at hafa til at fremja seiðinn' (ibid., 206–7).

²⁰⁸ Guðni Jónsson and Bjarni Vilhjálmsson read 'þeir eru þar upp á þriðja vetr' ('they remain there into the third winter'), suggesting that the events that follow take place in winter (Guðni Jónsson and Bjarni Vilhjálmsson, *Fornaldarsögur*, 2:7). Slay, however, has 'þeir voru þar [vppa/vppi] iij vetur' ('they were there for three winters [i.e. years]'), reading a cardinal numeral and taking the *a* or *i*, which is found in some witnesses only, as part of the adverb (Slay, *Hrólfs saga kraka*, 8).

temporal reference, however, it should be remembered that feasts in the sagas are fairly consistently organized in autumn or winter,[209] so that it may be safe to conclude that the author and audience of this text share an understanding that follows the same convention. Similarly, although *Orms þáttr Stórólfssonar* and *Ǫrvar-Odds saga* do not give prophecy a place in the seasonal cycle, these texts make clear that this activity is to take place 'um kveldit' ('in the evening', *Orms þáttr Stórólfssonar*, ch. 5)[210] or 'um nóttina' ('in the night'); the latter text even uses the term *náttfarsseiðr* ('night-travel witchcraft', *Ǫrvar-Odds saga*, ch. 2).[211] It is reasonable to conclude that prophecy in all these texts has an association with darkness, which explains the winter references in the first two or three texts and suggests that the last two at the very least should not be understood to refer to the bright summer evenings. A conceptual connection is thus implied between the darkest time of day during the darkest season, when society is reduced to the smallest domain, and the time at which higher powers may be consulted. However, prophecy in these texts is available from the social heart of the farmstead, and thus not dependent on immediate darkness or peripheral space; only the practitioner is socially peripheral.

Conclusions

This chapter has demonstrated that the Anglo-Saxon and early Icelandic literary traditions both describe winter as a time of intense activity in the periphery of the human domain. Their respective interests within this niche, however, differ somewhat.

Old English poems of various genres and themes use winter settings to express personal affliction. Rather than describe the effects of the cold and the sterile land on society as a whole, these texts employ winter's effects on the individual as vehicles by which to explore the psyche of a solitary protagonist. Most commonly, the poet taps into a branch of the elegiac mode, studying the individual as both a victim of the winter weather and a mind in agreement with this metaphor for melancholy. In these cases, it may seem that invoking winter as one phase of a seasonal cycle implies the imminence of better conditions, at least for a time. However, such relief is rarely depicted. In some cases, as with the melting sword of *Beowulf*, it is left to the reader to supply a metaphorical reading to the loosening of the bonds of winter, even though the coming of winter is frequently accompanied by descriptions of personal suffering. Only the Finnsburh episode makes

---

[209] Though this tendency is especially strong in the sagas of Icelanders, the pattern generally holds true for the legendary sagas as well except where occasional (for example funerary) feasts are concerned. See further above, pp. 52–61.
[210] Þórhallur Vilmundarson and Bjarni Vilhjálmsson, *Harðar saga*, 405.
[211] Guðni Jónsson and Bjarni Vilhjálmsson, *Fornaldarsögur*, 1:286–9.

detailed mention of the protagonist's emotional development into the warmer season, but here the homesickness of winter merely gives way to the vengeance of spring. Old English literature thus generally retains its focus on winter suffering even in texts that suggest seasonal progression. There is an acknowledgement of variation, but the attention remains fixated on one end of the cycle.

In contrast with the Anglo-Saxon focus on the solitary subject, the sagas of Icelanders explore winter's otherly connotations by contrasting them with society as a whole. Here, the function of the individual is mostly limited to a heroic confrontation with otherly categories on behalf of her or his community. The most categorical association of winter is with the dangerous supernatural, as hauntings in particular rarely occur outside the winter half-year and are closely associated with Christmas and the dark of night. The seasonality of social space is closely implicated in this tradition, since dangerous creatures, normally bound to mountainous habitats, impinge on the inhabited valleys along with the dark, the cold, and the snow of winter. The physical human domain is smallest at this time of year, and those who continue their work beyond the confines of the farm, shepherds especially, are the first to be affected by the hauntings. But as in classical and medieval European culture, where winter and the start of the year in particular was a prophetic time, the human sphere also benefits from the annual redrawing of its boundaries. Icelandic prognostics generally follow English and Continental examples in this regard, but the temporal distribution of the *vǫlva* motif places further emphasis on winter as the time of greatest access to prophecy. In this tradition, society may be spatially confined in winter, but it receives the benefit of a temporal extension beyond the present.

Despite close connections between the recurrent hall attacks of *Beowulf* and the seasonal hauntings of *Grettis saga* and related Scandinavian texts, it seems unlikely that the narrative underlying *Beowulf* was a winter tale like its northern analogues. Instead, the Old English poem employs one or both of the traditional Anglo-Saxon motifs of pathetic fallacy and the bonds of winter in the few episodes that mention the seasons. Its only temporal reference reminiscent of saga convention is Hengest's winter-induced exile in Frisia. Here, however, the subject matter itself indicates the implication of historical or pseudohistorical Scandinavians whose open-sea voyages would indeed have been restricted to the summer half-year. The defence of Heorot, although Scandinavian in its setting, is more universal in its subject matter and subject to seasonality only insofar as the monsters exclusively attack at night; its source tradition is not bound to any time of year.

Although many of the texts here discussed depict winter as a time of human confrontations with natural and supernatural outside threats, social tensions also develop within the human realm. On the one hand there is a continuation of hostilities between autonomous forces, in which the winter landscape fulfils a range of literary functions; this type of conflict often takes place with the season's ice and snow as its immediate setting. On the other hand, the confined social conditions of winter have a tendency to escalate suppressed antagonism, as may be seen in the Þórmóðr narratives, *Gísla saga*, and the Finnsburh episode. Winter is portrayed less as a military off-season than as a time of treachery requiring powerful individuals to be on their guard against friend and foe.

By its investigation of seasonal cycles in Anglo-Saxon and Old Icelandic literature, this chapter has confirmed the central role of winter in literary explorations of what lies beyond the human sphere, whether it is the natural world (more common in Old English literature) or the domain of the supernatural (a firmer association in Scandinavian texts). Not limited to the seasonally static geography described in the preceding chapter, these connections have been shown to hold also where one season gives way to the next, so that extrasocietal associations intensify at the start of winter and diminish as the dark season draws to a close.

The Icelandic literary corpus is not, however, limited to the lives of Icelanders, and English literature did not end with the Conquest. The genres in vogue in thirteenth- and fourteenth-century Europe found a market in Iceland as well as England. Some of these, among which the romance and the dream vision are especially notable, reveal very different assumptions regarding the seasonal and geographical backdrop of encounters with the natural and the supernatural. It is the aim of the following chapter to show that the rise of the romance aesthetic brought in summer as a rival setting to winter for explorations outside the human domain in a number of Middle English genres and to a lesser degree in Icelandic romance and legend. Although this new context for extrasocietal contact did not fully displace pre-existing conventions, it will be seen that it came to be the central seasonal setting for expeditions in Middle English verse.

— 4 —
Summer Adventure

Introduction

It was seen in the introduction that the early Germanic summer was a six-month season; in Iceland and Norway, it began around the second week of April on the Julian calendar.[1] It was also suggested that an associative consideration of the year tends to include the pleasant days of spring in the concept of summer. Perhaps in recognition of both facts, Middle English verse frequently references summer as an inclusive concept starting around April. This chapter will accordingly treat April and May as early summer (a concept still recognizable in Dutch *voorjaar* and borrowed into Danish as *foraar*)[2] except where spring and summer are clearly distinguished.

The associations of spring and summer in later-medieval literature are well documented. Above all, spring connotes love in Middle English verse.[3] In addition, the summer half-year claims centre stage in the popular topos of the nature opening,[4] itself a subtype of the *locus amoenus* or pleasant natural setting inherited from classical tradition.[5] These agreeable associations might tempt us to classify spring and summer as safe environments contrasting with the dangers of winter encountered in previous chapters.

---

[1] Natanael Beckman, 'Isländsk och medeltida skandinavisk tideräkning', in *Tideräkningen*, ed. Martin P:n Nilsson, Nordisk Kultur 21 (Stockholm: Albert Bonniers, 1934), 20–1, 26–7.

[2] Anderson, 'The Seasons of the Year', 238, 240; Der Boon and Geeraerts, *Woordenboek*, s.v. 'voorjaar'; Dahlerup and Jacobsen, *Ordbog*, s.v. 'foraar'.

[3] Wilhelm, *The Cruelest Month*; Alamichel, '*Sumer is icumen in*'; cf. Arthur Groos, '"Shall I Compare Thee to a Morn in May?": Walther von der Vogelweide and his Lady', *Publications of the Modern Language Association of America* 91, no. 3 (May 1976): 398–405.

[4] Werner Ross, 'Über den sogenannten Natureingang der Trobadors', *Romanische Forschungen* 65, nos. 1/2 (1953): 49–68; Barbara von Wulffen, *Der Natureingang in Minnesang und frühem Volkslied* (Munich: Max Hueber, 1963); Pearsall and Salter, *Landscapes and Seasons*, 165–7; Williams, 'The Nature Prologue in Welsh Court Poetry'.

[5] Ernst Robert Curtius, 'Rhetorische Naturschilderung im Mittelalter', *Romanische Forschungen* 56 (1942): 219–56; Ernst Robert Curtius, *Europäische Literatur und lateinisches Mittelalter*, 7th ed. (Bern and Munich: Francke, 1969), 191–209; Dagmar Thoss, *Studien zum 'locus amoenus' im Mittelalter*, Wiener romanistische Arbeiten 10 (Vienna and Stuttgart: Braumüller, 1972); Pearsall and Salter, *Landscapes and Seasons*, passim; Anne T. E. Matonis, 'Some Rhetorical Topics in the Early *cywyddwyr*', *Bulletin of the Board of Celtic Studies* 28 (1980): 42–56; Petra Haß, *Der 'locus amoenus' in der antiken Literatur: Zu Theorie und Geschichte eines literarischen Motivs* (Bamberg: Wissenschaftlicher Verlag Bamberg, 1998); Barrar, 'A Spacious, Green and Hospitable Land'. For the various functions fulfilled by the *locus amoenus*, see especially Curtius, 'Rhetorische Naturschilderung im Mittelalter', 246–9.

As we will see, however, the tendency in medieval romance and dream visions is instead to set confrontations with foreign elements, including moderately dangerous ones, in the warm season.

As in the two preceding chapters, here likewise a seasonal take on Bakhtin's concept of the chronotope may shed light on the dynamics of narrative space and time. The construct is particularly applicable to medieval romance, as Bakhtin recognized, because of the genre's extensive use of an adventure-space contrasting with the social environment that forms the protagonist's familiar sphere.[6] It is the seasonal implications of this adventure-space that will form the central object of study in what follows. It will furthermore be demonstrated that the functions and seasonality of the natural world in Middle English dream visions and debates have considerable overlap with those of romance.

In Middle English as in Old English literature, and to a degree in Old Norse literature, much of the narrative action takes place beyond the safety of the court, hall, or farmhouse. However, Middle English literature relies more heavily than either of the other corpora on the concept of adventure in the sense of unforeseen or chance events befalling a protagonist when he or she is already beyond the confines of the home. By contrast, narratives in Anglo-Saxon literature and the sagas of Icelanders imbue their heroes with more teleological purpose: whether it be the Israelites escaping from Egypt, Guthlac facing the wilderness and its demons, or a group of Icelandic farmers setting out to settle a score, the general tendency is for characters to know where they are going and why.

The Middle English convention in which narrators themselves undertake solitary journeys into wild or natural landscapes, especially prominent in visions and debates, has its literary roots in the Old French *chanson d'aventure*. This twelfth-century genre, whose Middle English counterpart gained popularity in the mid-fourteenth century, uses the solitary journey as a context for an encounter with another individual, most commonly a girl or religious authority, whose monologue or wooing forms the heart of the narrative. In the *chanson d'aventure* itself, English poets were less interested than their francophone counterparts in elaborating on the natural environment, although a rudimentary setting by the side of a forest or meadow is typically included, while spring (or May) and dawn or the morning are usually identified as the temporal setting.[7] This convention accordingly helps place the prominence of the adventure motif and its reliance on natural settings in later-medieval literature.

---

[6] Bakhtin, 'Forms of Time and of the Chronotope in the Novel', 151–5; see further Gurevich, 'Medieval Chronotope'.

[7] Helen Estabrook Sandison, *The chanson d'aventure in Middle English* (Bryn Mawr, PA: Bryn Mawr College, 1913), 1–33.

The reliance on chance encounters in this period created a need for new ways in which to draw solitary protagonists into the sorts of environment conducive to adventure. The home, whether it took the shape of a court, monastery, or farm, was a familiar, social space, and consequently permitted less deviation from realism than the unfamiliar outside world whose features could be beyond the reach of strict verification. In this respect, there is a continuity between all the corpora considered in this study that owes more to a universal among territorial species than to formative influence. After all, if unfamiliar spaces are home to predators and other dangers, the mind is more likely to err on the side of caution in their consideration by allowing for a wider range of contingencies, thus leaving room for the irrational and supernatural. What is new in Middle English literature and the foreign traditions on which the relevant genres relied, however, is outdoor recreation as a means of drawing individuals out into natural settings. In chivalric romance, it will be seen, adventure is often prompted by a mixed mode of recreation and purpose inasmuch as knights explicitly set out into the wilderness to win renown in whatever may come their way. This approach does not apply to visions and debates between birds, deities, or abstractions, which rely characteristically on unforeseen encounters. Protagonists within these genres thus need other excuses to find their way into spaces sufficiently removed from society to allow for such suspension of realism. Nature recreation is the typical answer to this need, doubly useful because it not only draws protagonists into the right sorts of landscape, but also provides sufficient leisure to explain their dozing off or their stopping to hear a full-length debate. Since most texts of this type were aimed at literate and educated audiences,[8] leisure and recreation were surely familiar concepts in the cultural sphere in which they were read or heard.

If the recreational activity engaged in was the hunt, it could take place at virtually any time of year, provided the plot did not require any particular species of game animal. More commonly, however, the protagonist is passively enjoying the scenery or resting from a journey. In these cases, spring and summer are natural choices of setting. This is particularly true of

---

[8] See, for example, Karl Brunner, 'Middle English Metrical Romances and their Audience', in *Studies in Medieval Literature in Honor of Professor Albert Croll Baugh*, ed. MacEdward Leach (Philadelphia, PA: University of Pennsylvania Press, 1961), 219–27. Chaucer in his dream visions makes such frequent intertextual references that he must have expected some part of his audience to understand them, though he frequently takes pains to explain, and sometimes himself misunderstands, classical myth. See the discussions in Michael St John, *Chaucer's Dream Visions: Courtliness and Individual Identity*, Studies in European Cultural Transition 7 (Aldershot: Ashgate, 2000), 13–17; Piero Boitani, 'Old Books Brought to Life in Dreams: *The Book of the Duchess, The House of Fame, The Parliament of Fowls*', in *The Cambridge Companion to Chaucer*, 2nd ed., ed. Piero Boitani and Jill Mann (Cambridge: Cambridge University Press, 2003), 58–77; A. C. Spearing, 'Dream Poems', in *Chaucer: Contemporary Approaches*, ed. Susanna Fein and David Raybin (University Park, PA: Pennsylvania State University Press, 2010), 160–3.

dream visions, which require that the protagonist fall asleep, a development especially plausible on a warm day.

Visions and Debates

As popular as the genres of (dream) vision and debate were in the high and later Middle Ages, it should be recognized that there was at least a general continuity in content and style between these and earlier incarnations of the same or related genres. Medieval vision literature is usually considered indebted to the biblical Apocalypse as well as to the visions of Peter and Paul dating back to the second and third centuries CE;[9] medieval debates are generally thought to have begun with the *Conflictus veris et hiemis* attributed to Alcuin,[10] itself a direct response to the singing contests in Virgil's *Eclogues*[11] but also contributing to a more uniform tradition of seasonal debates whose earliest known model is found among the Greek Aesopian texts.[12] Accordingly, the seasonal aspect of the literary contest was no invention of Middle English poets, as, for instance, the pastoral summer setting can be found in fully conventionalized form in Virgil's writings, while the personified debaters winter and spring are present in the Aesopian debate. Nevertheless, the spring opening came to take on specific functions in literary visions and debates of the Middle English tradition, and is as such especially well attested for England during the highly productive second half of the fourteenth century.

The eighth-century *Conflictus veris et hiemis* employs a brief pastoral form of the *locus amoenus*. Alcuin's only notable divergence from the Virgilian setting is found in the timeframe, which he moves from a hot summer's day to spring, though equally warm by implication, when the arrival of the cuckoo provides the occasion for the debate between the passing and the approaching season:

> Conveniunt subito cuncti de montibus altis
> pastores pecudum vernali luce sub umbra
> arborea pariter laetas celebrare camenas.
> Adfuit et iuvenis Dafnis seniorque Palemon;
> Omnes hi cuculo laudes cantare parabant.   (lines 1–5)

---

[9] Kamphausen, *Traum und Vision*, 76–82; Jiroušková, *Visio Pauli*, 7–17.
[10] John W. Conlee, ed., *Middle English Debate Poetry: A Critical Anthology* (East Lansing, MI: Colleagues, 1991), xiii. The edition consulted is Godman, *Poetry of the Carolingian Renaissance*, 144–8.
[11] A. J. Boyle, ed. and trans., *The 'Eclogues' of Virgil* (Melbourne: Hawthorn, 1976). The *Conflictus* is especially close in form to the third Eclogue.
[12] The Aesopian debate between winter and spring is edited in Ben Edwin Perry, ed., *Aesopica: A Series of Texts relating to Aesop or Ascribed to him or Closely Connected with the Literary Tradition that Bears his Name*, vol. 1, *Greek and Latin Texts* (Urbana, IL: University of Chicago Press, 1952), 425–6 (no. 271).

> In the spring light, all the cattle-herds from the high mountains suddenly convene in the shade of trees to celebrate the joyful Muses in equal measure. Young Daphnis was also present, and the older Palemon; they were all preparing to sing praises to the cuckoo.

By its participation in the pastoral tradition, this text also brings the seasonal debate into a natural setting, where the effects of seasonal variation are most visible.

From the twelfth century onwards, a range of Latin contests between seasons followed which likewise made use of Virgilian settings. Not all of these follow the *Conflictus* in setting the debate in a transitional season whose meteorological fluctuations are mimicked in the debate. Two related debates between winter and summer from the late-twelfth century, for instance, are set in the heat of summer.[13] A further text, likewise a late-twelfth-century poem identified in the manuscript as an 'altercatio yemis et estatis' ('debate between winter and summer'), is set in autumn but is resolved in peace rather than (as one might expect for this time of year) a victory at the hands of winter.[14] The genre by the twelfth century thus does not in all cases present the debate as a microcosmic representation of concurrent seasonal struggle but instead views the differences between summer and winter as more of a perpetual conceptual conflict.

The earliest known Middle English debate, *The Owl and the Nightingale* (c. 1200),[15] scarcely introduces its setting at all, let alone explain it. It does, however, find the space to specify a summer season. Before diving straight into the debate, the speaker only states,

> Ich was in one sumere dale,
> In one suþe diʒele hale;
> Iherde ich holde grete tale
> An hule and one niʒtingale.   (lines 1–4)

> I was in a summer valley, in a very secluded corner; I heard an owl and a nightingale engage in a vehement debate.

The extrasocietal setting is the more to be expected in this poem because it is the natural habitat of the protagonists. At the same time, it does set a generic precedent for other debates involving either natural or supernatural elements.

The humorous altercation that follows is not a debate between seasons like the Latin debates of its time, but it does implicitly compare the benefits

---

[13] Hans Walther, ed., *Das Streitgedicht in der lateinischen Literatur des Mittelalters*, Quellen und Untersuchungen zur lateinischen Philologie des Mittelalters 5.2 (Munich: Beck, 1920; reprinted with supplementary materials Hildesheim: Olms, 1984), 203–9; discussion at 41–4.

[14] Ibid., 191–203 (discussion at 37–41). Contrast winter's conquest of autumn in the Old English *Menologium* discussed above, pp. 146–7.

[15] Neil Cartlidge, ed. and trans., *The Owl and the Nightingale* (Exeter: University of Exeter Press, 2001); dating at xv. Cf. Conlee, *Middle English Debate Poetry*, xxi–xxii.

and disadvantages of summer and winter in the debaters' associations with those seasons. Its central interest is in the qualitative differences between the owl and the nightingale and in their relative benefit to mankind, involving the seasons in the debate inasmuch as the owl is associated with winter while the nightingale is only found in England in summer. In this matter, winter is unambiguously associated with gloom and hardship, but the owl defends her winter song by the observation that this is the season for carolling, while summer is merry enough as it is and in need of tempering lest men turn to sin (409–542). Although the debate ends undecided, the unpleasant associations of winter here recalled are certain to pull the nightingale ahead in the audience's favour.

Given the popularity of avian debates in Middle English, many of the later-fourteenth-century debates are set in the bird season, like the *Conflictus* and *The Owl and the Nightingale*. Unlike these earlier poems, however, the later texts show an increased interest in the physical setting of the debate,[16] developing a highly conventional form of the *locus amoenus* based around the solitary walk in a natural setting (following the *chanson d'aventure*), the riverside slumber, and the dream. In all these particulars, the debates strongly converge with the dream vision, and indeed dreams and debates frequently show up in conjunction in poems of this period. As both the *locus amoenus* and the *chanson d'aventure* are strongly associated with the summer season, these visions and debates have a marked interest in seasonal setting. Since the natural world they describe is an extrasocietal space or at least a cultivated imitation of one, there is commonly a touch of otherness to its depiction.

A typical dream-visionary setting is found in *Piers Plowman*, whose first two redactions were composed in the 1370s.[17] The long B-redaction of this poem opens with the following scene:

> In a somer seson, whan softe was þe sonne,
> I shoop me into shroudes as I a sheep were,
> In habite as an heremite vnholy of werkes,
> Wente wide in þis world wondres to here.
> Ac on a May morwenynge on Maluerne Hilles
> Me bifel a ferly, of fairye me þoʒte.
> I was wery ofwandred and wente me to reste
> Vnder a brood bank by a bournes syde;
> And as I lay and lenede and loked on þe watres,
> I slombred into a slepyng, it sweyed so murye.
> Thanne gan me to meten a merueillous sweuene.   (lines 1–11)

---

[16] Conlee, *Middle English Debate Poetry*, xxix–xxx.
[17] A. V. C. Schmidt, ed., William Langland, *'Piers Plowman': A Parallel-Text Edition of the A, B, C and Z Versions*, rev. ed., 2 vols (Kalamazoo, MI: Medieval Institute Publications, 2011); dating at 2:273–81.

> In a summer season, when the sun was soft, I clothed myself in an outfit as though I were I shepherd, in a habit like a hermit unholy of works; I travelled widely in this world to hear marvels. But on a May morning in the Malvern Hills, a strange thing happened to me which seemed magical to me. I was worn out from walking and went to rest myself along a wide bank by the side of a stream, and as I lay and reclined and looked at the water, I dozed off into a slumber, so pleasantly did it sound. Then a wondrous dream came to me.

The summer season is the first environmental aspect provided, and it is closely followed by the narrator's aim in setting out, namely 'wondres to here'. This is an adventurous aim, set in the season of the adventure poem, thus preparing the audience for a marvel through convention even before the marvel is announced outright ('me bifel a ferly, of fairye'). The May morning then further narrows down the temporal aspect, while also confirming that the bipartite year continued to be used (and indeed continued to be the norm)[18] in narrative poetry of the later-fourteenth century. The narrator rests by a brook, a convention whose constant murmur is bound to put him to sleep, and it is in this way that he experiences the poem's first vision.

Much the same convention may be recognized in the late-fourteenth- or early-fifteenth-century debate *Death and Liffe*.[19] Its narrator describes in detail his wanderings through a forest rich in flowers and with a river running through a meadow. Though he gives no reason for his excursion, his references to the joys of the scenery suggest its enjoyment is his aim: 'methought itt lengthened my liffe to looke on the bankes' ('it seemed to me that it prolonged my life to gaze at the banks', 29). Resting at last from his walk, he falls asleep by the riverside and enters into a visionary space (33–8) in which he witnesses a debate between Lady Life and Lady Death. Thus without reference to time of year or time of day, the *chanson d'aventure* motif and the narrator's dozing off connect the action with the time of floral beauty and the heat of the day.

The opening of *The Cuckoo and the Nightingale*, likewise written in the late-fourteenth century,[20] has certain critical aspects in common with that of *Death and Liffe*. Both are debates, yet both are set up as dream visions. *The Cuckoo and the Nightingale* is set in early May (42, 55), and again the excursion into the natural world is prompted by leisure: the speaker desires to hear the nightingale sing, and so he sets off 'unto a wode' (58), as he says,

> Til I came til a lavnde of white and grene;
> So faire one hade I neuer in bene,
> The grounde was grene, i-poudred with daise,

---

[18] Cf. Fischer, *'Sumer is icumen in'*.
[19] Joseph M. P. Donatelli, ed., *Death and Liffe* (Cambridge, MA: Medieval Academy of America, 1989); dating at 17.
[20] Conlee, *Middle English Debate Poetry*; dating at 249–50.

> The floures & þe grenes like heigh,
> Al grene and white; was noþing ellis sene. (lines 61–5)

Until I came to a clearing of white and green; I had never been in so fair a place. The ground was green, dotted with daisies. The flowers and the grass were of like height, all green and white; nothing else was seen.

The month of May, the outdoor leisure time, the search for the nightingale, and the *locus amoenus* are elements so thoroughly conventional that the events that follow could be anticipated by anyone familiar with the genre. The speaker decides to sit down in the clearing by the side of a stream, and the sounds of birdsong and rushing water soon induce a slumber (66–88). This state of half-waking, half-sleeping provides the elements necessary for the avian debate: the sleeper still hears the birds, but dreams he can interpret their intent (106–10).

Though the mid-fourteenth-century fragment *Wynnere and Wastoure*[21] is earlier than *Death and Liffe*, *The Cuckoo and the Nightingale*, and even *Piers Plowman*, which it influenced,[22] it demonstrates through subtle parody that the *chanson d'aventure* setting was already conventional by the middle of the century. Following a brief prologue on the prevalence of marvels in the present age, the poet sets the stage for a dream vision in the first person:

> Als I went in the weste wandrynge myn one,
> Bi a bonke of a bourne bryghte was the sonne,
> Vndir a worthiliche wodde by a wale medewe
> Fele floures gan folde ther my fote steppede.
> I layde myn hede one ane hill ane hawthorne besyde.
> The throstills full throly they threpen togedire,
> Hipped vp heghwalles fro heselis tyll othire,
> Bernacles with thayre billes one barkes thay roungen,
> Þe jay janglede one heghe, jarmede the foles,
> Þe bourne full bremly rane þe bankes bytwene.
> So ruyde were þe roughe stremys and raughten so heghe
> That it was neghande nyghte or I nappe myghte
> For dyn of the depe watir and dadillyng of fewllys.
> Bot as I laye at the laste þan lowked myn eghne
> And I was swythe in a sweuen sweped belyue. (lines 32–46)

As I walked in the wilderness, wandering by myself, the sun was bright by a riverbank. Many flowers folded where my foot trod along a splendid forest by a pleasant meadow. I laid my head down on a hill, beside a hawthorn. The thrushes compete amongst themselves most vigorously; woodpeckers leapt from one hazel to the next; barnacle geese munched on bark with their beaks; the jay twittered on high, the birds chirped, the river ran vigorously between the banks. So violent were the rough currents, and they reached so high up, that night was

---

[21] Stephanie Trigg, ed., *Wynnere and Wastoure*, EETS, os 297 (Oxford: Oxford University Press, 1990); dating at xxii–xxvii.

[22] Schmidt, *Piers Plowman*, 2:289–90.

drawing near before I was able to sleep for the sound of the deep water and the chatter of birds. But at last as I lay my eyes closed, and I was promptly swept into a dream without delay.

The references to flowers, birds, and the stream by a forest side all identify this setting as a *locus amoenus*; the reference to the bright sun in conjunction with the birds and flowers alerts the audience to the fact that the action must be situated in the warm season. Indeed, the audience may already have concluded that this is a Maytime setting, considering the prevalence of this calendrical detail in analogous texts. The parodical element in *Wynnere and Wastoure* is that rather than put him to sleep, as in *Piers Plowman* and *The Cuckoo and the Nightingale*, the birdsong and the sound of the running water keep the narrator awake until the evening, at which point he is finally able to sink into his dream, later in the day than is conventional.

Occasionally, the hunt was adduced as the motive for the conventional excursion into the natural world. This is seen, for instance, in *The Parlement of the Thre Ages*,[23] whose narrator spends a May morning (identified as 'the sesone of somere when softe bene the wedres', 'the season of summer when the weather is soft', 2) poaching in a private forest but falls asleep while guarding his buried catch against swine. Although he has come with an economic purpose, the poacher still has an eye for the natural world, which he describes as pleasant and in full bloom. Here as in other texts, the heat of the sun plays a role in the protagonist's dozing off (1–16, 91–103). A modified version of the motif is found in Paris's vision in the late-fourteenth-century *Destruction of Troy*,[24] which takes place during a summer hunt but after sunset, and his sleep is prompted by exhaustion from the day's exercise rather than the lazy enjoyment of a pleasant landscape (2340–79).

The long frame narrative of Chaucer's early poem *The Book of the Duchess*[25] does not deal with seasonal setting directly. Instead, it serves to set up the poem's theme of love. As *The Book of the Duchess* centres around a dialogue with a knight bereft of his lady, the frame narrative introduces this subject matter by telling how the speaker, unable to sleep for what must be interpreted as love-longing, turns to the tale of Alcyone's love for her husband Ceyx, lost at sea. By convention, of course, this subject matter belongs in spring. This seasonal identity is only made explicit within the speaker's dream, however, which contains a subtle transition between waking environment and dreamscape: although the dream's opening scene is set in the narrator's bed, this setting is brought as close to the outdoors as possible, with clear glass windows admitting bright sunlight, birdsong,

---

[23] M. Y. Offord, ed., *The Parlement of the Thre Ages*, EETS, os 246 (Oxford: Oxford University Press, 1959).
[24] Geo. A. Panton and David Donaldson, eds, *The 'Gest Hystoriale' of the Destruction of Troy: An Alliterative Romance*, EETS, os 39, 56 (London: Trübner, 1869–74; reprinted New York: Greenwood, 1969); dating at 1:liii–lxiii.
[25] Benson, *The Riverside Chaucer*, 329–46.

and the sounds of a nearby hunt (290–353). It is when the protagonist's dream-self rises and joins the hunting-party that he comes upon the knight whose story forms the focal element of the poem.

Where other dream visions emphasize the spring setting of the frame narrative, *The Book of the Duchess* introduces it only within the visionary space, demonstrating that the season has a role to play beyond that of portal into the otherworld, namely as the natural setting of that otherworld itself. This connection between the otherworld and the season of renewal is highly typical of the dream vision (and, it will be seen below, of other Middle English encounters with the supernatural). Chaucer employs it again in his *Legend of Good Women*,[26] a series of tales of female suffering framed by a dream-visionary gathering of legendary women in a springtime clearing. The central image in this poem's prologue is that of the daisy, a symbol for Alceste, whom Chaucer introduces as spouse to the god of love. The speaker recounts at length his love for daisies and his Maytime habit of visiting this flower (always in the singular) in the early mornings and the evenings (40–63). One night as he returns from a visit to his daisy, he has a bed made in an arbour, with flowers strewn about it; it is in this cultivated outdoor environment that he experiences his dream (197–211). The visionary space, however, is the same meadow in which the speaker spends his waking hours:

> Me mette how I lay in the medewe thoo,
> to seen this flour that I so love and drede;
> And from afer com walkyng in the mede
> The god of Love, and in his hand a quene.   (lines 210–13)
>
> Then I dreamed how I lay in the meadow, to see this flower that I so love and dread. And from afar there came walking in the meadow the god of love, and a lady at his arm.

Convention has it, of course, that May is the appropriate season for an encounter with the god of love, and a *locus amoenus* the appropriate setting. Since the work is also a dream vision, however, the connection of this genre with the spatio-seasonal context of a green spring environment is here likewise confirmed for both the frame narrative and the visionary space.

A further text making use of the *locus amoenus* in both these environments is *Pearl*.[27] Composed in the late-fourteenth century but in more northerly parts than Chaucer's visions,[28] this text has its speaker enter an 'erber grene' (38) with a rather different motivation than is customary, namely to mourn his lost daughter. The poem's allegorical style has this green environment

---

[26] Ibid., 587–630. References are to the F-text.
[27] E. V. Gordon, ed., *Pearl* (Oxford: Clarendon, 1953).
[28] Ibid., xliii–xlv.

as the location where the speaker has lost his pearl, as he says: 'þur3 gresse to grounde hit fro me yot' ('it went from me, through the grass and to the ground', 10). The straightforward reading is that the *erber* here is simply an abstraction of the cemetery which the speaker visits to mourn his daughter, rather than her actually having died in such a location. Even so, this poem, not at all interested in Chaucer's erotic brand of love, still makes use of the conventional pleasant landscape for its waking environment.

If carnal love is not an object in *Pearl*, the poem is nevertheless in need of a context that allows its protagonist to fall asleep. Not now bound to the May convention, the poet opts for the August grain harvest as his seasonal setting (39–40). Here, the visionary is beset by a sorrow-induced sleep that bears some thematic resemblance to the sleep enjoyed by Chaucer's love-starved protagonist in *The Book of the Duchess*. What *Pearl* shares with many other dream visions is that it takes an outdoor summertime environment to inspire a dream with a message from a world beyond our own.

The world which the visionary enters in his dream is presented as perfect in every way. Its description employs several of the characteristic features of the *locus amoenus*: forest, birds, and a stream, here further accompanied by tall cliffs. Not satisfied with mere repetition of the convention, however, the author takes great pains to stress that the beauty of this world is beyond human description. One of his ways of accomplishing this is that also found in the biblical depiction of the New Jerusalem (which indeed it is meant to represent),[29] namely by substituting gems for other, in this case natural, materials, and in other cases by comparing those materials to precious metals. Thus the leaves on the trees are like silver, the gravel underfoot consists of pearls, and the riverbed is likewise embellished with diverse precious stones. In addition, the visionary continually proclaims the beauty of the place, in one passage using the term *dubbement* ('splendour') four times in the space of fourteen lines (108–21). The central message of this description is that 'þe derþe þerof for to deuyse / nis no wi3 worþé þat tonge bere3' ('no tongued creature is worthy to describe its splendour', 99–100; cf. 69).[30] In all of this, the time of year is not once mentioned. However, the passage describes an unambiguous *locus amoenus*, a convention positively exclusive to spring and summer, as confirmed in this text by the forest in bloom, birdsong, and the fragrance of fruits.

Unlike most of the dream visions here discussed, *Pearl* describes a paradisal afterlife. Its participation in the *locus amoenus* trope therefore prompts the question to what degree the spring or summer setting represents only one of two types of dream poetry, complemented by unpleasant dreams connoting the winter half-year.

---

[29] Apc 21:18–21; cf. 21:11.
[30] The full landscape description prior to the introduction of the girl and the opposite bank extends across lines 65–136.

This question calls for two answers. The first is that winter dreams are exceedingly rare in Middle English poetry, and the genre of dream vision accordingly strongly linked to the summer half-year.[31] This presumably follows in part from an association between visions and the natural world, where one is unlikely to doze off in anything but warm and quiet weather. The other answer is that unpleasant dreamscapes do exist, in some instances employing a winter setting. The quantitative preference for summer landscapes therefore suggests that the genre is more commonly used to convey material lighter in tone. A darker vision is found, for instance, in the thirteenth-century debate *Als I lay in a winteris nyt*.[32] Although its seasonality is revealed only in the eponymous opening line, this poem uses its temporal setting to evoke a sentiment not fully present in any of the texts mentioned above, namely horror.[33] *Als I lay* is part of a popular subgenre of the medieval debate poem that pits the soul against its body following death in a frustrated accusation of having effected the soul's eternal damnation.[34] This genre cannot be detached from its didactic aim, which is to deliver the most urgent message of the medieval Church, namely for individuals to turn away from their sins in order to secure salvation. Accordingly, the imagery used is equally urgent, and the resulting horror considerably more intense and relatable than that of a romance encounter with superhuman challenges. Whereas romance narrative generally seeks the excitement of adventure without crossing over into horror, let alone conveying a sense of guilt, the audience of the body-and-soul debate would have been thoroughly aware that the message applied to them, and the poem's use of horror seeks to exploit this awareness.

As I lay demonstrates this tendency through a range of unpleasant associations, one of which is the seasonal image of cold and winter. In order of appearance, the poem's three central interests are the *ubi sunt* motif expressing the fleeting nature of earthly goods (13–120), the exploration through debate of the soul's lifelong struggle with its body to abstain from sin (121–464), and the torments that await the soul in hell (465–608). Along the way, however, there is some attention for the cold reality awaiting the corpse, a motif essential to medieval English body-and-soul debates.[35] Here as elsewhere, there is reference to the worms and the decay that will consume the body (46, 153) in conjunction with other discomforts of the grave as compared to life above ground:

---

[31] Cf. A. C. Spearing, *Medieval Dream-Poetry* (Cambridge: Cambridge University Press, 1976), 4 and discussions of individual poems in that work, such as at 26, 41, 130–1, 134.

[32] Conlee, *Middle English Debate Poetry*, 18–49.

[33] Ibid., xxix–xxx; Helen Phillips, 'Dream Poems', in *A Companion to Medieval English Literature and Culture: c. 1350–c. 1500*, ed. Peter Brown (Malden, MA: Blackwell, 2007), 377–8.

[34] Conlee, *Middle English Debate Poetry*, xxiv–xxvii.

[35] See, for example, *Soul I* (Krapp, Vercelli, 54–9); *The Grave* (Conlee, Middle English Debate Poetry, 3–6).

> Fram þe palays þat þou i lay,
> Wiþ wormes is now y-taken þin in;
> Þi bour is bilt wel cold in clay,
> Þe rof schal take to þi chin.   (lines 77–80)

> From the palace in which you lay, you have now taken up your lodging with worms. You have been quartered in clay, very cold; the roof will reach to your chin.

While the narrow confinement of the grave recalls the spatial constriction attributed to hell in Anglo-Saxon tradition,[36] its cold quality is another unpleasant negation of the palace previously inhabited by the body. The *winteris nyt* of the poem's opening line, however, is uncharacteristic of the genre in that it refers not to the temporal aspect of the graveyard setting but to a frame narrative in which the narrator witnesses the debate in a dream. The body-and-soul debate is here merged with the dream vision, and the poet has chosen to set the frame narrative on a winter's night. This choice of seasonal setting is telling, because it suggests that winter nights were considered appropriate for tales of horror in late-medieval England, as they were in late-medieval Iceland or the modern Western tradition. The deviation from the pleasant summer landscape of other dream visions is thus to be explained in terms of the aims of the genre. To bring the horror of damnation home to the poem's audience, it was appropriate to shock them with the psycho-geographical potential of winter imagery.

The Forest of Romance

ORIGINS AND INFLUENCES

Space in courtly romance is strongly dualistic. Although exceptions merit discussion below, the court typically functions as a safe haven, while the outside world is the backdrop for adventures. That outside world is remarkably homogeneous, the forest taking centre stage as the prime landscape of adventure.[37] Although the highways, foreign cities, and sea crossings of the military campaign trail may be thought of as equally valid geographical loci of romance, these do not allow for the individual adventures that establish a knight's worth,[38] as they are social spaces: the military campaign is a court on the move, a walled city in the wilderness[39] in which adventure is communal by default. In these settings,

---

[36] For example *Genesis B* 356–7 and the illustration on p. 36 of Oxford, Bodley, MS Junius XI.
[37] Marianne Stauffer, *Der Wald* (Bern: Francke, 1959), 11–12; Putter, *French Arthurian Romance*, 10–50; cf. Curtius, 'Rhetorische Naturschilderung im Mittelalter', 254.
[38] Corinne J. Saunders, *The Forest of Medieval Romance: Avernus, Broceliande, Arden* (Cambridge: Brewer, 1993), ix.
[39] This image is based on Paul Piehler, *The Visionary Landscape: A Study in Medieval Allegory* (London, 1971), 72–5; see further Saunders, *The Forest of Medieval Romance*, 40–1.

individual adventures take place only when the protagonist is separated from his companions or takes on an individual quest, as Gawain does when he meets Priamus in *The Alliterative Morte Arthure* (2513–716),[40] or Arthur when he confronts the giant at Mont Saint Michel in the same text (840–1221).[41] That the latter episode takes place not in a forest but on a rocky headland makes clear that the prominence of the forest, though pronounced, is not absolute.

The forest of medieval romance was informed by a variety of socio-economic and traditional factors, several of which have been described by Stauffer and Saunders.[42] This landscape possessed considerable economic value as a source of food, fuel, and construction materials and as pastureland, primarily for swine, while its clearance made way for further economic exploitation as arable land.[43] Accordingly, the rate of forest clearance generally kept up with population growth.[44] On a larger timescale, the reverse reasoning also holds true: since forest was the primary landscape of Western Europe prior to the spread of populous civilizations, most areas were woodland until they came within range of resource-intensive settlements; indeed, if left alone for long enough, they could return to forest.[45] In southern Britain, most land was turned to agricultural uses in the Bronze Age, with a further wave of deforestation taking place in Roman times;[46] on the Continent north of the Alps, woodland remained a far more prominent part of the landscape, with vast stretches surviving into the Middle Ages,[47] and other regions returning to their forest state

[40] Larry Dean Benson, ed., *King Arthur's Death: The Middle English 'Stanzaic Morte Arthur' and 'Alliterative Morte Arthure'* (Exeter: University of Exeter Press, 1986), 113–238.

[41] On the landscape of this episode, see Ralph W. V. Elliott, 'Landscape and Rhetoric in Middle-English Alliterative Poetry', *The Melbourne Critical Review* 4 (1961): 67.

[42] Esp. Stauffer, *Der Wald*, 54–104; Saunders, *The Forest of Medieval Romance*, 1–43.

[43] Jean R. Birrell, 'The Medieval English Forest', *Journal of Forest History* 24, no. 2 (April 1980): 78–85; Christian Schmid-Cadalbert, 'Der wilde Wald: Zur Darstellung und Funktion eines Raumes in der mittelhochdeutschen Literatur', in *Gotes und der werlde hulde: Literatur in Mittelalter und Neuzeit; Festschrift für Heinz Rupp zum 70. Geburtstag*, ed. Rüdiger Schnell (Bern and Stuttgart: Francke, 1989), 28–9.

[44] Philip H. Nicholls, 'On the Evolution of a Forest Landscape', *Transactions of the Institute of British Geographers* 56 (July 1972): 57–76; Kurt Mantel, *Wald und Forst in der Geschichte: Ein Lehr- und Handbuch* (Alfend and Hannover: Schaper, 1990), 52–64; Della Hooke, *Trees in Anglo-Saxon England: Literature, Lore and Landscape* (Woodbridge: Boydell, 2010), 113–18. For more recent illustrations of the same principle worldwide, see A. S. Mather and C. L. Needle, 'The Relationship of Population and Forest Trends', *The Geographical Journal* 166, no. 1 (March 2000): 2–13 and cf. Sven Wunder, *The Economics of Deforestation: The Example of Ecuador* (Basingstoke: MacMillan, 2000), 37–40.

[45] Mantel, *Wald und Forst*, 52; Richard Jones and Mark Page, 'Characterizing Rural Settlements and Landscape: Whittlewood Forest in the Middle Ages', *Medieval Archaeology* 47 (2003): 66. Forest regeneration in the absence of human activity is not, however, automatic: in temperate zones, the presence of wild herbivores precludes the formation at least of dense forests (Hooke, *Trees in Anglo-Saxon England*, 113).

[46] Petra Dark, 'Pollen Evidence for the Environment of Roman Britain', *Britannia* 30 (1999): 247–72.

[47] Karl Hasel, *Forstgeschichte: Ein Grundriß für Studium und Praxis*, Pareys Studientexte 48 (Hamburg and Berlin: Parey, 1985), 33–52; Schmid-Cadalbert, 'Der wilde Wald', 29–31; Mantel,

following the decline of the Roman Empire.[48]

The dualistic nature of romance space is an exaggeration of the old Continental environment, in which forest had simply been the space between settlements, the natural setting of the road.[49] However, it was precisely when the historical predominance of the European forest had ceased to be through extensive clearing that it began to assume such a prominent role in the literature.[50] On the Continent, the impressive but more isolated dense forests that in large part still survive today inspired the reimagining of a past in which this landscape covered much of Europe. In England, where extensive forests had long been cleared, the aristocrats in whose circles romances thrived[51] would have enjoyed enough mobility to take them through medieval forests the likes of the Weald or Forest of Dean even if they had not travelled abroad. With the rise of the royal hunting-forest, moreover, aristocrats of the high and later Middle Ages in Britain and Europe alike came to spend regular time in carefully protected woodlands,[52] some of which were planted specifically for the purpose of the hunt.[53] The popularity of the hunt from the eleventh century onwards may certainly be understood as both an inspiration for authors of romance and a point at which the literature resonated with its audience on the level of personal experience.

Since the forests constituted economic space and travelling-space but were less widely used as social space, they attracted activities best carried out outside the confines of society. Highwaymen took naturally to

---

Wald und Forst, 48; Ulrich Schraml and Georg Winkel, 'Germany', in *Forestry in Changing Societies in Europe*, ed. P. Pelkonen *et al.*, vol. 2, *Country Reports* (Joensuu: Joensuu University Press, 1999), 117; Hooke, *Trees in Anglo-Saxon England*, 116; cf. the Mediterranean situation described in, for example, Aline Durand and Marie-Pierre Ruas, 'La forêt Languedocienne (fin VIIIe siècle–XIe siècle)', in *Les forêts d'Occident du Moyen Âge à nos jours*, ed. A. Corvol-Dessert (Toulouse: Presses Universitaires du Mirail, 2004), 163–80. As has been pointed out, the spatial extent of Continental forests was not everywhere alike: eastern regions typically retained more forest cover by the early Middle Ages, and settlements were generally unevenly distributed across the region (Hasel, *Forstgeschichte*, 38–44; Schmid-Cadalbert, 'Der wilde Wald', 28).

[48] Roland Bechmann, *Trees and Man: The Forest in the Middle Ages*, trans. Katharyn Dunham (New York: Paragon, 1990), 76–7.

[49] Cf. Putter, *French Arthurian Romance*, 41–2.

[50] Schmid-Cadalbert, 'Der wilde Wald', 29–31; Putter, *French Arthurian Romance*, 16–17.

[51] Brunner, 'Metrical Romances'.

[52] Michael Billett, *A History of English Country Sports* (London: Hale, 1994), 81–3; Jean R. Birrell, 'Hunting and the Royal Forest', in *L'uomo e la foresta secc. XIII–XVIII: Atti della 'Ventisettesima Settimana di Studi', 8–13 maggio 1995*, ed. Simonetta Cavaciocchi (Florence: Le Monnier, 1996), 437–57; Aleks Pluskowski, 'Who Ruled the Forests? An Interdisciplinary Approach towards Medieval Hunting Landscapes', in *Fauna and Flora in the Middle Ages: Studies of the Medieval Environment and its Impact on the Human Mind, Papers Delivered at the International Medieval Congress, Leeds, in 2000, 2001, and 2002*, ed. Sieglinde Hartmann, Beihefte zur Mediaevistik 8 (Berlin: Peter Lang, 2007), 291–323.

[53] Saunders, *The Forest of Medieval Romance*, 6–9; but cf. Della Hooke, 'Medieval Forests and Parks in Southern and Central England', in *European Woods and Forests: Studies in Cultural History*, ed. Charles Watkins (Wallingford: CAB International, 1998), 19–32.

woodlands coinciding with roads, as these offered cover as well as food when needed. Poachers were drawn to forests for both sustenance and profit. Religious recluses and monastic communities settled in the forest because it represented the wilderness and primeval chaos, a place to be tested and tempted – like Christ[54] – by supernatural powers directly as opposed to through the evils of society.[55] Outlaws were driven to seek out economic spaces away from society, and often found these in the forests, where they had no choice but to live off the natural resources or the property of travellers. All these associations contributed to the psycho-geography of the forest to make it a place at once foreign and necessary, dangerous yet exciting, a place where the chaos of the subconscious could be confronted in the guise of a physical wilderness.[56]

The romance forest inherited some of its literary associations from classical literature, while others developed independently. In her book on the subject, Saunders describes how twelfth-century romance formed in part under direct influence from Virgil and Ovid, while also building on Celtic elements and the *roman d'Antiquité* tradition constituting an earlier-medieval reinterpretation of the late-Antique material. The chief difference as far as the forest is concerned is that the classical narratives depict it as a place where men could encounter pagan deities, an association abandoned by the later traditions, seemingly out of intolerance for pagan elements. In fact, the *romans d'Antiquité* abandoned the emphasis on the forest altogether, but this returned in the romance tradition under influence of the growing interest in chivalrous adventure. The supernatural aspect of the Roman forests had lived on in a more abstract guise as an association with unexpected turns of events, and was now merged with the Celtic interest in fairies and the otherworld.[57] Through its association with the Tristan material, in which it serves as a refuge for lovers, the forest gained a bipolar quality: normally an unfamiliar space where the irrational could be confronted, the similarly irrational quality of love made it familiar to lovers. In the same way, hermits and other exiles make the outside spaces their own, thereby relinquishing their bonds with society. It is important to observe that the forest's experiential value is able to change polarity within a text, so that the *locus amoenus* is a fleeting moment situated in a sheltered refuge within the larger landscape, which retains its hostile connotations.[58]

---

[54] The Old Saxon *Heliand* transforms the wilderness of Christ's temptation into a forest: Otto Behaghel, ed., *'Heliand' und 'Genesis'*, 10th ed., rev. Burkhard Taeger, Altdeutsche Textbibliothek 4 (Tübingen: Niemeyer, 1996), line 1124.

[55] Saunders, *The Forest of Medieval Romance*, 10–19; cf. Stauffer, *Der Wald*, 97–104.

[56] Piehler, *The Visionary Landscape*, 72–8; Saunders, *The Forest of Medieval Romance*, 19–24.

[57] Saunders, *The Forest of Medieval Romance*, 25–46.

[58] Ibid., 81–94, esp. 91–2.

SUMMER FORESTS, SUMMER FAIRIES

The experience of psycho-geographical injection, in which the individual is affected by a subjective evaluation of his or her surroundings, has the greatest force when undergone in isolation from other members of society. The larger the company, the more will the individual's confidence be bolstered against irrational impressions. A distinction should therefore be made between chivalric romances of individual adventure and social or military romances, in which much of the adventure centres on jousts and confrontations between large armies. The former type, in which a knight wins renown through individual achievement, is here of greater interest, although occasional episodes in the military romances likewise answer to the model of individual adventure. Two observations may be made that generally hold true for individual adventure: the forest is the central setting of adventure in its twin senses of chance events and heroic challenges, and the forest is normally a summer landscape, particularly where supernatural events and encounters with fairies are concerned.

The forest's role as a landscape of adventure follows from the premise, usually implicit, that heroism is proved outside the social sphere. In military romances, again, this is far less the case: in *Guy of Warwick*,[59] which centres heavily on large-scale battles, Guy's first instinct when told to prove his valour is to enter the jousting circuit (735–1074). Since Guy invariably wins both his numerous jousts and his many battles, however, the episodes of greatest narrative appeal are instead those whose development neither protagonist nor audience can foresee, and these tend to take place in the forest.

A key episode is that in which Guy first finds Tiri, soon to become his close friend. As Guy rides towards England with his men, coming upon a forest he orders his companions to find lodging in the nearby town while he enters the forest to enjoy the birdsong:

> Toward Inglond is Gij y-drawe,
> & wiþ him Herhaud, his gode felawe.
> Swiþe hastiliche þai gun ride,
> Þe weder was hot in somers tide.
> In May it was also ich wene,
> When floures sprede & springeþ grene:
> Into a forest sir Gij is go
> Neye a cite, nouȝt fer þer-fro.
> Þan seyd Gij to his meyney:
> 'Wendeþ swiþe wel an heye,
> Mine in to nim in þe cite;
> Ich wil a while here pleye me,

---

[59] Julius Zupitza, ed., *The Romance of Guy of Warwick: Edited from the Auchinleck MS. in the Advocates' Library, Edinburgh, and from MS. 107 in Caius College, Cambridge*, EETS, ES 42, 49, 59 (London: Trübner, 1883–91). Except where otherwise stated, the Auchinleck-redaction is cited.

> For to here þe foules singe.'
> Þer-in was þo his likeinge.   (lines 4499–5012)
>
> Guy travels to England, and his good friend Herhaud with him. They set off riding at great speed; the summer weather was warm. I believe it was in May, too, when flowers unfold and sprout green. Guy went into a forest near a city not far from there. Then Guy said to his retinue: 'Go in great haste, undermine the fortifications to take the city; I will amuse myself here for a while and listen to the birds sing.' Therein lay his delight then.

Had the poet continued by telling merely how Guy enjoyed the birdsong before returning to his companions, of course, the audience would have been disappointed: no romance would have its protagonist enter a forest by himself with such a limited narrative purpose. The episode is so designed that the audience anticipates an adventure, thereby heightening the suspense of this expedition into an extrasocietal space. The time of year is here introduced to convey the appeal of a forest ride, but combined with the heat of the day, the summer setting also exploits the convention, described below, of hot noontimes in or by the forest as foreshadowings of encounters with fairies and other unfamiliar agents. In this case, the text is not concerned with fairies but with human affairs, and Guy comes upon the wounded knight Tiri, which prompts him to rescue Tiri's lover from a band of outlaws and enter into a complex sequence of adventures to bring both Tiri and the lady to the safety (i.e. the social domain) of the town (4513–930). In this episode, the forest is employed both as a setting for adventures and as a hostile social space, the domain of outlaws and enemies. However, its natural beauty provides the occasion for the adventure, and the summer season makes this motif possible.

Elsewhere in the text, forest and season are employed in similar ways. It is 'opon a somers day' (4939) that Guy and Tiri learn that Tiri's father is under siege over Tiri's elopement with the duke's daughter, announcing a further sequence of adventures (4939–5504). The association of forest landscape with adventures and hostile encounters is further reinforced by a dangerous boar (6716–68), an ambush (1304–1518), and, in the Caius-manuscript, a lion and a dragon (4111–48);[60] in the last of these, the adventure is again prompted by Guy's desire for entertainment, although the term used, *play*, is usually associated with hunting and fowling when found in the context

---

[60] The motif of the knight rescuing a lion from a dragon was first used in Chrétien's *Yvain* (Wendelin Foerster, ed., *Yvain (der Löwenritter)*, 2nd ed. (Halle: Niemeyer, 1902)), but subsequently became a commonplace in romance, associated with various characters. In the Scandinavian retellings, for instance, the lion is saved by Trancival (*Ectors saga*, ch. 10: Agnete Loth, ed., *Late Medieval Icelandic Romances*, 5 vols (Copenhagen: Munksgaard, 1962–5), 1:122–4), Sigurðr þǫgli (*Sigurðar saga þǫgla*, chs 16–17: ibid., 2:138–44), and Vilhjálmr sjóðr (*Vilhjálms saga sjóðs*, ch. 13: ibid., 4:26–7) as well as by Íven himself (*Hærra Ivan*, lines 2691–752: Marianne E. Kalinke, ed., *Norse Romance*, 3 vols, Arthurian Archives 5 (Cambridge: Brewer, 1999), vol. 3; *Ívens saga*, ch. 10: ibid., 272–4). In all these cases, the setting for the encounter is a forest or forest clearing.

of natural landscapes, as it is here (4112).[61]

The search for forest adventures occurs also in *The Alliterative Morte Arthure*, a text that everywhere else bears an even stronger emphasis on military campaigns than *Warwick*. The adventure occurs during a campaign in Lorraine, in late July or early August (2390), when Gawain is sent into the wilderness with a few other men to obtain wildlife provisions for the army. At dawn, however, Gawain abandons his company 'wonders to seek' (2482–514, at 2514). He soon encounters an exotic knight named Priamus, and they wound each other severely before striking up a friendship. Both extrasocietal setting and summer season are once more emphasized when Gawain returns to his companions, who have been lulled to sleep by birdsong; the extraordinary (and therefore adventurous) nature of the encounter is demonstrated by Priamus's possession of a magic plant that heals their injuries (2690–709).

Summer encounters tend to be less desirable when it is women who venture into the forest or other extrasocietal space. *Sir Degaré*[62] is a good example of this. Degaré's mother, princess of Little Britain, is separated from her father's party on their way to the queen's tomb and dismounts in a forest clearing with no one but two handmaidens by her side. It is at this point that the morning heat is mentioned, a tell-tale sign of the otherworld encounter:

> Thai nist what hem was best to don.
> The weder was hot bifor þe non;
> Hii leien hem doun upon a grene,
> Under a chastein tre, ich wene,
> And fillen a-slepe everichone
> Bote the damaisele alone:
> She wente aboute and gaderede floures
> And herknede song of wilde foules;
> So fer in þe launde ȝhe goth, iwis,
> Þat ȝhe ne wot nevere whare ȝhe is.
> To hire maidenes ȝhe wolde anon.
> Ac hi ne wiste never wat wei to gon.   (lines 69–80)

They did not know what was their best course of action. The weather was warm before noon. They lay down on a meadow below a chestnut tree, I believe, and all fell asleep except the maiden alone. She went around and picked flowers and listened to the song of wild birds. Indeed, she goes so far into the woods that she has no idea where she is. She wanted to get to her attendants at once, but she had no idea which way to go.

---

[61] The lion and dragon also appear in the Auchinleck-manuscript, but they are there found 'toward a pleyn plas / þat bisiden a doun was' ('towards a level area that was beside a hill'); the knights encounter them while resting from their travels (4109–26). For *play* in the context of hunting and fowling, see lines 1203–12, 3147–54 of the Caius redaction.

[62] A. V. C. Schmidt and Nicolas Jacobs, eds, *Medieval English Romances*, 2 vols (New York: Holmes / Meier, 1980), 2:57–88.

In this *locus amoenus* turned hostile, the princess is approached by a man who politely introduces himself as a fairy knight, but goes on to make clear that he has come to have intercourse with her, which he does to her great distress (89–114). A similar episode sets the stage for the narrative of *Sir Orfeo*[63] when the queen entertains herself in the domesticated forest, the orchard:

> Bifel so in þe comessing of May
> (When miri & hot is þe day,
> & o-way beþ winter-schours,
> & eueri feld is ful of flours,
> & blosme breme on eueri bouȝ
> Ouer-al wexeþ miri anouȝ)
> Þis ich quen, Dame Heurodis,
> Tok to maidens of priis,
> & went in an vndrentide
> To play bi an orchard-side,
> To se þe floures sprede & spring,
> & to here þe foules sing.
> Þai sett hem doun al þre
> Vnder a fair ympe-tre,
> & wel sone þis fair quene
> Fel on slepe opon þe grene.
> Þe maidens durst hir nouȝt awake,
> Bot lete hir ligge & rest take.
> So sche slepe til after none,
> Þat vnder-tide was al y-done.   (lines 57–76)

It happened in the beginning of May – when the day is pleasant and warm, and winter's showers are over, and every field is full of flowers, and splendid blossom grows everywhere most pleasantly on every branch – this same lady, Dame Heurodis, took noble maidens with her and went one noontime to amuse herself by the side of an orchard, to see the flowers unfold and bloom, and to hear the birds sing. All three of them sat down below a beautiful orchard tree, and pretty soon this fair lady fell asleep in the meadow. The maidens dared not wake her but let her lie and have her rest. Thus she slept till after noon; the noontime was all over.

The seasonal setting is explicitly one of spring, and both the *locus amoenus* motif and the hot morning of fairy encounters are deployed right at the outset. Once awake, the queen is beyond herself with distress, as the king of fairies has come to her in her sleep, shown her his kingdom, and informed her that he will return the next day to take her away for good (77–174). This text thus overlaps with the genre of vision literature discussed above, but its interaction with a fairy otherworld makes it a romance first and foremost.

---

[63] A. J. Bliss, ed., *Sir Orfeo*, 2nd ed. (Oxford: Clarendon, 1966). The Auchinleck-redaction is cited throughout.

Not only do the fairies of *Sir Orfeo* strike on a hot May morning, their kingdom itself is a bright summer world whose likeness to the heavenly Jerusalem can hardly be overlooked. When Orfeo finds his way to the fairy kingdom after years of forest exile, self-imposed out of grief over his lost queen, he is faced with a brilliant sight:

> He com in-to a fair cuntray,
> As briʒt so sonne on somers day,
> Smoþe & plain & al grene
> – Hille no dale nas þer non y-sene.   (lines 351–4)

> He came into a fair country, as bright as the sun on a summer's day, smooth and plain and all green; neither hill nor valley was seen there.

The paradisal analogue begun with the absence of hills and valleys[64] continues with the description of the castle, which is inlaid with various gems like the heavenly Jerusalem, so that

> Al þat lond was euer liʒt,
> For when it schuld be þerk & niʒt
> Þe riche stones liʒt gonne
> As briʒt as doþ at none þe sonne.   (lines 369–72)[65]

> That whole land was perpetually light, for when it should have been dark and night, the precious stones lit up as brightly as the sun at noon.

The king's crown, moreover, shines 'as briʒt as þe sonne' ('as brightly as the sun', 152), and the royal couple's crowns and clothes 'schine so briʒt / þat vnneþe bihold he hem miʒt' ('shine so brightly that he could scarcely look at them', 415–16). The fairy kingdom is thus presented as universally bright, associated with summer and by implication devoid of seasonal variation; in all things it seems to Orfeo like 'þe proude court of Paradis' ('the magnificent courtyard of Paradise', 376).

The fairy encounter is found once again in *Sir Launfal*,[66] this time with a female fairy seeking the (now voluntary) favour of a knight. Launfal, having left Arthur's court because he does not get along with the new queen, Gwenore, rapidly spends his monetary reserves living in the town of Caerleon and becomes the scorn of all the townspeople. Ashamed of his situation, Launfal seeks comfort in a nearby forest clearing, as he says,

> Þat y myʒte confortede be
> By a launde unþer þys cyté,
> Al yn þys vnderntyde.   (lines 208–10)

> in order that I may be comforted by a clearing beside this city during the noontime.

---

[64] Cf. the Old English *Phoenix* 21–7.
[65] Cf. Apc 22:5.
[66] A. J. Bliss, ed., *Sir Launfal* (London and Edinburgh: Thomas Nelson, 1960).

Once there, the knight dismounts in precisely the type of setting that attracts fairies:

> Þe weþer was hot, þe vnderntyde;
> He ly3te adoun, & gan abyde
> Vnder a fayr forest;
> And, for hete of þe wedere,
> Hys mantell he feld togydere,
> And sette hym doun to reste.
> Þus sat þe kny3t yn symplyté,
> In þe schadwe, vnder a tre,
> Þer þat hym lykede best.   (lines 220–8)

> The weather was warm that noon; he alighted and halted by a pleasant forest. He folded up his cloak for the weather's heat and sat down to rest. Thus sat the knight in modesty in the shade, below a tree, where it pleased him best.

As he sits there reflecting on his misery, two fairy maidens approach him and ask him to follow them to their lady Tryamour, who lives in a forest pavilion and wants Launfal for her lover, showering him with riches in return (229–336). As Saunders observes, there is here less of the violence associated with the fairies in other texts; indeed, Launfal's life with Tryamour improves greatly on life in the human sphere, whether in Caerleon or at Arthur's court. The harsh nature of the fairy world is reflected only in Tryamour's instant disappearance when, against the instructions of the fairy princess, Launfal tells Gwenore that he has a lover, and in Tryamour's blinding of Gwenore after the latter is shown to have committed perjury in an attempt to bring Launfal into discredit (361–5, 673–810, 925–1008).[67] Whether dangerous or desirable, however, the fairy kingdom in this text, as in *Sir Degaré* and *Sir Orfeo*, is again accessed on a hot summer's day about noon. In this instance, it is worth remarking that the poem's source, Marie de France's *Lanval*, makes reference neither to the time nor to the heat of the day;[68] the English poet appears to have modified the material to conform to the broader convention, which is particularly well attested in English romances.

The hunt provides another fertile occasion for forest adventures. Previously discussed as the context of dream visions, this motif also shows up in knightly adventures such as *Sir Gawain and the Carle of Carlisle*.[69] Here, the hunt takes place during the 'grass-time of the yeere', when the deer have fattened up sufficiently to be desirable game (B19; cf. A31). This period began at the Nativity of St John, according to John Giffard,[70] so that the

---

[67] Saunders, *The Forest of Medieval Romance*, 145–7.
[68] Karl Wanke, ed., *Die 'lais' der Marie de France*, Bibliotheca normannica 3 (Halle: Niemeyer, 1925), 86–112; the relevant lines are 39–79.
[69] Auvo Kurvinen, ed., *Sir Gawain and the Carl of Carlisle* (Helsinki: Suomalaisen kirjallisuuden seura, 1951).
[70] In Giffard's reworking of the Middle English text of William Twiti's *L'art de venerie*, David

action of the poem is set in summer: the red hart chased by Gawain, Kay, and Bishop Bodwin was, according to the evidence gathered by Baillie-Grohman and Baillie-Grohman, not hunted after 14 September on the Julian calendar.[71] It thus seems to be an attachment to comfort or courtliness, not the cold of the season, that prompts Kay's insistence that the knights should seek out lodgings rather than sleep out of doors (B91–4). Accordingly, the group make their way to the carle of Carlisle, whose residence, a forest castle, is a typical otherworld location.[72] The audience's expectations in this regard soon prove correct, as the carle is a superhuman creature who has never yet allowed a guest to escape alive (B175–88, 409–15).

These examples show that the forest is the undisputed romance landscapes for contact with fairies and the superhuman. As part of this association, the forest is bound up with a number of further conventions of the genre. It is a landscape of isolation, for instance, in which characters tend to end up by themselves either by choice or through misadventure. In its capacity as a fairy landscape, the forest is also overwhelmingly a summer environment. In this respect, it joins and overlaps with the dream-visionary chronotope, which centres on the same season and a similar landscape category.

ADVENTURES IN OLD NORSE PROSE

As romance literature was translated into Old Norse, the configuration of the European adventure was left largely unaltered. Nevertheless, the Old Norse manifestation of the motif requires some discussion of its own in terms of the adoption into original Icelandic narratives of the genres of legendary saga and Nordic (as opposed to translated) romance.

Most importantly, the Old Norse narrative tradition already knew several motifs of seasonal adventure involving geographical distancing. Perhaps the most characteristic convention of this sort has a protagonist or group of protagonists spend the summer raiding, often in the Baltic region (referred to as *Austrvegr* or *Eystrasalt*, occasionally specifying an eastern Baltic region such as Kúrland). This pattern is found in the sagas of Icelanders and the kings' sagas, but is especially prominent in the legendary sagas. It tends to award the Baltic lands no supernatural or

---

Scott-Macnab, ed., *The Middle English Text of 'The Art of Hunting' by William Twiti*, Middle English Texts 40 (Heidelberg: Winter, 2009), 17, lines 97–8. For the sense of *grass-time*, see also *Middle English Dictionary*, s.v. 'grēs(e)', sense 2c.

[71] Wm A. Baillie-Grohman and F. Baillie-Grohman, eds, *The Master of Game* (London: Chatto / Windus, 1909), 254. Their information derives largely from an early-fifteenth-century translation of Gaston de Foix's *Livre de chasse*, itself begun in 1387 and thus contemporary with much of the literature discussed in this chapter (ibid., xii).

[72] Muriel Whitaker, 'Otherworld Castles in Middle English Arthurian Romance', in *The Medieval Castle: Romance and Reality*, ed. Kathryn Reyerson and Faye Powe (Dubuque, IA: Kendall / Hunt, 1984), 27–45; cf. Saunders, *The Forest of Medieval Romance*, 154.

other remarkable characteristics; in other words, the interest is purely in the adventure of raiding and warfare.[73]

A second motif, here particularly relevant, consists in journeys to Finnmǫrk in the farthest north, and sometimes to Bjarmaland east of Finnmǫrk; this motif too is particularly common in the legendary sagas. As was demonstrated above, the Sami are commonly associated with sorcery. Accordingly, journeys to northern and north-eastern lands are often journeys to a realm of the supernatural. When Eiríkr *blóðøx* first encounters Gunnhildr in Finnmǫrk, she explains she is there to learn witchcraft under the supervision of two Sami sorcerers.[74] The protagonist of *Bósa saga* is sent to obtain an ornamented vulture egg from Bjarmaland, here specifically near the River Dvina, which issues into the south-eastern part of the White Sea (chs 6–7).[75] The priestess who guards this egg is a prophetess and sorceress; her superhuman qualities in this respect are emphasized through her identification as a *troll*,[76] a concept with various referents, all tending towards the supernatural.[77] Similarly, when Ketill *hœngr* sails by Finnmǫrk, he has to put in to land on account of bad weather; he is awoken at night by a *trollkona* (*troll* woman) rocking his ship (ch. 3),[78] and he later experiences a series of adventures among the superhuman Sami inhabiting this region. A similar encounter is described in *Gríms saga loðinkinna*, whose title character wakes up first to a storm that chases off all game animals, and then to the laughter of two women identified as *jǫtnar* and *troll* (ch. 1).[79] In short, journeys to north-eastern Scandinavia have strong overtones of the supernatural and in this respect bear some similarity to the individual adventures of European romance.

---

[73] For example *Egils saga*, chs 19, 36, 46, 49: Bjarni Einarsson, *Egils saga*, 23, 49, 63, 70; *Njáls saga*, ch. 119: Einar Ólafur Sveinsson, *Brennu-Njáls saga*, 302; *Ynglinga saga*, chs 27, 31, 32: Bjarni Aðalbjarnarson, *Heimskringla*, 1:54, 60, 61; *Haralds saga hárfagra*, chs 24, 32: ibid., 1:123, 134; *Haralds saga gráfeldar*, chs 9, 12, 13: ibid., 1:213, 216, 217; *Óláfs saga Tryggvasonar*, chs 43, 90: ibid., 1:287, 338–41; *Óláfs saga helga*, chs 54, 62, 65: ibid., 1:71, 82, 83; *Gǫngu-Hrólfs saga*, chs 6, 38: Guðni Jónsson and Bjarni Vilhjálmsson, *Fornaldarsögur*, 2:374, 460; *Hálfdanar saga Eysteinssonar*, chs 1, 10, 12: ibid., 3:286, 297, 298; *Hversu Noregr byggðisk*, ch. 2: ibid., 2:142; *Ǫrvar-Odds saga*, ch. 23: ibid., 1:355–6; *Ragnars saga loðbrókar*, ch. 18: ibid., 1:143; *Ragnarssona saga*, ch. 2: ibid., 1:153; *Sǫrla þáttr*, ch. 4: ibid., 2:102; *Sturlaugs saga Starfsama*, ch. 24: ibid., 2:314; *Þorsteins saga Víkingssonar*, chs 7, 21, 22, 24, 25: ibid., 2:198, 233, 235, 241, 243.

[74] *Haralds saga hárfagra*, ch. 34: Bjarni Aðalbjarnarson, *Heimskringla*, 1:135; cf. *Egils saga*, ch. 37: Bjarni Einarsson, *Egils saga*, 50–1.

[75] Guðni Jónsson and Bjarni Vilhjálmsson, *Fornaldarsögur*, 2:475–6.

[76] Ch. 8: ibid., 2:478.

[77] Ármann Jakobsson, 'Hvað er tröll? Galdrar, tröll og samfélagsóvinir', in *Galdramenn: Galdrar og samfélag á miðöldum*, ed. Torfi H. Tulinius (Reykjavik: Hugvísindastofnun Háskóla Íslands, 2008), 95–118; Ármann Jakobsson, 'The Trollish Acts of Þorgrímr the Witch: The Meanings of *troll* and *ergi* in Medieval Iceland', *Saga-Book* 32 (2008): 39–68; P. S. Langeslag, '*Trǫll* and Ethnicity in *Egils saga*', in *Á austrvega: Saga and East Scandinavia; Preprint Papers of the 14th International Saga Conference, Uppsala, 9th–15th August 2009*, ed. Agneta Ney, Henrik Williams, and Fredrik Charpentier Ljungqvist, vol. 2, Institutionen för humaniora och samhällsvetenskaps, skriftserie 14 (Gävle: Gävle University Press, 2009), 560–7.

[78] Guðni Jónsson and Bjarni Vilhjálmsson, *Fornaldarsögur*, 1:251.

[79] Ibid., 1:270.

The first thing to observe about these journeying motifs is that they seem to have arisen independently of European influence. The raiding-motif is so omnipresent in saga tradition, and so prominent in medieval Scandinavian history, that there can be no doubt as to its Nordic origins. The motif of the supernatural northern or north-eastern realm, meanwhile, may rely on a spatial premise much like that of Continental romance, but the wider connections between the Sami and witchcraft, between *troll*, giants, and the north, are too widespread to be explained as an offshoot of a foreign tradition borrowed in the thirteenth century.[80] If anything, Old Norse journeys to Finnmǫrk are reminiscent of the Karelian-Finnish *Kalevala* cycle of poetry, which tells of nautical expeditions to a witch-governed northern land in order to recover a precious object.[81] Thus when Continental narratives of summer forests as sites of adventure and thresholds to a supernatural realm reached the north, an analogous tradition was already in place.

Even so, once the romance tradition came to Iceland, it did have an impact on the way journeys to the north and east were depicted. In Nordic romance as well as legendary sagas, foreign romance motifs were incorporated into a pre-existing Nordic geography and literary social order.[82] Accordingly, even if a Scandinavian tradition of spatial othering may be established, many individual instances of journeys to these regions are difficult to separate from the international romance tradition. A good example of this is found in *Helga þáttr Þórissonar*. Here, the protagonist loses his way in a maple forest not far from from Finnmǫrk (ch. 1).[83] The ensuing events were probably borrowed from the Lanval tradition[84] whose Middle English adaptation *Sir Launfal* was introduced above, although it differs from that narrative in particulars.[85] As in the other Lanval texts, the protagonist encounters a fairy-like maiden who invites him to be her lover. In the Icelandic text, however, the forest is set in northern Scandinavia near Finnmǫrk, and the maiden is the daughter of the superhuman King Guðmundr of Glæsisvellir, a region east of Bjarmaland representing an otherworld in many texts of this genre.[86]

---

[80] See Tolley, *Shamanism*. As is observed in that work (1:61), the Sami are not associated with magic in Greek and Latin sources until the mid-thirteenth century.

[81] See Nils Lid, 'The Mythical Realm of the Far North: As it Appears in the National Finnish Epic *Kalevala* and the Scandinavian *fornaldar-saga* Tradition', *LAOS* 1 (1951): 58–66.

[82] Rosemary Power, 'Journeys to the Otherworld in the Icelandic *fornaldarsögur*', *Folklore* 96, no. 2 (1985): 156.

[83] Guðni Jónsson and Bjarni Vilhjálmsson, *Fornaldarsögur*, 3:421–2; cf. Leiv Heggstad, Finn Hødnebø, and Erik Simensen, eds, *Norrøn ordbok*, 5th ed. (Oslo: Det norske samlaget, 2008), s.v. 'Vimund'.

[84] Rosemary Power, '*Le lai de Lanval* and *Helga þáttr Þórissonar*', *Opuscula* 8 (1985): 158–61.

[85] Cf. Wanke, *Die 'lais' der Marie de France*, 86–112.

[86] Cf. Power, 'Journeys to the Otherworld'; Rudolf Simek, 'Elusive Elysia; or: Which Way to Glæsisvellir? On the Geography of the North in Icelandic Legendary Fiction', in Rudolf Simek, Jónas Kristjánsson, and Hans Bekker-Nielsen, *Sagnaskemmtun*, 264–70.

Helga þáttr demonstrates how the season of encounters with the supernatural in legendary sagas coincides with that of European romance, but nevertheless comes across as a less immediate concern than in the romance tradition. In legendary sagas as in Continental romance, virtually all of the encounters take place in summer. However, this seasonality is presented in a considerably different way. Whereas in traditional romance the time of year only becomes relevant as a way of foreshadowing the supernatural encounter when the protagonist alights by a forest or in a clearing, Old Norse adventures typically describe the timing of expeditions relative to the seafaring season: it is after the winter that one sets sail, and the adventure must be complete, or else the journey interrupted, at the onset of winter.[87] Accordingly, *Helga þáttr* mentions the end of the summer only because it prompts the travellers to conclude their trading expedition to Finnmǫrk; it is on their return that Helgi encounters Guðmundr's daughter. The heat-of-the-day motif so consistently found in Middle English fairy encounters is found in the north only in translated romance, and only on rare occasions.[88] Like other texts of its genre, *Helga þáttr* is an amalgam of Nordic and European motifs, but the seasonality of the action, coinciding in both traditions, is presented in a characteristically Icelandic way.

EXILE

Forests in medieval romance do not function exclusively as thresholds to the world of fairies. Rather, as Saunders makes clear, they are home to a varied set of motifs.[89] Prominent among these is that of exile, as might be expected both from the sociohistorical role of the forest discussed above and from the binary division of romance space. As will be seen, forests are not exclusively lush and warm when described as places of exile; instead, natural winter landscapes remain a powerful image of personal deprivation.

Among the longer-standing traditions of self-imposed exile to the natural world is one that is not, perhaps, voluntary in a present-day legal sense, namely the exile of madness. The image of the powerful Babylonian king Nebuchadnezzar reduced to the state of a wild animal by divine punishment was well known throughout the Christian Middle Ages,[90] and Jerome claims that the association of madness with feral life in the fields and forests was common knowledge in his day.[91] The motif of a mad king

---

[87] Cf. *Konungs skuggsjá*, chs 22–3: Brenner, *Speculum regale*, 59–63.
[88] For example *Hektors saga*, ch. 5: Loth, *Late Medieval Icelandic Romances*, 1:92; *Viktors saga ok Blávuss*, ch. 1: ibid., 1:5–7.
[89] Saunders, *The Forest of Medieval Romance*.
[90] Penelope B. R. Doob, *Nebuchadnezzar's Children: Conventions of Madness in Middle English Literature* (New Haven, CT, and London: Yale University Press, 1974), 54–94; cf. Matthias Henze, *The Madness of King Nebuchadnezzar: The Ancient Near Eastern Origins and Early History of Interpretation of Daniel 4*, Supplements to the Journal for the Study of Judaism 61 (Leiden: Brill, 1999), esp. 179–201.
[91] *Patrologia Latina*, 25:513; Saunders, *The Forest of Medieval Romance*, 13.

relocating to the woods likewise had a strong presence in Celtic tradition, notably in the twelfth-century Irish text *Buile Shuibhne*, antecedents of which have been dated to the tenth century or earlier, and several Middle Welsh poems from the twelfth to fifteenth centuries, all of which are thought to have roots in the eleventh century or before.[92] One of the fullest expressions of the motif is found in Geoffrey of Monmouth's *Vita Merlini*, written about 1150.[93] In the opening scene of this Latin poem, King Merlin takes part in a large battle, repeatedly stopping to bewail the loss of his companions in a manner reminiscent of the Psalmist's lamentations (23–71). Upon victory, Merlin disappears to take up life in the forest, from which point onwards both the narrator and the other characters classify him as a madman (72–83, 299–304). He is repeatedly brought back to court and the nearby town by force, but when among men he always longs to return to the forest (for example 278–9, 499–500). Eventually cured after drinking from a magic spring, he attributes his gift of prophecy to his former madness (1136–68). Following his recovery, he is offered the opportunity to be restored to the throne, but he elects to continue living in the forest instead, now in the service of God (1259–91; cf. 1442–60). This narrative thus demonstrates the associative overlap between prophecy, madness, and religious seclusion.[94]

From the beginning of his exile, Merlin expresses distress at winter and its effects on his living conditions:

> Utitur herbarum radicibus, utitur herbis,
> utitur arboreo fructu morisque rubeti.
> Fit silvester homo quasi silvis deditus esset.
> Inde per estatem totam nullique repertus
> oblitusque sui cognatorumque suorum
> delituit silvis obductus more ferino.
> At cum venit yems herbasque tulisset et omnes
> arboreos fructus nec quo frueretur haberet,
> diffudit tales miseranda voce querelas:
> 'Celi Christe deus, quid agam? Qua parte morari
> terrarum potero cum nil quo vescar adesse
> inspicio, nec gramen humi nec in arbore glandes.
> Tres quater et juges septene poma ferentes
> hic steterant mali; nunc non stant. Ergo quis illas
> quis michi surripuit, quo devenere repente?

---

[92] J. G. O'Keeffe, ed., *Buile Śuibhne*, Mediaeval and Modern Irish Series 1 (Dublin: Dublin Institute for Advanced Studies, 1931), iii–v; Basil Clarke, ed. and trans., *Life of Merlin* (Cardiff: University of Wales Press, 1973), 1–5, 22–5.

[93] Clarke, *Life of Merlin* (dating and authorship at 36–42). For discussions of its relation to the wider tradition of wild men, see Ferdinand Lot, 'Études sur Merlin I: Les sources de la *Vita Merlini* de Gaufrei de Monmouth', *Annales de Bretagne* 16 (1900): 325–47; Richard Bernheimer, *Wild Men in the Middle Ages: A Study in Art, Sentiment, and Demonology* (Cambridge, MA: Harvard University Press, 1952); Philippe Walter, 'Sous le masque du souvage', in *Le devin maudit: Merlin, Lailoken, Suibhne*, ed. and trans. Philippe Walter *et al.* (Grenoble: Ellug, 1999).

[94] Cf. Doob, *Nebuchadnezzar's Children*, 134–207.

> Nunc illas uideo, nunc non. Sic fata repugnant;
> sic quoque concordant cum dant prohibentque videre.
> Deficiunt nunc poma michi, nunc cetera queque.
> Stat sine fronde nemus, sine fructu; plector utroque,
> cum neque fronde tegi valeo neque fructibus uti.
> Singula bruma tulit pluviisque cadentibus auster.
> Invenio si forte napes tellure sub ima
> concurrunt avideque sues aprique voraces
> eripiuntque napes michi quas de cespite vello.' (lines 78–101)

He eats the roots of grasses, he eats grasses, he eats the fruit of trees and mulberries of the thicket. He becomes a man of the woods, as though he had been consecrated to the woods. From then on throughout the summer, met by no one and forgetful of himself and of his acquaintances, he hid in the woods, enveloped in a beastly mode of life. But when the winter came and had borne off the plants and the fruits of the trees and he had nothing to eat, he poured out complaints like these in a pitiable voice: 'Christ, God of heaven, what shall I do? In what part of the world can I dwell when I find nothing on which I might feed, neither a plant of the earth nor acorns in a tree? Nineteen fruit-bearing apple trees stood here together; now they don't. Who then has taken them away from me, where have they suddenly gone? Now I see them, now I don't. Thus the fates oppose me; thus also they conspire against me, since they permit and forbid me to see. Now I am lacking in fruits and all other things. The wood remains without foliage, without fruit; I am punished in both respects, since I am able neither to be sheltered by the foliage nor to enjoy fruits. The winter and the south wind with its falling rains have carried them all off. If perhaps I find turnips below the deepest soil, pigs and voracious boars eagerly rush on and snatch away from me the turnips which I want from the turf.'

The severity of winter remains a theme for much of Merlin's life in the forest, as he repeatedly mourns the absence of plant foods in winter. He sees value in each of the four Julian seasons except winter, though spring receives the largest share of praise:

> O qui cuncta regis, quid est cur contigit ut non
> tempora sint eadem numeris distincta quaternis?
> Nunc ver jure suo flores frondesque ministrat,
> dat fruges estas, autumpnus micia poma.
> Consequitur glacialis yemps et cetera queque
> devorat et vastat pluviasque nivesque reportat.
> Singula queque suis arcet leditque procellis
> nec permittit humum varios producere flores
> aut quercus glandes aut malos punica mala.
> O utinam non esset hiems aut cana pruina!
> Ver foret aut estas, cuculusque canendo rediret
> Et Philomela pio que tristia pectora cantu
> mitigat et turtur conservans federa casta
> frondibus inque novis concordi voce volucres
> cantarent alie que me modulando foverent,

> dum nova flore novo tellus spiraret odorem
> gramine sub viridi levi; quoque murmure fontes
> diffluerent juxtaque daret sub fronde columba
> sompniferos gemitus irritaretque soporem.   (lines 146–64)[95]

O you who govern all, why does it happen that the seasons are not the same, distinct only in their fourfold number? As it is, spring by its law provides flowers and leaves, summer gives crops, autumn ripe fruits. The icy winter follows and devours each of the others and lays them waste and brings rains and snows. Each of them it encloses and injures with its storms, and it does not permit the earth to produce its various flowers or the oak to produce acorns or the apple tree to produce red apples. O would that there were no winter or white hoarfrost! That it were spring or summer, and the cuckoo would return with its singing, and the nightingale who softens sad hearts with her devout song, and the turtle dove keeping her chaste vows, and that other birds who soothe me with their song would sing among the new foliage with a harmonious sound, while the earth would breathe the fragrance of a new flower below new grass, green and smooth; also that the waters would flow off with a murmur and that near at hand a dove would produce sleep-inducing sighs below the foliage and incite a slumber!

Eventually, he asks his sister to provide a large forest mansion with food servants and scribes for the winters only. He makes clear that this is not because he cannot bear the cold; instead, the arrangements are meant only to prevent his running out of provisions (542–73).

A madness of a subtly different sort is that inspired by love and curable by its attainment. In *Sir Orfeo*, the forest serves not only as a portal to the fairy world, but also as the locale for Orfeo's self-imposed exile upon the abduction of his queen. The poet's discussion of the seasons is strongly reminiscent of that in the *Vita Merlini*, but the juxtaposition of court and forest is more marked:

> Now on hard heþe he liþ,
> Wiþ leues & gresse he him wriþ.
> He þat hadde had castels & tours,
> Riuer, forest, friþ wiþ flours;
> Now, þei it commenci to snewe & frese,
> Þis king mot make his bed in mese.
> He þat had y-had kniȝtes of priis
> Bifor him kneland, & leuedis,
> Now seþ he no-þing þat him likeþ,
> Bot wilde wormes bi him strikeþ.
> He þat had y-had plenté
> Of mete & drink, of ich deynté,
> Now may he al-day digge & wrote
> Er he finde his fille of rote.
> In somer he liueþ bi wild frut,

---

[95] For more references to and complaints of winter severity, see lines 416–18, 424–8, 535–73.

> & berien bot gode lite;
> In winter may he no-þing finde
> Bot rote, grases, & þe rinde.   (lines 243–60)

> Now he lies on the hard moor; he covers himself with leaves and grass, he who had possessed castles and towers, river, forest, park with flowers. Now, though it begin to snow and freeze, this king has to make his bed in the moss. He who had had noble knights kneel before him, and ladies too, now sees nothing that pleases him, but savage worms pass him by. He who had had an abundance of food and drink, of every delicacy, can now dig and grub all day before he finds his fill of roots. In summer, he lives on wild fruit and berries of but little merit; in winter he may find nothing but roots, grasses, and bark.

Noteworthy is the contrast between Orfeo's pre-exilic ownership of forests, which are mentioned among other landscapes of aristocratic entertainment, and his present condition of having made the forest his home, so that its delights are immediately lost among its discomforts. Although his exile is disagreeable the year round, winter is adduced as a time of particular hardship, both for its weather and because it withholds the fruits of the earth. Here as in the *Vita Merlini*, then, winter has associations of exilic deprivation comparable to those of Old English lyric, although both of the later texts take a more practical view of the season's effects on the exile in addition to its purely associative value.

Occasionally, exile is depicted as a circumstance preferable to life in society inasmuch as it permits arrangements not possible in the human domain. This is an integral argument of the Tristan romances, in which the young lovers can be together only in the forest. Owing to this desirable aspect of their exile, their forest habitat frequently displays limited *loca amoena* reflecting their love, even if the landscape as a whole remains a hostile territory.[96] Accordingly, summer landscapes make brief, repeated occurrences. The Middle English reworking of this originally Anglo-Norman tradition is *Sir Tristrem*,[97] a verse romance uniquely contained in the fourteenth-century Auchinleck-manuscript. The seasons are first evoked in its introduction, which describes how the beauty of the world and the best of its inhabitants must all give way to what comes after, just as the summer and its foliage turn grey in winter:

> This semly somers day,
> In winter it is nought sen;
> This greues wexen al gray,
> That in her time were grene.
> So dos this world, y say,

---

[96] Saunders, *The Forest of Medieval Romance*, 81–94, esp. 90–4; cf. Schmid-Cadalbert, 'Der wilde Wald', 24, 39.

[97] André Crépin, ed., *Sir Tristrem*, trans. Hélène Dauby, Medievales 17 (Amiens: Presses du Centre d'Études Médiévales, Université de Picardie-Jules Verne, 2002).

> Y wis and nought at wene,
> The gode ben al oway
> That our elders haue bene,
>   To abide.
> Of a knight is that y mene,
> His name, it sprong wel wide.   (lines 12–22)

This pleasant summer's day, it is not seen in winter. These groves, which were green in their time, all turn grey. So does this world operate, I say, certainly and without a doubt: our good ancestors are all gone for good. It is of a knight I speak; his reputation has travelled very widely.

The obvious implication is that Tristrem is one such shining example of the great men and women of a glorious past. In the process, however, the entire narrative is couched in a frame of figurative summer, in which all that is glorious exceeds the audience's standards of beauty, suspending realism for characters and narrative environment alike.

Since Ysonde is married to King Mark and the love between her and Tristrem is thus forbidden, the two can only give expression to it in private. Mostly, they seem to settle simply for Ysonde's bedroom, but they also exploit the outdoors, as in their orchard encounters (2058–61) and when they spend a week in a forest hideout (1915–22). The real *locus amoenus* is to be found in their extended forest habitation, however, after King Mark expels them from his kingdom on account of the apparent love that is between them (2438–569). The forest is replete with their love:

> A forest fled thai tille,
> Tristrem and Ysonde the schene.
> No hadde thai no won to wille
> Bot the wode so grene.
> Bi holtes and bi hille
> Fore Tristrem and the quene.
> Ysonde of ioie hath her fille
> And Tristrem, withouten wene,
>   As thare:
> So blithe al bidene
> Nar thai neuer are.   (lines 2454–64)

They fled to a forest, Tristrem and Ysonde the fair. They had no dwelling at their disposal except the wood so green. Tristrem and the lady lived by wood and by hill. Ysonde has her fill of joy then, and Tristrem too, without doubt; they had never been so completely happy before.

They occupy a cave, whose comforts are such as to invert the conventional qualities of the seasons:

> In winter it was hate;
> In somer it was cold.
> Thai hadden a dern gat
> That thai no man told.

> No hadde thai no wines wat,
> No ale that was old,
> No no gode mete thai at.
> Thai hadden al that thai wold
>   With wille.
> For loue ich other bihalt,
> Her non might of other fille.   (lines 2487–97)

> In winter it was warm; in summer it was cool. They had a hidden entrance of which they spoke to no-one. They had no drink of wine, nor ale that was old, nor did they eat good food. They had all their hearts' desire. Each gazed at the other in love; neither could get enough of the other.

This stanza expresses at once the comforts of the couple's living situation and the absence of other material comforts, namely their customary standards of food and drink. Thus the forest's assocation with deprivation as encountered in the *Vita Merlini* and *Sir Orfeo* recurs here in a less acute form and is immediately outweighed by the lovers' joy: although water, game, and grass is all their food and drink, 'swiche joie hadde thai never yete' ('they had never yet experienced such joy', 2500–8, at 2508). That the seasons are not remarked on in any further detail is primarily a function of the forest's role as the setting in which the lovers may fulfil their desires. The simple fare at their disposal serves as a reminder that the poet saw enough potential here to describe their exile as a miserable one if she or he so chose. Instead, however, the description of the seasons of cave life with their inverse polarity represents a deliberate choice to draw attention away from the more obvious seasons of life in the forest, whose afflictions in the narrative are eclipsed by the joy of the lovers' union.

The most detailed of the Norse accounts of this episode occurs in the thirteenth-century[98] *Tristrams saga ok Ísöndar*. This version is a close match to the English translation based on the same source, but subtle differences exist. Both texts point out the lovers' complete satisfaction with their fate, but whereas the English poem makes some mention of the poverty of their fare, the Icelandic prose text has them reject labour-based economics altogether, as they rely on God to provide sustenance:

> Ok íhuguðu þau þá lítt, hverr þeim skyldi fá vín ok vistir, þvíat Guð mun vilja gefa þeim nokkura næring, hvar sem þau váru.   (*Tristrams saga ok Ísöndar*, ch. 64)[99]

> And they gave little thought then to where they should obtain wine and provisions, because God would give them some sustenance wherever they were.

---

[98] Peter Jorgensen, ed., 'Tristrams saga ok Ísöndar', in Kalinke, *Norse Romance*, vol. 1, *The Tristan Legend*, 25.
[99] Jorgensen, 'Tristrams saga ok Ísöndar', 160.

Along with the couple's perfect satisfaction with their life together, this seemingly effortless access to food and drink with God's help is suggestive of prelapsarian life in Eden, where another couple was likewise in a position to eat 'of every tree' (Gn 2:16).[100] Indeed, next to the cave of the Icelandic text is 'a river welling up from the earth with wholesome water, and in the vicinity of the river grew the sweetest grasses with flowers as beautiful as one could want',[101] again recalling Eden. The difference is that in reality, the medieval lovers live 'í mikla eyðimörk' ('in a great wilderness'),[102] a landscape associated with the postlapsarian world as opposed to the safe garden of paradise, and therefore normally associated also with the toil of agriculture (Gn 3:17–18). The narrative world of Tristram and Ísönd is suspended from this reality by virtue of their love.

A second aspect in which the Icelandic account differs from the English text is that it presents the seasonality of the episode in a more realistic light. Rather than describe indoor pseudoseasons, it refers to the cold and the rain of the world outside, remarking that Tristram and Ísönd take shelter in their cave whenever such weather patterns occur. By contrast, good weather draws them out to the joys of forest and spring.[103]

The English and Icelandic retellings of the popular romance of Tristan and Iseult both derive from the Old French text by Thomas of Britain,[104] so that both contrast with Béroul's version of the story.[105] A significant difference between Thomas and Béroul is that the former has the enchantment that brings the lovers together last forever, while Béroul has it end after a period of three years. In Béroul, the end of this period announces itself during the couple's forest exile, yielding a powerful contrast in the lovers' perception of their surroundings before and after the potion expires: the forest idyll becomes a hateful exile (*Tristan* 2147–204). By comparison, the Thomas-derived versions place less emphasis on the subjective changeability of the forest habitat. Since Béroul does not have his lovers lament the season, however, his seasonal concerns are limited to space and lifestyle.

WINTER ROMANCE: *SIR GAWAIN AND THE GREEN KNIGHT*

If summer landscapes play a central role in chivalric adventures, that is not to say that the romance genre has no use for winter settings. It was

---

[100] 'Ex omni ligno.'

[101] 'Ein uppsprettandi á með heilsömu vatni, en umhverfis ána váru vaxin hin sætustu grös með fögru blómi, er maðr vildi kjósa.'

[102] Kalinke, *Norse Romance*, 1:160.

[103] Jorgensen, 'Tristrams saga ok Ísöndar', 160.

[104] Gesa Bonath, ed. and trans., *Thomas: 'Tristan'*, Klassische Texte des Romanischen Mittelalters in zweisprachigen Ausgaben 21 (Munich: Fink, 1985). For the textual relations see Kalinke, *Norse Romance*, 1:vii; Crépin, *Sir Tristrem*, 3.

[105] Norris J. Lacy, ed. and trans., *Béroul: 'The Romance of Tristan'*, Garland Library of Medieval Literature A 36 (New York and London: Garland, 1989).

seen above that winter remained a valuable motif by which to express the hardships of exile; it will now be seen that even otherworldly adventure itself may occur outside its typical seasonal chronotope of the summer forest.

The most striking negation of the paradigm of summer adventure here established would be a connection between midwinter and the supernatural, such as was found especially in the Icelandic sagas. This type of connection does indeed exist in the late-fourteenth-century[106] *Sir Gawain and the Green Knight*, the only Middle English romance adventure whose action is strongly concentrated around Christmastide. In Arthur's court, this festival is celebrated with fifteen days of merriment. On New Year's Day, the narrator explains, the king will not begin his meal before hearing of some adventure or marvel, or witnessing a jousting challenge. This is not a custom exclusive to New Year's Day, but rather one Arthur observes at every grand feast (85–106). Nevertheless, the poet has situated the episode on New Year's Day, and Arthur is to be treated to an adventure centrally pivoted on the Christmas season. The strange knight who rides into his court is all dressed in green, a colour reminiscent of the forest, though especially so in other seasons, and the holly branch he holds is 'grattest in grene when greuez are bare' ('the greatest thing in green when groves are bare', 207), another reminder of floral beauty in the season of its absence. The knight's request, that Arthur should join him in an exchange of axe blows, is introduced as 'a Crystemas gomen' ('a Christmas game') and explained by the fact that 'hit is ȝol and Nwe ȝer, and here ar ȝep mony' ('it is Yule and New Year, and there are many bold men here', 283–4). It may be, as Phelan suggests, that the axe which the Green Knight offers as a prize should be understood in the context of the New Year's gifts introduced in lines 66–70, likewise presented as a game, with mention of winning and losing.[107] In any case, the rules of the knight's game, which stipulate that the second player gets his turn only after a full year has passed (285–300), root the game even more firmly in the Christmas season as it involves two iterations but omits the intervening seasons. Indeed, the consequence of this rule is that Gawain, who accepts the challenge in Arthur's stead, spends a full year in the knowledge that he is to be struck with an axe on New Year's Day, thus giving the season a permanent place in his mind, as well as an ominous quality.[108]

---

[106] Tolkien and Gordon, *Sir Gawain and the Green Knight*, xxv–xxvi.

[107] Walter S. Phelan, *The Christmas Hero and Yuletide Tradition in 'Sir Gawain and the Green Knight'* (Lewiston, NY, Queenston, ON, and Lampeter: Edwin Mellen, 1992), passim. Emerson has proposed that the last two lines of the gift-giving scene concern the giving of kisses, which is a game closely analogous to that proposed by the Green Knight, not to mention the exhange of winnings at Hautdesert. Oliver Farrar Emerson, 'Notes on *Sir Gawain and the Green Knight*', *Journal of English and Germanic Philology* 21 (1922): 364–5; Tolkien and Gordon, *Sir Gawain and the Green Knight*, 74, n. to line 67; Edward Wilson, *The 'Gawain'-Poet* (Leiden: Brill, 1976), 118–19.

[108] Cf. A. V. C. Schmidt, '"Latent Content" and "The Testimony in the Text": Symbolic Meaning

Although the motif of an exchange of blows has been found elsewhere, two key temporal aspects to this sequence of events, the Christmas setting and the year's delay, are not found in conjunction in any of the analogues that have been proposed as sources. Three key texts may be distinguished for comparison with the beheading episode. A distant parallel is the ninth-century Old Irish *Fled Bricrend*,[109] which represents a tradition that may have influenced a second text, the Old French *Carados*, a section from the first continuation to Chrétien's *Parceval*.[110] That text in turn influenced *Sir Gawain and the Green Knight* directly,[111] while a further French text known as *La mule sans frein* has likewise been identified as a source.[112] For present purposes, the key difference between the four texts is temporal-structural. In this respect, *Fled Bricrend* stands out for not mentioning the time of year at all, while the return match in this text is to take place the next day, not after a year as in *Sir Gawain and the Green Knight*. *Carados* does specify a year's delay, but it situates each turn in the exchange of blows at Pentecost rather than on New Year's Day (7003–17, 7137–241). Pentecost is also the setting of *La mule sans frein*, though here the return blow again takes place the next morning (20, 559–633). As Benson notes, the *Gawain* poet's aim in moving the action from Pentecost to New Year's Day may lie in an association between that festival and the Round Table in Middle English romance.[113] If so, the unlooked-for consequence is that in terms of seasonality, *Sir Gawain and the Green Knight* has more in common with the dragon episode in *Hrólfs saga kraka* than with any of its models for the exchange of blows. Specifically, the sadness that comes over Arthur's court at the start of winter is reminiscent of the gloom at Hrólfr's court in *Hrólfs saga* as Yule approaches with its threat of a dragon attack (ch. 35).[114] By sharing this detail, the two texts attain a strongly convergent mood in which the Christmas season is dreaded for an associated superhuman threat.

in *Sir Gawain and the Green Knight'*, *Review of English Studies*, n.s., 38 (1987): 151–4.
[109] George Henderson, ed. and trans., *Fled Bricrend / The Feast of Bricriu* (London: Nutt, 1899); dating at xlvii–lxvii.
[110] William Roach and Robert H. Ivy, eds, *The Continuations of the Old French 'Perceval' of Chretien de Troyes*, vol. 2, *The First Continuation*, Romance Languages and Literatures, extra series 10 (Philadelphia, PA: University of Pennsylvania, Department of Romance Languages, 1949).
[111] Larry Dean Benson, 'The Source of the Beheading Episode in *Sir Gawain and the Green Knight*', *Modern Philology* 59, no. 1 (August 1961): 1–12.
[112] R. C. Johnston and D. D. R. Owen, eds, *Two Old French Gauvain Romances: 'Le chevalier à l'épée' and 'La mule sans frein'* (Edinburgh and London: Scottish Academic Press, 1972); the editors also identify points of contact with *Sir Gawain and the Green Knight*. For discussions of the various sources and analogues to the episode in *Sir Gawain and the Green Knight*, see George Lyman Kittredge, *A Study of 'Gawain and the Green Knight'* (Cambridge, MA: Harvard University Press, 1916), 9–76; Larry Dean Benson, *Art and Tradition in 'Sir Gawain and the Green Knight'* (New Brunswick, NJ: Rutgers University Press, 1965), 11–37. For translations of the relevant passages, see Elizabeth Brewer, ed. and trans., *Sir Gawain and the Green Knight: Sources and Analogues* (Cambridge: Brewer, 1992), 18–60.
[113] Benson, *Art and Tradition in 'Sir Gawain and the Green Knight'*, 26 and 266, n. 28.
[114] Guðni Jónsson and Bjarni Vilhjálmsson, *Fornaldarsögur*, 2:59–60.

What makes *Sir Gawain and the Green Knight* a forest romance is the fact that the remainder of the narrative is set outside Camelot, and therefore largely in the woods. After Gawain decapitates the Green Knight, who turns out to be resistant to such injuries, the stranger charges him to seek him out at the Green Chapel in a year's time for the return match (448–56). Although no further directions follow, it soon becomes clear that the chapel is to be reached through almost two months' journey on horseback from the mythical realm of Logres through North Wales and from there to the Wirral, finally to end in an unidentified forest environment that may be part of the Wirral but which, on account of its lack of specification, is best thought of as a return back into a literary landscape with limited relation to the real world (536–762).[115] The larger part of the poem takes place near the end of this journey, at and around the castle of Hautdesert, identified as a castle of adventure by its forest location and further connected with woodlands by the extensive hunting episodes in this section (763–2159). Finally, the poem's climax is set in a wild natural landscape turned pagan cultural landscape through the presence of a burial mound (2160–478). Thus the spatial setting of the poem is entirely in keeping with romance tradition, although its seasonal aspect is unconventional.

The winter setting in *Sir Gawain and the Green Knight* serves to create a starker contrast between safe and unsafe both spatially (indoor versus outdoor) and in temporal terms (summer versus winter). Ultimately, the first dimension of this opposition turns out to have been false, as it is in Hautdesert, an indoor setting and therefore perceived as safe, that the greatest danger lies.

A preference for summer over winter is first established in the poem's most extensive seasonal description, found in lines 500–35. Although the depiction or introduction of a single season is certainly conventional in Middle English poetry, this passage covers the full cycle of the year and is therefore likewise reminiscent of calendar illustrations of the medieval period,[116] and of calendar poems such as the Old English *Menologium*. The description stretches across the larger part of two stanzas, the first of which describes the movement from winter to summer while the second covers

[115] For discussions of the topograpy of Gawain's journey, see John McNeal Dodgson, 'Sir Gawain's Arrival in Wirral', in *Early English and Norse Studies Presented to Hugh Smith in Honour of his Sixtieth Birthday*, ed. Arthur Brown and Peter Foote (London: Methuen, 1963), 19–25; P. L. Heyworth, 'Sir Gawain's Crossing of the Dee', *Medium Ævum* 41 (1972): 124–7; W. A. Davenport, *The Art of the 'Gawain'-Poet* (London: Athlone, 1978), 147–51; J. 1983 Eadie, 'Sir Gawain's Travels in North Wales', *Review of English Studies* 34 (1983): 191–5; Ralph W. V. Elliott, 'Landscape and Geography', in *A Companion to the 'Gawain'-Poet*, ed. Derek Brewer and Jonathan Gibson, Arthurian Studies 38 (Cambridge: Brewer, 1997), 104–17. For the imprecise landscape description at the beginning and end of Gawain's journey, cf. esp. Dodgson, 'Sir Gawain's Arrival in Wirral', 19–20; Elliott, 'Landscape and Geography'.

[116] On calendar illustrations, see Véronique Frandon, 'Iconographie des saisons dans l'Occident médiéval', *Revue de la Bibliothèque nationale* 50 (1993): 2–8; Bridget Ann Henisch, *The Medieval Calendar Year* (University Park, PA: Pennsylvania State University Press, 1999).

the opposite progression:

> Forþi þis 3ol ouer3ede, and þe 3ere after,
> And vche sesoun serlepes sued after oþer:
> After Crystenmasse com þe crabbed lentoun,
> Þat fraystez flesch wyth þe fysche and fode more symple;
> Bot þenne þe weder of þe worlde wyth wynter hit þrepez,
> Colde clengez adoun, cloudez vplyften,
> Schyre schedez þe rayn in schowrez ful warme,
> Fallez vpon fayre flat, flowrez þere schewen,
> Boþe groundez and þe greuez grene ar her wedez,
> Bryddez busken to bylde, and bremlych syngen
> For solace of þe softe somer þat sues þerafter
>   bi bonk;
>   And blossumez bolne to blowe
>   Bi rawez rych and ronk,
>   Þen notez noble inno3e
>   Ar herde in wod so wlonk.
>
> After þe sesoun of somer wyth þe soft wyndez
> Quen Zeferus syflez hymself on sedez and erbez,
> Wela wynne is þe wort þat waxes þeroute,
> When þe donkande dewe dropez of þe leuez,
> To bide a blysful blusch of þe bry3t sunne.
> Bot þen hy3es heruest, and hardenes hym sone,
> Warnez hym for þe wynter to wax ful rype;
> He dryues wyth dro3t þe dust for to ryse,
> Fro þe face of þe folde to fly3e ful hy3e;
> Wroþe wynde of þe welkyn wrastelez with þe sunne,
> Þe leuez lancen fro þe lynde and ly3ten on þe grounde,
> And al grayes þe gres þat grene watz ere;
> Þenne al rypez and rotez þat ros vpon fyrst,
> And þus 3irnez þe 3ere in 3isterdayez mony,
> And wynter wyndez a3ayn, as þe worlde askez,
>   no fage,
>   Til Me3elmas mone
>   Watz cumen wyth wynter wage;
>   Þen þenkkez Gawan ful sone
>   Of his anious uyage.   (lines 500–35)

Therefore this Yule passed, and the following year, and each season in turn followed after the other. After Christmas came harsh Lent, which tests the flesh with fish and simpler fare. But then the weather of the world strives against winter: the cold shrivels up, the clouds are raised, brightly falls the rain in very warm showers, falling upon the fair meadow. Flowers appear there; green are the garments of both fields and groves; birds hasten to build, and sing cheerfully for the comfort of the soft summer that follows thereafter by the riverbank; and blossoms swell to bloom by the abundant and voluminous hedgerows; then very noble notes are heard in the forest so lush.

> Then the season of summer with its soft winds, when Zephyrus himself breathes on seeds and plants. Very lovely is the plant that grows out of that, when the moistening dew drips from the leaves to enjoy the bright sun's blissful blush. But then autumn hastens on, and soon hardens it, cautions it to ripen fully before the winter. With drought it causes the dust to rise up from the face of the earth to fly very high. An angry wind from the clouds wrestles with the sun; the leaves detach from the linden tree and land on the ground, and the grass that had previously been green turns entirely grey. Then all that had first risen ripens and rots, and so passes the year into so many yesterdays, and winter comes round again, without fail, as the world requires. Until the Michaelmas moon had come with the promise of winter; then Gawain soon remembers his troublesome journey.

When this passage is compared to the *Menologium*, two differences stand out. Firstly, the passage in *Sir Gawain and the Green Knight* is less concerned with accurate dating, concentrating instead on the perceptible progression of the year, with only the occasional nod at mankind's observance of the seasons. Secondly, the Middle English passage is more consistent in evaluating the seasons in subjective experiential terms. Lent, towards the end of the cold season, is *crabbed* ('harsh, unpleasant'), but when summer sets in it inspires *solace* in birds, whose *notez noble* are *bremlych* ('gloriously') executed in *wlonk* ('lovely') forests. A similar series of appreciative adjectives describes the summer harvest, but the coming of autumn is announced with words of hardening (*hardenen*), decaying (*roten*), and turning grey (*greien*). The full year's progression thus sets up a cycle between the two halves of the Christmas game in which the vivification of the natural world implies that Gawain is for a time able to forget about his supposed rendezvous with death. Once autumn comes on, however, there is a gradual fade back into a harsher reality. By Michaelmas, the dreaded mission has returned to the forefront of Gawain's mind (532–5); on All Saints' Day (coinciding with Samhain, a time of increased contact with the otherworld in Celtic tradition),[117] he announces he is to depart the next morning (536–49). Thus the seasonal progression is charged with an experiential evaluation triggering a pleasant forgetfulness in the summer, after which the protagonist wakes up to the threat of winter.[118]

After Gawain sets out to find the Green Knight, the hostility of the winter season is further brought out when the dangers of the road are described. In lines 713–39, we learn that Gawain encounters an enemy at virtually every ford, while superhuman creatures of various kinds likewise have to be overcome as part of the journey. Having depicted this aspect of the quest, which seems as much as any hero could take, the poet then makes clear that all these martial challenges are less daunting than the torments of winter:

---

[117] Jeffrey Gantz, trans., *Early Irish Myths and Sagas* (Harmondsworth: Penguin, 1983), 12–13.
[118] Cf. Putter, *French Arthurian Romance*, 12.

> For werre wrathed hym not so much þat wynter nas wors,
> When þe colde cler water fro þe cloudez schadde,
> And fres er hit falle myȝt to the fale erþe;
> Ner slayn wyth þe slete he sleped in his yrnes
> Mo nyȝtez þen innoghe in naked rokkez,
> Þer as claterande fro þe crest þe colde borne rennez,
> And henged heȝe ouer his hede in hard iisse-ikkles. (lines 726–32)
>
> Because war did not distress him so greatly that winter was not worse, when the cold, clear water poured from the clouds and froze before it could fall to the pale earth. Nearly overcome by the sleet, he slept many nights in his armour among the bare rocks, where the cold stream runs clattering from the crest and hung high over his head in solid icicles.

The passage not only makes use of the romance category of the forest as a hostile environment, but also appeals to the exilic association of winter. Rather than simply combining the two to increase the burden placed upon the hero, however, the poet introduces a hierarchy in which even dragons, bears, and trolls do not trouble Gawain as much as the winter season. Since this assessment of the winter experience contrasts greatly with the festivities taking place at Camelot in the same season, it serves to emphasize the difference between inside and outside especially at this time of year. Inside the castle, and in the social sphere, winter is the time of greatest festivity; however, it is the harshest time of year for camping out or travelling by oneself. Here as in the sagas of Icelanders, it is in winter that inside and outside form the starkest contrast. On Christmas Eve, therefore, Gawain prays to Mary that he may find 'sum wone' ('some dwelling', 733–9). When he comes upon Hautdesert, his escape from the elements adds to his illusion that the castle represents an inside and thus safety. In the hierarchy of dangers in his path, it turns out, winter is more daunting than knights and superhuman enemies, but moral lapse is the greatest danger of all.

Once characters are based inside, as at Hautdesert, the winter forest becomes an adventure to be sought out in the daytime through the pastime of the hunt.[119] The vivid and extensive hunting-descriptions in *Sir Gawain and the Green Knight* bring out the excitement of the sport and make clear that this is considered an excellent way for active men to prove their worth. It is therefore surprising at a first reading that Gawain does not join his host Bertilak on his hunt. Indeed, the exchange of winnings to which Gawain is challenged would have led the reader to assume that both would hunt, were it not that this challenge immediately follows Bertilak's directions that Gawain is to stay in bed and dine with his hostess while he himself hunts (1096–109). Thus Gawain spends seven days apparently without leaving the castle or undertaking anything at all, calling to mind the warning expressed in *The Alliterative Morte Arthure* that a knight who goes too long without

---

[119] Cf. ibid., 12–13.

adventure sacrifices his worldly esteem (247–58) and the medieval notion that the hunt keeps men from sin.[120] If inactivity may be permissible during Christmastide, the three days of hunting certainly appear to compare the protagonist unfavourably with Bertilak[121] until it becomes clear, at the Green Chapel, that Gawain's confrontations with Lady Bertilak had been his real test, and the conventional boundary between inside and outside, safe and unsafe, does not apply at Hautdesert, or arguably anywhere (2331–68). *Sir Gawain and the Green Knight* is thus not simply a chance exception to conventions of space and season, but rather its plot structure relies on the inversion of those expectations.

As Gawain gears up for the final stage of his journey, the harshness of winter weather is once more played up:

> Now neȝez þe Nw ȝere, and þe nyȝt passez,
> Þe day dryuez to þe derk, as Dryȝtyn biddez;
> Bot wylde wederez of þe worlde wakned þeroute,
> Clowdes kesten kenly þe colde to þe erþe,
> Wyth nyȝe innoghe of þe norþe, þe naked to tene;
> Þe snawe snitered ful snart, þat snayped þe wylde;
> Þe werbelande wynde wapped fro þe hyȝe,
> And drof vche dale ful of dryftes ful grete.
> Þe leude lystend ful wel þat leȝ in his bedde,
> Þaȝ he lowkez his liddez, ful lyttel he slepes;
> Bi vch kok þat crue he knwe wel þe steuen.   (lines 1998–2008)

> Now the New Year approaches, and the night passes; the day chases off the darkness, as the Lord commands, but savage weathers of the world awoke out of it. Clouds keenly cast the cold to the earth with enough harm from the north to afflict the bare flesh. Ferociously fell the snow that tormented the wild animals. The whistling wind blew from on high and filled each valley with massive snowdrifts. The man in his bed listened very closely. Although he has his eyes shut, he sleeps very little: at every cock that crows, he is well aware of both the time and the summons.

The passage highlights the boundary between inside and out by describing the weather from an indoor perspective. Apart from looking out, the description also looks ahead in time, as Gawain knows he will have to venture into the unforgiving outdoors. To him, and to a first-time audience, the transition is one from a safe indoors into an unsafe winter forest.[122] Only hindsight makes clear that Gawain's test is already over by this point, and that the snowy forest is a familiar space compared to the guest room at Hautdesert.

---

[120] Marcelle Thiébaux, *The Stag of Love: The Chase in Medieval Literature* (Ithaca, NY: Cornell University Press, 1974), 77–81.

[121] Cf. Davenport, *The Art of the 'Gawain'-Poet*, 139; Anne Rooney, 'The Hunts in *Sir Gawain and the Green Knight*', in Brewer and Gibson, *A Companion to the 'Gawain'-Poet*, 157–8.

[122] Cf. Putter, *French Arthurian Romance*, 13.

Indeed, winter imagery plays a decidedly smaller role in the remainder of Gawain's journey. Once at the Green Chapel, the snow on the ground (found in lines 2234 and 2315) is only one of the descriptors of the location, which is characterized by a brook and a crag in addition to the mound that represents the landscape's focal point. Tension is allowed to build up through cultural elements, or elements perceived as cultural, rather than the natural environment. Initially it is the interior of the mound, judged by Gawain to be a 'corsedest kyrk', that instils a sense of terror (2175–96); then it is the sound of an axe being ground out of sight that further leads up towards the poem's climax (2199–226). The snow has a final function to fulfil when the decisive axe blow falls, and Gawain sees his blood drip onto the snow:

> Þe scharp schrank to þe flesche þurȝ þe scyre grece,
> Þat þe schene blod ouer his schulderes schot to þe erþe;
> And quen þe burne seȝ þe blode blenk on þe snawe,
> He sprit forth spenne-fote more þen an spere lenþe.   (lines 2313–16)

The sharp blade cut to the flesh through the pale fat, so that the bright blood shot over his shoulders to the earth. And when the man saw the blood gleaming in the snow, he leaps forward, feet together, more than a spear's length.

As the sight of the blood indicates to Gawain that he has survived the blow, he realizes that he has fulfilled the agreement and is not bound to submit himself to any further violence. At the same time, the image of blood on snow, red on white, has powerful resonances in more than one tradition.

The image of blood dripping onto snow is a common folk-motif surfacing in both Irish and Continental texts. Relevant in the light of Celtic elements in *Sir Gawain and the Green Knight* is a passage in the Middle Irish *Longes Mac nUislenn*[123] in which Derdriu observes a raven drinking calf blood from the snow on a winter's day, prompting a longing for a man with snow-white skin, pitch-black hair, and blood-red cheeks (§7).[124] The variant that has received the bulk of scholarly attention, however, occurs in Chrétien de Troyes's twelfth-century *Conte du graal*,[125] in which Perceval witnesses a raven attacking a goose and is sent into a day-long transfixation by the mingling of three drops of goose blood with the snow, which reminds him of the complexion of his beloved Blancheflor (4162–293). As in *Sir Gawain and the Green Knight*, the setting in this text is atypical: the forest setting

---

[123] The work in its surviving form has been dated to about the year 1000, though a hypothetical earlier version has been assigned to the eighth or ninth century. Vernam Hull, ed. and trans., *Longes Mac N-Uislenn / The Exile of the Sons of Uisliu*, Modern Language Association of America Monograph Series 16 (New York: Modern Language Society of America, 1949; reprinted New York: Kraus, 1971), 29–32.

[124] Ibid., 43; translation at 62–3.

[125] William Roach, ed., *Le roman de Perceval; ou Le conte du graal*, second rev. ed., Textes littéraires français (Geneva and Paris: Droz / Minard, 1959).

is appropriate for any encounter whose significance the poet wishes to emphasize, but the frost and snow are unusual both in romance settings of wonder and in early summer, the chronological setting of the episode.[126] The sight of the blood on the snow sends Perceval into a contemplative mode that has been the subject of extensive critical discussion, not in the last place because the moment constitutes a structural marker in the narrative.[127] Freudian analysis has been a common denominator in the criticism, which asserts not only that the red-and-white contrast evokes thoughts of Blancheflor, as indeed the text makes clear it does, but specifically that the blood is suggestive of sexual intercourse, either in general or in the act of deflowering.[128] This reading is particularly central to Gallais's understanding of the passage, which proposes that the folk-motif in which the image is rooted is typically aimed at ensuring the future of the dynasty through the engendering of an heir, to which the finding of a spouse (with skin white as snow and cheeks, or lips, red as blood, as prompted by the image) is the first step.[129] Although deflowering is not itself of relevance to the Middle English narrative, Gawain's guilt certainly has a sexual component to it,[130] so one

[126] The central study of narrative time in Perceval is Hermann J. Weigand, 'Narrative Time in the Grail Poems of Chrétien de Troyes and Wolfram von Eschenbach: Five Essays with an Introduction', in *Wolfram's 'Parzival'*, ed. Ursula Hoffmann (Ithaca, NY, and London: Cornell University Press, 1969), 18–74, in which the time of the snowfall is calculated on the basis of internal chronology to take place a little over a month after Pentecost, and thus between mid-June and mid-July (pp. 26–31). In Wolfram's Middle High German reworking of the romance, the event is moved to a time between mid-September and mid-October. Weigand, 'Narrative Time', 58–9; Arthur Groos, *Romancing the Grail: Genre, Science, and Quest in Wolfram's 'Parzival'* (Ithaca, NY, and London: Cornell University Press, 1995), 130–2.

[127] See Trude Ehlert and Gerhard Meissburger, '*Perceval* et *Parzival*: Valeur et fonction de l'episode dit "des trois gouttes de sang sur la neige"', *Cahiers de civilisation médiévale Xe–XIIe siècles* 18 (1975): 197–227; Pierre Gallais, 'Le sang sur la neige (le conte et le rêve)', *Cahiers de civilisation médiévale Xe–XIIe siècles* 21 (1978): 37–42; Madeleine Jeay, 'Sanguine Inscriptions: Mythic and Literary Aspects of a Motif in Chrétien de Troyes's *Conte du graal*', in *Telling Tales: Medieval Narratives and the Folk Tradition*, ed. Francesca Canadé Sautman, Diana Conchado, and Giuseppe Carlo Di Scipio (New York: St. Martin's Press, 1998), 137–54; Matthias Meyer, 'Filling a Bath, Dropping into the Snow, Drunk through a Glass Straw: Transformations and Transfigurations of Blood in German Arthurian Romances', *Bibliographical Bulletin of the International Arthurian Society* 58 (2006): 410–16; and the literature cited especially in the first three of these items. For a discussion of the motif in the Middle High German *Perzival*, see Joachim Bumke, *Die Blutstropfen im Schnee: Über Wahrnemung und Erkenntnis im 'Parzival' Wolframs von Eschenbach*, Hermaea: Germanistische Forschungen, n.s. 94 (Tübingen: Niemeyer, 2001), esp. 1–14, 56–64, and the index of scholarship in n. 1 on pp. 1–2.

[128] Gallais, 'Le sang sur la neige'; Jeay, 'Sanguine Inscriptions', 140–4.

[129] Gallais, 'Le sang sur la neige'.

[130] While Bertilak categorically dismisses any guilt on Gawain's part in this respect (2360–8), Gawain treads a thin line in his bedroom encounters with Lady Bertilak and is certainly guilty of indulging in the sexual subtext of their interactions, as is demonstrated in Harvey De Roo, 'Undressing Lady Bertilak: Guilt and Denial in *Sir Gawain and the Green Knight*', *Chaucer Review* 27, no. 3 (1993): 305–24; cf. Jane Gilbert, 'Gender and Sexual Transgression', in Brewer and Gibson, *A Companion to the 'Gawain'-Poet*, 62–9. Although Gawain asserts, without explanation, that he may be excused for being deceived by a woman, his catalogue of Old Testament men ruined through their various interactions with women suggests that in all these cases, it is man's inability to 'luf hom wel and leue hem not' ('love them well and do not trust them [i.e. women]') that led to their downfall – and his own (*Sir Gawain and the Green Knight* 2414–28).

need not commit to Freudian psychoanalytics to see a connection between the blood of Gawain's punishment and the carnal temptation which it repays. Indeed, another direct source of the poem, the Old French *Chevalier à l'épée*,[131] which recounts a version of the narrative lacking an exchange of blows, has Gawain wounded by an enchanted sword specifically because he tries to take a girl's virginity (514–673). There is thus considerable support for the idea that the image of the blood on the snow is one part sexual.

However, an associative set of blood and snow that was at least as prominent in medieval culture, but sustained by a different institution, consists in the religious connotations of these elements. Blood and snow are common as separate images both in the Bible and in patristic writings. Snow is most commonly used to signal purity and innocence.[132] While blood signals martyrdom from Cain to the medieval martyrologies, it is also used to express guilt and sin.[133] In this usage, blood, or the colour red, is contrasted with the innocence of snow, or the colour white, as in Isaiah 1:18: 'if your sins were like scarlet, they will be whitened like snow'.[134] Thus if Gawain's blood reminds the reader of the sexual context of his transgression, a stronger implication is the ethical view that his customary virtue is stained by the sin of his dealings at Hautdesert. Indeed, the poet seems to be playing on the latter association when he describes how 'þe schene blod ouer his schulderes schot to þe erþe' (2314), *schulder* ('shoulder') evoking *schulde* ('guilt'). Whether in the sexual or the moral reading, however, the snow has none of the foreignness and hostility associated with winter in the remainder of the poem. Instead, the pure white of the snow is without fault; it is only the human element of blood that gives the image its overtones of guilt and desire. Two traditions are merged in this poem; one employs winter imagery for its hostile qualities, while the

---

[131] Johnston and Owen, *Two Old French Gauvain Romances*.

[132] Iob 9:30; Ps 50:9; Lam 4:7. Patristic authors widely pick up on the gospel observation that Christ's clothes are made white as snow ('alba sicut nix', Mt 17:2) when he meets Moses and Elijah on the mountain. Ambrose, for instance, observes that this indicates 'quod peccatum non cognoverit' ('that he did not know sin', *Apologia prophetae David*: *Patrologia Latina*, 14:876a). Since the Apocalypse furthermore indicates that virtuous people will walk with Christ in white robes (Apc 3:4–5; see also Apc 4:4), Lactantius (and others) reasoned that 'transformabit Deus homines in similitudinem angelorum, et erunt candidi sicut nix' ('God will transform men into the likeness of angels, and they will be white as snow', *De vita beata*: *Patrologia Latina*, 6:814b).

[133] For the biblical motif, see Gn 4:10; Ps 5:7; 25:9–10; 54:24; 58:3; 138:19; Sap 14:25; Sir 34:25; Is 1:15; 4:4; 59:3; Ez 7:23; 9:9; 22:2–5; 24:6–14; Mi 3:10; Na 3:1; Hab 2:12; Hbr 12:4. It should be noted that the comparatively straightforward imagery of the Old Testament undergoes an inversion in the New, where the blood of Christ is frequently said to wash away sins (for example I Io 1:7; Apc 1:5; 7:14, 22:14). This latter image is surely the most popular among patristic authors, but the Old Testament usage continues to be discussed and repeated, as in Augustine, *Enarrationes in Psalmos* (D. Eligius Dekkers and Iohannes [Johannes] Fraipont, eds, *Sancti Aurelii Augustini 'Enarrationes in Psalmos', I–L*, Aurelii Augustini opera 10.1, Corpus Christianorum, Series Latina, 38 (Turnhout: Brepols, 1956), 23); Pseudo-Augustine, *Sermones ad fratres in eremo commorantes*: *Patrologia Latina*, 40:1258.

[134] 'Si fuerint peccata vestra ut coccinum, quasi nix dealbabuntur.'

other uses the abstract colour symbolism of snow to evoke associations almost diametrically opposed to those found in Old English and Old Norse literature. When Gawain leaves Hautdesert, the snow is his enemy; when the final axe stroke falls, it pleads on his behalf.

It is clear from this discussion that *Sir Gawain and the Green Knight* stands out in its genre for its strongly divergent seasonal settings and imagery. However, it is equally remarkable how strongly convergent its employment of the seasons is with both Old English and Old Norse traditions. The poem shares its concentration of superhuman threats in the Christmas season with a range of Scandinavian texts and folktales, while its description of Gawain's travels recalls the hardship of exile as described in Anglo-Saxon sources. Although it is not inconceivable in view of the poem's northern English origins that it has incorporated motifs from both Anglo-Saxon and Scandinavian traditions, it is worth observing that the poem does not need such models to arrive at winter as a time of hardship and trials. After all, the conceptual boundary between society and the world outside becomes more pronounced in winter regardless of literary convention. It is therefore not surprising if an author turns to the dark and the cold to express superlative personal challenges. If anything, the mystery of Middle English romance is that this is not done more often.

Conclusions

If the seasonal interests of Middle English poetry as a whole show a striking inversion of Anglo-Saxon poetic preoccupations, this inversion is especially prominent in the extra-societal functions of seasonality studied here. The hoarfrost and the cold that characterize Old English expeditions of various kinds are in the Middle English corpus of narrative poetry largely limited to descriptions of exile. Meanwhile, Middle English verse celebrates the summer half-year, and particularly the month of May, not just as a framework for expressions of love but also as a context for fairy encounters, adventurous expeditions, debates, and dream visions. In all of these, the central spatial setting is the outdoors, usually in the shape of the forest. The summer forest is thus the central seasonal chronotope of Middle English poetic expeditions. Just as striking as the great number of references to summer expeditions in this corpus is the consistency of the convention. The reliability with which fairies are found near forests on sunny days towards noon, for instance, suggests above all a high level of intertextuality. That this subtype of the convention is less consistent in the French models than in their English derivatives furthermore suggests that there was a strong anglophone component to this intertextuality.

The association of the supernatural with summer forests contrasts with the monster habitats of *Beowulf*, but it has its strongest point of contrast in the Old Norse sagas, which show the same level of consistency in restricting hauntings to winter. This difference demonstrates that multiple configurations of seasonal motifs are possible and none is either universal or fully determined by external circumstances. At the same time, Iceland's greater seasonal variations in daylight and its lack of forests will certainly have played a role in making the dark of winter the most relatable unfamiliar setting, and therefore perceived as the most susceptible to supernatural threats. In England, similar considerations may be adduced to explain winter imagery in such poems as *Andreas* and *Beowulf*, while later romances show that the Celtic othering of forest landscapes was similarly potent in medieval English culture. Some basic tools and limitations may thus be provided by a society's physical surroundings, but the literary imagination has free rein to shape conventions within those broad boundaries.

This point is made more palpable by *Sir Gawain and the Green Knight*, the most striking exception to the seasonal chronotope of the summer forest in Middle English romance. Here, woodlands are still the central landscape of adventure, but the action now takes place almost exclusively at Christmastide. At least two factors may have contributed to this shift, of which the first is traditional in nature, while the other is proper to the aim of this poem. *Sir Gawain* leans heavily on Celtic traditions, among other things for its exchange-of-blows challenge. Although the known analogues to this motif either make no reference to the time of year or situate it at Pentecost, the Celtic supernatural does have a connection with the Celtic New Year (Samhain), so it is not inconceivable that the seasonal element was likewise derived from Celtic tradition. At the same time, winter is the time of greatest contrast between inside and outside, a contrast at the heart of the deception recounted in *Sir Gawain*. Christmas also provides an explanation for the amount of leisure enjoyed at Hautdesert, again crucial for plot development because it facilitates the meetings between Gawain and Lady Bertilak. These are thus creative considerations which the poet may have consulted in planning his work, while the original seasonality of some of his borrowed motifs may likewise have determined his choice of season.

One seasonal function retaining a high level of uniformity between Old and Middle English literature is that of exile, which maintains a strong connection with the winter season on account of its deprivation. If Old English poetry has a higher proportion of seasonally flavoured exile passages than Middle English verse, this may be attributed to the preoccupations of the elegiac genre, and perhaps to cultural concerns, too: the observation that Anglo-Saxon poets display considerable interest in the theme of exile is neither new nor controversial. Middle English instances of this motif, as well as later Latin texts such as the *Vita Merlini*, demonstrate only that winter hardship has an appeal extending well beyond the Anglo-Saxon horizon. Indeed, the discomforts of extreme heat and cold are surely universal literary topoi, and they have received due attention in visions of hell across the Christian world. As such, it is worth emphasizing that the Anglo-Saxon predilection for winter suffering is a quantitatively remarkable application of a qualitatively universal motif.

The existence of another universal is suggested by the seasonal setting of *Als I lay in a winteris nyt*. This soul-and-body debate employs the connotations of the dark winter night to reinforce the mood of horror expressed at the soul's impending doom. This combination of setting and sentiment may fruitfully be compared with those of Old English elegy and Old Norse winter hauntings. There is nevertheless some affinity with the summer landscape of romance inasmuch as both concern confrontations with alien and dangerous forces. What sets the soul-and-body debate apart is its intensity as well as its direct implications for the audience. That the winter setting is only sporadically found in Middle English narrative poetry thus may signal an interest on the part of its poets and audiences in adventures that could be enjoyed without the disturbing immediacy of horror.

In view of the various seasonal functions available to medieval authors, one thing that becomes clear from the differences between Anglo-Saxon and later literary traditions is how strong a tradition of its own each of the corpora has, even within a conceptual field as narrowly defined as the seasons. Once again, the relative uniformity among members of each of these traditions speaks to the strength of each, and consequently to the high level of intertextuality practised within each of these cultural spaces. While linguistic criteria alone rarely form the outer limits of a cultural tradition, this suggests that there is some validity in the degree to which some of these vernaculars tend to be studied in isolation from their neighbours. Nevertheless, it is in comparison with those neighbours, as undertaken in the present book, that a tradition's characteristics may be put into perspective. It is in this process that a literary tradition may be most fully delineated.

Conclusions

A community's social and cultural life is given to seasonal patterns representing a complex interplay between economic demands and traditional (for example religious) influences. Where such seasonality is found in literature, its representation is further shaped by the author's conscious aims and interests as well as his or her sensitivity to the powerful but typically unspoken dynamic between self and environment. In the study of any one text, the analysis of this dynamic and its seasonal implications may be an effective guide to the psychological assumptions on which the plot is built. When applied to a genre or cultural corpus as a whole, however, connotations of space and season provide information about the intersubjective map shared by the culture in which these texts have their origin. Although the world represented in narrative literature should not be understood to correspond without qualification to reality as its authors and audience saw it, that literary world nevertheless stems from the culture's mental map of the world and demands to be explained by it. The combined set of seasonal chronotopes employed in the literary output of a given society is in large part an exaggeration of the psychological associations of landscapes and seasons that had currency in that culture, thus aiding the construction of a psychological anthropology.

Sedentary societies are naturally given to some degree of core-and-periphery thinking: regardless of its spatial configuration, an inhabited area will be more familiar to its residents than the world beyond it. That extrasocietal spaces are associated with threats and monsters is therefore not surprising. However, the psychological and narrative functions of these spaces may be better understood once it is recognized that they are not all equal. Instead, they are subject to various evaluations and literary functions depending on the landscape category and the season represented. By studying the narrative functions of specific landscapes and seasons, we may attain a more detailed understanding of literary genre while contributing a literary body of evidence for the study of a culture's psychological reflexes to season and environment.

In our perception of the world, the sedentary universal of core-and-periphery thinking combines with the heuristic universal of category simplification. Peripheral landscape categories are grouped with other untrusted concepts, including the monsters we postulate as the agents behind natural threats. Because winter traditionally forces people to spend more time indoors, it compresses the sedentary core and expands the reach of the hostile domain accommodating the natural and the supernatural.

Since heat and light are the most salient features of immediate seasonal experience, their extreme representatives summer and winter are the salient seasons in an associative model of the solar cycle. These are not therefore chronologically bounded; instead, summer becomes conceptually valid whenever we judge the weather to be pleasant, while any cool day connotes winter. Sensual clues that connote either extreme are likewise recruited for associative categorization, so that the sound of birdsong and the smell of grass suffice to evoke summer. These associations are as valid today as they were for the medieval poets who dubbed the cuckoo the herald of summer.

The vernacular traditions of medieval northern Europe nevertheless present a special test case in view of their traditional reliance on a bipartite year. If binary categorization is a universal heuristic strategy, cultures relying on two administrative seasons do deal in temporal binaries more commonly than those that count four seasons. The connections made in Old English and Old Norse literature between winter, danger, and isolation, or between summer and the supernatural in Middle English romance, do not, of course, automatically follow from this background. However, they may be presumed to have been informed by the seasonal reality behind that binary taxonomy, particularly in northern Scandinavia, where a two-part calendar may be said to be a more accurate representation of the meteorological year.

A primarily spatial application of a bipartite associative year is widespread in Old English poetry, where winter environments are commonly invoked to contrast with the human sphere, but typically without reference to the succession of the seasons and often without mentioning the narrative time of year at all. Instead, references to cold or hoarfrost alone conjure up an environment suitable for exile, heroic expeditions, or monsters. All these motifs characterize the winter landscape as an ominous inversion of the human domain.

An unfavourable characterization of winter landscapes is also found in Old Norse narratives, which associate social categories perceived as hostile and supernatural, namely giants and Sami, with high altitudes and latitudes, as well as with elements of winter directly. In addition, however, the sagas provide a temporal mode of seasonal othering not made explicit in Old English poetry, identifying winter as the season for hauntings and divination. There is a real spatial dimension to these phenomena as well that is typical of winter, as this season reduces the human domain to the farmstead, while the dark valley outside is given over to revenants or the unknown, much as in Bede's parable of the sparrow. In the case of prophecy, the supernatural even makes its way into the farmstead itself, providing the social heart of the settlement with a way to contact the outside realm of the supernatural. However, the strong concentration of the Scandinavian supernatural in the winter months means that this season is associated with outside threats to the human domain more emphatically than in Old English poetry, whose winter motifs rarely employ a cyclical timeframe.

The Old English and Old Norse tendency to associate the extrasocietal experience with winter is thrown into proper relief when compared with other traditions. In Middle English literature, this connection is not often found; instead, adventures, visions, and the supernatural in this corpus are all associated with flourishing outdoor landscapes, and above all with Maytime woodlands. Where winter does surface, however, its connotations are no different from those in the neighbouring corpora. *Sir Gawain and the Green Knight* employs both the temporal concentration of the supernatural found in the sagas and the hostile, exilic functions of winter landscapes found in Old English poetry, and the latter element recurs in various other texts from post-Conquest Britain. Moreover, the soul-and-body debate *Als I lay in a winteris nyt* makes clear that the horror associated with winter and nighttime in nineteenth-century literature was likewise recognized in thirteenth-century England, suggesting that the reason why it is so rarely found in medieval romance is that horror is not normally an authorial aim in the genre. Instead, much of Middle English verse seeks to engage its audience through wonder and excitement of a less unsettling kind, for which the alien but inviting qualities of the summer forest render it the appropriate setting.

If the connection between winter and horror in *Als I lay* is typical of the seasonal chronotopicity of Middle English verse, then winter is chosen as a setting when the author aims for a higher degree of extradiegetic psychogeographical injection. This may be defined as a universal property of narrative winter settings within certain geographical and cultural bounds, applying at least to Old and Middle English as well as Old Norse, but equally valid in more recent English and Germanic literature. Shakespeare knew to situate King Lear's exile and the apparition of Hamlet's father during cold nights. Similarly, the Romantic predilection for hauntings, horror, and the sublime had authors like Poe and Dickens turn to this season more than to any other.[1] The season's functions in these texts are not so different from those found in Icelandic tales of hauntings or Old English verse studies in exile. There are certain higher-latitude universals here at work, but the seasonal conventions of a given literary culture result from a complex interplay between circumstance and cultural vogue which can sometimes be explained, but rarely predicted. If the Anglo-Saxon poetic preoccupation with the winter of exile may find an explanation in political circumstance whether ongoing or remembered, the arrival in fourteenth-century England of the Black Death and climatic fluctuation did not therefore prompt a similar response in literature. Instead, the dominant popular genres of the later-fourteenth century build on twelfth-century

---

[1] Cf. Gopnik, *Winter*, 1–50.

models by celebrating the adventurous potential of summer landscapes, confirming the mid-twentieth century conviction that convention plays a prominent role in the literary depiction of landscape.

That conventions are not immutable is apparent in the fact that English literature is in some respects more concerned with the seasons than its Continental sources. This is true of Anglo-Saxon literature, which appears to embrace the notion of a paradise without either summer or winter more fully than Continental tradition; it also seems to be the case in Middle English romance, which uses the motif of the hot summer's day even where its sources do not, as in *Sir Launfal*. However, Old English poetry is rarely interested in determining the narrative time of year, so that its seasonal chronotopes are primarily landscape settings with seasonal overtones. Middle English literature specifies the time of year where specific seasonal conventions are used, in addition to more general temporal markers such as royal and ecclesiastical feasts or the season of warfare. Old Norse is the most persistent in its seasonal references, making use of annual events and seasonal identities to structure its narratives, which often run from Winter Nights to Christmas to general assembly (in the case of the sagas of Icelanders) or from raiding season to raiding season (in the case of the legendary sagas and the raiding episodes in the sagas of Icelanders). Here the geographical differences between England and Iceland may certainly play a role: summer and winter are more distinct in Iceland not only in terms of temperature and darkness, but especially in their social implications, which include limits to travel (particularly overseas) in winter as well as advantages to holding political events at the time of least darkness. Accordingly, the seasonal chronotope of the sagas of Icelanders and of the contemporary sagas is the closest in all the genres here discussed to being a 'historical' chronotope of the sort Bakhtin sought to establish. With such a distinct social seasonality in place, these texts also permit a close study of the relationship between historical and narrative seasonality. The latter includes the supernatural elements of monsters and prophecy as well as the spring miracles in the bishops' sagas, many of which may be traced back to real concerns such as winter burial and the availability of spring grazing.

Where the narrative time of year plays no important role, mention of seasonal elements, such as hoarfrost, ice, or cold, possess heightened connotative value, since – with the notable exception of metrical considerations – the author has no circumstantial reasons to introduce them. Accordingly, winter landscapes and cold landscapes in *Beowulf*, *Andreas*, and other texts should not be brushed off as incidental: the poet is using them to craft a highly connotative setting. In the sagas, conversely, where the seasonality of the action is regularly noted for structural or pragmatic purposes (such as setting off at the start of the sailing season, or seeking accommodation at its end), no conclusions can be drawn from a single seasonal reference: here strength lies in numbers, as conventions across texts help determine the conventional value of individual occurrences. In some cases, of course, the seasonal emphasis of a single text is so apparent that the connection need not be questioned. *Grettis saga* is not the only example of strong seasonal bias, but it pursues one particular set of seasonal conventions with the greatest persistence, containing such a large number of hauntings and hostile encounters set at Christmas that the seasonal associations in this text are not only unmistakable, but unmistakably conscious. The existence of multiple Icelandic analogues to the pattern of hauntings found in this text confirms that the motif transcended the interests of a single author and was indeed a literary commonplace.

The grouping of seasonal elements with affectively charged categories of a different class likewise helps identify a season's connotations. The grouping of hostile categories (landscapes, seasons, and the supernatural) is especially useful as an anthropological artefact where an author uses it to explain or supplement natural phenomena. This is seen in the coincidence of the sailing off-season with the time when Sami are held to be especially dangerous, and it appears to underlie the popularity of revenant hauntings in Iceland, which may have an explanation in the difficulty of complying with Christian burial rites in winter. Connections of this type exploit a literary playground to explore real-world concerns involving perceived outside threats to society and its members. Such connections should, however, only be admitted where the texts themselves present sufficient evidence. Reading all the monsters of (say) *Beowulf* as personifications of seasonal threats is not warranted, though it is reasonable to extrapolate from the totality of seasonal and thermal references in the poem and conclude that the domain of winter contributes to the hostile associations of its monsters.

The comparison of Icelandic texts with analogues from the British Isles has long served to establish whether or not such texts share a common origin, and if so, what the nature of the relationship is. When the same texts are studied for thematic trends, however, it is sometimes possible to discern differences between the narrative interests current in the respective traditions. In this context, the fact that several Icelandic texts situate hauntings around Christmas where their foreign analogues consistently resist seasonal placement demonstrates not only the strength of the Icelandic connection between hauntings and winter, but also the extent to which the sagas of Icelanders rely on seasonal markers for their structure. Conversely, it underscores the lack of interest in narrative seasonality in the corresponding Anglo-Saxon and Irish traditions. The overall effect of such insights is to help delineate the literary traditions of the various North Atlantic vernaculars and shed light on the cultures that produced them. If the comparison furthermore helps identify lines of transmission between the various witnesses to a motif, this demonstrates the value of an integrated and comparative approach to literature.

The prism of seasonal imagery thus adds a valuable spectrum of insights to the study of literary tradition, but its range of implications extends well beyond the world of literature. As seasonal variation itself functions as an interface between planetary physics, climate, the economy, ritual, and psychology, its reflections in writing are a human response to all of these phenomena. Of course, methodological and paradigmatic differences preclude the straightforward conversion of data between the disciplines involved: attempts to adduce documentary data in the study of past climate demonstrate just a few of the challenges to be faced. Even so, many disciplines permit the researcher to consult neighbouring fields and push for a more holistic understanding of her subject. This book has attempted to demonstrate that such an approach is indispensable in literary studies. Just as a diegetic self or society cannot be defined without reference to its literary environment, so also literature itself has to be understood in the full context of the material and cultural reality in which it was conceived.

Bibliography

Adams, Gwenfair Walters. *Visions in Late Medieval England: Lay Spirituality and Sacred Glimpses of the Hidden Worlds of Faith*. Studies in the History of Christian Traditions 130. Leiden: Brill, 2007.
Adderley, W. Paul, Ian A. Simpson, and Orri Vésteinsson. 'Local-Scale Adaptations: A Modeled Assessment of Soil, Landscape, Microclimatic, and Management Factors in Norse Home-Field Productivities'. *Geoarchaeology* 34, no. 4 (2008): 500–27.
Alamichel, Marie-Françoise. '*Sumer is icumen in*: Chants et saisons dans la Grande-Bretagne médiévale'. In Carruthers, *La ronde des saisons*, 51–60.
Anderson, Earl R. *Folk-Taxonomies in Early English*. Cranbury, NJ, London, and Mississauga, ON: Associated University Presses, 2003.
—— 'The Seasons of the Year in Old English'. *Anglo-Saxon England* 26 (1997): 231–63.
Anderson, S. Axel. 'Iceland's Industries'. *Economic Geography* 7, no. 3 (July 1931): 284–96.
Andersson, Theodore M. 'The Discovery of Darkness in Northern Literature'. In Burlin and Irving, *Old English Studies in Honour of John C. Pope*, 1–14.
Anlezark, Daniel. 'Poisoned Places: The Avernian Tradition in Old English Poetry'. *Anglo-Saxon England* 36 (2007): 103–26.
—— ed. and trans. *The Old English Dialogues of Solomon and Saturn*. Anglo-Saxon Texts. Cambridge: Brewer, 2009.
Ármann Jakobsson. 'Hvað er tröll? Galdrar, tröll og samfélagsóvinir'. In *Galdramenn: Galdrar og samfélag á miðöldum*, ed. Torfi H. Tulinius, 95–118. Reykjavik: Hugvísindastofnun Háskóla Íslands, 2008.
—— 'The Trollish Acts of Þorgrímr the Witch: The Meanings of *troll* and *ergi* in Medieval Iceland'. *Saga-Book* 32 (2008): 39–68.
Arngart, O., ed. *The Proverbs of Alfred*. Vol. 2, *The Texts Edited with Introduction, Notes and Glossary*. Lund: Gleerup, 1955.
Árni Björnsson. *Saga daganna*. 2nd ed. Reykjavik: Mál og menning, 2000.
—— *Þorrablót*. Reykjavik: Mál og menning, 2008.
Assmann, B., ed. *Angelsächsische Homilien und Heiligenleben*. Bibliothek der angelsächsischen Prosa 3. Kassel: Wigand, 1889; reprinted with an introduction by Peter Clemoes, Darmstadt: Wissenschaftliche Buchgesellschaft, 1964.
Aståas, Reidar, ed. *Stjórn: Tekst etter håndskriftene*. 2 vols. Norrøne tekster 8. Oslo: Riksarkivet, 2009.
Axford, Yarrow, *et al.* 'Climate of the Little Ice Age and the Past 2000 Years in Northeast Iceland Inferred from Chironomids and Other Lake Sediment Proxies'. *Journal of Paleolimnology* 41 (2009): 7–24.
Bähr, Dieter. 'Altenglisch *īsig* (*Beowulf*, Zeile 33)'. *Zeitschrift für Anglistik und Amerikanistik* 19 (1971): 409–12.
Baillie-Grohman, Wm A., and F. Baillie-Grohman, eds. *The Master of Game*. London: Chatto / Windus, 1909.

Baker, Peter S., and Michael Lapidge, eds. *Byrhtferth's 'Enchiridion'*. EETS, ss 15. Oxford: Oxford University Press, 1995.
Bakhtin, M. M. 'Forms of Time and of the Chronotope in the Novel: Notes towards a Historical Poetics'. In *The Dialogic Imagination: Four Essays*, ed. Michael Holquist, translated by Caryl Emerson and Michael Holquist, 84–258. Austin, TX: University of Texas Press.
Banham, Debby, and Rosamond Faith. *Anglo-Saxon Farms and Farming*. Medieval History and Archaeology. Oxford: Oxford University Press, 2014.
Barber, Paul. *Vampires, Burial, and Death: Folklore and Reality*. New Haven, CT: Yale University Press, 1988.
Barrar, Kathleen. 'A Spacious, Green and Hospitable Land: Paradise in Old English Poetry'. *Bulletin of the John Rylands University Library of Manchester* 86, no. 2 (2004): 105–25.
Bately, Janet, ed. *The Anglo-Saxon Chronicle: A Collaborative Edition*. Vol. 3: MS A. Cambridge: Brewer, 1986.
—— ed. *The Old English 'Orosius'*. EETS, ss 6. London: Oxford University Press, 1980.
—— 'Time and the Passing of Time in *The Wanderer* and Related OE Texts'. *Essays & Studies*, n.s., no. 37 (1984): 1–15.
Battles, Paul. '*Genesis A* and the Anglo-Saxon "Migration Myth"'. *Anglo-Saxon England* 29 (2000): 43–66.
Baume, Andrew. 'Lancastrian Normandy and the Calendar of Medieval Warfare'. In Carruthers, *La ronde des saisons*, 61–8.
Bechmann, Roland. *Trees and Man: The Forest in the Middle Ages*. Translated by Katharyn Dunham. New York: Paragon, 1990.
Beckman, N., and Kr. Kålund, eds. *Alfræði íslenzk II: Rímtöl*. Copenhagen: Møller, 1914–18.
Beckman, Natanael. 'Isländsk och medeltida skandinavisk tideräkning'. In *Tideräkningen*, ed. Martin P:n Nilsson, 5–76. Nordisk Kultur 21. Stockholm: Albert Bonniers, 1934.
Behaghel, Otto, ed. *'Heliand' und 'Genesis'*. 10th ed. Rev. Burkhard Taeger. Altdeutsche Textbibliothek 4. Tübingen: Niemeyer, 1996.
Benedictow, Ole J. *The Black Death 1346–1353: The Complete History*. Woodbridge: Boydell, 2004.
Benson, Larry Dean. *Art and Tradition in 'Sir Gawain and the Green Knight'*. New Brunswick, NJ: Rutgers University Press, 1965.
—— ed. *King Arthur's Death: The Middle English 'Stanzaic Morte Arthur' and 'Alliterative Morte Arthure'*. Exeter: University of Exeter, 1986.
—— 'The Originality of *Beowulf*'. In *The Interpretation of Narrative: Theory and Practice*, ed. Morton W. Bloomfield, 1:1–43. Harvard English Studies. Cambridge, MA: Harvard University Press, 1970.
—— ed. *The Riverside Chaucer*. 3rd ed. Boston: Houghton Mifflin, 1987.
—— 'The Source of the Beheading Episode in *Sir Gawain and the Green Knight*'. *Modern Philology* 59, no. 1 (August 1961): 1–12.
Bernheimer, Richard. *Wild Men in the Middle Ages: A Study in Art, Sentiment, and Demonology*. Cambridge, MA: Harvard University Press, 1952.
Berretty, Patricia M., Peter M. Todd, and Laura Martignon. 'Categorization by Elimination: Using Few Cues to Choose'. In Gigerenzer and Todd, *Simple Heuristics*, 235–54.

Bertelsen, Henrik, ed. *Þiðriks saga af Bern*. 2 vols. Copenhagen: Møller, 1905–11.
Bethmann, L., and Georg Waitz, eds. 'Pauli Historia Langobardorum'. In *Saec. VI–IX*, 12–192. Monumenta Germaniae Historica, Scriptores rerum langobardicarum et italicarum 1. Hannover: Hahn.
Bethurum, Dorothy. 'Episcopal Magnificence in the Eleventh Century'. In *Studies in Old English Literature in Honor of Arthur G. Brodeur*, ed. Stanley B. Greenfield, 162–70. Eugene, OR: University of Oregon Books, 1963.
Bibire, Paul. 'Freyr and Gerðr: The Story and its Myths'. In Rudolf Simek, Jónas Kristjánsson, and Hans Bekker-Nielsen, *Sagnaskemmtun*, 19–40.
Billett, Michael. *A History of English Country Sports*. London: Hale, 1994.
Birket-Smith, Kaj. *The Eskimos*. Enlarged and rev. ed. Translated by W. E. Calvert and C. Daryll Forde. London: Methuen, 1959.
Birrell, Jean R. 'Hunting and the Royal Forest'. In *L'uomo e la foresta secc. XIII–XVIII: Atti della 'Ventisettesima Settimana di Studi', 8–13 maggio 1995*, ed. Simonetta Cavaciocchi, 437–57. Florence: Le Monnier, 1996.
—— 'The Medieval English Forest'. *Journal of Forest History* 24, no. 2 (April 1980): 78–85.
Bjarni Aðalbjarnarson, ed. *Heimskringla*. 3 vols. Íslenzk fornrit, 26–8. Reykjavik: Hið íslenzka fornritafélag, 1941–51.
Bjarni Einarsson, ed. *Ágrip af Nóregskonunga sǫgum*. Íslenzk fornrit 29. Reykjavik: Hið íslenzka fornritafélag, 1984.
—— ed. *Egils saga*. London: Viking Society for Northern Research / University College London, 2003.
Björn K. Þórólfsson and Guðni Jónsson, eds. *Vestfirðinga sǫgur*. Íslenzk fornrit 6. Reykjavik: Hið íslenzka fornritafélag, 1943.
Björn Þorsteinsson. *Íslenzka þjóðveldið*. Reykjavik: Heimskringla, 1953.
—— 'Tollr'. *KLNM* 18 (1974): 452–4.
Blake, Martin, ed. *Ælfric's 'De temporibus anni'*. Anglo-Saxon Texts 6. Cambridge: Brewer, 2009.
Blake, N. F., ed. and trans. *Jómsvíkinga saga*. London: Nelson, 1962.
Blatt, Franz, ed. *Die lateinischen Bearbeitungen der 'Acta Andreae et Matthiae apud anthropophagos'*. Gießen: Töpelmann, 1930.
Bliss, A. J., ed. *Sir Launfal*. London and Edinburgh: Thomas Nelson, 1960.
—— ed. *Sir Orfeo*. 2nd ed. Oxford: Clarendon, 1966.
Boberg, Inger M. *Motif-Index of Early Icelandic Literature*. Bibliotheca Arnamagnaeana 27. Copenhagen: Munksgaard, 1966.
Boitani, Piero. 'Old Books Brought to Life in Dreams: *The Book of the Duchess, The House of Fame, The Parliament of Fowls*'. In *The Cambridge Companion to Chaucer*, 2nd ed., ed. Piero Boitani and Jill Mann, 58–77. Cambridge: Cambridge University Press, 2003.
Bolland, Joannes [Jean], et al., eds. *Acta sanctorum quotquot toto orbe coluntur, vel a catholicis scriptoribus celebrantur*. 68 vols. Paris and Rome: Palmé, 1643–1940.
Bonath, Gesa, ed. and trans. *Thomas: 'Tristan'*. Klassische Texte des Romanischen Mittelalters in zweisprachigen Ausgaben 21. Munich: Fink, 1985.
Bonnemaison, Joël. *Culture and Space: Conceiving a New Cultural Geography*. Translated by Josée Pénot-Demetry. London and New York: Tauris, 2005.
Borowski, Oded. *Agriculture in Iron Age Israel*. Winona Lake, IN: Eisenbrauns, 1987.

Bosworth, Joseph, ed. *An Anglo-Saxon Dictionary*. Rev. T. Northcote Toller. Oxford: Oxford University Press, 1898.
Boyle, A. J., ed. and trans. *The 'Eclogues' of Virgil*. Melbourne: Hawthorn, 1976.
Bradley, Raymond S., Malcolm K. Hughes, and Henry F. Diaz. 'Climate in Medieval Time'. *Science*, n.s., 302, no. 5644 (17 October 2003): 404–5.
Bragi Halldórsson *et al.*, eds. *Íslendinga sögur: Orðstöðulykill og texti*. 2nd ed. CD-ROM. Reykjavik: Mál og menning, 1998.
Branch, Michael P., and Scott Slovic. 'Surveying the Emergence of Ecocriticism'. In *The ISLE Reader: Ecocriticism, 1993–2003*, ed. Michael P. Branch and Scott Slovic, xiii–xxiii. Athens, GA, and London: University of Georgia Press, 2003.
Brenner, Oscar, ed. *Speculum regale: Ein altnorwegischer Dialog nach Cod. Arnamagn. 243 Fol. B und den ältesten Fragmenten*. Munich: Kaiser, 1881.
Brewer, Derek, and Jonathan Gibson, eds. *A Companion to the 'Gawain'-Poet*. Arthurian Studies 38. Cambridge: Brewer, 1997.
Brewer, E. Cobham. *A Dictionary of Miracles: Imitative, Realistic, and Dogmatic*. Philadelphia, PA: Lippincott, 1884.
Brewer, Elizabeth, ed. and trans. *Sir Gawain and the Green Knight: Sources and Analogues*. Cambridge: Brewer, 1992.
Brill, W. G., ed. *Van Sinte Brandane*. Bibliotheek van Middelnederlandsche letterkunde 6. Groningen: Wolters, 1971.
Brooke, Stopford A. *The History of Early English Literature: Being the History of English Poetry from its Beginnings to the Accession of King Ælfred*. New York and London: Macmillan, 1892.
Brooks, Kenneth R., ed. *'Andreas' and 'The Fates of the Apostles'*. Oxford: Clarendon, 1961.
Brunner, Karl. 'Middle English Metrical Romances and their Audience'. In *Studies in Medieval Literature in Honor of Professor Albert Croll Baugh*, ed. MacEdward Leach, 219–27. Philadelphia, PA: University of Pennsylvania Press, 1961.
Buckland, P. C., T. Amorosi, L. K. Barlow, A. J. Dugmore, P. A. Mayewski, T. H. McGovern, A. E. J. Ogilvie, J. P. Sadler, and P. Skidmore. 'Bioarchaeological and Climatological Evidence for the Fate of Norse Farmers in Medieval Greenland'. *Antiquity* 70 (1996): 88–96.
Bugge, Sophus. 'Studien über das Beowulfepos'. *Beiträge zur Geschichte der deutschen Sprache und Literatur* 12 (1887): 1–112, 360–75.
Bumke, Joachim. *Die Blutstropfen im Schnee: Über Wahrnemung und Erkenntnis im 'Parzival' Wolframs von Eschenbach*. Hermaea: Germanistische Forschungen, n.s. 94. Tübingen: Niemeyer, 2001.
Burke, Kenneth. *A Grammar of Motives*. London: Prentice-Hall, 1945. Berkeley and Los Angeles: University of California Press, 1969.
Burlin, Robert B. 'Inner Weather and Interlace: A Note on the Semantic Value of Structure in *Beowulf*'. In Burlin and Irving, *Old English Studies in Honour of John C. Pope*, 81–9.
—— and Edward B. Irving Jr, eds. *Old English Studies in Honour of John C. Pope*. Toronto: University of Toronto Press, 1974.
Burton, Richard. 'Nature in Old English Poetry'. *Atlantic Monthly* (1894): 476–87.
Buss, David M. *Evolutionary Psychology: The New Science of the Mind*. 3rd ed. Boston: Pearson, 2008.
Butts, Richard. 'The Analogical Mere: Landscape and Terror in *Beowulf*'. *English*

Studies 68, no. 2 (1987): 113–21.
Byock, Jesse, ed. *Medieval Iceland: Society, Sagas, and Power*. Berkeley, CA: University of California Press, 1988.
Caciola, Nancy. 'Wraiths, Revenants and Ritual in Medieval Culture'. *Past & Present* 152, no. 1 (August 1996): 3–45.
Cahill, Paul, ed. *Duggals leiðsla*. Reykjavik: Stofnun Árna Magnússonar, 1983.
Calder, Daniel G. 'Setting and Mode in *The Seafarer* and *The Wanderer*'. *Neuphilologische Mitteilungen* 72 (1971): 264–75.
Cameron, Angus, Ashley Crandell Amos, Antonette diPaolo Healey, *et al*., eds. *Dictionary of Old English: A to G*. Toronto: Dictionary of Old English Project, 2007. Accessed 15 March 2015. http://doe.utoronto.ca/.
Cameron, M. L. *Anglo-Saxon Medicine*. Cambridge Studies in Anglo-Saxon England 7. Cambridge: Cambridge University Press, 1993.
Campbell, John Gregorson, ed. *The Fians; Or, Stories, Poems, & Traditions of Fionn and his Warrior Band*. Waifs and Strays of Celtic Tradition: Argyllshire Series 4. London: Nutt, 1891.
Carney, James. *Studies in Irish Literature and History*. Dublin: Dublin Institute for Advanced Studies, 1955.
Carruthers, Leo, ed. *La ronde des saisons: Les saisons dans la littérature et la société anglaises au Moyen Age*. Cultures et Civilisations Médiévales 16. Paris: Presses de l'Université de Paris-Sorbonne, 1998.
Cartlidge, Neil, ed. and trans. *The Owl and the Nightingale*. Exeter: University of Exeter Press, 2001.
Celander, Hilding, and Kustaa Vilkuna. 'Lucia'. *KLNM* 10 (1965): 704–10.
Chambers, R. W. *Beowulf: An Introduction to the Study of the Poem with a Discussion of the Stories of Offa and Finn*. 3rd ed. With a supplement by C. L. Wrenn. Cambridge: Cambridge University Press, 1959.
—— 'Beowulf's Fight with Grendel, and its Scandinavian Parallels'. *English Studies* 11 (1929): 81–100.
—— ed. *Widsith: A Study in Old English Heroic Legend*. Cambridge: Cambridge University Press, 1912.
Chardonnens, László Sándor, ed. *Anglo-Saxon Prognostics, 900–1100*: Study and Texts. Brill's Studies in Intellectual History 153: Brill's Texts and Sources in Intellectual History 3. Leiden: Brill, 2007.
Charles, R. H., ed. *The Book of the Secrets of Enoch: Translated from the Slavonic*. Translated by W. R. Morfill. Oxford: Clarendon, 1896.
Chater, Nick, and Paul Vitányi. 'Simplicity: A Unifying Principle in Cognitive Science?' *TRENDS in Cognitive Sciences* 7, no. 1 (January 2003): 19–22.
Christiansen, Reidar Th. *Folktales of Norway*. Translated by Pat Shaw Iversen. Chicago: University of Chicago Press, 1964.
—— *The Dead and the Living*. Studia Norvegica 2. Oslo: Aschehoug, 1946.
—— *The Migratory Legends: A Proposed List of Types with a Systematic Catalogue of the Norwegian Variants*. Helsinki: Suomalainen tiedeakatemia, 1958.
Cigman, Gloria. 'The Seasons in Late Medieval Literature: Mutability and Metaphors of Good and Evil'. *Études anglaises* 51, no. 2 (1998): 131–42.
Clark Hall, J. R., ed. *A Concise Anglo-Saxon Dictionary*. 4th ed. With a supplement by Herbert D. Meritt. Cambridge: Cambridge University Press, 1960.
Clarke, Basil, ed. and trans. *Life of Merlin*. Cardiff: University of Wales Press, 1973.

Cleasby, Richard, and Gudbrand Vigfusson [Guðbrandur Vigfússon], eds. *An Icelandic-English Dictionary*. 2nd ed. With a supplement by William A. Craigie. Oxford: Clarendon, 1957.

Clemoes, Peter, ed. *Ælfric's Catholic Homilies: The First Series*. EETS, ss 17. Oxford: Oxford University Press, 1997.

Clunies Ross, Margaret, ed. *Old Norse Myths, Literature and Society*. Odense: University Press of Southern Denmark, 2003.

—— 'Snorri Sturluson's Use of the Norse Origin-Legend of the Sons of Fornjótr in his *Edda*'. *Arkiv för nordisk filologi* 98 (1983): 47–66.

—— 'Two Old Icelandic Theories of Ritual'. In Clunies Ross, *Old Norse Myths, Literature and Society*, 279–99.

—— Kari Ellen Gade, Guðrún Nordal, Edith Marold, Diana Whaley, and Tarrin Wills, eds. *Skaldic Poetry of the Scandinavian Middle Ages*. Accessed 15 March 2015. https://www.abdn.ac.uk/skaldic/.

Coffin, Richard Neal. '*Beowulf* and its Relationship to Norse and Finno-Ugric Beliefs and Narratives'. Unpublished doctoral thesis, Boston University, 1962.

Colgrave, Bertram, ed. and trans. *Felix's 'Life of Guthlac'*. Cambridge: Cambridge University Press, 1956.

—— and R. A. B. Mynors, eds. *Bede's 'Ecclesiastical History of the English People'*. Oxford: Clarendon, 1969.

Conlee, John W., ed. *Middle English Debate Poetry: A Critical Anthology*. East Lansing, MI: Colleagues, 1991.

Cook, Patrick. '*Woriað þa winsalo*: The Bonds of Exile in *The Wanderer*'. *Neophilologus* 80 (1996): 127–37.

Cormac, Margaret. 'Christian Biography'. In *A Companion to Old Norse–Icelandic Literature and Culture*, ed. Rory McTurk, 27–42. Oxford: Blackwell, 2005.

Cornell, Muriel. 'Varieties of Repetition in Old English Poetry: Especially in *The Wanderer* and *The Seafarer*'. *Neophilologus* 65, no. 2 (1981): 292–307.

Coverley, Merlin. *Psychogeography*. Harpenden: Pocket Essentials, 2006.

Crépin, André, ed. *Sir Tristrem*. Translated by Hélène Dauby. Medievales 17. Amiens: Presses du Centre d'Études Médiévales, Université de Picardie-Jules Verne, 2002.

Cronin, T. M., et al. 'Medieval Warm Period, Little Ice Age and 20th Century Temperature Variability from Chesapeake Bay'. *Global and Planetary Change* 36 (2003): 17–29.

—— 'The Medieval Climate Anomaly and Little Ice Age in Chesapeake Bay and the North Atlantic Ocean'. *Palaeogeography, Palaeoclimatology, Palaeoecology* 297 (2010): 299–310.

Curtin, Jeremiah, trans. *Hero-Tales of Ireland*. London: MacMillan, 1894.

Curtius, Ernst Robert. *Europäische Literatur und lateinisches Mittelalter*. 7th ed. Bern and Munich: Francke, 1969.

—— 'Rhetorische Naturschilderung im Mittelalter'. *Romanische Forschungen* 56 (1942): 219–56.

Czerlinski, Jean, Gerd Gigerenzer, and Daniel G. Goldstein. 'How Good are Simple Heuristics?' In Gigerenzer and Todd, *Simple Heuristics*, 97–118.

Dahlerup, Verner, and Lis Jacobsen. *Ordbog over det danske Sprog: Historisk ordbog 1700–1950*. 28 vols. Copenhagen: Det danske sprog- og litteraturselskab, 1918–56. Accessed 15 March 2015. http://ordnet.dk/ods/.

Dale, Edmund. *National Life and Character in the Mirror of Early English Literature*. Cambridge: Cambridge University Press, 1907.
Danielli, Mary. 'Initiation Ceremonial from Norse Literature'. *Folk-Lore* 56, no. 2 (1945): 29–45.
Danstrup, John, et al., eds. *Kulturhistorisk leksikon for nordisk middelalder: fra vikingetid til reformationstid*. 22 vols. Copenhagen: Rosenkilde / Bagger, 1956–78.
Dark, Petra. 'Pollen Evidence for the Environment of Roman Britain'. *Britannia* 30 (1999): 247–72.
Darwin, Charles. 'A Biographical Sketch of an Infant'. *Mind* 2, no. 7 (July 1877): 285–94.
Davenport, W. A. *The Art of the 'Gawain'-Poet*. London: Athlone, 1978.
Davies, Constance. 'Beowulf's Fight with Grendel'. *The Times* (9 November 1935): Literary Supplement, 722.
De Roo, Harvey. 'Undressing Lady Bertilak: Guilt and Denial in *Sir Gawain and the Green Knight*'. *Chaucer Review* 27, no. 3 (1993): 305–24.
De Vogüé, Adalbert, and Paul Antin, eds. *Grégoire le grande: 'Dialogues'*. 3 vols. Sources chrétiennes, 251, 260, 265. Paris: Cerf, 1978–80.
De Vries, Jan, ed. *Altnordisches etymologisches Wörterbuch*. Leiden: Brill, 1962.
Debord, Guy-Ernest. 'Introduction à une critique de la géographie urbaine'. *Les lèvres nues* 6 (September 1955): 11–15. Reprinted in *Les lèvres nues: Collection complète* (1954–8), Paris: Plasma, 1978.
Degnboll, Helle, et al., eds. *Ordbog over det norrøne prosasprog / A Dictionary of Old Norse Prose*. Copenhagen: Den arnemagnæanske kommission, 1989–. Accessed 15 March 2015. http://onp.ku.dk.
Dekkers, D. Eligius, and Iohannes [Johannes] Fraipont, eds. *Sancti Aurelii Augustini 'Enarrationes in Psalmos', I–L*. Aurelii Augustini opera 10.1, Corpus Christianorum, Series Latina, 38. Turnhout: Brepols, 1956.
Der Boon, Ton, and Dirk Geeraerts, eds. *Van Dale Groot woordenboek der Nederlandse taal*. 14th ed. CD-ROM. 's-Hertogenbosch: C-Content, 2005.
Dewing, H. B., ed. and trans. *Procopius: 'History of the Wars'*. 3 vols. London: Heinemann, 1914–19.
Diamond, Jared. 'Ecological Collapses of Past Civilizations'. *Proceedings of the American Philosophical Society* 138, no. 3 (1994): 363–70.
Diel, Paul. *Fear and Anxiety: Primary Triggers of Survival and Evolution*. Translated by Brigitte Donvez. Claremont, CA: Hunter House, 1989.
Dinzelbacher, Peter. *Vision und Visionsliteratur im Mittelalter*. Monographien zur Geschichte des Mittelalters 23. Stuttgart: Hiersemann, 1981.
Doane, A. N., ed. *Genesis A: A New Edition*. Rev. ed. Madison, WI: University of Wisconsin Press, 2013.
—— ed. *The Saxon Genesis: An Edition of the West Saxon 'Genesis B' and the Old Saxon 'Vatican Genesis'*. Madison, WI: University of Wisconsin Press, 1991.
Dobbie, Elliott van Kirk, ed. *The Anglo-Saxon Minor Poems*. Anglo-Saxon Poetic Records 6. New York: Columbia University Press, 1942.
Dodgson, John McNeal. 'Sir Gawain's Arrival in Wirral'. In *Early English and Norse Studies Presented to Hugh Smith in Honour of his Sixtieth Birthday*, ed. Arthur Brown and Peter Foote, 19–25. London: Methuen, 1963.
Dombart, Bernardus [Bernard], and Alphonsus [Alphonse] Kalb, eds. *Sancti Aurelii Augustini 'De civitate Dei'*. 2 vols. Corpus Christianorum, Series Latina, 47–8: Aurelii Augustini opera, 14. Turnhout: Brepols, 1955.

Donatelli, Joseph M. P., ed. *Death and Liffe*. Cambridge, MA: Medieval Academy of America, 1989.
Doob, Penelope B. R. *Nebuchadnezzar's Children: Conventions of Madness in Middle English Literature*. New Haven, CT, and London: Yale University Press, 1974.
Dresbeck, LeRoy. 'Techne, labor et natura: Ideas and Active Life in the Medieval Winter'. *Studies in Medieval and Renaissance History*, s.s. 2 (1979): 81–119.
—— 'Winter Climate and Society in the Northern Middle Ages: The Technological Impact'. In *On Pre-Modern Technology and Science: A Volume of Studies in Honour of Lynn White, Jr.*, ed. Bert S. Hall and Delno C. West, 177–99. Malibu: Undena, 1976.
Dronke, Ursula. 'Art and Tradition in *Skírnismál*'. In *English and Medieval Studies: Presented to J. R. R. Tolkien on the Occasion of his Seventieth Birthday*, ed. Norman Davis and C. L. Wrenn, 250–68. London: Allen / Unwin, 1962.
—— ed. *The Poetic Edda*. 3 vols. Oxford: Clarendon, 1969–2011.
Dubois, Marguerite-Marie. 'Le rondeau du coucou'. In Carruthers, *La ronde des saisons*, 15–21.
Dudley, Donald R., and Graham Webster. *The Roman Conquest of Britain AD 43–57*. Chester Springs, PA: Dufour, 1965.
Dunn, Marilyn. *The Christianization of the Anglo-Saxons c. 597–c. 700: Discourses of Life, Death and Afterlife*. London: Continuum, 2009.
Dunning, T. P., and A. J. Bliss, eds. *The Wanderer*. London: Methuen, 1960.
Durand, Aline, and Marie-Pierre Ruas. 'La forêt Languedocienne (fin VIIIe siècle–XIe siècle)'. In *Les forêts d'Occident du Moyen Âge à nos jours*, ed. A. Corvol-Dessert, 163–80. Toulouse: Presses Universitaires du Mirail, 2004.
Dyer, C. C. *Making a Living in the Middle Ages: The People of Britain 850–1520*. New Haven and London: Yale University Press, 2002.
—— 'Seasonal Patterns in Food Consumption in the Later Middle Ages'. In *Food in Medieval England: Diet and Nutrition*, ed. C. M. Woolgar, D. Serjeantson, and T. Waldron, 201–14. Oxford: Oxford University Press, 2006.
Eadie, J. 1983. 'Sir Gawain's Travels in North Wales'. *Review of English Studies* 34 (1983): 191–5.
Ebbinghaus, Ernst A. Review of *Heyne-Schückings 'Beowulf'*. *Journal of English and Germanic Philology* 62 (1963): 676–8.
Ehlert, Trude, and Gerhard Meissburger. '*Perceval* et *Parzival*: Valeur et fonction de l'episode dit "des trois gouttes de sang sur la neige"'. *Cahiers de civilisation médiévale Xe–XIIe siècles* 18 (1975): 197–227.
Einar Ólafur Sveinsson, ed. *Brennu-Njáls saga*. Íslenzk fornrit 12. Reykjavik: Hið íslenzka fornritafélag, 1954.
—— ed. *Laxdœla saga*. Íslenzk fornrit 5. Reykjavik: Hið íslenzka fornritafélag, 1934.
—— ed. *Vatnsdœla saga*. Íslenzk fornrit 8. Reykjavik: Hið íslenzka fornritafélag, 1939.
—— and Matthías Þórðarson, eds. *Eyrbyggja saga*. Íslenzk fornrit 4. Reykjavik: Hið íslenzka fornritafélag, 1935.
Elliott, Ralph W. V. 'Landscape and Geography'. In Brewer and Gibson, *A Companion to the 'Gawain'-Poet*, 104–17.
—— 'Landscape and Rhetoric in Middle-English Alliterative Poetry'. *The Melbourne Critical Review* 4 (1961): 65–76.
Emerson, Oliver Farrar. 'Grendel's Motive in Attacking Heorot'. *The Modern Language Review* 16, no. 2 (April 1921): 113–19.

—— 'Notes on *Sir Gawain and the Green Knight*'. *Journal of English and Germanic Philology* 21 (1922): 363–410.
Endter, W., ed. *König Alfreds des Grossen Bearbeitung der 'Soliloquien' des Augustinus*. Bibliothek der angelsächsischen Prosa 11. Hamburg: Grand, 1922.
Enkvist, Nils Erik. *The Seasons of the Year: Chapters on a Motif from 'Beowulf' to 'The Shepherd's Calendar'*. Helsinki: Societas Scientiarum Fennica, 1957.
Ergang, Robert R. *Herder and the Foundations of German Nationalism*. Studies in History, Economics and Public Law 341. New York: Columbia University Press, 1931.
Étaix, Raymond, ed. *Gregorius Magnus: 'Homiliae in evangelia'*. Corpus Christianorum, Series Latina, 141. Turnhout: Brepols, 1999.
Farris, William Wayne. *Japan's Medieval Population: Famine, Fertility, and Warfare in a Transformative Age*. [Honolulu]: University of Hawai'i Press, 2006.
Faulkes, Anthony, ed. *Snorri Sturluson: 'Edda'*. 4 vols. London: Viking Society for Northern Research / University College London, 1988–99.
Finch, R. G., ed. and trans. *Vǫlsunga saga / The Saga of the Volsungs*. Icelandic Texts. London: Nelson, 1965.
Finnbogi Guðmundsson, ed. *Orkneyinga saga*. Íslenzk fornrit 34. Reykjavik: Hið íslenzka fornritafélag, 1965.
Finnur Jónsson, ed. *Den norsk-islandske skjaldedigtning*. 4 vols. Copenhagen: Villadsen / Christensen, 1912–15. Copenhagen: Rosenkilde and Bagger, 1967.
—— *Den oldnorske og oldislandske litteraturs historie*. 2nd ed. Vol. 2. Copenhagen: Gad, 1923.
—— ed. *Hauksbók*. Copenhagen: Thiele, 1892–6.
—— ed. *'Saga Óláfs Tryggvasonar' af Oddr Snorrason, munk*. Copenhagen: Gad, 1932.
Fischer, Andreas. '*Sumer is icumen in*: The Seasons of the Year in Middle English and Early Modern English'. In *Studies in Early Modern English*, ed. Dieter Kastovsky, 79–95. Topics in English Linguistics 13. Berlin and New York: Mouton de Gruyter, 1994.
FitzPatrick, Mary Cletus, ed. and trans. 'Lactanti *De ave phoenice*: With an Introduction, Text, Translation, and Commentary'. Unpublished doctoral dissertation, University of Pennsylvania, 1933.
Foerster, Wendelin, ed. *Yvain (der Löwenritter)*. 2nd ed. Halle: Niemeyer, 1902.
Fontaine, Jacques, ed. *Isidore de Seville: Traité de la nature*. Bibliothèque de l'École des hautes études hispaniques 28. Bordeaux: Féret, 1960.
Ford, Simon. *The Situationist International: A User's Guide*. London: Black Dog, 2005.
Foster, Herbert Baldwin, ed. *Dio's 'Roman History'*. Translated by Earnest Cary. London: Heinemann, 1924.
Frandon, Véronique. 'Iconographie des saisons dans l'Occident médiéval'. *Revue de la Bibliothèque nationale* 50 (1993): 2–8.
Frankis, P. J. 'The Thematic Significance of "enta geweorc" and Related Imagery in *The Wanderer*'. *Anglo-Saxon England* 2 (1973): 253–69.
Frere, Sheppard. *Britannia: A History of Roman Britain*. London: Routledge / Kegan Paul, 1967.
Friis-Jensen, Karsten, and Peter Zeeberg, eds. and trans., *Saxo Grammaticus: Gesta Danorum / Danmarkshistorien*. 2 vols. Copenhagen: Gad, 2005.
Fritzner, Johan. *Ordbog over det gamle norske Sprog*. Kristiania [Oslo]: Den norske Forlagsforening, 1883–96.

Fry, Donald K., ed. *Finnsburh: Fragment and Episode*. London: Methuen, 1974.
—— 'The Art of Bede: Edwin's Council'. In King and Stevens, *Saints, Scholars, and Heroes*, 1:191–207.
Fuglesang, Signe Horn. 'Iconographic Traditions and Models in Scandinavian Imagery'. Lecture presented at the 13th International Saga Conference, Durham and York, 6–12 August 2006. Accessed 15 March 2015. http://web.archive.org/web/20080227124110/http:/www.dur.ac.uk/medieval.wwww/sagaconf/fuglesangekphrasis.pdf.
Fulk, R. D., Robert E. Bjork, and John D. Niles, eds. *Klaeber's 'Beowulf' and 'The Fight at Finnsburg'*. Toronto: University of Toronto Press, 2008.
Furneaux, Henry, ed. *Cornelii Taciti 'Annalium libri I–IV'*. 2nd ed. Oxford: Clarendon, 1904.
Gallagher, Edward J., trans. *The Lays of Marie de France*. Indianapolis, IN: Hackett, 2010.
Gallais, Pierre. 'Le sang sur la neige (le conte et le rêve)'. *Cahiers de civilisation médiévale Xe–XIIe siècles* 21 (1978): 37–42.
Gantz, Jeffrey, trans. *Early Irish Myths and Sagas*. Harmondsworth: Penguin, 1983.
Garmonsway, G. N., and Jacqueline Simpson, trans. *'Beowulf' and its Analogues*. London and New York: Dent / Dutton, 1968.
Gelsinger, Bruce E. *Icelandic Enterprise: Commerce and Economy in the Middle Ages*. Columbia, SC: University of South Carolina Press, 1981.
Gigerenzer, Gerd. 'Fast and Frugal Heuristics: The Tools of Bounded Rationality'. In *Blackwell Handbook of Judgment and Decision Making*, ed. Derek J. Koehler and Nigel Harvey, 62–88. Malden, MA: Blackwell, 2004.
—— and Peter M. Todd. 'Fast and Frugal Heuristics: The Adaptive Toolbox'. In Gigerenzer and Todd, *Simple Heuristics*, 3–34.
—— eds. *Simple Heuristics that Make us Smart*. Oxford: Oxford University Press, 1999.
Gilbert, Jane. 'Gender and Sexual Transgression'. In Brewer and Gibson, *A Companion to the 'Gawain'-Poet*, 53–69.
Girvan, Ritchie. *Finnsburh*. Sir Israel Gollancz Memorial Lecture. Oxford: Oxford University Press, 1941.
Glotfelty, Cheryll. 'Literary Studies in an Age of Environmental Crisis'. In *The Ecocriticism Reader: Landmarks in Literary Ecology*, ed. Cheryll Glotfelty and Harold Fromm, xv–xxxvii. Athens, GA, and London: The University of Georgia Press, 1996.
Godden, Malcolm. 'Biblical Literature: The Old Testament'. In *The Cambridge Companion to Old English Literature*, 2nd ed., ed. Malcolm Godden and Michael Lapidge, 214–33. Cambridge: Cambridge University Press, 2013.
—— and Susan Irvine, eds. *Boethius: An Edition of the Old English Versions of Boethius's 'De Consolatione Philosophiae'*. 2 vols. Oxford: Oxford University Press, 2009.
Godman, Peter, ed. *Poetry of the Carolingian Renaissance*. London: Duckworth, 1985.
Goldsmith, Margaret E. *The Mode and Meaning of 'Beowulf'*. London: Athlone, 1970.
Gopnik, Adam. *Winter: Five Windows on the Season*. CBC Massey Lectures. Toronto: Anansi, 2011.
Gordon, E. V., ed. *Pearl*. Oxford: Clarendon, 1953.
—— ed. *The Battle of Maldon*. London: Methuen, 1937.
Granlund, John. 'Midsommar'. *KLNM* 11 (1966): 612–14.
—— 'Veckoräkning och veckoår'. *ARV* 11 (1955): 1–37.

Green, Martin. 'Man, Time, and Apocalypse in *The Wanderer, The Seafarer,* and *Beowulf*'. *Journal of English and Germanic Philology* 74, no. 4 (1975): 502–18.

Greenfield, Stanley B. '*Sylf,* Seasons, Structure and Genre in *The Seafarer*'. *Anglo-Saxon England* 9 (1981): 199–211.

— 'The Old English Elegies'. In Stanley, *Continuations and Beginnings,* 142–75.

Greentree, Rosemary. 'The Wanderer's Horizon: A Note on *ofer wapema gebind*'. *Neophilologus* 86 (2002): 307–9.

Gregory, Derek. *Geographical Imaginations*. Cambridge, MA, and Oxford: Blackwell, 1994.

Grienberger, Theodor von. 'Bemerkungen zum *Beowulf*'. *Beiträge zur Geschichte der deutschen Sprache und Literatur* 36 (1910): 77–101.

Grimm, Jacob. *Deutsche Mythologie*. 4th ed., ed. Elard Hugo Meyer. 3 vols. Berlin: Dümmler, 1875–8.

Groos, Arthur. *Romancing the Grail: Genre, Science, and Quest in Wolfram's 'Parzival'*. Ithaca, NY, and London: Cornell University Press, 1995.

— '"Shall I Compare Thee to a Morn in May?": Walther von der Vogelweide and his Lady'. *Publications of the Modern Language Association of America* 91, no. 3 (May 1976): 398–405.

Grotefend, H. *Zeitrechnung des deutschen Mittelalters und der Neuzeit*. 2 vols. Hannover: Hahn, 1891–8.

Grottanelli, Cristiano. 'Agriculture'. In *Encyclopedia of Religion,* 2nd ed., ed. Lindsay Jones, 231–63. Detroit, MI: MacMillan, 2005.

Grove, Jean M. 'Glacial Geological Evidence for the Medieval Warm Period'. *Climatic Change* 26 (1994): 143–69.

— *Little Ice Ages: Ancient and Modern*. 2nd ed. 2 vols. London and New York: Routledge, 2008.

— 'The Initiation of the "Little Ice Age" in Regions round the North Atlantic'. *Climatic Change* 48 (1999): 53–82.

Guðni Jónsson, ed. *Grettis saga Ásmundarsonar, Bandamanna saga, Odds þáttr Ófeigssonar*. Íslenzk fornrit 7. Reykjavik: Hið íslenzka fornritafélag, 1936.

— and Bjarni Vilhjálmsson, eds. *Fornaldarsögur norðurlanda*. 3 vols. Reykjavik: Bókaútgáfan forni, 1943–4.

Guðrun Ása Grímsdóttir, ed. *Biskupa sögur III*. Íslenzk fornrit 17. Reykjavik: Hið íslenzka fornritafélag, 1998.

Gunnar Karlsson. *Iceland's 1100 Years: History of a Marginal Society*. Reykjavik: Mál og menning, 2000.

Gunnell, Terry. '*Grýla, grýlur, grøleks* and *skeklers*: Medieval Disguise Traditions in the Early Middle Ages?' *ARV* 57 (2001): 33–54.

— 'Ritual Space. Ritual Year. Ritual Gender: A View of the Old Norse and New Icelandic Ritual Year'. In *First International Conference of the SIEF Working Group on the Ritual Year: Proceedings, Malta, March 20–24, 2005,* ed. George Mifsud-Chircop, 285–302. San Gwann, Malta: Publishers Enterprises Group, 2005.

— 'The Coming of the Christmas Visitors . . . Folk Legends Concerning the Attacks on Icelandic Farmhouses Made by Spirits at Christmas'. *Northern Studies* 38 (2004): 51–75.

— 'The Season of the *dísir*: The Winter Nights and the *dísablót* in Early Medieval Scandinavian Belief'. *Cosmos* 16, no. 2 (2000): 117–49.

Gunnell, Terry. 'Viking Religion: Old Norse Mythology'. In North and Allard, *'Beowulf' and Other Stories*, 379–403.
Gurevich, Aaron J. 'Medieval Chronotope'. *Theoretische geschiedenis* 22, no. 3 (1995): 225–40.
Hall, Alaric. 'The Images and Structure of *The Wife's Lament*'. *Leeds Studies in English* 33 (2002): 1–29.
Hallberg, Peter. *The Icelandic Saga*. Translated by Paul Schach. Lincoln, NE: University of Nebraska Press, 1962.
Hallgerður Gísladóttir. *Íslensk matarhefð*. Reykjavik: Mál og menning, 1999.
Halsall, Maureen, ed. *The Old English 'Rune Poem': A Critical Edition*. McMaster Old English Studies and Texts 2. Toronto: University of Toronto Press, 1981.
Halvorsen, Eyvind Flejd. 'Freyr'. *KLNM* 4 (1959): 618–20.
—— 'Vǫlva'. *KLNM* 20 (1976): 355–7.
Hamilton, Hans Claude, ed. *'Historia rerum Anglicarum' Willelmi Parvi, Ordinis Sancti Augustini canonici regularis in Cœnobio beatæ Mariæ de Newburgh in agro Eboracensi*. 2 vols. London: [English Historical] Society, 1856.
Hammond, Paul, ed. *Shakespeare's Sonnets: An Original-Spelling Text*. Oxford: Oxford University Press, 2012.
Hanscom, Elizabeth Deering. 'The Feeling for Nature in Old English Poetry'. *Journal of English and Germanic Philology* 5 (1903–5): 439–63.
Hansen, Finn. 'Naturbeskrivende indslag i *Gísla saga Súrssonar*'. *Scripta Islandica* 29 (1978): 45–9.
Harris, Richard L. 'The Deaths of Grettir and Grendel: A New Parallel'. *Scripta Islandica* 24 (1973): 25–53.
Harvey, Barbara, and Jim Oeppen. 'Patterns of Morbidity in Late Medieval England: A Sample from Westminster Abbey'. *Economic History Review* 54, no. 2 (2001): 215–39.
Harvey, P. D. A. '*Rectitudines singularum personarum* and *Gerefa*'. *English Historical Review* 108, no. 426 (1993): 1–22.
Hasel, Karl. *Forstgeschichte: Ein Grundriß für Studium und Praxis*. Pareys Studientexte 48. Hamburg and Berlin: Parey, 1985.
Haß, Petra. *Der 'locus amoenus' in der antiken Literatur: Zu Theorie und Geschichte eines literarischen Motivs*. Bamberg: Wissenschaftlicher Verlag Bamberg, 1998.
Hastrup, Kirsten. 'Temporal Categories'. In *Culture and History in Medieval Iceland*, 17–49. Oxford: Clarendon, 1985.
Hayes, Carlton J. H. 'Contributions of Herder to the Doctrine of Nationalism'. *The American Historical Review* 32, no. 4, 719–36.
Hecht, Hans, ed. *Übersetzung der 'Dialoge' Gregors des Grossen über das Leben und die Wundertaten italienischer Väter und über die Unsterblichkeit der Seelen*. 2 vols. 1900–7. Darmstadt: Wissenschaftliche Buchgesellschaft, 1966.
Heggstad, Leiv, Finn Hødnebø, and Erik Simensen, eds. *Norrøn ordbok*. 5th ed. Oslo: Det norske samlaget, 2008.
Helder, William. 'The Song of Creation in *Beowulf* and the Interpretation of Heorot'. *English Studies in Canada* 13, no. 3 (September 1987): 243–55.
Helgi Þorláksson. *Vaðmál og verðlag: Vaðmál í utanlandsviðskiptum og búskap Íslendinga á 13. og 14. öld*. Reykjavik: Helgi Þorláksson, 1991.
Henderson, George, ed. and trans. *Fled Bricrend / The Feast of Bricriu*. London: Nutt, 1899.

Henisch, Bridget Ann. *Fast and Feast: Food in Medieval Society*. University Park, PA: Pennsylvania State University Press, 1976.
—— *The Medieval Calendar Year*. University Park, PA: Pennsylvania State University Press, 1999.
Henze, Matthias. *The Madness of King Nebuchadnezzar: The Ancient Near Eastern Origins and Early History of Interpretation of Daniel 4*. Supplements to the Journal for the Study of Judaism 61. Leiden: Brill, 1999.
Hermann Pálsson. 'Odinic Echoes in *Gísla saga*'. In *Gudar på jorden: Festschrift till Lars Lönnroth*, ed. Stina Hansson and Mats Malm, 97–118. Stockholm and Stehag: Brutus Östling, 2000.
—— *Úr landnorðri: Samar og ystu rætur íslenskrar menningar*. Studia Islandica 54. Reykjavik: Bókmenntafræðistofnun Háskóla Íslands, 1997.
Hess-Lüttich, Ernest W. B. 'Text Space: Holistic Texts?' In *Signs & Space: An International Conference on the Semiotics of Space and Culture in Amsterdam*, ed. Ernest W. B. Hess-Lüttich, Jürgen E. Müller, and Aart van Zoest, 341–51. Kodikas/Code, supplement 23. Tübingen: Narr, 1998.
Heyworth, P. L. 'Sir Gawain's Crossing of the Dee'. *Medium Ævum* 41 (1972): 124–7.
Hilbig, Benjamin E., Sabine G. Scholl, and Rüdiger F. Pohl. 'Think or Blink: Is the Recognition Heuristic an "Intuitive" Strategy?' *Judgment and Decision Making* 5, no. 4 (July 2010): 300–9.
Hill, Paul. *The Viking Wars of Alfred the Great*. Barnsley: Pen & Sword, 2008.
Hill, Thomas D. 'The Anchor of Hope and the Sea of this World: *Christ II*, 850–66'. *English Studies* 75, no. 4 (1994): 289–92.
—— 'The Tropological Context of Heat and Cold Imagery in Anglo-Saxon Poetry'. *Neuphilologische Mitteilungen* 69 (1968): 522–32.
Hollander, L. M. '*Beowulf* 33'. *Modern Language Notes* 32, no. 4 (April 1917): 246–7.
Holthausen, Ferdinand. 'Zum *Beowulf* (v. 33)'. *Beiblatt zur 'Anglia'* 14 (1903): 82–3.
Holton, Frederick S. 'Old English Sea Imagery and the Interpretation of *The Seafarer*'. *The Yearbook of English Studies* 12 (1982): 208–17.
Hooke, Della. 'Medieval Forests and Parks in Southern and Central England'. In *European Woods and Forests: Studies in Cultural History*, ed. Charles Watkins, 19–32. Wallingford: CAB International, 1998.
—— *Trees in Anglo-Saxon England: Literature, Lore and Landscape*. Woodbridge: Boydell, 2010.
Howe, Nicholas. *Migration and Mythmaking in Anglo-Saxon England*. New Haven, CT: Yale University Press, 1989.
Hødnebø, Finn. 'Juleskrå'. *KLNM* 8 (1963): 19–20.
Hughes, J. Donald. *The Mediterranean: An Environmental History*. Nature and Human Societies. Santa Barbara, CA: ABC-Clio, 2005.
Hughes, Jane M. *An Eskimo Village in the Modern World*. Ithaca, NY: Cornell University Press, 1960.
Hughes, Malcolm K., and Henry F. Diaz. 'Was there a "Medieval Warm Period", and if so, where and when?' *Climatic Change* 26 (1994): 109–42.
Hull, Vernam, ed. and trans. *Longes Mac N-Uislenn / The Exile of the Sons of Uisliu*. Modern Language Association of America Monograph Series 16. New York: Modern Language Society of America, 1949; reprinted New York: Kraus, 1971.
Hume, Kathryn. 'The "Ruin Motif" in Old English Poetry'. *Anglia* 94 (1976): 339–60.

Hunger, Ulrich. 'Die altdeutsche Literatur und das Verlangen nach Wissenschaft: Schöpfungsakt und Fortschrittsglaube in der Frühgermanistik'. In *Wissenschaftgeschichte der Germanistik im 19. Jahrhundert*, ed. Jürgen Fohrmann and Wilhelm Voßkamp, 236–63. Stuttgart and Weimar: Metzler, 1994.

Huot, Sylvia. 'A Tale Much Told: The Status of the Love Philtre in the Old French Tristan Texts'. *Zeitschrift für deutsche Philologie* 124, Sonderheft (2005): 82–95.

Hurst, D., ed. 'In Cantica canticorum'. In *In Tobiam, In Proverbia, In Cantica canticorum*, 165–375. Bedae venerabilis opera 2; Corpus Christianorum, Series Latina, 119B. Turnhout: Brepols, 1983.

Hutton, Ronald. *The Stations of the Sun: A History of the Ritual Year in Britain*. Oxford: Oxford University Press, 1996.

Ingi Sigurðsson and Jón Skaptason, eds. *Aspects of Arctic and Sub-Arctic History: Proceedings of the International Congress on the History of the Arctic and Sub-Arctic Region, Reykjavík, 18–21 June 1998*. Reykjavik: University of Iceland Press, 2000.

Jakob Benediktsson, ed. *Íslendingabók, Landnámabók*. Íslenzk fornrit 1. Reykjavik: Hið íslenzka fornritafélag, 1986.

James, Montague Rhodes, ed. *Apocrypha anecdota: A Collection of Thirteen Apocryphal Books and Fragments*. London: Christophers, 1935.

James, Montague Rhodes, C. N. L. Brooke, and R. A. B. Mynors, eds. and trans. *Walter Map: De nugis curialium / Courtiers' Trifles*. Oxford: Clarendon, 1983.

Jansen, Eystein, et al. 'Palaeoclimate: The Physical Science Basis'. *Contribution of Working Group I to the Fourth Assessment Report of the Intergovernmental Panel on Climate Change*, ed. S. Solomon et al., 433–97. Cambridge: Cambridge University Press, 2007.

Jansson, Sam Owen. 'Nyår'. *KLNM* 12 (1967): 410–11.

Jeay, Madeleine. 'Sanguine Inscriptions: Mythic and Literary Aspects of a Motif in Chrétien de Troyes's *Conte du graal*'. In *Telling Tales: Medieval Narratives and the Folk Tradition*, ed. Francesca Canadé Sautman, Diana Conchado, and Giuseppe Carlo Di Scipio, 137–54. New York: St. Martin's Press, 1998.

Jenness, D. *The Life of the Copper Eskimos: Southern Party, 1913–16*. Report of the Canadian Arctic Expedition 1913–18 12. Ottawa: Acland, 1922.

Jensen, Helle, ed. *Eiríks saga víðfǫrla*. Editiones arnamagnæanæ B 29. Copenhagen: Reitzel, 1983.

Jesch, Judith. *Women in the Viking Age*. Woodbridge: Boydell, 1991.

Jiroušková, Lenka. *Die 'Visio Pauli': Wege und Wandlungen einer orientalischen Apokryphe im lateinischen Mittelalter*. Mittellateinische Studien und Texte 34. Leiden and Boston: Brill, 2006.

Jóhannes Halldórsson, ed. *Kjalnesinga saga*. Íslenzk fornrit 14. Reykjavik: Hið íslenzka fornritafélag, 1959.

Johnston, R. C., and D. D. R. Owen, eds. *Two Old French Gauvain Romances: 'Le chevalier à l'épée' and 'La mule sans frein'*. Edinburgh and London: Scottish Academic Press, 1972.

Jón Árnason, ed. *Íslenzkar þjóðsögur og ævintýri*. 2nd ed. Rev. Árni Böðvarsson and Bjarni Vilhjálmsson. 6 vols. Reykjavik: Bókaútgáfan þjóðsaga, 1954–61.

Jón Jóhannesson, ed. *Austfirðinga sǫgur*. Íslenzk fornrit 11. Reykjavik: Hið íslenzka fornritafélag, 1950.

——— *Íslendinga saga: A History of the Icelandic Commonwealth*. Winnipeg: University of Manitoba Press, 1974.

Jón Jóhannesson, Magnús Finnbogason, and Kristján Eldjárn, eds. *Sturlunga saga*. 2 vols. Reykjavik: Sturlunguútgáfan, 1946.
Jón Sigurðsson and Guðbrand[u]r Vígfusson, eds. *Biskupa sögur*. 2 vols. Copenhagen: Hið íslenzka bókmenntafélag, 1858–78.
Jónas Kristjánsson, ed. *Eyfirðinga sǫgur*. Íslenzk fornrit 9. Reykjavik: Hið íslenzka fornritafélag, 1956.
Jones, Charles W., ed. *Opera didascalica II: De temporum ratione liber*. Corpus Christianorum, Series Latina, 123B: Bedae venerabilis opera, 6. Turnhout: Brepols, 1977.
Jones, Richard, and Mark Page. 'Characterizing Rural Settlements and Landscape: Whittlewood Forest in the Middle Ages'. *Medieval Archaeology* 47 (2003): 53–83.
Jones, Thomas Gwynn. *Welsh Folklore and Folk-Custom*. Cambridge: Roman & Littlefield, 1930.
Jordan, James W. 'Arctic Climate and Landscape ca. AD 800–1400'. In *The Northern World AD 900–1400*, ed. Herbert Maschner, Owen Mason, and Robert McGhee, 7–29. Salt Lake City: University of Utah Press, 2009.
Jorgensen, Peter, ed. 'Tristrams saga ok Ísöndar'. In Kalinke, *Norse Romance*, vol. 1, *The Tristan Legend*, 28–226.
Kalinke, Marianne E., ed. *Norse Romance*. 3 vols. Arthurian Archives 5. Cambridge: Brewer, 1999.
Kamphausen, Hans Joachim. *Traum und Vision in der lateinischen Poesie der Karolingerzeit*. Lateinische Sprache und Literatur des Mittelalters 4. Frankfurt: Peter Lang, 1975.
Kålund, Kristian. *Bidrag til en historisk-topografisk Beskrivelse af Island*. 2 vols. Copenhagen: Gyldendal, 1877–82.
Kelchner, Georgia Dunham. *Dreams in Old Norse Literature and their Affinities in Folklore*. Cambridge: Cambridge University Press, 1935.
Kemble, John M., ed. *The Anglo-Saxon Poems of 'Beowulf', 'The Travellers Song' and 'The Battle of Finnesburh'*. 2nd ed. 2 vols. London: Pickering, 1835–7.
Kendall, Calvin B. 'Imitation and the Venerable Bede's *Historia Ecclesiastica*'. In King and Stevens, *Saints, Scholars, and Heroes*, 1:161–90.
Kennedy, Patrick, ed. *Legendary Fictions of the Irish Celts*. 2nd ed. London: MacMillan, 1891.
Ker, N. R. *Catalogue of Manuscripts Containing Anglo-Saxon*. Oxford: Clarendon, 1957.
Keyser, R., and P. A. Munch, eds. *Norges gamle love indtil 1387*. Christiania [Oslo]: Grøndahl, 1846–95.
King, Margot H., and Wesley M. Stevens, eds. *Saints, Scholars, and Heroes: Studies in Medieval Culture in Honour of Charles W. Jones*. 2 vols. Collegeville, MN: Hill Monastic Manuscript Library, 1979.
Kittredge, George Lyman. *A Study of 'Gawain and the Green Knight'*. Cambridge, MA: Harvard University Press, 1916.
—— 'Arthur and Gorlagon'. *Harvard Studies and Notes in Philology and Literature* 8 (1903): 149–275.
Klaeber, Frederick, ed. *'Beowulf' and 'The Fight at Finnsburg'*. 3rd ed. Boston: Heath, 1950.
—— 'Notizen zur jüngeren *Genesis*'. *Anglia* 37 (n.s. 25) (1913): 539–42.
—— 'Zur jüngeren *Genesis*'. *Anglia* 49 (n.s. 37) (1925): 361–75.

Klein, W. F. 'Purpose and the "Poetics" of *The Wanderer* and *The Seafarer*'. In Nicholson and Frese, *Anglo-Saxon Poetry*, 208–23.

Klinck, Anne L., ed. *The Old English Elegies: A Critical Edition and Genre Study*. Montreal: McGill-Queen's University Press, 1992.

Knowlton, E. C. 'Nature in Older Irish'. *Publications of the Modern Language Association of America* 44, no. 1 (1929): 92–122.

Knudsen, Karen, et al. 'Palaeoceanography and Climate Changes off North Iceland during the Last Millennium: Comparison of Foraminifera, Diatoms and Ice-Rafted Debris with Instrumental and Documentary Data'. *Journal of Quaternary Science* 24 (2009): 457–68.

Köberl, Johann. 'The Magic Sword in *Beowulf*'. *Neophilologus* 71, no. 1 (January 1987): 120–8.

Kock, Ernst A. *Jubilee Jaunts and Jottings: 250 Contributions to the Interpretation and Prosody of Old West Teutonic Alliterative Poetry*. Lunds Universitets Årsskrift, n.s. section 1 14.26. Lund: Gleerup, 1918.

Krapp, George Philip, ed. *The Junius Manuscript*. Anglo-Saxon Poetic Records 1. New York: Columbia University Press, 1931.

—— ed. *The Vercelli Book*. Anglo-Saxon Poetic Records 2. New York: Columbia University Press, 1932.

—— and Elliott van Kirk Dobbie, eds. *The Exeter Book*. Anglo-Saxon Poetic Records 3. New York: Columbia University Press, 1936.

Krause, Wolfgang. 'Die Inschrift auf der Urne von Niesdrowitz'. *Altschlesien* 6 (1936): 239–53.

—— *Runeninschriften im älteren Futhark*. Schriften der Königsberger Gelehrten Gesellschaft, Geisteswissenschaftliche Klasse 13.4. Halle: Niemeyer, 1937.

Kremenetski, K. V., et al. 'Medieval Climate Warming and Aridity as Indicated by Multiproxy Evidence from the Kola Peninsula, Russia'. *Palaeogeography, Palaeoclimatology, Palaeoecology* 209 (2004): 113–25.

Krogmann, Willy. 'Ae. īsig'. *Anglia*, n.s., 44 = 56 (1932): 438–9.

Kühnemann, Eugen, ed. *J. G. Herders 'Ideen zur Philosophie der Geschichte der Menschheit'*. Berlin: Deutsche Bibliothek, 1914.

Kunitz, Stephen J. 'Speculations on the European Mortality Decline'. *The Economic History Review*, n.s., 36, no. 3 (July 1983): 349–64.

Kurath, Hans, et al., eds. *Middle English Dictionary*. Ann Arbor, MI: University of Michigan Press, 1956–2007. Accessed 15 March 2015. http://quod.lib.umich.edu/m/med/.

Kurvinen, Auvo, ed. *Sir Gawain and the Carl of Carlisle*. Helsinki: Suomalaisen kirjallisuuden seura, 1951.

Lacy, Norris J., ed. and trans. *Béroul: 'The Romance of Tristan'*. Garland Library of Medieval Literature A 36. New York and London: Garland, 1989.

Lagerholm, Åke, ed. *Drei 'lygisǫgur': 'Egils saga einhenda ok Ásmundar berserkjabana', 'Ála flekks saga', 'Flóres saga konungs ok sona hans'*. Halle: Niemeyer, 1927.

Lamb, H. H. 'Britain's Climate in the Past'. In *The Changing Climate: Selected Papers*, 170–95. London: Methuen, 1966.

—— *Climate: Present, Past, and Future*. 2 vols. London: Methuen, 1972–7.

—— *Climate, History and the Modern World*. 2nd ed. London and New York: Routledge, 1995.

—— 'Northern Europe: The Last Thousand Years'. In *Weather, Climate and Human*

Affairs: A Book of Essays and Other Papers, 27–39. London: Routledge, 1998.
Landers, John. *The Field and the Forge: Population, Production, and Power in the Pre-Industrial West*. Oxford: Oxford University Press, 2003.
Langeslag, P. S. 'Monstrous Landscape in *Beowulf*'. *English Studies* 96, no. 2 (2015): 119–38.
—— '*Trǫll* and Ethnicity in *Egils saga*'. In *Á austrvega: Saga and East Scandinavia; Preprint Papers of the 14th International Saga Conference, Uppsala, 9th–15th August 2009*, ed. Agneta Ney, Henrik Williams, and Fredrik Charpentier Ljungqvist, 2:560–7. Institutionen för humaniora och samhällsvetenskaps, skriftserie 14. Gävle: Gävle University Press, 2009.
Larrington, Carolyne, and Peter Robinson, eds and trans. 'Anonymous: *Sólarljóð*'. In *Poetry on Christian Subjects*, ed. Margaret Clunies Ross, 1:287–357. Skaldic Poetry of the Scandinavian Middle Ages 7. Turnhout: Brepols, 2007.
Lawrence, William Witherle. '*Beowulf*' *and Epic Tradition*. Cambridge, MA: Harvard University Press, 1928.
—— 'The Haunted Mere in *Beowulf*'. *Publications of the Modern Language Association of America* 27, no. 2 (1912): 208–45.
Le Goff, Jacques. 'Discorso di chiusura'. In *Popoli e paesi nella cultura altomedievale: 23–29 aprile 1981*, 805–38. Settimane di studio del centro Italiano di studi sull'alto medioevo 29. Ed. not given. Spoleto: Presso la sede del Centro, 1983.
—— *La naissance du purgatoire*. Bibliothèque des histoires. Paris: Gallimard, 1981.
Lee, Alvin A. *The Guest-Hall of Eden: Four Essays on the Design of Old English Poetry*. New Haven and London: Yale University Press, 1972.
Lehmann, W. P. '*Beowulf* 33, *isig*'. *Modern Language Notes* 74, no. 7 (November 1959): 577–8.
Leslie, R. F., ed. *The Wanderer*. Manchester: Manchester University Press, 1966.
—— ed. *Three Old Englies Elegies: 'The Wife's Lament', 'The Husband's Message', 'The Ruin'*. Manchester: Manchester University Press, 1961.
Liberman, Anatoly. 'Beowulf – Grettir'. In *Germanic Dialects: Linguistic and Philological Investigations*, ed. Bela Brogyanyi and Thomas Krömmelbein, 353–401. Amsterdam Studies in the Theory and History of Linguistic Science 4. Amsterdam and Philadelphia, PA: Benjamins, 1986.
—— 'The "Icy" Ship of Scyld Scefing: *Beowulf* 33'. In *Bright is the Ring of Words: Festschrift für Horst Weinstock zum 65. Geburtstag*, ed. Clausdirk Pollner, Helmut Rohlfing, and Frank-Rutger Hausmann, 183–203. Bonn: Romanistischer Verlag, 1996.
Lid, Nils. 'The Mythical Realm of the Far North: As it Appears in the National Finnish Epic *Kalevala* and the Scandinavian *fornaldar-saga* Tradition'. *LAOS* 1 (1951): 58–66.
Liebermann, F., ed. *Die Gesetze der Angelsachsen*. 3 vols. Halle: Niemeyer, 1903–16.
Linderholm, Hans W., and Björn E. Gunnarson. 'Summer Temperature Variability in Central Scandinavia during the Last 3600 Years'. *Geografiska Annaler* 87a1 (2005): 231–41.
Lindsay, W. M., ed. *Isidori Hispalensis episcopi 'Etymologiarum sive Originum libri XX'*. 2 vols. Oxford: Clarendon, 1911.
Liquori, Donna. 'Where Death Comes in Winter, and Burial in the Spring'. *New York Times* (1 May 2005): Late Edition, East Coast, Section 1, p. 41.
Liuzza, Roy. 'Anglo-Saxon Prognostics in Context: A Survey and Handlist of Manuscripts'. *Anglo-Saxon England* 30 (2001): 181–230.

Liuzza, Roy. 'The Tower of Babel: *The Wanderer* and the Ruins of History'. *Studies in the Literary Imagination* 36, no. 1 (Spring 2003): 1–35.
Lockett, Leslie. *Anglo-Saxon Psychologies in the Vernacular and Latin Traditions*. Toronto: University of Toronto Press, 2011.
Lönnroth, Lars. *Njáls saga: A Critical Introduction*. Berkeley, Los Angeles, and London: University of California Press, 1976.
Lot, Ferdinand. 'Études sur Merlin I: Les sources de la *Vita Merlini* de Gaufrei de Monmouth'. *Annales de Bretagne* 16 (1900): 325–47.
Loth, Agnete, ed. *Late Medieval Icelandic Romances*. 5 vols. Copenhagen: Munksgaard, 1962–5.
Lucas, Peter J., ed. *Exodus*. London: Methuen, 1977.
Lúðvík Kristjánsson. 'Fiskveiðar Íslendinga 1874–1940: Lauslegt yfirlit'. *Almanak hins Íslenzka þjóðvinafélags* (Reykjavik) 70 (1944): 65–111.
Lund, Allan A., ed. P. *Cornelius Tacitus: 'Germania'*. Heidelberg: Winter, 1988.
Lynnerup, Niels. *The Greenland Norse: A Biological-Anthropological Study*. Meddelelser om Grønland: Man and Society 24. Copenhagen: Commission for Scientific Research in Greenland, 1998.
Mac Airt, Seán, and Gearóid Mac Niocaill, eds and trans. *The Annals of Ulster (to AD 1131)*. Vol. 1, Text and Translation. Dublin: Dublin Institute for Advanced Studies, 1983.
MacDougall, James, ed. and trans. *Folk and Hero Tales*. Waifs and Strays of Celtic Tradition: Argyllshire series 3. London: Nutt, 1891.
Machan, Tim William, ed. *Vafþrúðnismál*. 2nd ed. Durham Medieval and Renaissance Texts 1. Durham: Centre for Medieval and Renaissance Studies, Durham University, 2008.
MacInnes, D., ed. and trans. *Folk and Hero Tales*. Waifs and Strays of Celtic Tradition: Argyllshire Series 2. London: Nutt, 1890.
Magennis, Hugh. *Anglo-Saxon Appetites: Food and Drink and their Consumption in Old English and Related Literature*. Dublin: Four Courts, 1999.
—— *Images of Community in Old English Poetry*. Cambridge Studies in Anglo-Saxon England 18. Cambridge: Cambridge University Press, 1996.
Magerøy, Hallvard. '*Ynglingatal*'. *KLNM* 20 (1976): 362–4.
Magnús Fjalldal. *The Long Arm of Coincidence: The Frustrated Connection between 'Beowulf' and 'Grettis saga'*. Toronto: University of Toronto Press, 1998.
Major, Tristan. '1 Corinthians 15:52 as a Source for the Old English Version of Bede's Simile of the Sparrow'. *Notes & Queries* 54, no. 1 (2007): 11–16.
Malmberg, Lars. '*The Wanderer: waþema gebind*'. *Neuphilologische Mitteilungen* 71 (1970): 96–9.
Malone, Kemp. 'Finn's Stronghold'. *Modern Philology* 43, no. 1 (August 1945): 83–5.
—— 'Hildeburg and Hengest'. *ELH: A Journal of English Literary History* 10, no. 4 (December 1943): 257–84.
Mann, Michael E., et al. 'Proxy-Based Reconstructions of Hemispheric and Global Surface Temperature Variations Over the Past Two Millennia'. *PNAS* 105, no. 36 (September 2008): 13252–7.
Mantel, Kurt. *Wald und Forst in der Geschichte: Ein Lehr- und Handbuch*. Alfend and Hannover: Schaper, 1990.
Marsden, Richard, ed. *The 'Old English Heptateuch' and Ælfric's 'Libellus de veteri testamento et novo'*. Vol. 1, *Introduction and Text*. EETS, os 330. Oxford: Oxford

University Press, 2008.
Marteinn Helgi Sigurðsson. 'Þórr's Travel Companion in *Hymiskviða*'. *Gripla* 16 (2005): 197–208.
Martin, B. K. 'Aspects of Winter in Latin and Old English Poetry'. *Journal of English and Germanic Philology* 68, no. 3, 375–90.
Marx, Karl, and Friedrich Engels. *Werke*. 13 vols. Ed. not given; commissioned by the Institut für Marxismus-Leninismus beim ZK der SED. Berlin: Dietz, 1956–90.
Masson-Delmotte, V., M. Schulz, A. Abe-Ouchi, J. Beer, et al. 'Information from Palaeoclimate Archives: The Physical Science Basis'. *Working Group I Contribution to the Fifth Assessment Report of the Intergovernmental Panel on Climate Change*, ed. Thomas F. Stocker et al., 383–464. Cambridge: Cambridge University Press, 2013.
Mather, A. S., and C. L. Needle. 'The Relationship of Population and Forest Trends'. *The Geographical Journal* 166, no. 1 (March 2000): 2–13.
Matonis, Anne T. E. 'Some Rhetorical Topics in the Early *cywyddwyr*'. *Bulletin of the Board of Celtic Studies* 28 (1980): 42–72.
Mattisson, Anki. *Ordbok över svenska språket*. Stockholm: Svenska Akademien, 1898–. Accessed 15 March 2015. http://www.saob.se/.
Mazzuoli Porru, G. '*Beowulf*, v. 33: īsig ond ūtfūs'. In *Studi linguistici e filologici per Carlo Alberto Mastrelli*, ed. Luciano Agostiniani, Vittoria Grazi, and Alberto Nocentini, 263–74. Pisa: Pacini, 1985.
McConchie, R. 'Grettir Ásmundarson's Fight with Kárr the Old: A Neglected *Beowulf* Analogue'. *English Studies* 63, no. 6 (1982): 481–6.
McCormick, Michael. *Origins of the European Economy: Communications and Commerce, A.D. 300–900*. Cambridge: Cambridge University Press, 2001.
McCreesh, Bernadine. 'Good Weather, Bad Weather: The Use of the Natural World in *Gísla saga*', lecture presented at New Directions in Medieval Scandinavian Studies: The 30th Annual Conference of the Center for Medieval Studies, Fordham University, 28 March 2010.
McGovern, Thomas H. 'Management for Extinction in Norse Greenland'. In *Historical Ecology: Cultural Knowledge and Changing Landscapes*, ed. C. Crumley, 127–54. Santa Fe: School of American Research Monographs, 1994.
—— et al. 'Landscapes of Settlement in Northern Iceland: Historical Ecology of Human Impact and Climate Fluctuation on the Millennial Scale'. *American Anthropologist* 109, no. 1 (March 2007).
McKinnell, John. *Meeting the Other in Norse Myth and Legend*. Cambridge: Brewer, 2005.
—— '*Vǫluspá* and the Feast of Easter'. *Alvíssmál* 12 (2008): 3–28.
Meissner, Rudolf. *Die Kenningar der Skalden: Ein Beitrag zur skaldischen Poetik*. Rheinische Beiträge und Hülfsbücher zur germanischen Philologie und Volkskunde 1. Bonn and Leipzig: Schroeder, 1921.
Mellinkoff, Ruth. 'Cain's Monstrous Progeny in *Beowulf*, Part I: Noachic Tradition'. *Anglo-Saxon England* 8 (1979): 143–62.
—— 'Cain's Monstrous Progeny in *Beowulf*, Part II: Post-Diluvian Survival'. *Anglo-Saxon England* 9 (1980): 183–97.
Meritt, H. D., ed. *Old English Glosses: A Collection*. New York: Modern Language Association of America, 1945.

Meulengracht Sørensen, Preben. 'The Sea, the Flame, and the Wind: The Legendary Ancestors of the Earls of Orkney'. In *At fortælle Historien: Studier i den gamle nordiske litteratur*, ed. Michael Dallapiazza, Olaf Hansen, and Gerd Wolfgang Weber, 221–30. Hesperides 16. Trieste: Parnaso, 2001.

—— 'Thor's Fishing Expedition: Towards a Dialogue between Archaeology and History of Religion'. In *Words and Objects*, ed. Gro Steinsland, 257–78. Oslo: Norwegian University Press, 1986.

Meyer, Matthias. 'Filling a Bath, Dropping into the Snow, Drunk through a Glass Straw: Transformations and Transfigurations of Blood in German Arthurian Romances'. *Bibliographical Bulletin of the International Arthurian Society* 58 (2006): 399–424.

Michelet, Fabienne. *Creation, Migration, and Conquest: Imaginary Geography and Sense of Space in Old English Literature*. Oxford: Oxford University Press, 2006.

Migne, J. P., ed. *Patrologiae cursus completus: Series Latina*. Paris: Migne, 1841–65.

Miller, Edward, and John Hatcher. *Medieval England: Rural Society and Economic Change 1086–1348*. London: Longman, 1978.

Mombritius, Boninus [Bonino Mombrizio], ed. *Sanctuarium seu Vitae sanctorum*. 2 vols. Paris: Fontemoing, 1910. Hildesheim and New York: Olms, 1978.

Moorman, Frederic W. *Nature*. Quellen und Forschungen zur Sprach- und Culturgeschichte der germanischen Völker 95. Strasbourg: Trübner, 1905.

Mora, Maria José. 'Un invierno entre los hielos: Los paisajes de la poesía anglosajona'. *Cuadernos del CEMYR* 7 (1999): 225–42.

Mörður Árnason, ed. *Íslensk orðabók*. 4th ed. Reykjavik: Edda, 2007.

Moreschini, Claudio, ed. *Boethius: 'De consolatione Philosophiae', Opuscula theologica*. 2nd ed. Munich and Leipzig: Saur, 2005.

Morris, R., ed. *The Blickling Homilies*. 3 vols. EETS, os 58, 63, 73. London: Trübner, 1874–80; reprinted in one volume 1967.

Mullen, Karen A. '*The Wanderer*: Considered Again'. *Neophilologus* 58, no. 1 (January 1974): 74–81.

Müllenhoff, Karl. 'Der Mythus von Beóvulf'. *Zeitschrift für deutsches Altertum* 7 (1849): 419–41.

Mundal, Else. 'Coexistence of Saami and Norse Culture: Reflected in and Interpreted by Old Norse Myths'. In *Old Norse Myths, Literature and Society: Proceedings of the 11th International Saga Conference, 2–7 July 2000, University of Sydney*, ed. Geraldine Barnes and Margaret Clunies Ross, 346–55. Sydney: Centre for Medieval Studies, 2000.

Murphy, Gerard, ed. *Duanaire Finn / The Book of the Lays of Fionn*. Vol. 3. Irish Texts Society 43. Dublin: Irish Texts Society, 1953.

Neckel, Gustav, ed. *Edda: Die Lieder des Codex Regius nebst verwandten Denkmälern*. Vol. 1, Text. 5th ed. Rev. Hans Kuhn. Heidelberg: Winter, 1983.

Neidorf, Leonard, ed. *The Dating of 'Beowulf': A Reassessment*. Cambridge: Brewer, 2014.

Nettle, Daniel. 'Error Management'. In *Evolution and the Mechanisms of Decision Making*, ed. Peter Hammerstein and Jeffrey R. Stevens, 69–79. Cambridge, MA: MIT Press, 2012.

Netzer, Katinka. *Wissenschaft aus nationaler Sehnsucht: Verhandlungen der Germanisten 1846 und 1847*. Heidelberg: Winter, 2006.

Neville, Jennifer. *Representations of the Natural World in Old English Poetry*. Cambridge Studies in Anglo-Saxon England 27. Cambridge: Cambridge University Press, 1999.

—— 'The Seasons in Old English Poetry'. In Carruthers, *La ronde des saisons*, 37–49.
Nicholls, Philip H. 'On the Evolution of a Forest Landscape'. *Transactions of the Institute of British Geographers* 56 (July 1972): 57–76.
Nicholson, Lewis E., and Dolores Warwick Frese, eds. *Anglo-Saxon Poetry: Essays in Appreciation; for John McGalliard*. Notre Dame and London: University of Notre Dame Press, 1975.
Niles, John D. 'The Problem of the Ending of *The Wife's Lament*'. *Speculum* 78, no. 4 (2003): 1107–50.
Nilsson, Martin P. 'Folkfesternas samband med år och arbetsliv'. In *Årets högtider*, ed. Martin P. Nilsson, 1–13. Nordisk kultur 22. Stockholm: Bonniers, 1938.
—— *Primitive Time-Reckoning: A Study in the Origins and First Development of the Art of Counting Time among the Primitive and Early Culture Peoples*. Lund: Berling, 1920.
Nordberg, Andreas, ed. *Jul, disting och förkyrklig tideräkning: Kalendrar och kalendariska riter i det förkristna Norden*. Acta academiae Regiae Gustavi Adolphi 91. Uppsala: Kungliga Gustav Adolfs Akademien för svensk folkkultur, 2006.
Nordland, Odd. 'Prognostica'. *KLNM* 13 (1968): 496–8.
North, Gerald R., et al. *Surface Temperature Reconstructions for the last 2,000 Years*. Washington, DC: National Academic Press, 2006. Accessed 5 March 2015. http://www.nap.edu/catalog/11676.html.
North, Richard, ed. *Heathen Gods in Old English Literature*. Cambridge Studies in Anglo-Saxon England 22. Cambridge: Cambridge University Press, 1997.
—— and Joe Allard, eds. *'Beowulf' and Other Stories: A New Introduction to Old English, Old Icelandic and Anglo-Norman Literatures*. 2nd ed. Harlow: Pearson Education, 2011.
Nørlund, Poul. *Buried Norsemen at Herjolfsnes: An Archaeological and Historical Study*. Meddelelser om Grønland 67.1. Copenhagen: Rietzel, 1924.
—— 'Kirkegaarden paa Herjolfsnæs: Et bidrag til diskussionen om klimateorien'. *Historisk tidsskrift* 27 (1927): 385–402.
—— *Viking Settlers in Greenland*. Translated by W. E. Calvert. London and Copenhagen: Cambridge University Press / Gad, 1936.
Ó Carragáin, Éamonn, and Richard North. '*The Dream of the Rood* and Anglo-Saxon Northumbria'. In North and Allard, *'Beowulf' and Other Stories*, 160–88.
O'Donoghue, Heather. *Old Norse–Icelandic Literature: A Short Introduction*. Oxford: Blackwell, 2004.
Oxford English Dictionary Online. Oxford: Oxford University Press. Accessed 15 March 2015. http://www.oed.com/.
Offord, M. Y., ed. *The Parlement of the Thre Ages*. EETS, os 246. Oxford: Oxford University Press, 1959.
Ogilvie, A. E. J. 'Climate and Farming in Northern Iceland, ca. 1700–1850'. In Ingi Sigurðsson and Jón Skaptason, *Aspects*, 289–99.
—— 'Climate and Society in Iceland From the Medieval Period to the Late Eighteenth Century'. Unpublished doctoral thesis, University of East Anglia, 1981.
—— 'Climatic Changes in Iceland AD c. 865 to 1598'. *Acta Archæologica* 61 (1990): 233–51.
—— and Graham Farmer. 'Documenting the Medieval Climate'. In *Climates of the British Isles: Present, Past and Future*, ed. Mike Hulme, 112–33. London: Routledge, 1997.

Ogilvie, A. E. J., and Trausti Jónsson. '"Little Ice Age" Research: A Perspective from Iceland'. *Climatic Change* 48 (2001): 9–52.

Ogilvie, A. E. J., and Gísli Pálsson. 'Mood, Magic, and Metaphor: Allusions to Weather and Climate in the Sagas of Icelanders'. In *Weather, Climate, Culture*, ed. Sarah Strauss and Benjamin Orlove, 251–74. Oxford and New York: Berg, 2003.

O'Keeffe, J. G., ed. *Buile Suibhne*. Mediaeval and Modern Irish Series 1. Dublin: Dublin Institute for Advanced Studies, 1931.

Ólafur Halldórsson. *Jómsvíkinga saga*. Reykjavik: Jón Helgason, 1969.

—— ed. *Óláfs saga Tryggvasonar en mesta*. 3 vols. Editiones arnamagnæanæ A, 1–3. Copenhagen: Munksgaard, 1958–2000.

Olsen, Magnus. 'Fra gammelnorsk myte og kultus'. *Maal og minne* 1 (1909): 17–36.

Orchard, Andy. *Pride and Prodigies: Studies in the Monsters of the 'Beowulf'-Manuscript*. Cambridge: Brewer, 1995

—— *A Critical Companion to 'Beowulf'*. Cambridge: Brewer, 2003.

—— 'Not what it was: The World of Old English Elegy'. In *The Oxford Handbook of the Elegy*, ed. Karen Weisman, 101–17. Oxford: Oxford University Press, 2010.

—— 'Reconstructing *The Ruin*'. In *Intertexts: Studies in Anglo-Saxon Culture Presented to Paul E. Szarmach*, ed. Virginia Blanton and Helene Scheck, 45–68. Medieval and Renaissance Texts and Studies 334; Arizona Studies in the Middle Ages and the Renaissance 24. Tempe, AZ: Arizona Center for Medieval and Renaissance Studies / Brepols, 2008.

—— 'Re-reading *The Wanderer*: The Value of Cross-References'. In *Via Crucis: Essays on Early Medieval Sources and Ideas in Memory of J. E. Cross*, ed. Thomas N. Hall, 1–26. Morgantown: West Virginia University Press, 2002.

—— trans. *The Elder Edda: A Book of Viking Lore*. London: Penguin, 2011.

—— 'The Word Made Flesh: Christianity and Oral Culture in Anglo-Saxon Verse'. *Oral Tradition* 24, no. 2 (2009): 293–318.

Owen-Crocker, Gale R. *The Four Funerals in 'Beowulf' and the Structure of the Poem*. Manchester and New York: Manchester University Press, 2000.

Page, R. I. 'Anglo-Saxon Paganism: The Evidence of Bede'. In *Pagans and Christians*, ed. T. Hofstra, L. A. J. R. Houwen, and A. A. MacDonald, 99–129. Germania Latina 2. Groningen: Forsten, 1995.

—— ed. *The Icelandic Rune-Poem*. London: Viking Society for Northern Research / University College London, 1999.

—— 'The Use of Double Runes in Old English Inscriptions'. In *Runes and Runic Inscriptions: Collected Essays on Anglo-Saxon and Viking Runes*, 95–104. 1962. Woodbridge: Boydell, 1995.

Páll Bergthórsson. 'The Effect of Climatic Variations on Farming in Iceland'. In Ingi Sigurðsson and Jón Skaptason, *Aspects*, 264–9.

Panton, Geo. A., and David Donaldson, eds. *The 'Gest Hystoriale' of the Destruction of Troy: An Alliterative Romance*. EETS, os 39, 56. London: Trübner, 1869–74; reprinted New York: Greenwood, 1969.

Pausas, Juli G., and Jon E. Keeley. 'A Burning Story: The Role of Fire in the History of Life'. *BioScience* 59, no. 7 (July–August 2009): 593–601.

Payne, John W., James R. Bettman, and Eric J. Johnson. *The Adaptive Decision Maker*. Cambridge: Cambridge University press, 1993.

Pearsall, Derek, and Elizabeth Salter. *Landscapes and Seasons of the Medieval World*. Toronto and Buffalo, NY: University of Toronto Press, 1973.

Pearson, Kathy L. 'Nutrition and the Early-Medieval Diet'. *Speculum* 72, no. 1 (January 1997): 1–32.
Peiper, Rudolf, ed. *Alcimi Ecdicii Aviti Viennensis episcopi opera quae supersunt*. Vol. 2. Monumenta Germaniae Historica, Auctores antiquissimi 6. Berlin: Weidmann, 1883.
Perdikaris, Sophia, and Thomas H. McGovern. 'Cod Fish, Walrus, and Chieftains: Economic Intensification in the Norse North Atlantic'. In *Seeking a Richer Harvest: The Archaeology of Subsistence Intensification, Innovation, and Change*, ed. Tina L. Thurston and Christopher T. Fisher, 193–216. New York: Springer, 2006.
Perry, Ben Edwin, ed. *Aesopica: A Series of Texts relating to Aesop or Ascribed to him or Closely Connected with the Literary Tradition that Bears his Name*. Vol. 1, *Greek and Latin Texts*. Urbana, IL: University of Chicago Press, 1952.
Pertz, Georgius Heinricus, ed. *Chronicon Hugonis monachi Virdunensis et Divionensis, abbatis Flaviniacensis*, 280–503. Monumenta Germaniae Historica, Scriptores 8. Hannover: Hahn, 1848.
Petersen, Robert. 'Burial-Forms and Death Cult among the Eskimos'. *Folk* 8–9 (1966–7): 259–80.
Pfister, C., *et al.* 'Winter Air Temperature Variations in Western Europe during the Early and High Middle Ages (AD 750–1300)'. *The Holocene* 8, no. 5 (1998): 535–52.
Pfister, C., G. Schwarz-Zanetti, and M. Wegmann. 'Winter Severity in Europe: The Fourteenth Century'. *Climatic Change* 34 (1996): 91–108.
Phelan, Walter S. *The Christmas Hero and Yuletide Tradition in 'Sir Gawain and the Green Knight'*. Lewiston, NY, Queenston, ON, and Lampeter: Edwin Mellen, 1992.
Phillips, Helen. 'Dream Poems'. In *A Companion to Medieval English Literature and Culture: c. 1350–c. 1500*, ed. Peter Brown, 374–86. Malden, MA: Blackwell, 2007.
Piehler, Paul. *The Visionary Landscape: A Study in Medieval Allegory*. London, 1971.
Pluskowski, Aleks. 'Who Ruled the Forests? An Interdisciplinary Approach towards Medieval Hunting Landscapes'. In *Fauna and Flora in the Middle Ages: Studies of the Medieval Environment and its Impact on the Human Mind; Papers Delivered at the International Medieval Congress, Leeds, in 2000, 2001, and 2002*, ed. Sieglinde Hartmann, 291–323. Beihefte zur Mediaevistik 8. Berlin: Peter Lang, 2007.
Poestion, Josef Calasanz, ed. *Isländische Märchen*. Vienna: Carl Gerold's Sohn, 1884.
Pope, John C., ed. *Homilies of Ælfric: A Supplementary Collection*. 2 vols. EETS, os 259–60. London: Oxford University press, 1967–8.
—— ed. *Seven Old English Poems*. Indianapolis and New York: Bobbs-Merill, 1966.
Power, Rosemary. 'Journeys to the Otherworld in the Icelandic *fornaldarsögur*'. *Folklore* 96, no. 2 (1985): 156–75.
—— '*Le lai de Lanval* and *Helga þáttr Þórissonar*'. *Opuscula* 8 (1985): 158–61.
Puhvel, Martin. *'Beowulf' and the Celtic Tradition*. Waterloo, ON: Wilfrid Laurier University Press, 1979.
Putter, Ad. *'Sir Gawain and the Green Knight' and French Arthurian Romance*. Oxford: Clarendon, 1995.
Raith, Josef, ed. *Die altenglische Version des halitgar'schen Bussbuches*. Hamburg: Grand, 1933. Darmstadt: Wissenschaftliche Buchgesellschaft, 1964.
Rannveig Sigurdardóttir *et al. The Economy of Iceland*. Reykjavik: Sedlabanki, 2007.
Rat, Jean-Michel. 'Les activités maritimes du Haut Moyen Age en relation avec les saisons'. In Carruthers, *La ronde des saisons*, 23–35.
Ratzel, Friedrich. *Politische Geographie*. Munich and Leipzig: Oldenbourg, 1897.

Rauer, Christine, ed. *The Old English Martyrology: Edition, Translation and Commentary*. Anglo-Saxon Texts. Cambridge: Brewer, 2013.
Renoir, Alain. 'The Old English *Ruin*: Contrastive Structure and Affective Impact'. In *The Old English Elegies: New Essays in Criticism and Research*, ed. Martin Green, 148–73. Rutherford, NJ: Fairleigh Dickinson University Press, 1983.
Roach, William, ed. *Le roman de Perceval; ou Le conte du graal*. Second rev. ed. Textes littéraires français. Geneva and Paris: Droz / Minard, 1959.
Roach, William, and Robert H. Ivy, eds. *The Continuations of the Old French 'Perceval' of Chretien de Troyes*. Vol. 2, *The First Continuation*. Romance Languages and Literatures, extra series 10. Philadelphia, PA: University of Pennsylvania, Department of Romance Languages, 1949.
Robertson, D. W., Jr. 'The Doctrine of Charity in Mediaeval Literary Gardens: A Topical Approach through Symbolism and Allegory'. *Speculum* 26, no. 1 (January 1951): 24–49.
Robinson, Fred C. 'Possible Biblical Resonances in Bede's Presentation of the Conversion of the English'. In *Text and Language in Medieval English Prose: A Festschrift for Tadao Kubouchi*, ed. Jacek Fisiak and John Scahill, 207–13. Studies in English Medieval Language and Literature 12. Frankfurt: Peter Lang, 2005.
Rodkinson, Michael Levi, ed. and trans. *The Babylonian Talmud*. 2nd ed. 18 vols. New York: New Talmud Publishing Company, 1918.
Roll, Susan K. *Toward the Origins of Christmas*. Kampen: Kok Pharos, 1995.
Rommel, Floribert, and Charles Morel, eds. *Grégoire le Grand: 'Règle pastorale'*. 2 vols. Sources chrétiennes 381. Paris: Cerf, 1992.
Rooney, Anne. 'The Hunts in *Sir Gawain and the Green Knight*'. In Brewer and Gibson, *A Companion to the 'Gawain'-Poet*, 157–79.
Rosier, James L. 'The Literal-Figurative Identity of the Wanderer'. *Publications of the Modern Language Association of America* 79, no. 1 (March 1964): 366–9.
Ross, Werner. 'Über den sogenannten Natureingang der Trobadors'. *Romanische Forschungen* 65, nos. 1/2 (1953): 49–68.
Roth, Jonathan P. *The Logistics of the Roman Army at War*. Columbia Studies in the Classical Tradition 23. Leiden: Brill, 1998.
Roth, Leland M. *Understanding Architecture: Its Elements, History, and Meaning*. 2nd ed. Boulder, CO: Westview, 2007.
Rowe, Elizabeth Ashman. 'Origin Legends and Foundation Myths in Flateyjarbók'. In Clunies Ross, *Old Norse Myths, Literature and Society*, 198–216.
Rudolf Simek, Jónas Kristjánsson, and Hans Bekker-Nielsen, eds. *Sagnaskemmtun: Studies in Honour of Hermann Pálsson*. Vienna: Böhlau, 1986.
Safriel, Uriel N. 'Dryland Development, Desertification and Security in the Mediterranean'. In *Desertification in the Mediterranean Region: A Security Issue*, ed. William G. Kepner *et al.*, 227–50. NATO Security through Science Series, C: Environmental Security. Dordrecht: Springer, 2006.
Salmon, Vivian. 'Some Connotations of *cold* in Old and Middle English'. *Modern Language Notes* 74, no. 4 (1959): 314–22.
Sandison, Helen Estabrook. *The chanson d'aventure in Middle English*. Bryn Mawr, PA: Bryn Mawr College, 1913.
Sands, Roger. *Forestry in a Global Context*. Cambridge, MA: CABI, 2005.
Sauer, C. O. 'Fire and Early Man'. *Paideuma* 7, no. 8 (November 1961): 399–407.
Saunders, Corinne J. *The Forest of Medieval Romance: Avernus, Broceliande, Arden*.

Cambridge: Brewer, 1993.
Schach, Paul. 'The Anticipatory Literary Setting in the Old Icelandic Family Sagas'. *Scandinavian Studies* 27, no. 1, 1–13.
—— 'The Use of Scenery in the *Íslendinga sǫgur*'. Unpublished doctoral dissertation, University of Pennsylvania, 1949.
Schaubert, Else von, ed. *Heyne–Schückings 'Beowulf'*. 17th ed. Paderborn: Schöningh, 1961.
Schenkl, Carolus [Karl], ed. *S. Ambrosii opera*. Vol. 1. Corpus Scriptorum Ecclesiasticorum Latinorum. Vienna: Tempsky, 1897.
Schmeidler, Bernhard, ed. *Adam von Bremen: Hamburgische Kirchengeschichte*. 3rd ed. Scriptores rerum germanicarum 2. Hannover: Hahn, 1917.
Schmid-Cadalbert, Christian. 'Der wilde Wald: Zur Darstellung und Funktion eines Raumes in der mittelhochdeutschen Literatur'. In *Gotes und der werlde hulde: Literatur in Mittelalter und Neuzeit; Festschrift für Heinz Rupp zum 70. Geburtstag*, ed. Rüdiger Schnell, 24–47. Bern and Stuttgart: Francke, 1989.
Schmidt, A. V. C. '"Latent Content" and "The Testimony in the Text": Symbolic Meaning in *Sir Gawain and the Green Knight*'. *Review of English Studies*, n.s., 38 (1987): 145–68.
—— ed. *William Langland, 'Piers Plowman': A Parallel-Text Edition of the A, B, C and Z Versions*. Rev. ed. 2 vols. Kalamazoo, MI: Medieval Institute Publications, 2011.
—— and Nicolas Jacobs, eds. *Medieval English Romances*. 2 vols. New York: Holmes / Meier, 1980.
Schmidt, Jean-Claude. *Ghosts in the Middle Ages: The Living and the Dead in Medieval Society*. Translated by Teresa Lavender Fagan. Chicago: University of Chicago Press, 1998.
Schraml, Ulrich, and Georg Winkel. 'Germany'. In *Forestry in Changing Societies in Europe*, ed. P. Pelkonen *et al.*, vol. 2, Country Reports, 115–38. Joensuu: Joensuu University Press, 1999.
Schulz, Katja. *Riesen: Von Wissenshütern und Wildnisbewohnern in Edda und Saga*. Heidelberg: Winter, 2004.
Schuster, Mary Faith. 'Bede and the Sparrow Simile'. *The American Benedictine Review* 8, no. 1 (1957): 47–50.
Scott, Jonathan. 'EarthTools'. August 2005. Accessed 15 March 2015. http://www.earthtools.org.
Scott-Macnab, David, ed. *The Middle English Text of 'The Art of Hunting' by William Twiti*. Middle English Texts 40. Heidelberg: Winter, 2009.
Scowcroft, R. Mark. 'The Hand and the Child: Studies of Celtic Tradition in European Literature'. Unpublished doctoral dissertation, Cornell University, 1982.
—— 'The Irish Analogues to *Beowulf*'. *Speculum* 74, no. 1 (January 1999): 22–64.
Scragg, Donald, ed. *The Battle of Maldon*. Manchester: Manchester University Press, 1981.
—— ed. 'The Battle of Maldon'. In *The Battle of Maldon: 991 AD*, ed. Donald Scragg, 15–36. Oxford: Blackwell, 1991.
—— ed. *The Vercelli Homilies*. EETS, os 300. Oxford: Oxford University Press, 1992.
Seaver, Kirsten. *The Frozen Echo: Greenland and the Exploration of North America ca. AD 1000–1500*. Stanford, CA: Stanford University Press, 1996.
See, Klaus von, *et al.*, eds. *Kommentar zu den Liedern der 'Edda'*. Heidelberg: Winter, 1993–.

Seierstad, Andr. 'Jul'. *KLNM* 8 (1963): 6–17.
Selmer, Carl, ed. *Navigatio Sancti Brendani abbatis: From Early Latin Manuscripts*. Notre Dame, IN: University of Notre Dame Press, 1959.
Semple, Ellen Churchill. *Influences of Geographic Environment on the Basis of Ratzel's System of Anthropo-Geography*. New York: Holt / Rinehart / Winston, 1911.
Shaw, Philip A. *Pagan Goddesses in the Early Germanic World: Eostre, Hreda and the Cult of Matrons*. Studies in Early Medieval History. London: Bristol Classical Press, 2011.
Shippey, Tom, ed. *Old English Verse*. London: Hutchinson University Library, 1972.
Short, William R. *Icelanders in the Viking Age: The People of the Sagas*. Jefferson, NC, and London: McFarland, 2010.
Sievers, Eduard. 'Gegenbemerkungen zum *Beowulf*'. *Beiträge zur Geschichte der deutschen Sprache und Literatur* 36 (1910): 397–434.
—— 'Lückenbüsser'. *Beiträge zur Geschichte der deutschen Sprache und Literatur* 27 (1902): 572.
Sigurður Nordal, ed. *Orkneyinga sǫgur*. Copenhagen: Møller, 1913–16.
—— *Snorri Sturluson*. Helgafell: Víkingsprent, 1973.
—— ed. *Þjóðsagnabókin: Sýnisbók íslenzkra þjóðsagnasafna*. 3 vols. Reykjavik: Almenna bókafélágið, 1971–3.
—— and Guðni Jónsson, eds. *Borgfirðinga sǫgur*. Íslenzk fornrit 3. Reykjavik: Hið íslenzka fornritafélag, 1916–18.
Sigurgeir Steingrímsson, Ólafur Halldórsson, and Peter Foote, eds. *Biskupa sögur I*. 2 vols. Íslenzk fornrit 15. Reykjavik: Hið íslenzka fornritafélag, 2003.
Silverstein, Theodore. *Visio Sancti Pauli: The History of the Apocalypse in Latin together with Nine Texts*. London: Christophers, 1935.
Simek, Rudolf. *Altnordische Kosmographie: Studien und Quellen zu Weltbild und Weltbeschreibung in Norwegen und Island vom 12. bis zum 14. Jahrhundert*. Ergänzungsbände zum Reallexikon der Germanischen Altertumskunde 4. Berlin and New York: De Gruyter, 1990.
—— 'Elusive Elysia; or: Which Way to Glæsisvellir? On the Geography of the North in Icelandic Legendary Fiction'. In Rudolf Simek, Jónas Kristjánsson, and Hans Bekker-Nielsen, *Sagnaskemmtun*, 247–75.
Simpson, Ian A., W. Paul Adderley, Garðar Guðmundsson, Margrét Hallsdóttir, Magnús Á. Sigurgeirsson, and Mjöll Snæsdóttir. 'Soil Limitations to Agrarian Land Production in Premodern Iceland'. *Human Ecology* 30, no. 4 (December 2002): 423–43.
Simpson, Jacqueline, ed. and trans. *Icelandic Folktales and Legends*. Berkeley and Los Angeles: University of California Press, 1972.
Skeat, Walter W., ed. *Ælfric's Lives of Saints: Being a Set of Sermons on Saints' Days Formerly Observed by the English Church*. 4 vols. EETS, os 76, 82, 94, 114. London: Oxford University Press, 1881–1900; reprinted in two volumes 1966.
—— ed. *The Gospel According to Saint Matthew*. Cambridge: Cambridge University Press, 1887. Darmstadt: Wissenschaftliche Buchgesellschaft, 1970.
Slay, D., ed. *Hrólfs saga kraka*. Editiones Arnamagnæanæ B 1. Copenhagen: Munksgaard, 1960.
Smith, A. H., ed. *English Place-Name Elements*. 2 vols. Cambridge: Cambridge University Press, 1970.
Smith, Anthony D., ed. *Nationalist Movements*. London: Macmillan, 1976.

—— 'Neo-Classicist and Romantic Elements in the Emergence of Nationalist Conceptions'. In Smith, *Nationalist Movements*, 74–87.
—— 'The Formation of Nationalist Movements'. In Smith, *Nationalist Movements*, 1–30.
Smith, Kevin P. '*Landnám*: The Settlement of Iceland in Archaeological and Historical Perspective'. *World Archaeology* 26, no. 3 (February 1995): 319–47.
Smith, Neil. *Uneven Development*. 3rd ed. Athens, GA: University of Georgia Press, 2008.
Sobecki, Sebastian I. *The Sea and Medieval English Literature*. Studies in Medieval Romance 5. Cambridge: Brewer, 2008.
Sørensen, Bent. *A History of Energy: Northern Europe from the Stone Age to the Present Day*. Abingdon and New York: Earthscan, 2012.
Spearing, A. C. 'Dream Poems'. In *Chaucer: Contemporary Approaches*, ed. Susanna Fein and David Raybin, 159–78. University Park, PA: Pennsylvania State University Press, 2010.
—— *Medieval Dream-Poetry*. Cambridge: Cambridge University Press, 1976.
Spinner, Katharina. 'Die Ausdrücke für Sinnesempfindungen in der angelsächsischen Poesie verglichen mit den Bezeichnungen für Sinnesempfindungen in der altnordischen, altsächsischen und althochdeutschen Dichtung'. Unpublished doctoral thesis, University of Halle, 1924.
Squatriti, Paolo. *Water and Society in Early Medieval Italy, AD 400–1000*. Cambridge: Cambridge University Press, 1998.
Squires, Ann, ed. *The Old English 'Physiologus'*. Durham Medieval Texts 5. Durham: Durham Medieval Texts, 1988.
St John, Michael. *Chaucer's Dream Visions: Courtliness and Individual Identity*. Studies in European Cultural Transition 7. Aldershot: Ashgate, 2000.
Stanley, E. G., ed. *Continuations and Beginnings: Studies in Old English Literature*. London: Nelson, 1966.
—— 'Old English Poetic Diction and the Interpretation of *The Wanderer, The Seafarer* and *The Penitent's Prayer*'. *Anglia* 73.4 (n.s. 61.4) (1956): 413–66.
Stauffer, Marianne. *Der Wald*. Bern: Francke, 1959.
Stedman, Douglas. 'Some Points of Resemblance between *Beowulf* and the *Grettla* (or *Grettis saga*)'. *Saga-Book* 8 (1913–14): 6–26.
Steen, Janie. *Verse and Virtuosity: The Adaptation of Latin Rhetoric in Old English Poetry*. Toronto: University of Toronto Press, 2008.
Stefán Karlsson. '*Bóklausir menn*: A Note on Two Versions of *Guðmundar saga*'. In Rudolf Simek, Jónas Kristjánsson, and Hans Bekker-Nielsen, *Sagnaskemmtun*, 277–86.
Stein, Howard F. *Developmental Time, Cultural Space: Studies in Psychogeography*. Norman, and London: University of Oklahoma Press, 1987.
Stern, Sacha. *Calendars in Antiquity: Empires, States, and Societies*. Oxford: Oxford University Press, 2012.
Stitt, J. Michael. *'Beowulf' and the Bear's Son: Epic, Saga, and Fairytale in Northern Germanic Tradition*. Albert Bates Studies in Oral Tradition 8. New York and London: Garland, 1992.
Storå, Nils. *Burial Customs of the Skolt Lapps*. Folklore Fellows' Communications 210. Helsinki: Suomalainen tiedeakatemia, 1971.
Stork, Gustav, ed. *Islandske annaler indtil 1578*. Christiania [Oslo]: Grøndahl, 1888.
Ström, Folke. 'Diser'. *KLNM* 3 (1958): 101–3.

Suphan, Bernhard, ed. 'Ueber den Fleiß in mehreren gelehrten Sprachen'. In *Herders sämmtliche Werke*, 1:1–7. Berlin: Weidmann, 1877–13.

Sveinbjörn Egilsson, ed. *Lexicon poeticum antiquæ linguæ septentrionalis*. Copenhagen: Det kongelige nordiske oldskriftselskab, 1860.

Sveinbjörn Egilsson and Finnur Jónsson, eds. *Lexicon poeticum antiquæ linguæ septentrionalis / Ordbog over det norsk-islandske skjaldesprog*. 2nd ed. Copenhagen: Møller, 1931.

Sveinbjörn Rafnsson. *Ólafs sögur Tryggvasonar: Um gerðir þeirra, heimildir og höfunda*. Reykjavik: Háskólaútgáfan, 2005.

Sweet, Henry, ed. *King Alfred's West-Saxon Version of Gregory's 'Pastoral Care'*. 2 vols. EETS, os 45, 50. London: Oxford University Press, 1871.

Talentino, Arnold V. 'Moral Irony in *The Ruin*'. *Papers on Language & Literature* 14, no. 1 (Winter): 3–10.

Tangl, Michael, ed. *Epistolae selectae in usum scholarum I: S. Bonifatii et Lulli epistolae*. Berlin: Weidmann, 1916.

Taylor, A. R. 'Two Notes on *Beowulf*'. *Leeds Studies in English* 7–8 (1052): 5–17.

Taylor, Paul Beekman. 'Heorot, Earth, and Asgard: Christian Poetry and Pagan Myth'. *Tennessee Studies in Literature* 11 (1966): 119–30.

Tepper, Leo. 'The Monster's Mother at Yuletide'. In *Monsters and the Monstrous in Medieval Northwest Europe*, ed. by K. E. Olsen and L. A. J. R. Houwen, 93–102. Leuven: Peeters, 2001.

Thiébaux, Marcelle. *The Stag of Love: The Chase in Medieval Literature*. Ithaca, NY: Cornell University Press, 1974.

Thomas, R. J., G. A. Bevan, and J Gareth Thomas. *Geiriadur Prifysgol Cymru*. 61 vols. Cardiff: Gwasg Prifysgol Cymru, 1950–2002.

Thomson, R. L., ed. *Pwyll pendeuic Dyuet*. Mediaeval and Modern Welsh Series 1. Dublin: Dublin Institute for Advanced Studies, 1957.

Thoss, Dagmar. *Studien zum 'locus amoenus' im Mittelalter*. Wiener romanistische Arbeiten 10. Vienna and Stuttgart: Braumüller, 1972.

Tille, Alexander. *Yule and Christmas: Their Place in the Germanic Year*. London: Nutt, 1899.

Tolkien, J. R. R., and Alan Bliss, eds. *Finn and Hengest: The 'Fragment' and the 'Episode'*. London: Allen & Unwin, 1982.

Tolkien, J. R. R., and E. V. Gordon, eds. *Sir Gawain and the Green Knight*. 2nd ed. Rev. Norman Davis. Oxford: Clarendon, 1967.

Tolkien, J. R. R., and Joan Turville-Petre, eds. *The Old English 'Exodus': Text, Translation, and Commentary*. Oxford: Clarendon, 1981.

Tolley, Clive. *Shamanism in Norse Myth and Magic*. 2 vols. Folklore Fellows' Communications, 296–7. Helsinki: Suomalainen tiedeakatemia, 2009.

Toswell, M. J. 'Bede's Sparrow and the Psalter in England'. *ANQ* 13, no. 1 (2000): 7–12.

Trautmann, Moritz. 'Auch zum *Beowulf*: Ein Gruß an Herrn Eduard Sievers'. *Bonner Beiträge zur Anglistik* 17 (1905): 143–74.

—— 'Beiträge zu einem künftigen Sprachschatz der altenglischen Dichter'. *Anglia* 33 (1910): 276–82.

—— 'Berichtigungen, Vermutungen und Erklärungen zum *Beowulf*: Erste Hälfte'. *Bonner Beiträge zur Anglistik* 2 (1899): 121–92.

Travis, David J., Andrew M. Carleton, and Ryan G. Lauritsen. 'Contrails Reduce Daily Temperature Range'. *Nature* 418, no. 6898 (August 2002): 601.

Trigg, Stephanie, ed. *Wynnere and Wastoure*. EETS, os 297. Oxford: Oxford University Press, 1990.
Turner, Andrew J., and Bernard J. Muir, eds and trans. *Eadmer of Canterbury: Lives and Miracles of Saints Oda, Dunstan, and Oswald*. Oxford: Clarendon, 2006.
Turville-Petre, Gabriel, ed. *Hervarar saga ok Heiðreks*. London: Viking Society for Northern Research / University College London, 1976.
Tuve, Rosemond. *Seasons and Months: Studies in a Tradition of Middle English Poetry*. 1933. Cambridge: Brewer, 1974.
Þórhallur Vilmundarson and Bjarni Vilhjálmsson, eds. *Harðar saga*. Íslenzk fornrit 13. Reykjavík: Hið íslenzka fornritafélag, 1991.
Þorleifur Hauksson, ed. *Sverris saga*. Íslenzk fornrit 30. Reykjavík: Hið íslenzka fornritafélag, 2007.
Unwin, Tim. 'Saxon and Early Norman Viticulture in England'. *Journal of Wine Research* 1, no. 1 (1990): 61–75.
Vasey, Daniel E. 'Population, Agriculture, and Famine: Iceland, 1784–1785'. *Human Ecology* 19, no. 3 (September 1991): 323–50.
Verdon, Jean. *Night in the Middle Ages*. Translated by George Holoch. Notre Dame: University of Notre Dame Press, 2002.
Vésteinn Ólason. 'Introduction'. In *'Gisli Sursson's Saga' and 'The Saga of the People of Eyri'*, translated by Judy Quinn and Martin S. Regal, vii–xlvi. London: Penguin, 1997.
Vickrey, John F. 'The Narrative Structure of Hengest's Revenge in *Beowulf*'. *Anglo-Saxon England* 6 (1977): 91–103.
Vigfusson, Gudbrand [Guðbrandur Vigfússon], ed. *Icelandic Sagas and Other Historical Documents Relating to the Settlement and Descents of the Northmen on the British Isles*. Vol. 1. London: H. M. Stationary Office, 1887.
Vilhjálmur Finsen, ed. *Grágás: Efter det Arnamagnæanske haandskrift nr. 334 fol., Staðarhólsbók*. Copenhagen: Gyldendal, 1879.
——— ed. *Grágás: Islændernes lovbog i fristatens tid*. Copenhagen: Berling, 1852; reprinted in one volume Odense: Odense universitetsforlag, 1974.
Viswanathan, S. 'On the Melting of the Sword: *wæl-rāpas* and the Engraving on the Sword-Hilt in *Beowulf*'. *Philological Quarterly* 58, no. 3 (summer 1979): 360–3.
Vries, Oebele. 'De âldfryske ivichheidsformule'. In *Miscellanea Frisica: A New Collection of Frisian Studies*, ed. N. R. Århammar, P. H. Breuker, Freark Dam, A. Dykstra, and T. J. Steenmeijer-Wielenga, 89–96. Fryske Akademy 634. Assen: Van Gorcum, 1984.
Wachsler, Arthur A. 'Grettir's Fight with a Bear: Another Neglected Analogue of *Beowulf* in the *Grettis sage Asmundarsonar*'. *English Studies* 66, no. 5 (1985): 381–90.
Wagenaar, Jan A. *Origin and Transformation of the Ancient Israelite Festival Calendar*. Beihefte zur Zeitschrift für altorientalische und biblische Rechtsgeschichte 6. Wiesbaden: Harrassowitz, 2005.
Wagner, Albrecht, ed. *Visio Tnugdali: Lateinisch und altdeutsch*. Erlangen: Deichert, 1882.
Wallis, Faith, trans. *Bede: 'The Reckoning of Time'*. Translated Texts for Historians 29. Liverpool: Liverpool University Press, 1999.
Walter, Philippe. 'Sous le masque du souvage'. In *Le devin maudit: Merlin, Lailoken, Suibhne*, ed. and trans. Philippe Walter, Jean-Charles Berthet, Christine Bord, and Nathalie Stalmans. Grenoble: Ellug, 1999.

Walther, Hans, ed. *Das Streitgedicht in der lateinischen Literatur des Mittelalters.* Quellen und Untersuchungen zur lateinischen Philologie des Mittelalters 5.2. Munich: Beck, 1920; reprinted with supplementary materials Hildesheim: Olms, 1984.

Wanke, Karl, ed. *Die 'lais' der Marie de France.* Bibliotheca normannica 3. Halle: Niemeyer, 1925.

Weber, Robert, ed. *Biblia sacra iuxta vulgatam versionem.* 5th ed. Rev. Roger Gryson. Stuttgart: Deutsche Bibelgesellschaft, 2007.

Weigand, Hermann J. 'Narrative Time in the Grail Poems of Chrétien de Troyes and Wolfram von Eschenbach'. In *Wolfram's 'Parzival': Five Essays with an Introduction,* ed. Ursula Hoffmann, 18–74. Ithaca, NY, and London: Cornell University Press, 1969.

Weinhold, Karl, ed. *Die deutschen Monatnamen.* Halle: Waisenhaus, 1869.

Weyer, Edward Moffat, Jr. *The Eskimos: Their Environment and Folkways.* New Haven: Yale University Press, 1932.

Whitaker, Ian. 'Late Classical and Early Mediaeval Accounts of the Lapps (Sami)'. *Classica et mediaevalia* 34 (1983): 283–303.

—— '"Scridefinnas" in *Widsið*'. *Neophilologus* 66, no. 4 (October 1982): 602–8.

Whitaker, Muriel. 'Otherworld Castles in Middle English Arthurian Romance'. In *The Medieval Castle: Romance and Reality,* ed. Kathryn Reyerson and Faye Powe, 27–45. Dubuque, IA: Kendall / Hunt, 1984.

Whitbread, L. 'A Medieval English Metaphor'. *Philological Quarterly* 17, no. 4 (October 1938): 365–70.

Wilhelm, James J. *The Cruelest Month: Spring, Nature, and Love in Classical and Medieval Lyrics.* New Haven, CT, and London: Yale University Press, 1965.

Williams, David. *Cain and Beowulf: A Study in Secular Allegory.* Toronto: University of Toronto Press, 1982.

Williams, J. E. Caerwyn. 'The Nature Prologue in Welsh Court Poetry'. *Studia Celtica* 24–5 (1989–90): 70–90.

Williams, R. A. *The Finn Episode in 'Beowulf': An Essay in Interpretation.* Cambridge: Cambridge University Press, 1924.

Wilmanns, W., ed. 'Disputatio regalis et nobilissimi iuvenis Pippini cum Albino scholastico'. *Zeitschrift für deutsches Alterthum* 14 (1869): 530–55.

Wilson, Edward. *The 'Gawain'-Poet.* Leiden: Brill, 1976.

Wolf, Kirsten. '*Visio Tnugdali*'. In *Medieval Scandinavia: An Encyclopedia,* ed. Phillip Pulsiano, 705–6. New York and London: Garland, 1993.

Woolf, Rosemary. 'Saints' Lives'. In Stanley, *Continuations and Beginnings,* 37–66.

—— '*The Wanderer, The Seafarer,* and the Genre of *planctus*'. In Nicholson and Frese, *Anglo-Saxon Poetry,* 192–207.

Wormald, Francis, ed. *English Kalendars before AD 1100.* London: Henry Bradshaw Society, 1934.

Wrenn, C. L., ed. *Beowulf: With the 'Finnesburg Fragment'.* Boston, MA, and London: Heath / Harrap, 1953.

Wright, Charles D. *The Irish Tradition in Old English Literature.* Cambridge Studies in Anglo-Saxon England 6. Cambridge: Cambridge University Press, 1993.

Wright, William Aldis, ed. *The Metrical Chronicle of Robert of Gloucester.* 2 vols. Rerum Britannicarum medii ævi scriptores 86. London: Her Majesty's Stationery Office, 1887. New York: Kraus, 1965.

Wulffen, Barbara von. *Der Natureingang in Minnesang und frühem Volkslied*. Munich: Max Hueber, 1963.
Wunder, Sven. *The Economics of Deforestation: The Example of Ecuador*. Basingstoke: MacMillan, 2000.
Wyatt, A. J., and R. W. Chambers, eds. *Beowulf: With the 'Finnsburg Fragment'*. Cambridge: Cambridge University Press, 1915.
Wyatt, Ian, and Jessie Cook, eds. *Two Tales of Icelanders: Ögmundar þáttr dytts og Gunnars helmings, Ǫlkofra þáttr*. Durham Medieval Texts 10. Durham: Durham Medieval Texts, Department of English, 1993.
Zangemeister, Carolus [Karl], ed. *Paulus Orosius: 'Historiarum adversum paganos libri VII', accedit eiusdem 'Liber apologeticus'*. Hildesheim: Olms, 1967.
Zupitza, Julius, ed. *Aelfrics 'Grammatik' und 'Glossar'*. Berlin: Weidmann, 1880.
—— ed. *The Romance of Guy of Warwick: Edited from the Auchinleck MS. in the Advocates' Library, Edinburgh, and from MS. 107 in Caius College, Cambridge*. EETS, ES 42, 49, 59. London: Trübner, 1883–91.
Zycha, Iosephus [Joseph], ed. *De Genesi ad litteram libri duodecim*. Corpus Scriptorum Ecclesiasticorum Latinorum, 28 (3, no. 2). Vienna: Tempsky, 1894.

Index

Adam of Bremen 52
Aesopian fable 164
aetiology 39–40, 44–5, 62, 106
agriculture 2, 24, 25, 29, 61–2
  in biblical and patristic
     tradition 30–1, 47–8, 193
  in early Germanic cultures 6–7, 9
  in England 17–21, 25, 48, 50, 174
  in Iceland, Scandinavia, and Old
     Norse tradition 17–24, 25, 42–3,
     47, 48, 57
  in Israel 47–8
Ágrip 52–3, 55–6
Alcuin 142, see also *Conflictus veris et hiemis*
Alfred of Wessex 25 n. 104, 108–9
Alliterative Morte Arthure 173–4, 179,
   199–200
Als I lay in a winteris nyt 172–3, 206,
   209
alþingi 23, 57, 60, 61, 114, 210
Andreas 73 n. 46, 81–2, 89–90, 110,
   144, 145–6, 205, 210
angels 31–2, 122, 203 n. 132
Assembly see *alþingi, haustþing, várþing*
Atlakviða 89 n. 106
Augustine of Hippo 30–2
Ælfric of Eynsham 21, 88
Æsir 41, 45–67, 149

Bakhtin, Mikhail see chronotope
Battle of Maldon 83–4
Bede see *Historia ecclesiastica, De temporum ratione*
Beowulf see also cave episode, defence
   of the hall, Finnsburh episode,
   Grendel and his mother, Heorot
   analogues 128–37
  lack of seasonal chronology 129,
     134

line 33 *isig* 97–100
  swimming contest 90–2
  use of seasons 137–41
binary categories 9–13, 173–4, 186,
   208, see also calendar, heuristics
Blickling Homilies 94–5, 100
blood on snow 201–4
boasts 60–1, 154–5
bonds of winter 137–48
Book of the Duchess 169–70
Bósa saga ok Herrauðs 184
Brennu-Njáls saga 58–9, 60, 151, 153
Buile Shuibhne 187
burial rites see funerary practices
Byrhtferth of Ramsey 88

calendar
  associative 9–13
  economic see economics
  military 24–5
  ritual 47–61
  systems 4–9
Candlemas 53, 58, 120
Carados 195
Carmen de ave phoenice 35, 85 n. 91
cave episode 129–31, 132, 134
chanson d'aventure 162, 166, 167, 168
Chaucer 16, 65, see also *Book of the
   Duchess, Legend of Good Women,
   Parliament of Fowls*
Chevalier à l'épée 203
Chrétien de Troyes 178 n. 60, 195,
   201–2
Christ and Satan 33, 38
Christ B 82–3
Christmas 5, 12, 48, 52–3, 56, 57, 61,
   114–25, 128–9, 133–4, 136, 151,
   154–6, 158, 194–200, 204, 205, 210,
   211, see also Yule
Christmas Visitors 123–5

chronotope, seasonal 66, 68–9, 207, 209–10
  applied to summer settings 162, 183, 193–4, 204–5
  applied to winter settings 127, 137, 148, 193–4, 205, 209–10
climate 1–4, 26, 47, 105, 127
  determinism *see* environmental determinism
  history 4, 13–17, 18, 22, 126
clothing *see* dress
cold 16, 23, 100, 104–5, 115, 144–6, 157, 173, 193, 204, 205–6
  absence from Eden or heaven 30–1, 33–6
  as a seasonal feature 1–2, 4–5, 11–12, 21, 31, 40, 158, 189, 197, 200
  association with horror, sorrow, and the extrasocietal 71, 80–100, 100, 102, 113, 141, 149, 172–3, 204, 206, 208–9
  figurative uses 32, 78, 149, *see also* bonds of winter
  foreboding violence 115, 154
  practical implications 1, 16, 24–5, 125–8, 148
  punitive 33–4, 36–9, 47, 70, *see also* hell
  water 77–89, 90–5, 97, 110–11
Conflictus veris et hiemis 79, 164–5
Consolation of Philosophy 76 n. 62, 86, 88, 98
Conte du graal 201–2
crampons 150, 152–3
Cuckoo and the Nightingale 167–8, 169

darkness 114
  as a seasonal or cyclical element 4–5, 11–12, 25, 31–2, 51, 52, 57–8, 72, 91–2, 95, 113, 117–18, 122–3, 134 n. 109, 144, 146, 156–8, 200, 205, 206, 208, 210
  as an unfamiliar or hostile domain 31–2, 67, 70, 91–2, 95, 113, 114, 117–18, 122–3, 134 n. 109, 135, 146, 156–8, 204, 205, 206, 208

figurative uses 31–2, 40, 48, 57–8, 73–5
  of hell 31–3, 37, 70
De temporibus anni 21, 88
De temporum ratione 7–8, 49–51
Death and Liffe 167
Death of Edward 84
defence of the hall 129, 131–4
Degaré, Sir 179–80
Destruction of Troy 169
Dialogues of Gregory the Great 24, 87 n. 97
dísablót 54, 55
divination 154–7, 158
dream vision 32–9, 164–73
dress 34, 124, 150–1, 181, 203 n. 132
Droplaugarsona saga 57
Dryhthelm 33, 36–7
Duggals leiðsla 37–8

Easter 6, 23, 47–8, 51, 52–3, 55
Ecclesiastical History of the English People see Historia ecclesiastica
Eclogues of Virgil 164
ecocriticism 64
economics 2, 6–7, 17–25, 27, 47, 50, 61–2, 148, 192, 207
economy, organic 4, 17, 25, 29, 61–2
Edda, Poetic *see Atlakviða, Hávamál, Hymiskviða, Hyndluljóð, Lokasenna, Skírnismál, Vafþrúðnismál, Vǫluspá*
Edda, Prose 40–2, 45–6, 101 n. 157, 103, 104–6
Eden 29–33, 35–6, 40, 47, 61, 70, 85, 135, 193, 210
Edwin of Deira 70, 73–5
Egils saga Skallagrímssonar 22, 54, 55, 59, 152
Eiríks saga rauða 121, 125–8, 156
Eiríks saga víðfǫrla 61
elegy 69–80, 110, 140, 146–7, 205–6
elements, four 88
Élivágar 103–6
elves 123
energy infrastructure 1–2, 4, 16, 17, 25, 29

Index

environmental determinism 1–3, 25, 37 n. 41, 61, 63–4, 65
Epiphany 55, 115, 117, 120
eternity oaths 107
Etymologiae 142
euhemerism 53, 149
exile 70, 77–9, 140, 158, 176, 181, 186–93, 204, 205, 208, 209, *see also* Fall of Man
Exodus, Old English 84–5, 89
Eyrbyggja saga 22, 119–20, 121–2 Table 1, 151–2, 153

fairies 176, 177–8, 180–3, 185–6, 189, 204
Fall of Man 29–31, 40, 70, 134–5, 193
fellivetr 22
fertility cults and rites 23–4, 42–3, 47, 49, 55
fimbulvetr 40–2
Finnar *see* Sami
Finnmǫrk 108 n. 187, 125, 184–6
Finnsburh episode 137–40, 143, 145, 148, 157–8, 159
fishery 18–19, 21, 22, 61–2, 85
Fled Bricrend 195
Flóamanna saga 60–1, 121, 134–7
flood 87, 90, 94
folktales and folk elements 117, 118, 123–5, 131–4, 201–2, 204
forests 7, 69, 93, 162, 167, 168–9, 171, 173–83, 185–202
Fornjótr 43–7, 66
Fóstbrœðra saga 59–60, 139, 146, 152, 153
Freyr 23 n. 91, 42–3, 46, 54, 154
Fundinn Noregr 43–7, 66
funerary practices 125–8, 210, 211

Gawain and the Carle of Carlisle, Sir 182–3
Gawain and the Green Knight, Sir 193–204, 205, 209
Genesis A 34 n. 31, 38, 87
Genesis B 33–4, 38, 69–70, 110, 135
Geoffrey of Monmouth 187, *see also Vita Merlini*

Germania 6–8, 20 n. 76, 43, 49
Gesta Danorum 108–9, 129, 150–1
giants 42–3, 45, 47, 94, 100–6, 110, 174, 185, 208
Ginnungagap 104–5
Gísla saga Súrssonar 23 n. 91, 58, 152, 153–4, 159
Glámr 114–19, 121–2 Table 1, 123, 124, 125, 127, 128
Glæsisvellir 185
Góiblót 45
Grágás 8, 107–8
Gregory the Great 32, 83, *see also Dialogues* of Gregory the Great
Grendel and his mother 81, 92–6, 97 n. 133, 116, 118, 128–31, 134–5, 136, 140–1
Grettis saga Ásmundarsonar 59–60, 108, 114–31, 133, 134, 139, 152, 153, 158, 211
Gríms saga loðinkinna 184
Grœnlendinga saga 59
Guðmundar saga Arasonar 23
Guðmundr of Glæsisvellir 185
Guðrún Ósvífrsdóttir 59, 120–1
Gulaþingslǫg 55, 108, 127
Gull-Þóris saga 131
Gullbrá og Skeggi 118, 131
Gusir, King of the Sami 108 n. 187, 125
Guy of Warwick 177–9

hail 34, 35, 36, 37, 44, 72, 76, 77, 78, 103, 144–6, 199
hail-rune 99, 144 n. 145
Hákonar saga góða 53
Hákonar saga herðibreiðs 151
Hand and the Child, the 132–4
Haralds saga ins hárfagra 108, 110
Harðar saga ok Hólmverjar 131
hauntings 113–37, 158, 204–5, 206, 208, 209, 211
haustþing 57
Hávamál 102
Hávarðar saga Ísfirðings 117, 121–2 Table 1, 124

heat 71, 81, 84–5, 87 n. 97, 96, 104–6, 141, 155, 191–2, 205–6, *see also* Medieval Warm Period
  absence from Eden or heaven 30, 33–5
  artificial 75–6
  as a seasonal feature 2, 4–5, 10, 11–12, 40, 70, 147–8, 177–82, 197, 208
  figurative uses 32, 78–80, 90
  of adventure-space 81, 164–9, 177–82, 210
  punitive 34, 36–9, 47, 70, 95, *see also* hell
heating and heat preservation 1–2, 4, 17, 74–5
heaven 29–36, 47, 77–8, 80, 142, 181
Heiðarvíga saga 108, 137
Heimskringla see Hákonar saga góða, Hákonar saga herðibreiðs, Haralds saga ins hárfagra, Óláfs saga helga, Ynglinga saga
heitstrenging 60–1, 154–5
Helga þáttr Þórissonar 185–6
hell 29, 31, 33, 36–9, 41, 70, 78, 93 n. 121, 94–5, 99–100, 135, 145, 172, 173, 205–6
Heorot 128–9, 131–4, 135, 158
heuristics 10–13, 207–8
Historia ecclesiastica gentis Anglorum 33, 36, 73–6
historicism 63–4
History of the Wars 52, 108–9, 118 n. 20
Hænsa- Þóris saga 20 n. 78, 22 n. 87, 61
hrímþursar see giants
Hrólfs saga kraka 117, 121–2, 124, 129, 131, 133, 137, 156, 195
hrosfellisvetr 22
huldufólk 123
hunt 18, 25, 163, 169–70, 175, 178–9, 182–3, 196, 199–200
Husband's Message 79–80, 140
Hversu Noregr byggðisk 43–7, 66
Hymiskviða 102, 103
Hyndluljóð 41

ice 23, 94–5, 97–100, 104–5, 137–8, 141, 143, 146, 147–53, 159
ice-rune 99
insulation *see* heating and heat preservation
Isidore of Seville 88, 142
Íslendinga saga 152–3

Jerome 186
John the Baptist, Nativity of 52–3, 56, 114, 182
jóladrykkja and *jólaǫl* 55
Jómsvíkinga saga 42 n. 58, 61
Jóns saga ins helga 23–4
jǫtnar see giants

Kalevala 185
kennings and circumlocutions 66 n. 20, 81–2, 98, 101 n. 157, 106, 130 n. 90, 143
Ketils saga hœngs 108 n. 187, 109–10, 125, 184
knattleikr 60, 152

Lactantius 35, 85 n. 91, 203 n. 132
Landnámabók 22
Lárentíus saga Kálfssonar 23–4
Launfal, Sir 181–2, 185, 210
Laxdæla saga 58, 59, 120–2
Legend of Good Women 170
Lent 21, 197–8
light 105
  artificial 74–6
  as a seasonal or cyclical element 4, 11–12, 31, 51, 52, 91–2, 114, 117–18, 138, 140, 147, 148, 164–5, 197–8, 205, 208
  as an element of adventure-space 168–70
  figurative uses 31–2, 40, 48, 57–8, 83, 92
  miraculous 130–1
  of heaven 33, 181
  of the moon 124 n. 59
  punitive 34
Little Ice Age 14–16

livestock 18, 20–3, 25, 50, 54, 114–15, 116, 119, 155
locus amoenus 27, 31, 32, 35, 79, 85, 140, 151, 161, 164–71, 173, 176, 179–80, 190–1
Lokasenna 89 n. 106, 102 n. 160
Longes Mac nUislenn 201
Lucia 58

madness 186–7
Map, Walter 122
Maxims I 147–8
Maxims II 21
Medieval Warm Period 4, 14–16
Menologium 50, 146–7, 196, 198
Merlin 187–9, 205
Metres of Boethius 86, 88
Michaelmas 52–3, 197–8
Midsummer 56, 58, 114–16
modraniht 51
month names 49–51
Moving Days 23, 116 n. 10
mule sans frein, La 195
Muspellr and Muspellsheimr 104–5
myth 26–7, 29–47, 62, 85, 97 n. 133, 99–106, 149, 196

nature opening 161, 164–9
nautadauðavetr, nautfellisvetr 22
Navigatio Sancti Brendani 39
Nebuchadnezzar 186
Niflheimr 104–5
Njáls saga see *Brennu-Njáls saga*
noon 178–82, 204

Óðinn 39, 40–1, 53, 55, 102
Óláfs saga helga 53
Óláfs saga Tryggvasonar by Oddr Snorrason 109
Óláfs saga Tryggvasonar en mesta 108, 124
Orfeo, Sir 180–1, 182, 189–90, 192
Orkneyinga saga 43–6, 108
Orms þáttr Stórólfssonar 131, 157
Ovid 176
Owl and the Nightingale 165–6
Ǫrvar-Odds saga 157

paradise see Eden, heaven
Parlement of the Thre Ages 169
Parliament of Fowls 9, 35
pathetic fallacy 70, 140, 158
Pearl 170–1
Phoenix 34–5, 85–6, 110
Physiologus 90
Piers Plowman 166–7, 168, 169
precipitation see hail, rain, snow
Procopius see *History of the Wars*
prognostication 154–7, 158
psycho-geography 67–8, 70, 71, 75, 95, 111, 173, 176, 177, 209
Pwyll pendeuic Dyuet 133–4

Ragnarǫk 41–2
Ragnarr *loðbrók* 150–1
raiding 24, 83, 118–19, 183–5, 210, see also warfare
rain 4, 24, 29, 34–5, 41, 58, 71, 74, 76 n. 61, 104–5, 119, 188–9, 193, 197, 199
Reis van Sente Brandane 39
revenants see hauntings
risar see giants
ritual 21, 26, 29, 42–3, 47–61, 99–100, 114, 125–8, 212
roman d'Antiquité 176
romance 60 n. 172, 62, 65, 68–9, 150, 159, 162–4, 172, 173–86, 189–205, 206, 208–10
Ruin 71–3, 76, 97, 110
Rune poems 99–100, 144 n. 145

salience 11–12, 208
Sami 46, 100–1, 106–11, 125, 126 n. 68, 156, 184–5, 208, 211
Samsons saga fagra 131
Satan 38, 90, 135
Saturnalia 48
Saxo Grammaticus see *Gesta Danorum*
sea see under water
Seafarer 9, 76–82, 86, 87–8, 97, 110, 140, 144, 145–6
Shakespeare 10, 26, 63, 209

skiing 2, 106–9, 150, 153
Skilful Companions 133–4
Skírnismál 42–3
Snjár *inn gamli* 46
Snorri Sturluson *see* Edda, Hákonar saga góða, Hákonar saga herðibreiðs, Haralds saga ins hárfagra, Óláfs saga helga, Ynglinga saga
snow 57, 58, 74, 77, 103, 106–9, 114–15, 117, 126–7, 134 n. 109, 144–7, 150–4, 158, 159, 200–4
snowshoes 46, 108, 152, 153
Sólarljóð 38
Solomon and Saturn II 144–5
sorcery 101, 109–10, 111, 118, 128, 154, 156–7, 184–5
Soul and Body I 89
sparrow simile 73–6, 110, 208
Stjórn 30 n. 4
Sturlunga saga *see* Íslendinga saga, Þorgils saga skarða
subsistence farming 19–20
Surtr 105
Sverris saga 150, 152–3

Tacitus *see* Germania
temperatures *see* Medieval Warm Period, Little Ice Age
time-reckoning 4–9
trade 18–21, 25, 85
travel 12, 24–5, 57–8, 82 n. 75, 85, 116, 138–9, 148, 153, 156–7, 175–6, 186, 199, 204, 210
Tristan and Isolde 60 n. 172, 176, 190–3
troll 117 n. 15, 124, 128, 184–5

Þiðranda þáttr ok Þórhalls 124
Þorgils saga skarða 56
Þorrablót 45

underntide 178, 179–82, 204

Vafþrúðnismál 39–41, 42, 101–2, 103–6
Vanir 42
várþing 57
Vatnsdœla saga 109, 156
vetrnætr *see* Winter Nights
Víga-Glúms saga 42–3 n. 60, 54
Virgil 164–5, 176
Visio Sancti Pauli 32–3, 36
Visio Tnugdali 33, 37–8, 39
vision literature 32–9, 164–73
Vita Merlini 187–9, 205
Vǫlundarkviða 108
vǫlur 156–7, 158
Vǫluspá 35–6, 41–2

Wanderer 71–3, 75–6, 77–8, 80, 81, 86, 87–8, 97, 110, 140, 142–4, 145, 146
warfare 24–5, 42, 51, 53, 55, 73 n. 46, 82, 83–4, 100, 137–9, 148–54, 159, 173, 177, 179, *see also* raiding
water *see also* rain
  for consumption 86–7, 192, 193
  holy 125–6
  settings and landscape features 80–97, 103, 105–6, 110, 130–1, 138 n. 123, 142–7, 150–1, 167–9, 189, 193
Wife's Lament 70–1, 75–6, 79–80, 86, 87–8, 110
William of Newburgh 122
Winter Nights 42 n. 58, 53–9, 61, 114–17, 121–2 Table 1, 124–5, 210
witchcraft *see* sorcery
Wynnere and Wastoure 168–9

year *see* calendar
Yggdrasill 102–3
Ynglinga saga 45 n. 79, 46, 53, 149
Ynglingatal 46
Yule, pre-Christian 51, 53, 54–5, 56, 60 n. 179, 124, 125, 154–5, 195, *see also* Christmas

www.ingramcontent.com/pod-product-compliance
Lightning Source LLC
Chambersburg PA
CBHW051609230426
43668CB00013B/2044